Theatre
at the Crossroads

Other Books by John Gassner:

Form and Idea in the Modern Theatre
Twenty Best European Plays on the American Stage
The Theatre in Our Times
Producing the Play
Best American Plays Library (5 volumes)
A Treasury of the Theatre (3 volumes)
Human Relations in the Theatre
Great Film Plays (with Dudley Nichols)
Best Film Plays of 1945 (with Dudley Nichols)
Best Film Plays of 1943-44 (with Dudley Nichols)
Comedies of Molière
English Comedies
Twenty Best Film Plays (with Dudley Nichols)
Our Heritage of World Literature (with Stith Thompson)
Masters of the Drama

JOHN GASSNER

Theatre
at the Crossroads

Plays and Playwrights
of the Mid-Century
American Stage

HOLT, RINEHART
AND WINSTON
NEW YORK

for Joanne

who sustains her grandfather

at the crossroads

PREFACE

I owe the publication of this book to the initiative of my friend Stanley
Burnshaw, the interest of Walter Bradbury of Henry Holt and Company,
the suggestions and ministrations of Mrs. Joyce Bermel, and the final
editorial supervision of Joseph M. Fox and Louise Waller at the publishers' offices, and the assistance of my wife and indefatigable theatre
companion. But my indebtedness does not end with this brief roll-call.
My gratitude must be extended to include theatre associates who sharpened my thinking, editors of publications in which my thoughts had
their inception recently, public occasions (at The Johns Hopkins University, The University of Michigan, and The University of Detroit),
and friends who argued points with me.

For reasons that I hope will be satisfactory as well as apparent to the
reader I have attempted to stay as close as possible to the provocations of
specific theatrical events and discussions. Most of the problems examined
in this book may have had their beginnings in the last three decades of
the nineteenth century, but I have been concerned here primarily with
the theatre that has been shaping and reshaping, or unshaping, itself in
recent decades. The productions to which I have given detailed notice
appeared on our Broadway and off-Broadway stages during the Fifties.
The book, then, is essentially a review of mid-century theatre and mid-
century situations.

I should explain, however, that I make no pretense of completeness in
the chronicle-criticism that is the substance of the second part of the
volume. I have omitted comment not only on productions I have deemed

unworthy of notice, but on a number of well-regarded plays on which I could offer description rather than criticism, or on which my comments contribute nothing in particular to my theme or argument. No slight is intended by the omissions, which are repaired here and there by brief references to the plays. The limitation is mine and not the authors'; it is *my* fault that I did not feel particularly bright about some attractive works whereas I could find sermons in stones. The reader who requires a complete summary of the past decade or of the postwar period since 1945 will turn, of course, to the annual Dodd, Mead *Best Plays* volume started by the late Burns Mantle and continued by his accommodating successors John Chapman and Louis Kronenberger.

I take special pleasure in noting my indebtedness to Robert Corrigan of the *Tulane Drama Review* and to Barnard Hewitt, H.D. Albright, Hubert Heffner, and James Clancy of the *Educational Theatre Journal* for the interest they have often evinced in my views.

—JOHN GASSNER
May, 1960

CONTENTS

INTRODUCTION

This is an optimistic book. Its argument is predicated upon a belief that the theatre is one of the few popular institutions still worth taking seriously. Or worth addressing seriously. Men and women are creatively involved with it in spite of the extreme pressures of our time and place. They even take a large view of the theatre and of their own particular endeavors, successes, and failures. In the world of the professional, community, and university stage will be found persons who maintain perspectives on the past, present, and future. They are concerned with knowing where they are in this moment of history, how they got there, and where they are going. This means that they take pride in their art and regard their participation in it with self-respect. They are capable of improving their own particular work and the enterprise of theatre as a whole because they combine creative effort with critical intelligence and an inquiring spirit.

It is possible to hold conversations with these men and women, and also with a portion of their public, so that criticism need not be a monologue and the critic need not feel alienated from them when he speaks his mind. He is anticipated by the responsible critic in the creator himself and by the responsible critic in the spectator. Granted that creators and spectators of this caliber are anything but superabundant, it is nonetheless encouraging that they exist at all.

Theatre at the Crossroads was not written, however, to sustain an optimistic viewpoint. It is simply an assessment of the mid-century theatre as viewed from the vantage point of Broadway and off-Broadway stage production since World War II. It starts with a series of general essays, several of which offer perspectives that take us back to the beginnings of modern drama. It concludes with discussions of specific productions that comprise a chronicle of the New York stage during the 1950-1960 period. Above all, the book consists of questions raised (more or less inadvertently, to be sure) by these productions.

A point of view concerning the mid-century stage, however, cannot easily be achieved, for the theatre has been in one of the most eclectic phases of its history. Our slogan throughout this recent period could well have been "anything goes!" Almost anything "went" or didn't "go" for good reasons, bad ones, or no apparent reasons whatsoever; and this situation is not to be attributed solely to the anarchy so often and so correctly noted in the conditions of theatrical production. The modern theatre has been in existence for a long time. Over a hundred years have elapsed since the beginnings of realism in France and England, eighty years since the publication of *A Doll's House*. No other age has had a continuous history on a comparable scale for so long, and in so many countries and languages, too. To expect any marked degree of uniformity, rather than an extreme mingling of tastes and styles, would be unrealistic. If anything, it is remarkable that one dramatic style—that of representational realism or naturalism—should have maintained some kind of dominance for approximately a century.

A continuing tension between naturalism and a variety of alternatives of dramatic stylization has characterized the century's theatre. It has led to intense partisanship and to some extremism in the form of extravagant expressionist or surrealist plays and productions. But tolerance for contradictory approaches and styles in the contemporary theatre has enriched the interest of the stage. I, for one, can heartily endorse the search for new dramatic form and style on the one hand, while also finding merit in Elizabeth Bowen's generalization that, "We want the naturalistic surface, but with a kind of internal burning."

My attitude, I grant, is somewhat ambivalent, but no more so than the actual endeavors and achievement of the mid-century stage. A division of aim and style has surely been apparent in the work of, let us say, O'Neill, O'Casey, Williams, and Miller, as well as of many an earlier playwright and stage director such as Ibsen, Strindberg, Hauptmann, Reinhardt, Copeau, and even Stanislavski.

When people talk about the theatre of the present, however, I am not sure I know what they are talking about. So much of the theatre of the present is the theatre of the past. And when they talk about the theatre of the future, I am equally puzzled. Many of the avant-garde plays and productions adhere to styles forty, sixty, or seventy years old, or are conservative by comparison with plays staged then.* Although the theatre has been at the crossroads in the 1945-1960 period, it was also uncomfortably and provocatively situated there in almost every other decade of the twentieth century. The modern theatre may yet go down in history as the theatre of permanent crisis.

We might as well get used to the possibility that the crisis will vanish only with the modern age, because intrinsic to modern dramatic art is the contradiction of our wanting a theatre that deals with contemporary reality and that, at the same time, has a universal and poetic quality. But it is even more important to realize that states of crisis have not precluded the possibility, nor exempted human beings from the necessity, of finding effective means for expressing their divided aims and partial realizations. It is possible to take the measure of our theatre without enervating fatalism.

It is no easy thing to take the measure of the modern drama. The very standards of measurement have been changing before our eyes, and old reputations and appreciations disappearing with older generations. For the generation of the Forties and Fifties there is no longer any magic left in the playwrights and causes that sustained the American theatre of the Thirties and Twenties. O'Neill's reputation was severely challenged until a succession of stage productions toward the end of the Fifties wrung respect from the new generation. Many European culture-heroes matter no longer to the young; only the names of Chekhov and O'Casey retain much luster in America. Even the reputations of Ibsen and Strindberg stand in peril.

Constancy has been no greater in other lands. In England, as in

* As partial evidence one can cite Maeterlinck's *Pelléas et Mélisande* at the Théâtre de l'Oeuvre in 1893; Alfred Jarry's presurrealist parody *Ubu Roi* at the Théâtre de l'Oeuvre in December, 1896; Strindberg's ultraexpressionist *To Damascus* in 1898, and his *A Dream Play* in 1902 (first staged in Stockholm in 1906); Meyerhold's break with Stanislavski, and the beginning of Reinhardt's career at Berlin in 1902; and Apollinaire's surrealist *Les Mamelles de Tirésias,* 1903, staged in Paris in 1917.

America, John Galsworthy seems virtually forgotten, and Shaw, to whom
we continue to be faithful in our realistic manner and musical-comedy
fashion, has come under suspicion in Great Britain. Hardly two years
had elapsed since his death in 1950 when a British critic, Raymond
Williams, declared that "Shaw's dynamic as a dramatist is surely weakening, and it seems impossible that it can, as a major force, survive the
period of which he was a victim." The author of this statement, for whom
T.S. Eliot was the reigning arbiter of taste, quoted the latter's edict:
"Shaw was a poet—until he was born, and the poet in Shaw was still-
born . . . Shaw is dramatically precious and poetically less than immature."* In America a *Partisan Review* writer, William Barrett, had less
confidence in the feasibility of dispensing with Bernard Shaw while
calling him "the King of the Middlebrows" who was "no thinker but an
intelligent and tireless journalist of ideas." According to Mr. Barrett,
"Ould Barney was a tiresome noodle, spinning out ideas with a brisk
and extrovert cheerfulness never daunted by a poet's sense of the obscure
and dense substance of life that all very clear ideas must violate." In
view of the Shaw revival, however, it is apparent that "for a retrograde
audience" Shaw is "still daring . . ."**

New gods have seemed to be supplanting the old and one avant-garde
favorite has displaced another with great rapidity. While Americans
were still discovering Giraudoux and Anouilh, playgoers in France were
transferring their allegiance to Beckett, Genet, and Ionesco; and by the
time we were beginning to familiarize ourselves with the work of the
latter, Europeans were advancing the claims of Adamov and other "new"
avant-gardists.

No concerted effort has been made to enable the theatre to "speak
out" completely and use language as the prime dramatic medium it has
been in the past great ages. Even the principle that "the stage is poetry in
action" has been only sporadically observed. No grammar of dramatic art
has developed to take the place of the babel of tongues with which the
theatre has tried to communicate with its public. We can assent, indeed,
to a conclusion reached half a century earlier by the French novelist and
playwright Paul Bourget that, "Dramatic Art has followed the same road
as the art of the novel, but it has not advanced with the same rapidity."

* Raymond Williams, *Drama from Ibsen to Eliot*, London, 1953.
** "Theatre Chronicle: A Plausible Irishman," *Partisan Review*, Winter, 1957, p.
102.

A conviction that there is no dramatic art where there is no stylization has gained ground in some quarters. This awareness of style is related to the growth of a new public and of new theatrical groups throughout the land. These are preponderantly university-educated groups that have been introduced to dramatic art in the classroom as well as in the green-room. That their aims and principles are not exactly new and were entertained more than half a century before does not greatly matter. New endeavor can make them new. Anything would indeed be welcome that would improve upon the tacitly accepted realistic style Robert Edmond Jones so aptly described as, "a record of life at low ebb, viewed in the sunless light of day."

Still, the implications of the search for stylization remain to be explored further. How is realism to be displaced without banishing reality from the theatre? How can theatricality be restored to the theatre without cultivating triviality and preciosity? How is *poetry* rather than some customary theatrical substitute of symbolic props, atmospheric lighting, or decorative language to return to the stage? How is such poetry to be introduced into the American theatre without bringing the contemporary poets into it and encouraging them to use their talent to the full instead of parking it at the stage door and stammering like captive men of the naturalistic stage?

Neither the theatrical handsprings of showmen nor the willed idiosyncrasies of bohemianism are of particular avail in accomplishing this. Nor will a multitude of critical manifestoes bring about what only talent and labor can be expected to accomplish. Even for creation on a less exalted level, the playwright will have to have something to say that can be said dramatically. That these requirements cannot easily be met in a period of waning enthusiasms and convictions should surprise no one.

Theatre at the Crossroads is also a *pessimistic* book, and many chapters point directly or indirectly at some softness or error, if not worse than error, in the theatre of the Forties and Fifties. A decline in American social drama after a sparse flurry of quasi-political liberal comedy around 1945 is symptomatic of estrangement from contemporary social reality. At the same time the American theatre of the period has not shown a particular inclination toward concern with universals or absolutes. An impending renascence of poetic drama in English under the leadership of T.S. Eliot and Christopher Fry has failed to materialize. Fry's efforts to enthrone dramatic poetry have become less and less productive of gratifying drama since *The Lady's Not for Burning*. T.S. Eliot, after having written about a third of a very good play in *The Cocktail Party* in the high-comedy vein of Noel Coward, has virtually settled for verse which he hoped would be indistinguishable from prose.

Nor has there been much progress in any other special style either. Giraudoux died in 1944 without leaving any noticeable impression on the postwar theatre after productions of *The Madwoman of Chaillot*, except for the moderate Broadway success of *La Guerre de Troie n'aura pas lieu* (*Tiger at the Gates*), a play written some twenty years earlier. Existentialist French drama had a brief career in France and hardly any in America. Even Sartre has failed to establish himself in our theatre.

As of the end of 1959, Brecht's sole American success is an off-Broadway production of Marc Blitzstein's adaptation of *The Threepenny Opera*. Even Western Europe, where Brecht's East German theatrical company, the Berliner Ensemble, made a strong impression, gave no indication that his example has proved productive in the field of dramatic writing. Brecht's own productivity as a playwright was virtually over by 1945, and when he died in 1956 it looked very much as if he had been the last of the very few "epic" dramatists.

Enthusiasm for the Swiss writer Friedrich Duerrenmatt's *The Visit* in 1958 can be tempered by the reflection that expressionist contrivance reached its peak more than thirty years before. This leaves the theatre with only a few Beckett and Ionesco left-bank samples of original writing. Although the failure of these playwrights to establish themselves in the American theatre of the Fifties is a discredit to Broadway rather than to Beckett and Ionesco, we can hardly say that the avant-garde writers, including the gifted Jean Genet, the author of *The Maids, Deathwatch,* and *The Balcony*, approach the stature of major dramatists or seem likely to exert great influence on the American stage.

In the United States we have witnessed the more or less impressive emergence of new dramatic talent between 1945 and 1950, climaxed by the success of Williams, Miller, and Inge. But evidence of growth in their case after *A Streetcar Named Desire, Death of a Salesman,* and *Come Back, Little Sheba* is spotty, while evidence of devolution rather than evolution is abundant in the work of their elders. Successful productions are not conclusive because success is often achieved on Broadway with more than a little help from sensational writing and stage production. Many a successful play has seemed artificially inflated with psychological and social pseudo-significance and has had no more conviction when platitudinously clear than when muddily ambiguous.

It is evident that the postwar period has gleaned a lean harvest in the important areas of tragedy and high comedy—even if we stretch our definitions sufficiently to certify as tragedies *Death of a Salesman* and *A Streetcar Named Desire* in America and *The Lark* and *The Visit* in Europe. And it should be observed that more or less gratifying Broadway and off-Broadway seasons were pyramided on such a collection of modern plays written *before* World War II as *Tiger at the Gates* (*La Guerre de Troie n'aura pas lieu*), *Ivanov*, *A Month in the Country*, *The Threepenny Opera*, and *Man and Superman*.

The art of stage production has not made any significant advances with the possible exception of the development of arena staging, a style of presenting plays in the midst of the audience actually elaborated in the Thirties by Glenn Hughes in America and Okhlopkov in Russia. The conditions of professional and commercial stage production have become increasingly forbidding, as mounting costs make "smash-hit" success mandatory. Ibsen, Strindberg, and Chekhov, not to mention Synge and Lorca, could not survive as playwrights under comparable conditions.

One can conclude only that if the postwar theatre claims our interest in general it is because the mélange has been sometimes exciting and sometimes even arresting. A season's or a decade's playgoing is replete with partial gratifications, and with supplementary ones such as the miming of Marcel Marceau, the one-man shows of a variety of other performers, and individual performances by a Gwen Verdon, a Gretchen Wyler, or a Menasha Skulnik. For these reasons it is possible to accept the paradox that *Theatre at the Crossroads* can render a report on the mid-century stage both pessimistic and optimistic.

PART ONE

Interrogations and

Persuasions

1 SCRIPT OR SPOTLIGHT?

Half a century of theatre and drama is a vast subject, and half a century of *modern* theatre and drama is an intimidating one. But the defense against intimidation is temerity, and the cure for confusion is simplification. I supply the temerity by asserting that there are no mysteries in modern theatre and drama that cannot be plumbed by informed common sense. If the practice of the theatre arts requires a variety of skills, these call for competence rather than for profundity.

The drama of any period usually lags behind developments in the realm of ideas, unless these are transfigured by a good playwright who is also a true poet. Ideas usually seem new in the theatre only after they have ceased to be new anywhere else.

Although much of the history of modern theatre is an intrusion upon the realm of ideas, it is not necessary to analyze the ideas themselves. The theatre's dabblings in sociology and psychology have been too superficial to excite even dilettantes. Nothing is apt to seem more faded today than the journalistic content once expected to assure modernity to the drama. Intellectualism is less a characteristic of modern drama than was once thought to be the case. It is not the *what* of the content, but the *how* of the presentation that really matters.

But the *how* need not overawe us. Whether we have in mind the organization of a play or the style of a production, the esthetic problem is how to achieve an arresting sequence of pictures, actions, and experiences. The high-sounding programs of symbolism, expressionism, surrealism, constructivism, and the like may occupy theatrical scholars for the remainder of the century. But they are simplicity itself by comparison with similar phenomena in poetry and fiction. To realize this we need

1

only compare O'Neill's elementary interior monologues in *Strange Interlude* with the complicated stream-of-consciousness texture of James
Joyce's *Ulysses,* or the thin poetic style of T.S. Eliot's most successful stage
play, *The Cocktail Party,* with the texture of "The Waste Land," *Ash
Wednesday,* and *Four Quartets.*

It is a paradox that the American professional theatre of the past fifty
years should have begun to lose its mass basis precisely when it began to
express modern ideas, using advanced methods of production style. Local
stock companies began to vanish from the American scene, and touring
companies became rare, leaving a vacuum in many a large city. Professional enterprise became confined to a square mile around Times Square,
and in recent decades even Broadway productions suffered reduction by
two-thirds. Advances in dramatic art after 1910 were mainly accomplished
by a few off-Broadway little theatre groups, by the early Theatre Guild
built on a subscription audience that rarely exceeded 30,000 persons, and
later by the Group Theater (1931-1941) which had only three moderate
successes, *Men in White, Awake and Sing!* and *Golden Boy.* In time, our
professional theatre could be described as the Sahara of the Golden East
competing unequally with the growing film industry, the Sahara of the
Golden West.

It is not surprising that the history of twentieth-century American
theatre should show numerous efforts to compensate for the desiccation
of professional theatre. The results are a gratifying growth of noncommercial and semi-professional productions in the regional, community, and
college and university theatres. A small professional nucleus, recently
once more augmented by so-called off-Broadway theatre and a large but
indistinct mass of semiprofessional, student, and amateur production
makes up U.S. theatre.

Elsewhere in the Western world the condition of the theatre has seemed
more favorable, but only in two areas has this been conclusively the case:
in Germany, where many cities have maintained a tradition of subsidized
theatre, and in Soviet Russia, where the state has supported numerous
theatrical groups—but with almost uninterrupted party-line dictation.

The theatre has been overshadowed as a mass art by its parvenu relations, motion pictures, radio, and television. The interchange between
the theatre and its relatives has had its effects, but it is questionable

whether these have been notably gratifying. On the whole, radio, television, and motion pictures have adulterated the plays they have adapted, nor can it be maintained that they have materially improved the crafts of playwriting or production.

In association with the mass-communication media, however, dramatic art comprises an enormously ramified assault upon entire nations. It is a second paradox that by adulteration, diffusion, and reconstitution as radio, television, and motion picture drama, theatrical enterprise has gained control of the consciousness and taste of the public. Never before in history has dramatic performance proved so potent an instrument of propaganda, mass-mesmerism, and indoctrination. Never before, except possibly in Athens in the 5th century B.C., has the theatre possessed such power actually to influence its age. A heavy responsibility rests upon the theatre. But with the advent of the mass-communication media on the one hand and the rise of totalitarian dictatorships on the other, dramatic art—except on the legitimate stage—has been subverted by big business and big government. We may say that theatre on the stage contracted only to become a vastly expanded enterprise as theatre on the screen and on the air waves.

In shrinking, however, the stage became the one outpost of free expression in democratic countries. Theatre has been the province of the individual operator who is under no obligation to consider corporate interests. Since the legitimate stage cannot hope to be patronized by every man, woman, and child, theatrical producers do not feel obliged to descend to the lowest common denominator of feeling and intelligence. Integrity has been possible to a greater degree on the stage than on the screen and the air waves. In nontotalitarian states, the theatre usually has been unintimidated by governments, free-booting politicians, demagogues, and pressure groups. It has not shut its doors against minorities and political dissidents. Nor has the stage been closed to experimentation, however wild or negativistic. It is worth noting that many experiments have been carried on in the center of the commercial theatre, so often denounced as smugly unimaginative and pusillanimous. All of Giraudoux' plays presented during his lifetime were produced by Louis Jouvet, who graduated from Copeau's little Théâtre du Vieux Colombier to the big boulevard theatres of Paris. Both *Our Town* and *The Skin of Our Teeth,* Wilder's boldest departures from conventional realism, were first produced by Broadway managements. Tennessee Williams owed his first success with *The Glass Menagerie* to the former song-and-dance man Eddie Dowling and his partner Louis Singer, a real-estate operator, as well as to that mesmeric veteran of the Broadway stage, the late Laurette Taylor.

The hazardous operations of individual managements, from the Moscow Art Theatre that introduced Chekhov at the turn of the century to the latest Kermit Bloomgarden or Alfred de Liagre production in Manhattan, account for most of the theatre's distinction in our century. The smallness of the business has been directly related to the greatness and independence of the art. Theatre has been one of the few things in the twentieth century to escape thorough standardization except when enslaved by the super-state.

If there have been some paradoxes in the twentieth-century theatre's external situation, there have also been contradictions in its very character and development as an art. A significant one has been the fact that whereas the nineteenth-century theatre increasingly affirmed realism often only to violate it in practice, the twentieth-century stage *disavowed* realism only to keep it essentially intact; only to strengthen it with anti-naturalistic techniques, as in the use of expressionism to intensify the social reference of a *Waiting for Lefty* or *Death of a Salesman*.

We might clarify an involved situation here by dividing the century-long history of modern theatre into *two* movements—the one leading dramatic art toward realism, and the other drawing it away. Between 1880 and 1900 the two trends crystallized into a so-called independent theatre and a so-called art theatre movement. The independent theatre elected for everyday life and for prose. The art theatre fostered imaginative art, exotic experience, and poetry of drama and theatre. The one movement was officially dedicated to truth, the other to beauty.

The independent theatre acquired headquarters at André Antoine's Théâtre Libre, founded in Paris in 1887; the Freie Bühne formed by Otto Brahm and others in Berlin in 1889; the Independent Theatre of London (which produced Shaw's first play, *Widowers' Houses,* in 1892); and the Moscow Art Theatre, established by Stanislavski and Dantchenko in 1898. The early outposts of the art theatre movement were the little Théâtre des Arts in Paris, organized in 1890 by the poet Paul Fort; Lugné-

Poë's Théâtre de l'Oeuvre, which presented Maeterlinck's *Pelléas et Mélisande* in 1892; Max Reinhardt's Kleines Theatre of Berlin which also favored *Pelléas et Mélisande* with a production in 1903; and Jacques Copeau's Théâtre du Vieux Colombier, started in Paris in 1913.

The independent or free theatre leaders sought to achieve a more or less thorough illusion of reality by using box sets as well as environmental detail, and by separating the stage from the audience. Above all, they came to assume an imaginary fourth wall between the stage and the auditorium which forbade the playwright to soliloquize, or the actor to play to the public or even concede awareness of its presence in the darkened house. The realists' *internal* means of reforming the stage consisted of that deepening of emotional response and identification with dramatic characters nowadays both famous and infamous under such terms as the Stanislavski System of acting and The Method.

Conversely, the art theatre production program under the leadership of Gordon Craig, Reinhardt, Copeau, Meyerhold, and others developed strategies of stylization that would make expressive use of the theatre, giving theatrical artifice various degrees of prominence. It was this program that sparked the century's fascinating experiments, and it is with these experiments that we have tended to identify *modernism*. Realistic illusionism was thus replaced by a new principle—that of the "theatre theatrical." The new modernists from the latter-day Strindberg to O'Neill, Cocteau, and Giraudoux were bent upon "re-theatricalizing" the theatre that the realists of the nineteenth century had officially "de-theatricalized."

The strategies of re-theatricalization were many and varied. At one extreme, they involved no fundamental change in dramatic structure and only minor alterations in prevalent realistic types of staging and acting. The classic example is Rostand's *Cyrano de Bergerac* at the turn of the century. All that was required for this kind of theatricalization was the invention of a theatrical subject and plot. Cyrano's character is as histrionic as his first dramatic appearance or his famous death scene. By placing such colorful personalities in suitably theatrical situations and assigning to them some suitably bravura speeches (such as Cyrano's great speech on noses), it was possible to re-theatricalize the drama without violating the fourth-wall convention, and without atmospherically blurring or expressionistically distorting the outlines of reality. The method consisted in the recovery of romantic élan and the substituting of poetic high relief for prosaic low relief. The theatre was still expected to produce an illusion of reality, and the playgoer was expected to be grateful because the illusion was beautiful and noble.

This romanticism, revived with or without ironic overtones and controlled rhetoric, has never deserted the twentieth-century theatre. The romantic afflatus has not been less apparent in relatively recent work, such as Maxwell Anderson's historical verse plays and Cocteau's *The Eagle Has Two Heads,* than in the turn-of-the-century plays of Rostand and D'Annunzio. It is perhaps significant that New York welcomed the 1957-58 revival of Schiller's *Maria Stuart* in English and a French production of Hugo's *Marie Tudor,* while two of the most successful of the off-Broadway productions were James Forsyth's British drama *Heloise* and the vibrant Circle in the Square revival of Edwin Justus Mayer's *Children of Darkness.* Note also the romanticism of Christopher Fry's verbally ornamental plays, especially *The Lady's Not for Burning;* of many a poetic Irish drama by Synge and Yeats; of Molnar's successful blending of bland romance and sophisticated irony; and of the rueful French plays of Obey, Giraudoux, and Anouilh. "Romanticism and Realism," wrote Harvard's learned Professor Charles H. Grandgent, "do not succeed each other, as the text-books say; they exist side by side. Sometimes one is on the surface, sometimes the other, but they are both there all the time."

We continue to regard the theatre of the twentieth century as a branch of modern realistic art. Yet the decades since Coquelin's production of *Cyrano de Bergerac* in 1897 have also comprised one of the great periods of romantic theatre. Romantic drama has won new resources and acquired new attractions in the previously mentioned plays, and in many other works by such differently oriented playwrights as Maeterlinck, James M. Barrie, Gerhart Hauptmann, Hugo von Hofmannsthal, García Lorca, the mystical Paul Claudel, and the Nietzschean Henry de Montherlant. I submit that a theatrical period which contains so much romantic literature should not be denounced as prosaic and banal.

The revolt against realistic theatre, however, followed less familiar and more extreme courses than the revival of romanticism. It is unnecessary to dwell here on the symbolist, expressionist, dadaist, futurist, surrealist, constructivist, pirandellian, formalist, and epic realist programs. We can now look upon the 1890-1910 symbolist movement as an attempt to create a poetry of nuance and suggestion, and to inculcate into the theatre, whether by atmospheric playwriting or atmospheric lighting, a sense of the universal and the infinite. We can realize that works such as *Pelléas et Mélisande* and James M. Barrie's *Dear Brutus* and *Mary Rose* did more to dilute or dissolve the theatre than to revolutionize it. In stage-craft the effect of symbolism was considerable. Scenic design and lighting became expressively simplified. But again it must be noted that except for brief flurries of excitement in the case of some early Reinhardt or Robert Edmond Jones productions, it was possible for the realistic stage to absorb symbolist stagecraft. Suggestiveness and simplification, far from undermining the realistic theatre, actually tended to improve its effective-ness by suppressing the irrelevant.

The leaders of realism tended to welcome or join rather than repel the symbolist playwrights and artists. It is significant that Stanislavski pro-duced a number of Maeterlinck's plays and gave Gordon Craig an oppor-tunity to stage *Hamlet* at the Moscow Art Theatre in his most extravagant abstract style. Ibsen turned to symbolist playwriting without visible strain, and Maeterlinck could compliment the father of dramatic realism as a superlative symbolist—a fact sufficiently evident to anyone following Ibsen's work after *The Wild Duck*. It is worth noting that symbolist playwriting did not even entail any particular sacrifice of character analysis or social realism in Ibsen's case. The symbolist challenge actually enriched dramatic realism and extended its life.

Much the same thing can be said about the more drastic challenge of expressionist style and other experiments in new dramaturgy. As the recent favorable reception of Duerrenmatt's *The Visit* would indicate, expressionist art is no longer regarded as particularly esoteric or difficult to understand. It simply passes for theatre.

It is true that the expressionists used a dream-formation technique of distortion, fantastic characters and actions, and depersonalized or frenzied speech. What happened was simply that the theatre acquired one more technique to be variously employed for social protest or satire, as in Kaiser's *From Morn to Midnight,* Elmer Rice's *The Adding Machine,* Kaufman and Connelly's *Beggar on Horseback,* and O'Casey's *The Silver Tassie*. It was also used for the rendering of subjective tensions and fantasies, as in *The Emperor Jones,* and for numerous other purposes, including those of American musical-comedy entertainment as in *Lady in the Dark* and the first-act conclusion of *Oklahoma!* Tamed or untamed,

expressionism, having failed to displace realism, ended by serving the
realistic objectives of the period. Playwrights used expressionist stylization
for vividly projecting character problems, social disturbances, and other
familiar disorientations of twentieth-century man.

Many another bold program for the reformation of dramatic art dribbled out. As a matter of fact, a reverse tendency to move back to more or
less representational theatre, has also been observable in modern times.
Strindberg, Hauptmann, and others, including O'Neill, returned from
expressionist or symbolist excursions to the stringent or modified realism
of such plays as *The Dance of Death, Rose Bernd,* and *Long Days' Journey into Night.* Poets as captivated by formalistic drama as Masefield
and Lorca turned to the poetic naturalism of *The Tragedy of Nan* and
The House of Bernarda Alba. And the noteworthy blossoming of the
American musical theatre tended to bring even this intrinsically nonrealistic genre within the orbit of realism. The tendency was apparent in
Pal Joey, the Kurt Weill musical version of *Street Scene,* Blitzstein's
Regina, Menotti's *The Consul* and *The Saint of Bleecker Street,* and
several sociologically slanted Rodgers and Hammerstein musicals.

It is not my contention that the paradoxical survival of realistic theatre
art has been all gain and no loss—far from it. In Shakespearian production, especially, all gain came in departures from nineteenth century
realism, and all loss from an unimaginative adherence to that constricting
style. And there was enormous profit in artistry from the imaginative
staging of other classics, from the baroque fantastication of a Giraudoux,
and from the power of imagination in many a social drama. We soon
discovered that a sociological intention did not preclude imaginative
theatre whether symbolical as in O'Casey's *Within the Gates* and Werfel's *Goat Song,* lyrico-dramatic as in many an epic theatre demonstration
by Bertolt Brecht, or expressionist as in Miller's *Death of a Salesman.*

There can be no doubt that realism in both playwriting and play production owed its survival in large part to noteworthy changes in its own
texture that might not have arisen but for the challenge of the art theatres
and their antinaturalistic programs. A poetic or atmospheric naturalism
or realism became manifest at the turn of the century, most notably in
the work of the Moscow Art Theatre and its principal author, Anton
Chekhov. His contrapuntal technique, his touches of symbolism incorporated in the very titles of such plays as *The Sea Gull* and *The Cherry*

Orchard, and his compassion and humor sublimated naturalism with no loss of character or social reality.

Chekhov's example became an influence in twentieth-century dramatic realism. We have encountered it for half a century, with or without evidence, in many works from Russia to England and Ireland. With or without Chekhov, there could be little doubt that poetry and truth were not unreconcilable in the modern theatre. An irradiated realism has sustained the theatre from decade to decade in the twentieth century, although it has not sustained it often enough.

When we also take into account the pressures of external circumstance (the journalistic and scientific temper of the times and the social and political tensions of the age) it is not in the least surprising that the century that started disavowing the realistic theatre should have also started reëstablishing it from the beginning, rehabilitating it even while harboring romantic playwriting and briefly succumbing to the allurements of other non-naturalistic styles. It is true that ours has been an eclectic century, and our eclecticism has carried us so far indeed that an Elia Kazan can stage a thoroughly naturalistic drama of sexual tension and legacy hunting such as *Cat on a Hot Tin Roof* with considerable physical stylization, including the use of a skeletal stage setting. But we have wandered away from essential realism by experimenting with various styles only to return to it again and again, and the over-all results arouse mixed feelings of gratification and frustration.

In today's theatre we do not often ascend the tragic heights. Most of our high tragedies are low, unless they are reminiscently romantic, like Maxwell Anderson's or embedded in folk tradition like Lorca's *Blood Wedding.* In modern theatre the distinction between tragedy and comedy has often been indistinct, as in *The Cherry Orchard, Juno and the Paycock,* and *The Plough and the Stars.*

Verbal poetry, in general, does not thrive in our milieu; it is either absent or watered down. The realms of the poet and the dramatist are kept distinct, even though now and then a Claudel, Eliot, or Fry tries to cross the boundaries and sometimes succeeds. In Classic Greece and Elizabethan England the poets were playwrights and the playwrights poets. In twentieth-century Europe and America, as a rule, the poets aren't playwrights and the playwrights aren't poets. Poetry seeps into the colloquial language and prose of modern plays as atmosphere, mood, or intimation. The most pervasive and usually the most effective poetry is not one of words, but of the theatrical organization of the play and the production elements, the stylized setting and performance, involved in its presentation. Poetry, in brief, is mainly in Cocteau's words a *"poésie de théâtre,"* and can easily become a specious tour de force on the part of an overly impetuous or unscrupulous ambitious stage director.

As a result of scenic artistry and other factors, such as the advances in electric lighting, the art and craft of stage production has never attained more frequent excellence, richer resources, and greater possibilities than in our century. Nor has any period of theatrical history been richer in plays of general worth, while being relatively poor in masterpieces. The dramatic compositions of the age are at their best exciting or fascinating without being overpowering. They are, with few exceptions, the work of journeymen rather than masters, while our technologically accomplished world position manifests itself abundantly in the supplementary stage arts. The baby spotlight outshines the verbal icon and the poetry of language. Genius of the first order in this theatre tends to be electronic rather than literary. No one then can render a favorable verdict on the theatre of our century without conceding these qualifications. They are not few, and they are not negligible.

2 PLAYWRITING
AT THE CROSSROADS

Our mid-century theatre has been in a state of more or less constant crisis. In no respect has it been more disappointing than in the caliber of most new plays. Like other contemporary writers the playwright has been disoriented, but more than other writers he has betrayed his disorientation because he works under extreme disadvantages. He must address a large public, which responds to his work manifestly under the influence of the time spirit. He must also satisfy excessive requirements imposed by the extravagant faith placed in him (from eighty-five thousand to a hundred and fifty thousand dollars' worth in the case of a Broadway production) and by the extreme insecurity of theatrical production.

Rarely does the playwright complete a final preproduction version without having followed extensive suggestions from his producer. Usually he must rework his play during the rehearsal and try-out periods because of pressure from the stage director. Many of the author's afterthoughts simply cannot be incorporated in the playing text because it is too late for his actors to discard old lines and learn new ones. Rarely does the playwright work under even moderately favorable conditions.

His situation in our time goes well beyond the normal hazards of his complex and chronically harassed craft. It is an error to assume that the craft itself can remain stable or that it encounters the same opportunities and challenges in one period that it does in another. In the theatre instability is particularly marked, and the incidence of diminishing returns for certain kinds of substance and style is extraordinarily high. Interest and taste, the very orbit of cultural life, may undergo radical changes

within a single decade. The playwright who has much meaning for one
brief period may have little for another.

Instinctively or from occupational experience effective writers are aware
of this fact to some degree, and they cannot long remain effective in the
theatre without reconsidering and readjusting their perspectives. Arthur
Miller and Tennessee Williams are giving serious thought to their problems both as writers in an age of anxiety and failure and as relative new-
comers in the modern theatre with more than three-quarters of a century
of trial and error behind it.

As a rule, however, playwrights need to be made aware of the situation
in their craft, because they tend to confuse a perspective with mere
accommodation to fashion. The practical playwright is usually responsive
to current interests rather than to the broad stream of development in
his art, and since the rise of realism in the nineteenth century he has
been peculiarly inclined to view his obligation as one of echoing popular
interests. He succumbs to mediocrity to the degree that mediocrity is
inherent in his subject. Alfred North Whitehead wrote that "Tennyson
was a great poet with a mediocre subject," namely, Victorian England.
Playwrights often suffer the same fate. Moreover, they are acutely susceptible to the seductions of the moment.

Playwrights must realize that they are standing at the crossroads of
modern drama. They are called upon to choose one of two ways of writing
for the stage—the way of the *reporter* and the way of the *creator*. They
must choose the latter if the stage is to survive the severe and growing
competition of the mass media. Just as playwrights, especially in America,
can no longer compete with routine farces and melodrama, now the
stock in trade of television and films, so they can no longer compete
against the camera's facsimile reproductions of humdrum reality.

The average playwright hesitates at the crossroads. He does so because
the way of the reporter once proved satisfactory, or at least profitable, and
was equated with truthfulness and significance. At the same time, he is
wary of flights into imaginative art because these have so often represented a retreat from reality, a rejection of popular theatre, or a sterile
Bohemianism. More than he realizes his preference for so-called down-to-
earth reportorial drama is the result of misconceptions. In writing conventionally, he confuses the drama of stencils with the dramatic realism
that gave theatre its modernity and claim to importance after 1880.

He fails to realize that the masters of realistic drama were creators of life *in the drama* rather than sedulous imitators of life *outside the theatre.* The modern masters shaped an experience out of the substance of their passion and intellect, instead of setting up a camera in the streets or the family parlor and letting the camera click mechanically. The new playwright, especially in the American theatre, fails to distinguish sharply enough between an Ibsen or a Chekhov and any of the numerous mediocrities who have taken the name of realism in vain. He does not distinguish either between the pseudo-poetic artificers and true poets of the theatre. He concludes from the most doubtful avant-garde aberrations of expressionists, surrealists, and decadent exhibitionists that these represent the *only* alternatives to his "honest" kind of still-life or dead-life realism.

Antirealists, reacting to pseudo-realism, have drawn their own erroneous conclusions. Too many of them conclude that it is high time to swing from a flying trapeze and thumb noses at the public as a reliable method of creating a new dramatic art. They assume that anything that contravenes realism is ipso facto art, thus mistaking ambiguity for profundity and sensationalism for creative potency.

Today the novelty has worn off both realism and antirealism as principles of dramatic composition. The realistic playwright can no longer count on making an impression because he has provided an accurate picture of surface reality. Nor can any antirealistic playwright startle us into delight merely because he has distorted it. It is time to realize that the sensationalism of realism and the sensationalism of antirealism are by now equally passé.

Most important to the state of dramatic art, however, is not that a playwright can no longer win success or esteem on factitious grounds of novelty, but that certain factors that once gave impetus to his writing are no longer sufficiently operative. I have in mind the need of some fresh stimulus. Writers for the stage need a sense of relatedness. They must feel that they are not creating in a void, and for a vaulting mind and spirit even the theatre considered as an autonomous institution is essentially a vacuum. "Theatre for theatre's sake" has never been able to nourish memorable playwriting. As John Livingston Lowes wisely declared, "the imagination never operates in a vacuum." A sense of extratheatrical purpose is as marked in the work of an effective antirealist like Bertolt Brecht as in the work of a great realist like Ibsen, and is as decisive in the comic genius of a Bernard Shaw as in the tragic sense of an O'Neill. These playwrights believed with Moussorgsky that, "Art is not an end in itself, but a means of addressing humanity." It is to the weakening of extra-theatrical purpose, to the loss of creative incentives which mere show business cannot provide that we must attribute at least some of the flatness of contemporary playwriting.

The modern drama was born in rebellion and cradled in criticism. Intelligence, vigor, and vivacity were attendant upon its development in the last quarter of the nineteenth century. One reason why pioneering modern realism was not flaccid, as most realistic plays have been since the Forties, is that it was *critical* realism. The critical spirit led to adventurousness in dramatic art itself. Personal passion produced individuality of style. And the need for making a special view apparent produced changes in dramatic structure that carried realistic dramaturgy well beyond the mere adoption of the fourth-wall convention of pretending that actions transpire on the stage exactly as they do off stage.

We may recall the highly individual style and form of Ibsen, Strindberg, Chekhov, Shaw, and the young O'Casey. To realize their distinctiveness we need only observe Ibsen's development of a retrospective, stock-taking, discussion-pyramided type of drama which first appeared in *A Doll's House* and culminated in *John Gabriel Borkman*; or Strindberg's intense concentration on dramatic crisis to the exclusion of other elements of plot in such plays as *Miss Julie* and *Creditors*; or Chekhov's contrapuntal weave of action; or Shaw's dialectical brilliance in melodrama, farce, and comedy of ideas; or O'Casey's lyrical pathos and mordant humor. These and other distinctive realists did not lose a distinctive style whenever they chose to forsake the realistic theatre. When Ibsen adopted symbolism, when Strindberg turned to expressionism, or when Shaw wrote *Heartbreak House* as "A Fantasia in the Russian Manner on English Themes," to cite his own somewhat dubious subtitle, each was still bent on having his say in his own manner.

Also associated with critical realism was the sheer pleasure of intellectualism, most conspicuous in Shaw's writing. Intellect was once considered a distinction rather than a detriment. A playwright was expected to have a mind, in which he gloried. Moreover, the advanced theatre believed a playwright could not be modern unless he possessed integrity. He could not be modern if he moderated or vulgarized reality for the sake of approval, which explains the critic Shaw's contemptuous description of the pseudo-Ibsenist Pinero as a playwright who had no idea "beyond that of doing something daring and bringing down the house by running away from the consequences."

Not surprisingly, then, the true modernist in the theatre between 1880 and 1939 usually had his pioneering work produced by experimental stage groups. In Europe such work was less taxed by the requirement of serving commercial enterprise because the play appeared in repertory, whereas nowadays, particularly on Broadway, a play that does not win immediate success is quickly laid in lavender. Too often if a play does not promise popular success in our high-cost theatre, the work is either tailored to suit the market or denied a professional stage production. Only in recent years has there been a slight swing away from this commodity-philosophy of play production. Yet laudable as such off-Broadway enterprises as the Circle in the Square or the Cherry Lane in New York have been, they are still no substitute for the repertory system.

A sense of discovery was also a powerful ferment of dramatic modernism, whether discovery took the form of naturalistic scientism and sociology or of psychological exploration, such as Strindberg and Wedekind undertook. Nor should we slight the efforts of playwrights to discover the common earth and the common man. The discovery of unfashionable life for the theatre gave us the plays of Synge and O'Casey, Tolstoi's *The Power of Darkness* and Gorky's *The Lower Depths,* and the first plays of O'Neill and Odets.

Finally, the playwrights were likely to benefit from the stimulus of visionary optimism. They had an active faith in man, however greatly scientific determinism tended to reduce his tragic stature. Without that faith there would have been little point in Ibsen's or Shaw's prodding or haranguing modern man, or in exposing his frustrations in a particular society. It may be argued that the pioneering playwrights were deluded, that they suffered from the fallacy and pathos of modern liberalism. It cannot be denied, however, that they derived purposefulness, passion, and even exuberance from their faith. Believers in progress may become the dupes, even the victims, of progress, but confidence and a sense of engagement promote dramatic vigor. Can one doubt this conclusion after comparing the difference in voltage between the early and late plays of Clifford Odets, or between the plays Shaw wrote before 1914 and those he wrote after 1930?

That the pervasive disenchantment of our world should have affected

playwrights is hardly surprising. It is understandable that in the contemporary situation playwrights are now wary of the social prescriptions
popular in the theatre of the Thirties. One does not expect writers to *will*
themselves into believing untenable postulates for man or society. But
many young writers seem to be immobilized at the crossroads of modern
theatre because they have not yet learned to make anything even out of
their disbelief. Without trying to account for current apathy, I venture
to describe the condition as one of intellectual sloth, as hesitancy to let
the mind or spirit assert itself even in disenchantment. It may be that
the alternative to the old critical realism sparked by optimism is a new
critical realism sparked by disillusion. As yet our playwrights have shown
little aptitude for this second kind of realism. Only in Europe has this
aptitude appeared on the stage, in the plays of Beckett, Ionesco, Gênet,
and Duerrenmatt.

Since Western theatre is now eclectic, our playwrights can elect a
nonrealistic style of theatre as an alternative. They can even elect dramatic estheticism without necessarily disintegrating the modern stage.
The test, however, must be the same as for realism, namely, the quality
of the achievement.

Nihilism or alienation became pronounced in nonrealistic European
dramaturgy during and after World War I. It became marked in the
case of the expressionists, dadaists, and surrealists. Ranging from the fin
de siècle cult of symbolism to the cultivation of frenzy after 1914, antirealism proved largely arid only at this latter end of the spectrum. Estheticism maintained at least a belief and an adventurousness in art, besides
correcting the excesses of naturalism. Dedication to art is considerably
more fruitful than the dedication to precisely nothing which characterizes
the commercial stage in our time. An art for art's sake policy, if carried
to logical conclusions, may be a sign of decadence, but we should not
overlook the fact that estheticism has its own assertiveness, too. It demands
integrity from the artist; it requires him to respect his sensibility and to
strive for a high degree of artistry in the service of style and form. The
pursuit of art for art's sake, which is paralleled by a theatre for theatre's
sake principle, has obvious limitations but can be in some respects affirmative and humanistic. It is not surprising, therefore, that the esthetic
movement of the 1890's left a small legacy to playwrights of the present
generation. Beckett's, Ionesco's, and Tennessee Williams' estheticism at-
tests to the vitality of the legacy.

There is no reason to assume that estheticism cannot draw upon the resources of modern realism even while discarding realistic dramaturgy and peephole stage conventions. The vital elements of realism remained in force, for example, when the late Jean Giraudoux wrote imaginative plays infused with his considerable critical intelligence. There is no essential conflict between the aims of modern realism and of poetic extravaganza or fantasy in *The Madwoman of Chaillot* or the *Don Juan in Hell* interlude of *Man and Superman*. There is no reason why contemporary theatre should be limited to two bad choices: the artistic ineptitude of would-be realists and the mental vacuousness of would-be esthetes.

If playwrights, especially in America, seem incapable of availing themselves of the possibilities inherent in modern nonrealistic art, the reason is twofold. Faith in art as a sufficient goal has been at a low ebb in the commercial theatre ever since the social idealism of the Thirties discredited an art for art's sake viewpoint. But the infusion of nonrealistic dramaturgy with the critical spirit never made much headway in the American theatre after the Twenties. Today the critical spirit is so enervated that it does not invigorate nonrealistic drama any more than it invigorates realistic drama. Tennessee Williams' *Camino Real,* the most recent American experiment in the symbolist-expressionist style, was as transparent in its thinking as in its literary effusiveness. If British poetic drama as written by Eliot and Fry cannot be charged with transparency, it is not exempt from another charge: that of sterility. I would make a grudging exception only in favor of *The Cocktail Party* and *The Lady's Not for Burning.* Strong claims have been made for the work of Jean Anouilh in France, but as yet I cannot wholly validate them myself, and I am inclined to doubt that posterity will. Not one of his plays, except his early *Thieves' Carnival* and his one-act tragedy *Medea,* has seemed to me completely satisfactory. In no country's theatre, except the French in which Beckett and Ionesco have made advances since those made by Giraudoux and Anouilh, can I discern any unique dramatic stylization distinguished by vitality.

Playwriting has been enfeebled in the mid-century theatre because neither the realistic nor the esthetic legacy has manifested sufficient potency. Both styles of modern theatre have suffered much deterioration from within—realism because it became too commonplace, estheticism because it became too empty and pretentious. The failings of each mode

of modernism were inherent in the mode—observe the dry texture of
Ibsen's realistic plays and the vaporous quality of Maeterlinck's symbolist
efforts. In many instances their successors merely exaggerated the faults,
latter-day realists increasing the commonplaceness while latter-day antirealists increased the vapor. The contemporary social and political situation has undoubtedly debilitated playwriting, making it placid and eva-
sive or agreeably superficial. But its deficiencies and defects have been
intrinsic to modern dramatic art itself; inherited tendencies exact their
toll and the past must share the blame for present failure. Bad example
stalemated realism and discredited estheticism.

Standing between seedy realism and motley theatricalism, the contemporary playwright is likely to be cross-ventilated with no particular benefit
to his art or his public. Especially is this true in the American professional
theatre where the unstimulating realistic play usually expires on the
boards and the stylized play rarely reaches them. Nodding in the direction
of debased realism an Elmer Rice has both an artistic and financial fiasco
with *The Winner* or with an earlier problem play such as *A New Life*.
Gazing in the opposite direction of symbolic estheticism a Tennessee
Williams bravely runs into a fog with a *Camino Real*.

Where then may the playwright, whose plight is not entirely alien to
his colleagues in fiction and nondramatic poetry, take his stand? I cannot
adopt a Pisgah view in order to direct the new playwright toward the
Promised Land. But it is neither impossible nor impertinent to direct
his gaze toward possibilities suggested by past experience and present
exigency. The playwright might consider the following possibilities of
ending his present impasse:

Let him pursue the way of realism, if he inclines in that direction,
but let him reject photography. Let his *perception* and *apprehension*
be realistic. Whether he adopts the method of direct assault upon
reality or some indirect Chekhovian method, he is entirely free to avail
himself of an imaginative presentation. Without such presentation,
The Glass Menagerie would have been tenuous. Without the modified
expressionism Arthur Miller mingled with realism, *Death of a Salesman* would have been humdrum, especially in view of the representative commonplaceness of his Willy Loman.

A contemporary playwright's art does not have to be humdrum because his characters lack brilliance or some other glamorous attribute. His imagination should be able to give them dimension and stature; he should not shy away from suffering and exultation but remember that, as Masefield said, commonplace people "dare not suffer and cannot exult." Imaginative form can transfigure subject matter. The *form* can be poetic. The playwright can bring into being a "poetry of the theatre" in the action, organization, and sequence of the episodes. Treadmill playwriting, that is, walking the treadmills of an ordinary time sequence and routine exposition, is unnecessary. It can actually prove detrimental to the higher realism of exposing or expressing the truth about individuals and societies or, as Pascal put it, "the grandeur and misery of men."

Poetry can also be achieved in realistic drama by attention to nuance, atmosphere, and mood. Too many plays are written today without sensibility, without a dominant feeling or feeling-tone in individual scenes and in the play as a whole. Insufficient stress is placed on variety of scene within the unity of the play. Action is shown under a glare of white light without any concern for chiaroscuro. Language, too, is susceptible to enrichment and intensification without violence to artistic (as opposed to phonographic) plausibility. Both colloquial and formal dialogue can be modulated and accentuated, can be enriched with rhythm and imagery without resorting to reminiscent patterns or literary echoes.

Realism need not be cravenly imitative in portrayal and description. It can even be discreetly symbolic and suggestive, as in *The Wild Duck, The Sea Gull,* and *The Cherry Orchard* of the veteran realists, Ibsen and Chekhov. It is not necessary to present ideas with a massive retaliation technique; they can be parceled out, orchestrated, and counterpointed.

The play of ideas should *play* rather than bombard. It is conceivable that the bankruptcy of serious *ideas* in the theatre has been, to a degree, a bankruptcy of *method,* which began when intellection became confused with the vending of specific solutions. That the solutions have not worked out very well is no reason why the intellect must abdicate from the theatre. Nor is there any reason to seek the tether of uncritical traditionalism, by prescript from Eliot or anyone else. Because the freedom of modernism led the playwright, as well as his fellow citizens, into error is no reason for replacing inquiry with dogma. It would be better to reflect that realism erred because it became dogmatic rather than critical, prescriptive rather than exploratory.

Finally, there may well be a future for poetic drama, if it serves to illuminate modern life rather than to obscure it with windy exclamations or obscurantist metaphysics. But the poet needs a stern discipline for the modern theatre. He should not rely on traditional blank verse, for example, but on an idiom and meter attuned to contemporary speech. Ornate rhetoric should not be mistaken for dramatic poetry. If the contemporary theatre is to be redeemed by poetry the dramatic conception of the work, the characterization, and the specific situations must determine poetic expression. There is little sense in inviting contemporary poets into the theatre unless they learn to communicate content without elaborate exegesis, for which there is obviously no time during a performance. The poet must simply become a playwright if we are to have a sound alternative to dramatic realism. In order to be meaningful to our stage he will have to condescend a little to our common world. In aiming at universality he should not rule out contemporary realities and become merely historical.

The future of both realism and poetry depends upon developments a critic cannot insure. Perhaps it would be best to let Bernard Shaw have the last word. "From time to time," Shaw wrote, "dramatic art gets a germinal impulse. There follows in the theatre a spring which flourishes into a glorious summer. This becomes stale almost before its arrival is generally recognized; and the sequel is not a new golden age, but a barren winter that may last any time from fifteen years to a hundred and fifty. Then comes a new impulse; and the cycle begins again." We can only hope that it will begin soon.

3 WHAT PRICE EXALTATION?

A question that continues to agitate literary circles is whether it is possible to write tragedy in modern times, whether indeed it has been possible to produce tragedies at all ever since Ibsen's generation abandoned romanticism. The subject has become a vested interest of academic criticism, but has also involved nonacademic critics and creative writers. Those who deplore the vogue of realism or the absence of poetry on the stage are especially inclined to make the impossibility of writing tragedy an article of faith. They seem to exclude modern drama from the aristocracy of letters altogether. Since tragedy is the most aristocratic of dramatic genres, they conclude that a tragic playwright simply cannot thrive in the popular theatre.

It is not the theatre, but the modern world that receives criticism's first and most devastating fire. How indeed should the exalted art of tragedy, which has traditionally dealt with the fate of singular individuals, flourish in the age of the common man? How should the grandeur of the tragic hero and the splendor of tragic vision survive in a world leveled down by democracy and cheapened by mass-production and mass-consumption? But the leaders of this mandarin brand of criticism, many of whom have cherished ideals of classic or medieval unity, have been wont to observe that this world characterized by a distressing sameness is paradoxically a divided one. It is said to be incapable of providing the individual with a coherent view of himself and of his place in the universe.

The same critics who disdain a world grown irrevocably common are apt to deplore the absence of communion in it. They regret the lack of tradition and belief in our mongrel culture. With no myth or cult to assure the continuity of time-honored values, no religion to relate the individual unequivocally to the universe, no fixity of class structure to bind men to their place, we presumably cannot have significant dramatic action: it cannot be significant because it cannot be communally meaningful. The high concern with human fate that has characterized the tragic art of past ages must therefore make way for considerations of temporary and local conflict between ant-men who are paradoxically common without being representative.

A commonplace realism takes the place of the ideality to which the art of tragedy aspires by historical example since the time of Aeschylus and by critical prescript since the time of Aristotle. And it is a rare event indeed when the language of the modern stage does not reflect the commonplace view of mankind. The plot may pulsate with exciting events, as in the plays of O'Neill, but the language limps behind the action and limits the tragic resonance. Inarticulateness dooms the characters to a level of consciousness too low to sustain an impressive personality and a significant action.

That inarticulateness is itself a concomitant of choosing low-grade personalities for dramatic representation and of holding a low view of humanity. Henry James was surely correct when he declared in one of his prefaces that, "the agents in any drama are interesting only in proportion as they feel their respective situations," and feeling communicates itself mainly through language. The prose of modern drama, often commonplace if not indeed barbarically colloquial, is both a symptom of the absence of tragic art and a cause of its absence.

So runs the current argument, which also notes that science and sociology are antitragic. When behavior is explained largely by heredity, instinct, and environment man is deprived of any genuine responsibility for his actions that would make dramatic conflict humanistically relevant and calamity morally significant. There can be no tragic heroes in the bleak commonwealth of conditioned animals.

Nor is the individual given materially greater significance when he is treated as a psychological case history. His writhings in the grip of a neurosis or psychosis may gratify our curiosity but not our moral sense. He may be interesting as a specimen of morbidity, but his plight will exalt neither the character nor spectator. An heroic view of man is the last thing that sociology and psychopathology can supply, whereas it has been the peculiar triumph of tragic art in the past to affirm the wonder of man.

For ages, tragedy has been a high mystery by means of which defeat has been transformed into victory for the human spirit. In this mystery, which converts despair over the human condition into reconciliation with fate and leaves us exhilarated rather than dismayed, the protagonist is the sacrifice, and the sacrifice must be worthy of the rite. With respect to both the sacrificial victim and the humanity that the tragic rite redeems, modern rationalistic inquiry is held to be altogether too disillusioning.

But if the modern viewpoint is too depressing, it is also too optimistic for tragedy, for modern liberalism has been inveterately melioristic. Denying that evil and suffering are absolute and unalterable, the liberal viewpoint has proposed to remove or moderate the very conditions that make tragedy possible and its ministrations welcome. The modern viewpoint appears to be both too hard and not hard enough for tragedy.

The critics of liberal modernism cannot be completely represented by the arguments above, for they have set up their batteries not only on the literary heights but on the summits of theological disputation. They have wondered how modern writers, who are mostly of the liberal persuasion, could expect to write tragedy while rejecting the doctrine of original sin, failing to make characters accountable to God, or depriving man of the belief that his suffering has spiritual significance.

Some critics have also become amateur anthropologists in emphasizing the ritualistic character of a tragic performance. They believe that because tragedy developed out of religious ritual in Greece, the modern theatre, which is not at all pyramided upon any religious rites, is unable to engender tragic art. The error in this kind of reasoning is the familiar genetic fallacy, which assumes that a thing must remain what it was at its inception.

The genetic fallacy is not always conspicuously advanced. It is apt to be screened from view by the argument that a community of values (as best expressed in religion and ritual) is essential to the development of tragedy, and this is, on the surface, a reasonable belief. If the tragic experience demonstrates the calamitous results of a character's conduct, that conduct must obviously constitute a violation of a more or less accepted norm. In a community which sanctioned parricide and incest, Oedipus would not be a tragic character. And if a tragically misguided character is to arrive at restorative perceptions or redeeming realizations these must be acceptable to the public. Playwright and public must be in agreement on values, on what perceptions are restorative or what realizations are redemptive. The emphasis on such agreement becomes an argument against the possibility of writing tragedy today once the critic disallows modern diversity and scepticism. It is doubtful that such communion was ever absolute in the individualistic Athenian and Elizabethan periods, and perhaps communion is a religious experience that ought not to be confused with social conformity. History supplies many examples of ancient despotisms and modern totalitarian societies that failed to produce tragic art. But the conservative position, as laid down in previous decades by Hulme and T.S. Eliot, is indeed the final emplacement from which traditionalists offer resistance to the idea that modern playwrights can compose tragedy.

Traditionalists tend to be inflexible on this issue. They rarely admit that any modern dramatist has written a true tragedy, and a play dealing tragically with a commoner's fate, such as *Death of a Salesman*, is likely to be treated as pretentious vulgarity. A more moderate position grants a few deviations into tragedy by Ibsen, O'Neill, and perhaps a few other writers. But the advanced and more persistent traditionalist view holds that realistic dramaturgy and prose are incompatible with tragedy, as are liberalism, meliorism, unconditional sympathy with ordinary persons, scepticism, and modern individualism. According to this view, the would-be tragedian, unless he renounces the ambience of modern thought and popular art, will end up only with melodrama, propaganda, pathology, pathos and sentimentality, or just plain nastiness and bathos.

That is one side of the argument concerning tragedy in the modern theatre, and it is not difficult to understand why it should be supported with so much intellectual artillery. The fire is directed at the modern spirit, which presumably cannot have much worth if it does not produce tragic art—an assumption which would invalidate all but the three brief periods of human history that produced Attic, Elizabethan, and neoclassic French tragedy of the latter part of the seventeenth century.

But the other side of the argument, though less often maintained, has also been vigorously advanced. Implicit in the theatre's hopes and endeavors for the past three-quarters of a century has been the conviction that tragedy could be revitalized by sinking its roots deeper into modern consciousness and by relating it more closely to the immediate life of the times. I do not know of any comprehensive statement that adequately presented this viewpoint in the United States until Herbert J. Muller published his vigorous book, *The Spirit of Tragedy*, late in 1956. Presentations of the modern liberal position have been scattered in a variety of prefaces, letters, diaries, and reviews; liberal doctrine concerning tragedy has never been particularly impressive, even though such important writers as Hebbel, Zola, Strindberg, Galsworthy, and Arthur Miller have contributed to it. The real force of the argument must be sought in the works to which the theories were prefatory or supplementary. It resides in whatever realizations of tragedy can be found in modern plays.

A fundamental premise has been the opinion that a great deal of the tragic art of the past, while excellent as far as it went, belongs to the past. The pagan beliefs that served Attic tragedy twenty-five centuries ago are no longer acceptable to modern man. Neither are the beliefs of the Elizabethan period or the age of Louis XIV. *There is simply no single true philosophy of tragedy any more than there is a single inviolable tragic form.* Tragic art is subject to evolutionary processes, and tragedy created in modern times must be modern. The fact that it will be different from tragedy written three, five, or twenty-five centuries ago does not mean that it will no longer be tragedy; it will merely be different. It will be as different from earlier tragic literature as *Hamlet* differs from *Oedipus Rex*, or Racine's *Phèdre* from Euripides' *Hippolytus*.

Aristotle himself did not presume to legislate on tragedy for all time, but spoke modestly about tragic art as he knew it from the works of a number of Athenian playwrights. He spoke of tragedy as it had developed up to his time in Greece, rather than of an everlasting and invariable type of drama. In generalizing about tragic method he spoke of optimal approaches rather than of absolutes. In the *Poetics* he even countenanced a turn of fortune from bad to good as a possible (though not the most effective) pattern of a tragedy. It was apparent to him that the Greek plays differed in kind and degree of tragic artistry, whatever their external structural similarities. It could be apparent to us, too, if we did not invite the hobgoblin of consistency into literary theory and attribute to Greek tragedy a single form, quality, and effect. The leaders of the modern theatre after 1870 rejected esthetic absolutism. They envisaged not only the possibility of writing tragedy with modern minds, but of extending its range and enlarging its potentialities as a reflection of man and his world. Some apologists for modern drama could even maintain that antiquated Greek notions of fate had been replaced in the theatre by the sounder deterministic factors of instinct, heredity, and environment.

The modern view started with considerations of character and environment. Tragic art was allowed to focus on all, rather than on only class-privileged, representatives of the human race. By 1870 the destiny of nations was no longer being shaped exclusively by a dynasty or an aristocracy. It was virtually granted that a character's social status was secondary to his stature as a human being. Ibsen and his successors did not intend to repeat the error of early writers of bourgeois tragedy, such as Diderot and Lillo, who made common characters commonplace in feeling, will, and destiny. Many writers created passion-charged personalities, such as Ibsen's Hedda Gabler or O'Neill's Christine and Lavinia, the modern Clytemnestra and Electra of *Mourning Becomes Electra.*

Examples from the past favored latitude. It had been possible for Shakespeare to plumb human destiny with so divided a character as Hamlet. It had even proved possible to create tragedy with essentially antiheroic figures such as Richard II and Euripides' Electra. If the modern playwright tended more and more to focus on characters of divided will and thwarted desire, he was under no necessity to renounce all intention of giving them tragic prominence.

The generally nonheroic character could be revealed as heroic in some central aspect of his being and action. Strindberg's mentally tormented Captain in *The Father* is a clinical case. Yet he could be fully analyzed as a pathological character without lessening the force of his defense of masculinity in an overfeminized society. His personality and experiences were too intensely realized by Strindberg to generate pity without also producing fear. The Captain, as protagonist, fought too strenuously against his wife Laura, the antagonist, and he resisted his fate too forcefully to communicate pathos rather than passion. Lowly Willy Loman of *Death of a Salesman* could be tethered to the satchel of a traveling salesman and made to swallow the mental garbage of a materialistic society. But he could also be allowed to assert his sense of worth against his own littleness and to rage like a caged lion in his suburban home—and suburban mind. According to liberal doctrine modern dramatists could reveal more, rather than fewer, facets of humanity and with greater, rather than less, conviction.

That communication with modern audiences was henceforth to be attained on the maximum levels of understanding available to modern consciousness was indeed the ruling conviction of Ibsen, Strindberg, Shaw, Hauptmann, Curel, and other pioneers of the late nineteenth-century theatre, to which our own is still very largely bound. In their view it was preposterous to compose tragedy according to histrionic notions of heroism, and they consequently broke with romanticism as decisively as romantic writers had broken with neoclassicism. The moderns could admire Shakespeare without believing that the Elizabethan world-picture was correct or meaningful for the modern world; and they could find merit in classic tragedy or even employ its retrospective dramatic structure, as Ibsen did in *Ghosts*, without subscribing to Greek notions of fate. It seemed sounder as well as more honest to attempt to translate ancient concerns into present ones and old concepts into new ones. Aeschylus and Euripides had not hesitated to do this, and there was no particular reason why Ibsen and Strindberg or O'Neill and Arthur Miller should.

The proponents of modern drama could contend that they met the fundamental requirements of tragic art with considerable fidelity. They approached their subject with high seriousness; they motivated human conduct, they refrained from mere pathos by attending to social and psychological causation, and they made calamity a means for achieving significant revelations concerning the individual character and his world. For modern sociological and psychological writers error, evil, and suffering were never ends in themselves, useful only in providing the audience with a *frisson* and the playwright with an income. They knew that tragic perception was a necessary element in the tragic experience and proposed to provide dramatic realizations not by rote but by critical inquiry.

Sometimes it was the main character who was led from passion to perception or from suffering to understanding. Sometimes, however, the final comprehension, the tragic realization, belonged to *a group of secondary characters*, whose role was not radically different from that of a Greek chorus. Sometimes it was the *audience* that was expected to understand what the characters could not clearly comprehend or express. The means might differ in respect to the situation and the intelligence of the character, but suffering was not allowed to be devoid of meaning. In one way or another calamity produced tragic insight. Direct or indirect means supplied the awareness that the modern protagonist could not be allowed to articulate because he could not be convincingly given the intelligence of a Hamlet or the formal eloquence of the characters or choruses of classic formal tragedies.

Articulateness on the part of characters was indeed very much the concern of modernists for, as critics impatient with prose in the theatre tend to forget, verse-drama had become quite decadent in the nineteenth

century before it was abandoned. (It was not abandoned so absolutely
that an Ibsen, Hauptmann, or Maxwell Anderson would not go back to
verse.) Leaders of the modern theatre found it necessary to reject verse
and rhetorical prose not merely for the sake of fourth-wall verisimilitude,
but for the purpose of preserving simple artistic integrity. They could not
countenance the deterioration of feeling into bathos and the customary
use of eloquence as a screen for hollow content, a fault in a good deal of
nineteenth-century writing in which poetry and original sensibility and
thought rarely met. The decision to write prose-drama was the result of
clear deliberation on Ibsen's part. The author of *Brand* and *Peer Gynt*
laid aside a considerable reputation as a poet and a hard-won success as
a literary playwright when he entered upon the realistic, prose part of his
career in his fiftieth year. That his prose became a powerful instrument
for demonstrating the mental and emotional processes of his characters
is evident even in translation. The verbal exchanges between speakers,
the double meaning of many a line, and the symbolist stress on key words
or phrases, such as "vine-leaves in his hair" (Hedda's words), do not indicate indifference to the role of language in the drama.

The cumulative effect of Ibsen's and other writers' reformation of
dialogue could provide characters with an articulateness that had previously been attained only by means of set speeches, tirades, and soliloquies in prerealistic drama. Ibsen's successors, among them such masters
of dialogue as Shaw and O'Casey, continued to prove that prose could
be written for the theatre with compelling *brio*. Many a verse-drama of
the past three centuries sounds exceedingly flat with its familiar tropes
and metronomic regularity by comparison with the verbal explosions in
essentially realistic plays. And dramatic excitement was heightened by a
variety of poetic effects—by nuance, reverberations, and counterpoint.
Peasant dialect, as in the plays of Synge, lent a new music and a new
imagery for the theatre, as did city street colloquialism in the early work
of O'Casey and Odets. Symbolism as well could be imbedded in the soil
of realism whenever a playwright was capable of composing a *Rosmer-
sholm* or *John Gabriel Borkman*.

The search for a poetically charged prose need not exhaust the effort
to insure expressiveness on the modern stage. Developments in physical
production and in the art of acting have contributed imaginativeness and
power. Gordon Craig called for expressive stage design and Stanislavski
for *inner* realism in acting, and both were heeded. The masters of poetry

of the theatre could give scenic atmosphere and visual symbolization to tragic action. "A good scene design should not be a picture but an image," wrote Craig's American disciple Robert Edmond Jones; it could create "an expectancy, a foreboding, a tension" in the theatre. That acting could add emotional depth and stature to a dramatic character was evident whenever a Duse or Nazimova played an Ibsen part.

Finally, we should not overlook the modern playwright's use of new dramatic styles, fantastic invention, and expressive distortion of scenes and characters. Ever since the turn of the century there have been expressionist as well as realistic attempts to write tragedy. Playwrights who gravitated toward expressionism endeavored to give a tragic accent to such contemporary themes as the Oedipus complex, the alienation of the individual in a mechanized world, and the crises of war and revolution.

One can maintain that the boundaries of tragic art were extended by the adoption of a variety of techniques that exteriorized inner conflict, as well as by naturalistic presentations that closed a ring of inevitability around the dramatic action of an individual. If this argument does not prove that modern playwrights have written greater tragedies than Sophocles and Shakespeare (the reverse is obviously the case), it does suggest that modern drama may be relieved of the charge that it has extinguished the art of tragedy by simply being modern in content and style.

To mediate between the conflicting claims of promodern and antimodern factions is no easy matter. The value we place on specific works is the first and last consideration. There is no difficulty in claiming that the modern age can produce tragedy if we are prepared to qualify a considerable number of modern plays as tragedies. Conversely, it is easy enough to maintain that the modern spirit cannot support tragic writing once we disqualify these same plays.

An agile disputant can sustain his aristocratic distaste for the world of the common man by invalidating almost any modern play. All he has to do is to insist on absolute standards of high tragedy derived from a few masterpieces of the past and prove that a particular modern work deviates from these. He can then protest, often with good reason, that the hero of this modern play lacks the magnitude of spirit, or the tragic stature, needed to dignify humanity. With respect to many a modern stage character from Ibsen's Oswald Alving to O'Neill's Yank and Miller's Willy Loman it has been possible for fastidious critics to say, with Henry James, that,

"Our curiosity and our sympathy care comparatively little for what happens to the stupid, the coarse, and the blind."

The critic may indeed multiply his strictures without ever being entirely wrong. The plays may impress him as depressing rather than exalting, and as topical rather than universal. They may also strike him as too prosaic, too intellectual or too unintellectual, too active or too passive, too optimistic or too pessimistic. Any one of these attributes can be easily isolated for the purpose of invalidating tragic status for such modern works as *Ghosts, Hedda Gabler, The Father, The Power of Darkness, The Lower Depths, The Hairy Ape, Desire Under the Elms, Mourning Becomes Electra, The Iceman Cometh*—and perhaps even *Saint Joan*.

Advocates of a scrupulously restricted category of tragedy would probably certify only plays removed from the liberal-scientific spirit or deliberately set against it. They would approve peasant drama set far from industrial civilization, such as Synge's Aran Islands or Lorca's Spanish countryside. They would also qualify formally organized plays, preferably suggestive of ritual and rooted in theology or in myth. Among these would be Eliot's *Murder in the Cathedral* and *The Family Reunion*, some short poetic pieces by Yeats patterned after medieval Japanese drama, and a few antirealistic French plays such as Giraudoux' *Electra* and Cocteau's *The Infernal Machine*. To this one may add a genre of neoromantic verse-drama, represented by Maxwell Anderson's Elizabethan trilogy, *Elizabeth the Queen, Mary of Scotland,* and *Anne of the Thousand Days*; and his *Winterset*—plays well patterned after a tragic blueprint.

A strenuous exponent of the realistic and liberal persuasion could, in turn, cut a good deal of ground from under the literary opposition. Turning to specific works he could show us Cocteau and other French sophisticates leaning toward contrived tragicality and arriving at mere cleverness much more conclusively than at tragedy.

If the peril of writing tragedies under the modern liberal dispensation is an unliterary descent into banality, the peril of creating it under any other dispensation is a literary ascent into futility. Which is the greater misfortune cannot be determined, I suppose, without bias. (My own is, on the whole, democratic, while that of some men of letters for whom I have entertained the greatest admiration is largely aristocratic.) The two factions are not fated to remain completely apart, and there are areas of agreement available to reasonable exponents of either viewpoint. Liberals can agree that some inadequacies have attended the efforts of O'Neill, Ibsen, and the sociological playwrights to produce tragic literature, while conservatives can concede some measure of tragic power to Ibsen, Strindberg, Curel, O'Neill, and Benavente. It would certainly appear that some clearly definable tragedies and many plays more or less tragic in feeling such as Chekhov's *The Three Sisters* have been written.

We may also conclude that there is no compelling reason for the modern stage to strain toward tragedy. There are other honorable ways of responding to the human condition. Shaw followed the time-honored way of comedy so creditably in his comedies of ideas that they have overshadowed the work of many a tragedian of modern, Victorian, or Elizabethan times. The writing of comedies is as serious and intelligent a business as the writing of tragedies. Comedy, too, constitutes a criticism of life, incorporates values, and affords a catharsis. The comic viewpoint is at least as relevant as the tragic to man's life in society and perhaps even more representative of human conduct. The comic playwright need not spare us glimpses into the abyss of human nature or encounters with what Nietzsche called "the terrible wisdom of Silenus." Comedy is an art of notable variety; it runs from light to dark and from sweet to bitter.

There is also the way of *drame,* of serious drama without tragic pretensions. Many provocative social and psychological dramas as diversified as *Awake and Sing!* and *The Children's Hour* as well as imaginative works such as *Our Town* and *The Skin of Our Teeth* have filled a place in our theatre without conveniently fitting into pigeonholes of tragedy. Our modern age has generally found its sensibility and mood most adequately expressed by *drame.* We can only conclude that if plays such as *The Three Sisters, Juno and the Paycock, The Glass Menagerie,* and *Six Characters in Search of an Author* have not conformed to any blueprints of tragedy (and it is not likely that there was any intention on their author's part to achieve such conformity), this has been no loss to the theatre of our century. It is the value of the specific work and not the genre to which it conforms that matters to the playgoer. Not to prefer a distinguished nontragic composition to an undistinguished tragic one would be pedantry on the part of the critic, suicide on the part of the producer of plays, plain idiocy on the part of the playgoer.

Tragedies of one kind or another have been contributory to the interest and power of modern theatre. But the creative spirit of an age should be allowed, and indeed expected, to engender its own dramatic forms as well as to modify existent ones. Seemingly overawed by premises and promises of tragic grandeur, playwrights from D'Annunzio to Maxwell Anderson (or O'Neill when he composed *Dynamo* and *Lazarus Laughed*) have strained too much to produce high tragedy. They would have been well advised to leave their characters and situations in the nontragic categories that would have suited them better. Critics and scholars have tended to confuse playwrights by harping on categories of drama, glorifying one of these above all others and insufficiently noting the infrequent production of high tragedy throughout the ages and then rarely in pure form. Since everybody has been infected at some time or other with the desire to see the modern drama live beyond its spiritual income, it may yet become necessary to stress the *perils* rather than the possibilities of tragedy.

It may be necessary even to be irreverent toward some of the traditional tragic criteria few have questioned. Why must we try so hard to impress ourselves with our nobility? Why must we make a special effort to amass data on human error and evil, and why is it considered essential for the drama to exploit horrifying crimes and outrageous situations before amending Man's planetary record with evidences of nobility behind the mask of violence?

In 1929 the large-minded critic and scholar Joseph Wood Krutch expressed the conviction that tragedy was a dead art in the modern world. Whereas an "idea of nobility" had permeated the high tragedies of the past, some vision "ample and passionate" had disappeared from dramatic art as the leaders of modern thought came to consider man's soul commonplace and his emotions mean. Faced with disaster, which constitutes the final test of character, classical heroes had proved the human animal to be inherently noble. By contrast with this exalting affirmation, the failure and suffering of the characters in modern drama usually turned out to be merely depressing.

Ever since Mr. Krutch set down these conclusions in *The Modern Temper*, devotees of the stage with some claim to literacy have been at pains to reject his bitter pill, and he himself appeared to have rejected it partially when he acclaimed O'Neill as a tragic playwright. Various resistances to a strictly deterministic viewpoint made themselves felt, and Orville Prescott in reviewing a later book by Mr. Krutch, *Human Nature and the Human Condition*, in the September 4, 1959, issue of the New

York *Times,* expressed what I suppose is a majority middle-brow opinion: "Most of us do not believe that human character is formed solely by environment, heredity and conditioning. Most of us still do believe in some degree of free will and in moral values that are not solely a matter of local custom." The mid-century drama in America supports Mr. Prescott, for the emphasis on free will and moral responsibility has been strong in a number of plays by Miller, Kingsley, Hellman, Maxwell and Robert Anderson, Inge, Odets, Laurents, and even Tennessee Williams.

Yet Mr. Krutch would have no difficulty in pointing out that if our scepticism is perhaps less callow than it was in the debunking postwar period of the Twenties, our present-day despair of the human condition is, if anything, much deeper—and it is receiving constant support from the state of our strontium-90-conscious world. In spite of evidence of much heroic self-sacrifice in World War II, we are hardly moved to declaim with Sophocles that, "Nothing is more wonderful than man!" We cannot recover our pristine wonder at the human animal.

In the theatre it is plain that the most strenuously affirmative drama of the mid-century period, the existentialist drama in France, has also registered the bleakest despair. If the existentialist writers have trumpeted a gospel of free will by maintaining the view that men determine what they are by what they choose to do in a universe entirely indifferent to them, that view also condemns the individual to existentialist isolation and anguish. In so meaningless a universe as the existentialists', man's heroic acts look suspiciously like the gestures we might make in a mirror in order to impress ourselves. If we must act so in order to impress ourselves we are actually closer to desperation than to an exhilarating view of life.

We must more often question whether the vicarious exaltation of audiences traditionally associated with high tragedy is as essential or as valuable as our romantic imagination leads us to believe. The fetishists of high tragedy are anything but complimentary to humanity in assuming that man has to be regularly reminded by the theatre that he is a noble creature. We need intelligence and a comprehensive grasp of the realities of our times far more than we need metaphysical uplift. Feelings of nobility and heroic exaltation are among the cheapest and most easily whipped up emotions both in the theatre and outside it, and they require the strictest scrutiny wherever they appear. We may be sure that Hitler's young bravos felt extremely noble and exalted when they bombed Rotterdam, devastated Warsaw, and blitzed London's civilian population. They were supposedly serving their country and a great national destiny; they were confident, too, that they were saving Europe from materialism and ushering in a new heroic age. They displayed courage, loyalty, endurance; they had all the universally recognized heroic virtues. The virtues they lacked were the *unheroic* ones, without which there can be no civilization. I suspect that we have considerably more need for an intelligently critical theatre than for a tragic one.

When such a conclusion is entertained the very hierarchy of dramatic types that has grown up in our critical literature as well as in our unwritten assumptions about the drama may have to be questioned. One might ask whether there really is any reason to place *The Frogs* below *Antigone* in the order of creative achievement (not to mention the order of theatrical gratification), *King Henry IV* below *Coriolanus* or *Julius Caesar*, *The Misanthrope* below *The Cid* or *Andromache*, *What Price Glory?* below *Elizabeth the Queen* or *Winterset*, Giraudoux' *The Madwoman of Chaillot* below the same author's *Electra?* Tragedy, as a genre, may be pulled down from its eminence (which is not, however, the same thing as denigrating *Oedipus Rex* or *Hamlet*) by reflection on its limited range and primitive nature; it is married to violence and not a little fascinated with our primitive self. Or we may merely reflect that tragedy has marked limitations as a mirror of civilization and of human society.

In any case we may adopt the title of Karl Jaspers' little book, *Tragedy Is Not Enough*. Tragedy may be rich in truth, since it deals with an aspect of reality. But the knowledge it provides is only one stage in our process of self-education. It is also necessary to go *beyond* tragedy. There is surely considerable sense in making efforts to correct error and to reduce world-wide misery instead of treating all of it as irremediable except by the homeopathic process of swallowing misery pills in the theatre—which is what katharsis has been taken to mean. There are also alternatives to trying to transcend misery by drugging ourselves with the hashish of heroism, a procedure that has given us Fascists as well as tragedians. In many circumstances nontragic treatments of misfortune can be truer, more relevant, and even more profound than the inflationary techniques of high tragedy. When the reality in question consists of frustration and attrition rather than spectacular disaster, we may be grateful indeed that subtragic treatments such as Chekhov's have been available to the modern theatre. There are ways of considering the human condition that may be more profoundly represented by a *Waiting for Godot* than by *The Duchess of Malfi*. Yet invidious contrasts would not arise if it were not for romantic overvaluations of tragedy as a method of solemnly lifting ourselves up by our bootstraps.

4 REASONS FOR SOCIAL DRAMA

"Every man who is persuaded may persuade."—VICTOR HUGO

". . . without a stock of ideas, mind cannot operate and plays cannot exist."—BERNARD SHAW

". . . the artist should not prove a thesis but create examples."
—ERNST TOLLER

"The present ruling certainty is uncertainty." This sentence, written not in 1950 or 1960 but in 1843 by a German social philosopher and journalist, did not stop its author, Bruno Bauer, from writing voluminously about the state of the world. A similar conviction, widespread throughout Western society, has not prevented men and women from producing extensive commentaries on local, natural, or world problems. We are probably in the most problem-conscious period of world history. In 1945 we came to the end of one of civilization's major crises only to be thrust into a series of minor ones that could easily touch off a war of total extermination. Yet the theatre of this mid-century period has had less to say about the world and has been a poorer reflector of its tensions than ever before in our century.

Comment on this anomalous situation has been infrequent. If anything, play reviewers have often registered relief that the stage was uncluttered with problems. Only toward the end of the decade, in the summer of 1959, was there a flurry of concern in an influential publication, the New York *Times,* when Marya Mannes, theatre critic of the liberal weekly *The Reporter,* lamented that it would be impossible to form an impression of what America was like from the past season's plays. On the summits of recent scholarly criticism social drama has had virtually no status whatsoever. When society came up for consideration at all critic-savants in the Fifties usually concluded that the possibilities of art are diminished in egalitarian pseudocultures that lack a common tradition or faith. A leaning toward problem-writing carries the stigma of middle-brow art, naïve and bankrupt liberalism, or cryptocommunism, toward all of which the contributors to most literary quarterlies are apt to be severe, if not scornful.

Yet both the literary and the nonliterary press have continued to lament the frequent emptiness of our theatre. And they look askance at the one other source from which content has dribbled into the drama: interest in sexuality and its aberrations that has made Tennessee Williams the most successful playwright in America. (This, I admit, is too narrow a view to take of Williams' dramatic work. But it is the view that secured popularity for him whether or not he sought it. I believe that he did *not* seek it but got it as a bonus for his mordant playwriting.) The confusion of attitudes has indeed been a source of wonder.

The inconsistencies of the prevalent attitudes are especially grave in view of two ineluctable facts. One is that the modern theatre since Ibsen's middle period (about 1875) has subsisted to a large degree on its social relevance. The other is that the theatre continues to earn respect with productions that touch upon social questions.

The two greatest successes in the American theatre of the imaginative and urbane Jean Giraudoux after World War II were his social dramas *The Madwoman of Chaillot* and *Tiger at the Gates,* the latter a Chris-topher Fry translation of an antiwar play ironically titled *The Trojan War Will Not Take Place.* Ironically, too, the shades of Kurt Weill and Bertolt Brecht had to wait until the Fifties for the triumph of their musical satire of the Twenties, *The Threepenny Opera,* probably the most "subversive" play of the century exclusive of direct propaganda. Arthur Miller became an important playwright in America and John Osborne in England largely on the strength of direct and indirect con-tributions to the loosely defined genre we call social drama. Several of the best comedies and farces of the mid-century period (Lindsay and Crouse's *State of the Union* and Garson Kanin's *Born Yesterday* are the prime examples) made more than accidental contact with social realities, as did so deliquescent a farce as Gore Vidal's *Visit to a Small Planet,* and Peter Ustinov's bland fantastications on political themes. Paradoxically, in a decade when social drama has generally been considered an interloper in our entertainment business, the season of 1958-59 introduced one of the most promising new playwrights we have encountered in a quarter of a century when the twenty-eight-year-old Lorraine Hansberry's *A Raisin in the Sun* opened on Broadway. The play, which dealt with Negro life in a big city, won the New York Drama Critics Circle award in the spring of 1959 and received ample public support at the box office.

One may conclude from the postwar record that reports of the death of social drama have been journalistic and critical exaggerations, even if a social theatre movement is nowhere discernible except in Communist countries where no other philosophy of serious theatre has had any chance of survival. It would be surprising if our contemporary stage could cut itself entirely adrift from century-old moorings of some kind of social interest. One circumstance, however, dims all prospects for a return of socially slanted theatre: the young are not likely to support it. They already dismiss the proponents of social drama in the Thirties and Forties as sentimental and confused, and the new intelligentsia appears to be resolved never to be caught with its sympathies showing. Socially slanted theatre has always been a theatre of the young, and it is not likely to thrive when the young are old.

In reviewing the recent period of theatre one recalls play after play that expressed social awareness. One recalls the vigorous effort to create a socially-minded theatre during the Thirties and the high artistry of the Group Theater, which continues to influence the American stage although it has been defunct since 1941. One remembers the courageous stand of the democratic theatre of Prague until Hitler's march into Czechoslovakia, the struggle to maintain a free German-speaking theatre in Switzerland, the independence of the Scandinavian stage, the vigorous war effort of the Russian theatre between 1941 and 1945, the U.S.O. tours of American actors to the war fronts, and the perseverance of the blitzed English theatre which produced highhearted plays such as Irwin Shaw's *The Gentle People* and Robert Ardrey's *Thunder Rock*. Nor can we overlook the adeptness with which the wartime Parisian theatre managed to produce social dramas such as Sartre's *The Flies* under military occupation. In fact, no country in which the theatre manifested any vitality before and immediately after World War II has lacked playwrights who have treated the social scene.

It was apparent, however, in the very heyday of the social drama from

1930 to 1940 that there were areas of weakness and positive danger zones
in a theatre of prosaic protest and propaganda. Perhaps it is more necessary to protect the genre of social drama from its friends than from its
enemies. The former are likely to confuse art with sociology and drama
with preachment. They forget that social drama became a significant
modern art not by being didactic, which it had been as early as 1850
under Dumas fils, but by becoming exploratory; and not by being journalistic, which it had been as early as 1850 under the same leadership,
but by becoming expressive. It was *creation,* not *agitation,* that made
social drama a distinguished form of modern theatre. It was not the mere
presence or solution of a problem in a play that held out the promise of
vital dramatic art. If the social theatre is not ultimately destroyed by blind
partisanship, it stands a good chance of being annihilated by sheer bore-
dom. The trouble is simply that we can have too much conviction by
rote and too much passion via hysteria, usually the whipped-up hysteria
of a political party or nation. It doesn't matter where the clichés originate
or where the frenzied partisanship occurs; dramatic art is thereby debilitated whether it emanates from the political left or right.

The theatre of social awareness once brought into play the acute creative faculties of such individualists as Ibsen, Shaw, and Chekhov. But
the credit they brought to the modern theatre began to be whittled away
virtually from the start by pusillanimous practical showmen. Proficient
pseudo-Ibsenite playwrights, such as Pinero in England and Sudermann
in Germany, softened the impeachments of the pioneers of dramatic
modernism. Today the humdrum presentation of a milieu and its issues
seems to be distinctly in the ascendant; social drama has been less vigorous than it was thirty or even sixty years ago in many European countries.
The American theatre, which displayed great verve during the Twenties
and Thirties, became comparatively circumspect in the mid-century decades. The situation has been no different in countries where the social
responsibility of the theatre has received the greatest emphasis, that is, in
Russia and the nations most directly under her influence.

Caution or compromise in the arts used to be associated primarily with
bourgeois complacency and a timid or shrewd accommodation to the
status quo. But there has been at least as much absence of independent
criticism in the Communist theatre. In the latter, moreover, we have
witnessed the prevalence of a primarily utilitarian view of the theatre.
Socialist Realism, which has tethered playwrights to playwriting for use

rather than for creative expression, is far more likely to promote five-year plans for industrialization than to advance the theatre as an art.

There were risks in the social theatre from the beginning. Not the least was the danger that playwriting would be subverted to the objectives of some ruling ideology. That risk has proved to be particularly great in recent decades. A great risk, too, was that dramatic treatment of society would become reportage. It was likely that the drama would become enfeebled, if not invalidated as art, while gaining acceptance as an important social and political instrument. Thus arose the problem play, in which a problem was prosaically presented and didactically resolved, usually with the help of contrivances associated with the Scribean well-made play of intrigue and coincidences. Even Ibsen succumbed to this widely distributed type of blueprint dramatics when he wrote *The Pillars of Society*. The problem play lost caste with every reputable critic and was supposedly displaced by naturalism. Nevertheless, it has retained its hold whenever playwrights have tried to reform society, and the problem play has returned in an especially primitive and prosaic manner ever since Socialist Realism came to be officially sponsored as the one valid, nondecadent dramatic style of serious theatre in Russia. Cogent arguments may be urged against other exercises in social criticism. Consider the desiccated character of many naturalistic treatments of the social scene since Zola's time, the frequent hysterics of Central European social expressionism in the Twenties, the brassy hollowness of the agitprop drama of the Thirties, and the fainthearted liberalism of the Forties and Fifties.

Still, there is no reason to write off the social drama as a lost genre when we review the work of recent decades. On the contrary, the genre must be exceptionally sturdy if it has been able to withstand the assaults of its foes and friends, totalitarian regimentation, international tension, and war, as well as the seductions of commercial showmanship. Out of the social tensions of the Thirties, American writers led by Clifford Odets compounded a vigorous Depression Period theatre.

To the more or less vital work of the past two decades in England belong J.B. Priestley's haunting, semirealistic, and allegorical plays, *They Came to a City* and *An Inspector Calls*, as well as such contrasting realistic dramas as Emlyn Williams' *The Corn Is Green* and Terence Rattigan's *The Winslow Boy*, unquestionably the best plays written by these able writers for the commercial stage. *The Corn Is Green* was a vivid recollection of a university-educated woman's pioneering endeavor to educate the children of the Welsh coal-mining districts. *The Winslow Boy* was a stirring account of an ordinary family's extraordinary effort to secure justice from Parliament itself for a little son expelled from school. The concern for education, reform, and civil liberties to be found in England has been well reflected in these and other plays and the treatment has been typically moderate and, whenever possible, good-natured. It is with this type of drama, in which genre painting is an essential element, rather than in poetic writing, such as the youthful verse plays of Auden, Isherwood, and Spender, that the British social dramatists have been most effective. This is still the case, although some of the younger writers in Britain, such as John Whiting and John Osborne, have adopted a more vigorous style of attack in the Fifties.

In France the social drama has aroused great interest, even when the playwright has transcended realistic dramaturgy. Perhaps the best example is that set by Jean Giraudoux whose imagination took him back to classic times in his previously mentioned sardonic anticipation of World War II, *La Guerre de Troie n'aura pas lieu*. Both *Intermezzo*, unsuccessfully produced in New York under the title of *The Enchanted*, and *The Madwoman of Chaillot*, successfully adapted for Broadway by Maurice Valency, displayed Giraudoux' urbane social criticism in a context of fantasy. His scorn of philistine morals and of predatory materialism was all the more remarkable since it came from a right-wing, rather than left-wing, position. Giraudoux died in 1944, but the luminous and witty artistry he brought to the theatre of social criticism remains undimmed.

An effective imagination was also at work at the other extreme of contemporary French writing, in the moralistic critique and glum world-view of existentialist drama. The quest for engagement has raised severe social questions for Sartre, Camus, Robles, and others. Yet realism, powerfully employed in some cases, as in Sartre's drama of French Resistance *Morts sans sèpulture* (adapted by Thornton Wilder under the title of *The Victors*), has not been the dominant style of existentialist drama. Existentialism may be best remembered in the theatre for Sartre's highly imaginative early plays *Huis Clos* (called *No Exit* on Broadway) and *The Flies*.

Inevitably, too, social drama attracted Central European writers during their period of exile and since their return to Germany and Austria after

World War II. Georg Kaiser wrote some trenchant plays, the satirical *Klawitter* and *The Soldier Tanaka,* in which Japanese militarism was flayed; and Franz Werfel, living in America, was particularly effective with his "comedy" about the fall of France, *Jacobowsky and the Colonel.* Carl Zuckmayer turned increasingly from his favorite vein of folk comedy to political drama after his memorable satire on Prussian militarism, *The Captain of Koepenick,* produced in 1931. Especially effective both in Germany and in England after World War II has been his penetrative character study, *The Devil's General,* which dramatizes the disillusionment of a German military hero.

Until 1956, the German social theatre had Bertolt Brecht, the poet-playwright who explored most fully the possibilities of a unique dramatic form and distinctive theatrical style for social philosophy. This was epic realism, distinguished alike for analytical sharpness and poetic vigor. Whether or not one subscribes to Brecht's dramatic theories or to his Marxist politics, one cannot deny him the attributes of genius. *The Caucasian Chalk Circle* and *The Good Woman of Setzuan* are two of the most distinguished parables of the modern theatre, and *Mother Courage* may yet be considered the greatest antiwar play since Euripides produced *The Trojan Women.*

Writers of social drama have had many modes and styles at their disposal, and have been effective without dependency upon either a single dramatic style or a single ideology. Among them, there have been such poetic realists as Odets, such humorists as Giraudoux and Kataev, such grave writers as Afinogenov and Arthur Miller, such conservatives as Rattigan and Zuckmayer, and such far-to-the-left dramatists as Sartre and O'Casey. But those writers who have been artists rather than hacks have always been uniquely themselves, and it has been as impossible to imprison their artistry within a category as to kill their initiative with theories, whether of their own making or of some critic's or bureaucrat's. We can learn from them that the thinker-playwright, *le dramaturge-penseur,* needs no rules to represent the drama of man in society. We need only a climate of freedom in which a playwright may form his own art and draw his own conclusions.

In the American theatre of the Fifties, nevertheless, an ambivalent attitude did prevail and social drama was at low ebb except in the work of Arthur Miller. As previously noted, little notice was taken of social conflict in the decline of vigor, vitality, and sense of direction to which I shall call attention elsewhere in this volume.* The absence of ferment was noted with little regret by those who remembered only the excesses and defects but none of the merits of our social theatre in the Thirties. It is also probable that many American playgoers had only extremely vague impressions of a connection between the development of our stage in previous decades and its writers' awareness of social tension.

James Joyce's Bloom once demonstrated his political convictions: he "climbed up into a secure position amid the ramifications of a tree" in order to watch a political procession. That is about as far as most American playwrights and playgoers would have liked to go, even after the advent of modernity in our theatre *circa* 1910. They would have been content to look down on the procession of social conflict from a safe eminence, if it had not stretched out a feral claw and pulled them down from the tree.

Although modernity in theatre is generally dated from Ibsen's middle period of socially charged prose, we should be mistaken if we attributed the inspiration of the American vanguard to European realism. Our little theatre movement began under different auspices than the free theatres of Europe that established realism and social thinking on the stage. An art theatre ideal had supplanted realism in the affections of the cognoscenti by the first decade of the century, and it was less under the star of Ibsen than under the constellation of Craig, Appia, and Reinhardt that our new theatre was born.

The nascent progressive theatre in the United States babbled prettily in its cradle and its first words were experiment, art, decor, symbolism, atmosphere, and formal beauty. *Margaret Fleming* and other early indigenous realistic plays were considered passé by the avant-garde of 1910-1918. Symbolist or poetic playwrights were supposed to have set better examples than Ibsen and Hauptmann (the latter was enjoying a vogue less on the strength of *The Weavers* than on the Maeterlinckéd sweetness of *The Sunken Bell*). The early favorites of our little theatre movement were largely psychological *jeux d'esprit* such as Alice Gerstenberg's arch little comedy *Overtones*, poetic pieces such as Edna St. Vincent Millay's *Aria da Capo,* and atmospheric ones such as O'Neill's *The Moon of the Caribbees.*

Eventually, and quite contrary to the expectations of the art-for-art's-

* See "Entropy?" at the beginning of Part Two.

sake apostles, the professional theatre confronted the realities of the modern world because it had no other alternative to becoming hopelessly attenuated and feeble.* Little theatres hidden away in small towns could thrive on a steady diet of regional color for a time, but the professional theatre was metropolitan and could hardly remain impervious to the tensions of industrial society and the attitudes or ideas engendered by it. Those playwrights who were artists rather than hacks and wrote under some compelling motive felt alienated from the booming materialistic world of the Twenties. They reacted with Bohemian defiance and expatriation in the Twenties and confronted their Main Street environment with defensive scepticism or cynicism. American drama acquired its characteristic 1920 pattern of iconoclastic comedy, irreverent farce, and realism, to which the next decade added the flare of direct protest.

Even experiments in nonrealistic dramaturgy, such as *The Adding Machine, Beggar on Horseback, The Great God Brown, The Hairy Ape,* and *All God's Chillun Got Wings,* drew social questions within their orbit of imaginative theatre. The first two plays were obviously directed against the standardization of life in the machine age. And in spite of O'Neill's efforts to suspend the last three plays in the ether of metaphysics or extrasocial symbolism, *All God's Chillun* could not have been written without this playwright's awareness of racial conflict. Tragedy of alienation in materialistic society appeared in *The Great God Brown,* a play of masks and split personalities motivated by the author's search for integration in modern life.

Before long, social criticism became an accepted, even admired, feature of an American theatre which soon acquired the enviable reputation for vigor and vitality abroad that it retains to this day. We took social drama for granted and an energetic minority considered it the ultimate in dramatic expression. It was deprecated only when plays failed to rise above commonplaceness or melodrama, or when the gospel of salvation by economic readjustment or revolution became flagrantly simplified. Even politically conservative reviewers writing for journals unalterably opposed to New Deal policies applauded the fire of *Waiting for Lefty* and the theatrical vitality of *One-Third of a Nation.* So mild-mannered

* A similar development affected the Irish national theatre. When Yeats helped to establish it and became a leader of the Dublin Abbey Theatre around 1900 he dreamed of creating a poetic theatre. What he got was, in the main, a realistic or quasi-realistic one replete with peasant comedies and tragedies.

a gentleman as Burns Mantle campaigned vigorously for Paul Green's and Richard Wright's dramatization of *Native Son,* and the philosopher-critic Joseph Wood Krutch, who could never be taken in by any dogma or doxology, found it possible to praise the explosive rebelliousness of *Awake and Sing!*

In one way or another, playwrights, producers, and play reviewers were inclined to assume that a socially oriented theatre was an integral part of the American way. They even looked askance at the British stage with its continued penchant for mild comedy of manners, a sort of theatrical Chamberlainism, and at the French theatre for its admixture of left-bank estheticism and boulevardism. After the advent of Hitler in 1933 men came to look upon the American theatre as one of the last bulwarks of democratic expression. To a considerable degree the strength of the American stage was equated with its realism and social awareness.

The climate for this tradition began to change rapidly in 1948, and the storm signals have been up since then. It is possible to wonder whether this tradition is not going out of the American theatre, and whether another positive, that is, productive tradition can arise to take its place. Only anti-American propagandists or extravagantly misinformed Europeans could contend that a free theatre no longer exists in the United States. But aggravations of the cold war with communism, the Korean War, the rise of pressures from right-wing groups, and the growing affluence of the nation have exerted dampening influences on producers and playwrights who might otherwise have favored social questions. Plays of social content after 1948 have come to be viewed with misgivings by those who finance productions. An essentially moralistic play such as Arthur Miller's *All My Sons,* a principled, well-built drama voted the best play of its year by the New York Drama Critics Circle,* was banned for production abroad by our State Department in 1949.

We were on the brink of a suspicion that all social drama was the machination of a traitorous left wing. Caution seemed to invade an art that had hitherto fed passion into its marrow. Writers were in danger of casting about for themes to which they were temperamentally indifferent. Some playwrights were reduced to looking for protective neutral coloration, some to orchestrating lulling melodies, and some to blowing hot and cold air through the dramatic medium that used to be their trumpet.

* The only dissenters were the late George Jean Nathan, Richard Watts, Jr., and the writer, who favored O'Neill's *The Iceman Cometh.*

It was fortunate only that the Broadway theatre resisted popular hysteria and flagrant chauvinism. We may be grateful to Broadway for not returning to the trumpery melodrama of the "over-the-top" variety of plays that had proliferated during World War I.

The real defect in our theatre since 1948 has been the waning of passion and the dilution of critical intellect. There is little prospect of our being compensated for the loss of immediacy and strong involvement by an increase of poetic art divorced from mundane concerns. If other interests proved capable of nourishing plays that a normal intelligence could respect, there would be less need to worry. But this has by no means been the case.

Heterodoxy, as the Rev. Sydney Smith said, is the other fellow's doxy. Antipathy toward social drama is more often than not our resistance to *the other person's* brand of social drama. That social consciousness in our theatre has no perdurable masterpieces to its credit is secondary to its having kept our stage vigorous. That much of this drama has tended to descend to bathos and brummagem, that its authors have shared delusions with the rest of the world's citizenry, that it has not been notably profound—all this is inconsequential beside the fact that the alternative has been reliance upon mindless farces, musical entertainments, historical romances, and period pieces, comedies of manners occasionally as pleasant as *The Pleasure of His Company* but usually redolent of faded elegance, or comedies of good will such as *A Majority of One*. (Here the marketable sentiment hardly lives up to the promise of an idea quoted from Thoreau in the published epigraph, "Any man more right than his neighbors constitutes a majority of one.")

I have enough confidence in American institutions not to be frightened by the probability that there will be no change in the attitude that authors of American social drama have maintained, as a rule, virtually since the beginning of the century. This attitude is intrinsically critical of the status quo. It does not regard our national policies as infallible, it ferrets out injustices, and it does not put the same valuation upon capitalistic society as does the National Association of Manufacturers. The detachment of the artist from many accepted values, his attachment to ideal ways of life, his chronic antiphilistinism, and his refractory personality, especially if he happens to be a dramatist by temperament, cannot be altered without gelding him as an artist. We need not be troubled by this penchant for dissent if we do not grant him the authority of a sociologist, economist, or statesman—even if he should want to assume that authority on the grounds that he cannot make worse mistakes than the professionals. Provided his humanity is deep and wide enough and that his artistry does not become the captive of his politics, we can grant him our respect. If this defense of social criticism in plays has little to do with esthetics, it is nonetheless concerned with the life blood of the drama. Esthetic considerations are worth applying only to living entities, not to plays that have already had the life squeezed out of them.

A discussion of the role and value of social interest in the American theatre could go on endlessly without satisfying those who welcome out-and-out propaganda, provided it serves their particular faction. But discussion would no more satisfy the opposite camp (no doubt located on Parnassus) that hates to see the theatre tarnished with nonliterary elements. Yet literature suffers along with dramatic action when a vague unease takes the place of the directness we associate with social drama. One can do no better than to quote a British reviewer's recent comment on the talented J.D. Salinger's novel *The Catcher in the Rye*:

> The real objection to a romanticism of this kind is its unrealised, withdrawn quality ... [Salinger's writing] misses any outgoing urgency of purpose, any central direction. One feels that the driving force behind it is somehow unformulated, inchoate, and intensely personal ... His revolt has not hardened or taken on any definite shape but has turned on itself and been manifested in a vague kind of mystical vision of love and togetherness.[*]

It so happens that in the same issue of *Critical Quarterly* Raymond Williams published an excellent article on Miller, "The Realism of Arthur Miller."[**] In endeavoring to assess Miller's status as the playwright who "brought back into the theatre, in an important way, the drama of social questions," Williams reviews pertinent facts connected with the "widespread withdrawal from social thinking which came to its peak in the late nineteen-forties." The reasons given here and elsewhere for this withdrawal are not altogether convincing when they are limited to faults in the standard social drama of the left: "low-pressure naturalism," "angularity of the self-conscious problem play," and so on, since that

[*] Allun Jones in *Critical Quarterly*, Hull, England, Summer 1959, pp. 171–72.
[**] Pages 140–49.

drama had virtually become extinct by 1939. But the author is quite correct in saying that before the decline in social drama could be halted it was necessary to understand why the older forms of social drama had become inadequate. He is also correct in declaring that, "a revival, at depth and with passion, of the social thinking itself" was necessary. Arthur Miller, with his five plays and his prefaces (1947-60) broke the impasse, Williams declares, although the "break-out [is] still scattered and uncertain."

Miller's chief accomplishment has been his aptitude for translating social realities into personal ones, and personal situations into relationships that ultimately constitute a view of society as a moral reality. In Raymond Williams' apt sentences, "Every aspect of personal life is radically affected by the quality of the general life, yet the general life is seen at its most important in completely personal terms." Miller has presented social realities such as success-worship, moral cowardice, lack of integrity, and witch hunting "as living tissue" and has dealt with characters as "individuals who are ends and values in themselves."

For these reasons, as well as for his successful adaptation of techniques for the requirements of his subject (the most successful adaptation being his use of expressionism in dealing with the consciousness of Willy Loman in *Death of a Salesman**), Miller has been able to revitalize American social drama and has given encouragement to others. His example has kept the drama of social questions and conflicts in the foreground where it could be seen by young writers such as the author of *A Raisin in the Sun*. Regardless of any shortcomings to which we may allude in evaluating his work (and the greatest of these, I believe, is the lack of language equal to his aspirations), Miller has been a major figure in the Western theatre. He has been the mid-century playwright who gave private life a large reference and resonance in accordance with the principle he has defined so well in writing: "The end of drama is the creation of a higher consciousness and not merely a subjective attack upon the audience's nerves and feelings."

Postscript: I hear the usual objections like a continual susurration in the asphodels. These voices are apt to suggest ruefully that we already

---

* Miller reports in his introduction to his *Collected Plays* (Viking Press, 1957) that his first interest in *Death of a Salesman* was the protagonist's consciousness. His first image of the play was an "enormous face . . . which would appear and then open up, and we would see the inside of a man's head. In fact, *The Inside of His Head* was the first title."

have too many social dramatists. The answer is to take a look at the large number of plays that haven't a social question or reference beyond a crack at U.S. Republicans or the English welfare state. There is another still voice that tells us that social drama is altogether second-rate work and that no first-rate writer will touch it except out of sheer perversity (*i.e.*, Bernard Shaw). Yet the leading playwrights of France and Central Europe since the end of World War II (Sartre, Camus, Zuckmayer, Brecht, Duerrenmatt) have been social dramatists, the greatest living writer of the English-speaking stage has been O'Casey, and of the two leading living playwrights in America Arthur Miller has definitely been a social dramatist and Tennessee Williams has been trying very hard to become one, if *Camino Real, Orpheus Descending,* and *Sweet Bird of Youth* are any indication.

"I believe the best plays are about people and not about things," says Terence Rattigan in a symposium on "The Play of Ideas" in the March, 1950, issue of *The New Statesman and Nation.* What proponent of the play of ideas, (which term is inclusive enough to cover psychological and philosophical as well as social dramas), ever said that plays are about "things"? Rattigan also maintains that "the theatre that deals with people and stories instead of with ideas and theories is immortal." This statement too is shot through with fallacy. There is nothing immortal about the theatre that deals with people and stories—the world's worst plays, as well as its best, have dealt with people and stories. How many competently written plays of ideas does Mr. Rattigan know that *don't* deal with stories or (except in the case of special expressionist and surrealist plays) don't deal with *people?* It is not the expressionists who had reason to give us *R.U.R.* and *The Life of the Insects,* that Mr. Rattigan has in mind, but such writers as Ibsen and Shaw.

"Why is *Ghosts* a masterpiece? Because of what it says about syphilis or because of what it says about Mrs. Alving?" A loaded question, Mr. Rattigan. *Ghosts* is not about syphilis, and "what it says about Mrs. Alving" (about her learning that her submission to conventional morality had been a tragic error) is precisely what makes it a *play of ideas* or a *social drama.* The discovery that her son Oswald has inherited syphilis from the husband to whom she had returned in obedience to the conventional morality represented by Pastor Manders is only the last of the ironies that demonstrate the argument against the old morality. *Ghosts* is not a character drama any more than any other play in which the action and argument revolve around well-drawn characters. *Ghosts* is very much concerned with its superpersonal theme.

Mr. Rattigan goes on to say that, "From Aeschylus to Tennessee Williams the only theatre that has ever mattered is the theatre of character and narration." If this were the only question of value, Aeschylus must have been a dolt to strain so hard to establish moral, religious, and political principles in the *Oresteia* which is the peak of his known achievement as a dramatist and tragic poet, and Sophocles must have been inept to devote so much effort to the clash of principles in *Antigone*. Rattigan doesn't think "that ideas *per se,* social, political, or moral have a very important place in the theatre." But the catch lies in the *"per se,"* since ideas without the agency of narration and character have never had a place in the theatre at all. Mr. Rattigan's own most highly regarded play, *The Winslow Boy,* provides the best refutation of his argument that ideas "definitely take third place to character and narration anyway." Would the characters and narration of *The Winslow Boy* have had much value out of the context of the social drama of an ordinary English family making heroic efforts to secure justice for a little boy who had been wrongly expelled from school?

Shaw, Bridie, and O'Casey all disagree with Rattigan. But the final answer is simply that a play is about something the author establishes by means of his story and characters. It has a meaning, and in a good play the meaning is intrinsic to the life of the play, not superimposed on it. That meaning is more complex than any definition provided by critical discourse; it is not a bald statement or thesis but a significance that belongs to the complex organic organization called a play. The idea is something communicated through the experience of characters acting, reacting, and being acted upon, in short, the experience which is the play itself. When the action, which is the meaning, has marked social ramifications we get social drama.

A good social drama is a good play, a bad social drama is a bad play, and good plays may or may not be social dramas. The error of the faction that has clamored for the play of ideas or for social drama has always been its implicit or express exclusion of the possibility of merit in other kinds of plays. The error of the opposite faction has always been the assumption that a play of ideas or a social drama automatically condemns itself to a secondary status.

5 NEW TRAGIC PERSPECTIVES?

". . .in the evolution of the tragic hero we see a trend towards comedy."—FRIEDRICH DUERRENMATT

". . . if man is not tragic, his life is ridiculous and painful, 'comic' in fact, and by revealing his absurdity one can achieve a sort of tragedy."—EUGÈNE IONESCO

"A farce and a tragedy are alike in this, that they are a moment of intense life."—WILLIAM BUTLER YEATS

"It is about time someone wrote a new *Poetics*," my friend said. He was thinking of the exalted subject of tragedy, and he looked hopefully at me, or so my vanity led me to believe. How easy it would be to join this enterprise of drafting new or modified laws for tragedy, and how difficult to extricate oneself from it! There hasn't been a generation since the fifteenth century that hasn't tried to rewrite Aristotle's text, whether by interpretation or augmentation. Yet nothing absolute has ever been said on the subject that went perceptibly beyond the prejudices or ambitions of a period, a nation, a species of littérateur, or a class of playgoers and readers. The very effort to define the limits of tragedy appears to have introduced even more confusion into criticism and playwriting. Surely tragedy is never quite the same thing from place to place and from one playwright's work to another.

Even Sophocles, the ideal tragedian of most critics, did not conform to any tragic blueprint. Only the most superficial reading could fail to disclose differences of tragic vision between *Ajax* and *Antigone*. Are there not differences of tragic form when the protagonist is overthrown (*Oedipus the King*) or triumphant (Sophocles' *Electra*)? Would the

51

tragic status of the latter, in which the heroine is victorious at the expense of her mother's life, be the same if it had to be validated by rigorous definition or by present-day sentiments? If there are these distinct differences between one Sophoclean play and another, the differences in other dramatic tragic literature are even greater.

If we no longer lay down dogmatic principles for tragedy, there is still a tendency to cherish some ideal of tragedy. *Oedipus the King* represents this ideal in Aristotle's *Poetics* and in the opinion of many contemporary critics. Carried to the point of idolatry, however, respect for ideal tragedy becomes an inhibiting influence. It endorses the notion that a single work or single conception of drama sums up all the possibilities of tragic art. This conclusion, latent in every definition of ideal tragedy is made absurd by the facts. *Hamlet* includes elements of tragic experience and perception not cointained in *Oedipus the King*, and the reverse is also true. *Phèdre* has a concentration of feeling lacking in the *Hippolytus*, just as Euripides' play has a dimension of tragicality greatly reduced in Racine's drama. This much will probably be granted, but literary warfare is sure to be declared whenever we look at modern drama. We are in difficulties whenever we suggest that treatments of destructive femininity, such as *Hedda Gabler* and *The Father*, have added tragic elements not contained in *Phèdre* and the *Hippolytus*. I would not greatly hesitate to make this claim myself, with the understanding that the addition of a new dramatic element does not necessarily make a late play superior to an early one.

Another danger latent in idealization of a particular type of tragedy is the danger of regarding every other kind of play as a necessary descent from some isolated individual achievement (*Oedipus the King*, probably), or from some golden age (the fifth-century Attic period, no doubt) never recovered or recoverable. Such a dogmatic approach is altogether too rigid and fatalistic for dramatic art. Consistently maintained, this view leaves little room for the appearance of *Hamlet, Macbeth,* or *King Lear* and the emergence of an Elizabethan age of tragedy two thousand years after the death of Sophocles. It makes the writing of true tragedy conditional upon the recovery of esthetic and social norms that prevailed only once, centuries or millennia ago.

A major source of error may be our tendency to certify one work as *more* tragic than another, as if quantitative measures could possibly be as valid in art as they are in the physical sciences. To formulate judgments on this basis is to create a false hierarchy of values. For playwrights to think they must cut their cloth according to some pattern, Greek or Elizabethan, is to court academicism in the worst sense of the term. It encourages epigonal tendencies rather than the spontaneously creative spirit of the theatre. The late Maxwell Anderson especially favored the epigonal approach in most of his verse plays, but his popular success with *Elizabeth the Queen* or *Mary of Scotland* in the early 1930's had no effect on dramatic writing in our time. He had a number of predecessors in the nineteenth-century theatre such as George Henry Boker and Stephen Phillips, but none of these succeeded in revitalizing tragedy by adopting Elizabethan and romantic persiflage. To worry about how much more tragic one piece is than another can be utterly misleading. A more relevant question would be not how much *more* tragic but how *differently* tragic.

Common sense would suggest that we employ a theory of limits as an alternative to dogmatism—that we assume that some dramatic works are completely tragic whereas other works are only incompletely so. If this meant nothing more than that we rate some tragedies higher than others there would be no problem of definition. We would be saying nothing more than that we like one play better than another because its content, structure, or style impresses us more. But if we say that we like one play better than another because it is more tragic or that one play is less meritorious than another because it is less tragic, then we only compound our difficulties in arriving at sound judgment.

We omit too many values by making tragicality a major criterion unless we catch the playwright *evading* a tragic conclusion. Maxwell Anderson's verse play, *Elizabeth the Queen*, meets many long-accepted criteria for tragedy. The exalted lovers Elizabeth and Essex have all the nobility, all the tragic stature, that has long been required of the protagonists of a tragedy, and their action has magnitude in almost any sense of the term. A well-defined tragic flaw, or whatever equivalent we can find for *hamartia*, produces the downfall of Essex and the unhappiness of the Queen. The reversal of fortune in their case is the most tragic of possible reversals. It is caused by their own strong will; *proairesis* is in good order here, for the chief characters make decisive choices and are acutely aware of the consequences of their decisions, their *dianoia* and *ethos* dominate the action. Neither their intellectual nor ethical bent can be considered revolting, and their conduct does not outrage our sensibilities even at the point of highest tension. The "tragic rhythm" of "purpose, passion, and perception," (according to Kenneth Burke's and Francis Fergusson's well-known formulation) determines the movement of the action quite satisfactorily. When Essex dies he departs from life in a manner obviously calculated to elevate the public; the dignity of man is affirmed by his refusal to save his neck. One would suppose that the audience of the successful Theater Guild production of 1930, when Alfred Lunt and Lynn Fontanne played the leading roles, had experienced a *katharsis*.

We have no difficulty in certifying *Elizabeth the Queen* as a tragedy, whereas the same cannot be said of Euripides' *Electra*. It does not follow that the latter is the inferior, that is, the less penetrating and stirring, play. In calling *Electra* a melodrama in his noteworthy book on Greek tragedy, Professor Kitto did not deny that the play had an excellence of its own that was not to be slighted simply because he could not validate it as a tragedy. Similarly, in our own times, *A Streetcar Named Desire* is not to be considered inferior to *Elizabeth the Queen*.

It is conceivable that a play may be nontragic and yet more absorbing than a work we can certify as tragedy. Can there be any doubt about this matter when we compare the *Paolo and Francesca* of Stephen Phillips with *The Cherry Orchard*, which its author called a comedy, or *Juno and the Paycock*, in which the admixture of comic and tragic elements can be disconcerting only to purists? Then there are all the modern plays from *Ghosts* to *Death of a Salesman* whose tragic status has been questioned. How shall we account for their relative excellence and their patent superiority to many tragedies?

These reflections are obvious, but they remain heretical to those who employ tragedy as an honorific term. Such purists cannot abide the thought that a tragedy may be inferior to a nontragic work. For them there seems to be no such thing as a *bad* tragedy, even if the Elizabethan and Jacobean theatre abounded with exalted rubbish, as did the neo-classic theatres of France, England, and Germany after *Athalie*. The thesis is flagrantly circular; it amounts to saying that if the play is bad it cannot be a tragedy, and if it is a tragedy it cannot be bad.

Reasoning of this sort turns tragedy into a *value* rather than a *genre*. A rejected tragedy is then called a melodrama. Though it is apparent that the authors of such plays as *The Spanish Tragedy* or *The Revenger's Tragedy* had only the genre of tragedy in mind, it becomes necessary to locate a separate pigeonhole for them in order to preserve the ideal of tragedy from debasement or question. Should we differ as to the excellence of a play, one man's tragedy can become another man's melodrama. John Webster was dismissed by Bernard Shaw as a "Tussaud laureate." Those who agree with this judgment and employ the term tragedy honorifically have no choice but to deny that Webster was a tragic poet.

The honorific view of tragedy is conducive to imitative and inflationary writing. Why should Maxwell Anderson have thought that *Winterset* must fit the pattern of *Hamlet*? His first journalistic treatment of the Sacco-Vanzetti case, *Gods of the Lightning*, had a truer ring and possessed more integrity in action and dialogue than *Winterset*. In the latter a gangster speaks diluted Elizabethan verse, and an exposé of social injustice is jettisoned in the last act so that the play may end with a rabbinical sermon on the tragic dignity of man. The reductio ad absurdum materializes when, having come to the conclusion that the writing of a social drama is not a passport to immortality, the playwright tries to make trebly sure that his treatment will have the requisite tragic nobility and universality by combining the *Hamlet* theme with *Romeo and Juliet* and mad Lear motifs. It is a tribute to Maxwell Anderson's abilities that the fragments coalesce as well as they do. But *Winterset* exemplifies the danger of trying to write tragedy as high art, assuring significance, instead of simply trying to write a good play. Tragedy should be the product of a writer's struggle with his matter rather than of conscious conformity to patterns and principles that are considered uplifting.

It must be admitted that the tragic measure is handy. With it we can threaten to take the height and width of some plays that have been stretched artificially by sensation-mongering playwrights and stage directors. With it we can take soundings to ascertain whether there is any depth in a contemporary work presented to us with an air of profundity. For such purposes it is good to have a measure that does not shrink opportunistically to suit the market places of art, ideas, and ethics. Our concept of tragedy must not be cheapened in our time to conform to cheapness in feelings, ideas, and values.

But opportunism is not the sole alternative to dogmatism, and works of art are never wholly measurable. Our main problem is how to maintain reasonable standards without desiccating dramatic art by excluding new knowledge and awareness. New issues are needed, too, since the universal has to be embodied in the concrete if it is to be perceived freshly; if, in fact, it is to be *experienced* rather than conceived abstractly. In the theatre only the specific has stage-reality; the abstract, such as the eulogy on Man in Sophocles' *Antigone,* is dramatically immediate only in the context of the action.

Perhaps this is the moment to say a word on the tragic fallacy on which tragedy is supposed to have been nourished in past ages. The fallacy consisted in the assumption that man lived in a universe founded on reason, ruled by law, ordered by divine plan; that man's life had a meaning; that man's dignity was assured by his place in the very center of creation and by the moral structure of the world. This is the alleged tragic fallacy now supposedly lost forever as a result of the modern scientific view of life. Without the fallacy we are supposedly incapable of maintaining the dignity of man.

But this argument consists of two doubtful premises: one, that these ennobling assumptions had such sway in past ages, and two, that man could not attain dignity without them. The first assumption is a gross exaggeration of the belief of the Greeks, whose religion and mythology made human fate arbitrary, uncertain, and irrational. Even if the tragic fallacy had prevailed, there is insufficient evidence that the great tragedies —*Oedipus Rex, Hamlet,* and *Phèdre,* for example—were based or dependent on its premises. The second assumption, that human dignity is inconceivable without these ennobling assumptions, is also baseless. Atheists have been as heroic and have died as nobly as believers, and existentialist resisters to the German occupation of France sacrificed their lives no less than De Gaullists. Man's scientific mastery of nature has given him dignity, as has his confidence in being able to order the universe according to scientific hypotheses and mathematical formulations. A knowledge of the chemistry of the body has not destroyed the possibility of love among scientists, nor are physiologists forever banished from the paradise of romance. There has never been conclusive evidence that human dignity has been dependent on illusory notions of the grandeur of man in a universe that validates his grandeur. I believe that the theory of the tragic fallacy is itself a fallacy.

Psychology and sociology have indeed undermined the tragic fallacy, but it is questionable whether they have made the writing of tragedy impossible. If anything, they have presented new challenges to the tragic playwright. Ultimately, we shall come to realize that no interpretation of the *Poetics* and no new *Poetics* can have much positive value for our theatre unless it gives guidance to our century's major ventures in serious playwriting: to psychological drama and social drama. Our new knowledge will not require abdication from tragic distinction if new knowledge is assimilated into old principle—the very practical old principle that there shall be no suffering in the theatre that does not, in the end, enlighten and fortify the spectator. This is tantamount to saying that new knowledge must be transfigured into wisdom, as old knowledge used to be in the world's best tragic literature. Tragic wisdom must have its epiphany in a modern psychological and social theatre, about which it has too often been possible to say only that, "Knowledge comes but wisdom lingers."

A review of Ernest Jones's third volume of *The Life and Work of Sigmund Freud* (by David Baken in the December 9, 1957, issue of *The New Republic*) opens as follows:

> Freud once wrote that the world had experienced blows to its narcissism: the cosmological blow from Copernicus, the biological blow at the hands of Darwin, and the psychological blow from psychoanalysis. Each of these, from the vantage point of 1957, has had a paradoxical effect. In spite of the seeming abasement of man, each has, in its turn, increased man's power over the forces that govern him, and has thus served to enhance man's dignity.

Combined with the greater courage demanded of men deprived of comforting ignorance, the increase in men's awareness of themselves should make tragic art more possible, rather than less. Other factors in society will probably continue to act as deterrents to tragic vision, for there seems to be no ebb in the tide of togetherness and run-away materialism. "Blows to narcissism" may be interpreted as incentives to tragic creation. The drama of past ages would have been specious indeed if it had had to subsist on men's narcissism rather than on their sense of reality. It has been realized before that in some fundamental respects tragedy is our most realistic art, and not a mere device for cadging a bonus for our sufferings. There is no reason why we should not be able to face reality even with new knowledge undermining old egotism and traditional security.

So long as the individual is not dwarfed by social analysis or transformed into the puppet of social forces, *theme* in social drama is in little danger of being reduced to *thesis*. So long as theme is not whittled down to thesis, there is little danger of the characters being reduced to puppets. The real impediments to the writing of social drama on levels higher than those attained by the problem-play or thesis drama are want of talent and want of imaginative intelligence. Want of talent will result in the absence of life in the work, in abortive character creation, or even total absence of individualization. Want of imaginative intelligence will result in failure to surmount thesis. The playwright will be incapable of realizing the implications of the social situation and of letting his mind carry the initial social issue beyond its journalistic immediacy. He will see case histories rather than humanity, problems rather than the human condition. He may actually fail to apprehend the *moral* nature of the issues by contenting himself with their political and social character or their news value.

More than we may realize today the tragic imagination is actually a moral one. For example, John Wexley's spirited social drama, *They Shall Not Die,* about racial prejudice and the Scottsboro Case, could not be tragedy in a truly meaningful sense of the term because the author restricted his moral imagination while giving vent to his indignation. Mr. Wexley expressed his sense of morality in attacking a particular instance of social injustice with vigor and clarity. Beyond that he did not go and, considering the vogue of propaganda drama in the Thirties, did not think it necessary to go. But indignation alone (not that I doubt its ethical and social value!) carries us only as far as condemnation, so that we are enabled only to see the immediate issue, the victim, and the culprit, rather than humanity in its multidimensional reality. Imagination in high dramatic art begins where the clear-cut issue fades, where victim and culprit conclude their roles and begin to live, ideally also acquiring some degree of insight into themselves as rational members of the human race.

The great limitation of writers of social drama has been a limitation of the creative imagination. Condemnation is especially limiting because it simplifies everything to the point of banality. The greatest of all moral tragedians, Aeschylus, would have had little stature as a tragic poet if his *Agamemnon* had amounted to nothing more than a demonstration that it is wrong for a woman to murder her husband, or if the raison d'être of *The Libation Bringers,* the sequel to this tragedy, had been simply to inform Athenians that it is a crime to kill one's mother. Too much effort has been expended by writers of social drama in proving that which it requires little creative effort to demonstrate. The moral imagination is a form of *understanding*, whereas indignation is *judgment* signed and sealed. Tragedy, with its largeness of spirit, is an estate possible to social drama whenever the moral imagination takes precedence over indictments humanity richly deserves at all times and never more so than during the travail of social transition.

It has been especially difficult to perceive tragic possibilities in thesis drama, for thesis is the prose of drama whereas tragedy is its poetry. The difficulty vanishes when the prose of argument is interfused with the poetry of feeling. This has rarely been the case because the moralist or propagandist is rarely an artist. Tolstoi was a reformer by intention but an artist by instinct and long practice when he came to write his peasant drama, *The Power of Darkness*. This was a preachment against the loose morals of the peasantry, but since it is an authentic work of art it is not anomalous to actually speak of "thesis tragedy" in this particular case.

Another difficulty has been the tendency in thesis drama, if not in all social drama, to regard error and suffering as wholly eradicable by legislation or by a formal change of opinion, custom, or education. Playwrights have tended to disregard human nature itself as an obstacle to reform and to ignore nonsociological factors in human destiny, including those ironic and irrational elements that abound in the tragedies of Sophocles, Euripides, Shakespeare, and Racine.

Genuine tragedy has always been more realistic than melioristic or moralistic drama. Tragedy has always recognized that there is a built-in capacity for disaster in man and that life always has its impossibilities, whereas reformers have ever been concerned with its possibilities.

Tragedy may therefore come to be regarded as less *useful* than comedy and farce as a social instrument. The tragic sense of life might well be denounced as lack of faith, as antisocial defeatism, or as the vain indulgence of morbidity in periods of moral reformation, such as the period of the establishment of the Christian church. (Had there been any vogue of tragedy in St. Augustine's time the great Bishop of Hippo would probably have had to regard it as subversive as Manichaeism, unless he could have moralized tragedy and employed it to demonstrate original sin. The author of the *Confessions* might well have done so, but original sin is, of course, precisely what modern progressive writers, the scions of the eighteenth-century enlightenment, would have discounted before undertaking to produce thesis drama.) Tragedy may be the one luxury a society urgently in need of reformation can not afford—only to discover, after accumulating a harvest of blasted hopes, that tragedy is the one luxury it *can* afford!

Some of our contemporaries write about tragedy as though its outlook had to be almost desperately romantic. They give that impression when they refer to tragic art as idealistic, spiritual, elevating, or consolatory. Maxwell Anderson, for instance, sounded a familiar note in *The Essence of Tragedy* by declaring that the tragedian "must so arrange his story that it will prove to the audience that men pass through suffering purified, that, animal though we are, despicable though we are in many ways, there is in us all some divine, incalculable fire that urges us to be better than we are."

Professional critics in our time have also entertained more or less romantic interpretations by regarding the tragic outlook as ersatz belief for the religious faith that scientific thought has allegedly made untenable. Yet no one has seriously invalidated the hard realism of tragedy that connects life with suffering, crime with expiation, and lack of equilibrium (in the individual and in society) with painfully attained restorations of equilibrium.

Realism is held mainly culpable as the literary and theatrical movement that has given primacy to verisimilitude, illusionism, and intellectualism or rationalism. There is some validity in this indictment, which is by no means of recent origin. (It was applied to Euripides in the last quarter of the fifth century B.C.) Yet the indictment is not realy airtight. Verisimilitude is not intrinsically antitragic. What did the Athenian audiences get but verisimilitude when the self-blinded Oedipus stood before them, or when the Furies, at the close of *The Libation Bringers,* approached Orestes who had just murdered his mother? Verisimilitude is carried to its highest power in Lear's dying line, "Pray you, undo this button."

Illusionism is something even the Attic, the Elizabethan, the French neoclassic, and the Baroque stages endeavored to achieve in a variety of respects. Illusionism, like verisimilitude, is a highly relativistic concept. Technical devices and a manner of acting that would strike us as anything but illusionistic today provided sufficient illusion of reality for their own times. Garrick's Shakespearian acting would probably impress the New York playgoer as extravagant whereas Garrick's intelligent contemporaries acclaimed it as the high-water mark of realistic performance. Moreover, intellectualism and rationalism can encompass a concern for the passions. Witness Euripides and Racine. Did not Aristotle, who would have been the last person in Greece to overlook Euripides' intellectualism, call him the "most tragic" of the Greek poets?

Realism has also been blamed for the prevalence of prose drama and the rule of the fourth-wall convention. But do these factors really destroy the possibility of writing tragedy? Prose drama came into vogue long before Ibsen introduced genuine realism into the theatre—and surely the prevalence of verse drama in past ages did not automatically produce tragedy. Verse may provide a certain degree of formalism that can dignify a dramatic composition and may facilitate esthetic distance, but tragedy needs a great deal more than this.

Poetry, in the full sense of the term, is a different matter. Its absence may be accompanied by lack of imagination, universality, and reverberation in a work. Without these qualities a play, however serious and catastrophic the action, will be untragic. But it has been possible to write poetic drama such as *The Tragedy of Nan* and *The House of Bernarda Alba* without composing dialogue in verse. Realism, far from discouraging poetic prose in the theatre, has favored its use.

The fourth-wall convention may have limited the articulateness of dramatic characters by virtually outlawing soliloquies. A Hamlet so deprived would certainly be a lesser Hamlet, but it does not follow that theatrical articulateness depends upon the actor's freedom to address audiences directly. A psychological wall between the characters and audiences is in fact established the moment actors play a scene with each other. (It does not much matter whether the play is staged in the open or in an enclosed theatre, within a box set or on a platform stage, with scenery or without, and whether or not there are three other walls.) The moment the actors are in scene or in action, when they are truly interacting, they belong to themselves and not to the public. They are psychologically shut off from those who watch the performance. Actors must stylize their performance, adopt a sophisticated attitude and break their concentration up on each other in order to speak to the audience. They used to break through the psychological wall only by employing asides, a crude device at best for tragedy, although a successful one for comedy.

In tragedy the characters play for keeps rather than for the audience. With a few exceptions (such as certain speeches of Iago or Richard III) even the soliloquies are likely to establish a wall around the character. The "To be or not to be" and "Tomorrow and tomorrow and tomorrow" speeches were surely not intended to be dropped into the lap of the audience as a bouquet. Characters are perhaps never more isolated than when they deliver their soliloquies de profundis. This isolation of the tragic hero has contributed greatly to the power and significance of many a famous tragedy. Sophocles, Shakespeare, and Racine appear to have made a special effort to effect the tragic isolation of their characters; observe, for example, the lack of rapport between Antigone and the chorus or between Hamlet and his mother.

But it is unnecessary to pursue this argument further when it must be apparent that tragic expressiveness can be achieved without violating the fourth-wall convention of the realistic theatre. If necessary, the character can speak to others even at great length, as Hickey does in a fifteen-minute harangue to his friends in *The Iceman Cometh*. This monologue (the actor delivers it entirely without addressing the audience) is the most memorable episode in O'Neill's play, which is never more genuinely tragic than at that point. Dialogue always allows characters to express themselves behind the fourth wall. Anouilh, who did not hesitate to disregard the picture-frame stage in his *Antigone* (by using a Narrator who even delivers a lecture on the subject of tragedy to the audience), actually reached the peak of his effectiveness in that play with a long behind-the-fourth-wall discussion between Antigone and Creon.

So much for regarding the fourth wall as an impediment to the creation of tragedy. There is no reason to fear that the protagonist's *état d'âme* will remain hidden behind that wall. The really pertinent question is whether the playwright actually has an *état d'âme* to express or an inner personality and state of mind interesting enough to be worth expressing. I doubt that realism per se must destroy the tragic spirit; the realism of Tolstoi and Dostoevski, surely the greatest literary realism of the past century, did not do so in the modern novel. Man is often a paradox and the less reason he has to think well of himself the better he thinks of himself. It is a matter of history that men did not consider themselves insignificant even when the nineteenth-century mechanism and determinism found their widest theoretical acceptance. Also no creative writer is exclusively under the influence of his times. He may be the child of his own age, but he is also the proud heir of civilization. The creation of art is not yet a reflex conditioned solely by the present.

It is true that realism brings the common and ignoble elements of a society and of human nature into the action. But every age has contributed its meanness as well as its nobility to tragedies written in its time. The meanness and the gross values of our age cannot be regarded as an inexorable interdict against the existence of tragic art. The evil of modern times *belongs* to modern tragedy, just as the deplorable aspects of the Renaissance, including Machiavellism, belonged to Renaissance tragedy.

Without incorporating the undesirable qualities of men and their times, tragic literature would be literature in a void. We tend to spot heroic elements while ignoring the antiheroic in old masterpieces. We ennoble the tragic flaw and often play down that which is shameful about it or about the milieu that produced it. I like Cedric Whitman's reference to "the self-slain greatness" of the tragic character and endorse William McCollom's statement, in his recent book, *Tragedy,* that, "the hero's shame is the corollary of his genius." (But the role of the ignoble element in drama is still to be explored. We have yet to pick up the clue that Nietzsche left us in juxtaposing Dionysian and Apollonian elements in *The Birth of Tragedy.*)

The heroic quality or the genius of the tragic character should also receive due weight. But we must come to understand it a little better in contemporary characters such as Willy Loman, the salesman-hero of *Death of a Salesman.* Arthur Miller has insisted upon the tragic worth of this greatly flawed character, and anybody familiar with his struggles and not too sheltered or snobbish to be capable of sympathy should know what heroism is required of the Willy Lomans of the world. Willy Loman makes himself a tragic hero of sorts by his abundant capacity for suffering. He asserts a sort of tragic or semitragic dignity, with his fine resentment of slights and his battle for respect as well as for self-respect. He makes a claim for tragic intensity by his refusal to surrender all expectations of triumph for and through his son. Willy is passionately unwilling to resign himself to failure and the cheat of days. His very agony gives him tragic stature within the recognizable world of middle-class realities. Tragedy is no one's prerogative; it is *earned* damnation and redemption. The hero *makes himself tragic,* differently in different societies; he is not tragic by his status prior to the action of the play. Even the character's

awareness, the perception or tragic recognition upon which so much stress
has been placed of late, is bound to be different in the case of characters
differently conditioned by the social situation. Miller would be justified
in insisting that, within the limitations of his characters, themselves valid
dramatic factors in *Death of a Salesman,* Willy does struggle toward and
arrive at realizations convincingly his own.

Characters make themselves tragic *in collaboration with their world.*
In tragedy, as William McCollom has rightly observed, there is both "self-
determination" and "social determination." Willy seeks the truth about
himself and his situation. The search is his, for we must not ignore the
fact that all the flashbacks and hallucinations in *Death of a Salesman*
represent Willy's own anguished consciousness of failure. Willy pursues
truth and struggles against it within his personal and social limits no less
arduously and catastrophically than Oedipus. Thus Miller's protagonist
brings not only personal and social meanness into his play, but also personal stature and heroism.

The one thing Miller could not do—that his integrity would not allow
him to do—is to give Willy *an interesting mind.* It is chiefly this limitation,
along with a related limitation of language (because the character is an
urban commoner *and* because his author is rarely a poet), that makes me
contemplate the use of such a term as low tragedy. My intention is to
distinguish modern democratic drama from the aristocratic high tragedy
of earlier ages. Perhaps the genius of our century resides precisely in low
tragedy, if we are to risk a generalization concerning the taste and aptitude of the age.

There are differences of degree as well as of quality, in the exaltation
or liberation that different plays provide (e.g. *Death of a Salesman* and
King Lear although their respective protagonists have made equally gross
errors of judgment and have suffered as parents). Low tragedy is the
only term that may be sufficiently descriptive for such variously estimable
modern plays as *The Lower Depths, The Iceman Cometh, Desire Under
the Elms, Death of a Salesman,* and *John Gabriel Borkman* (or even
Giraudoux' *Electre,* Cocteau's *The Infernal Machine,* and Anouilh's *Antigone,* all plays in which high tragic substance is adulterated with low
tragic sophistication).

If low tragedy were employed descriptively rather than pejoratively,
it would call attention to a modern type of tragedy different from Classic
and Elizabethan high tragedy. Surely the term does not have to be deroga-

tory, since powerful tragic impressions have been created even by Ibsen's, Strindberg's and O'Neill's prosaic masonry. If there is a reason for dissatisfaction with contemporary playwriting it is not that our serious dramatists do not write high tragedy, but that they so often fail to create *any* sort of tragedy with their own resources of social and psychological awareness, historical consciousness, and moral relativism. (Even moral relativism need not be vulgarized; Ibsen proved that conclusively in *The Wild Duck*.) To say fatalistically that tragedy cannot be created with these resources is premature, if indeed such conclusion is not already disproved by some or all of the low tragedies listed above.

6 EUGENE O'NEILL: THE COURSE
OF A MAJOR DRAMATIST

Eugene O'Neill died at the age of sixty-five in Boston on November 27, 1953, but it is possible to maintain that he became the most alive playwright of the Fifties. More than any playwright of this decade, with the exception of O'Casey, his work revealed those comprehensive interests and intensive explorations of human experience that distinguish a major dramatist. He was one of the very few playwrights of the mid-century stage who could arouse with some labor the same interest in life that about a dozen writers did with some ease in modern fiction. It is not with a sense of loss but with a sense of lively recognition that we now associated O'Neill's name as play after play of his was revived or published and produced for the first time posthumously here and abroad.

It should be noted that one of the extremely rare twentieth-century dramatists of first rank was an American; this fact can only reinforce the widespread view that the contemporary American stage has been one of the most vigorous theatrical centers of the world. It is remarkable, too, that O'Neill won his reputation *twice* (once in the Twenties and once in the Fifties after his death), without coming up to the literary standards of the day or winning the approbation of literary critics.

The return of O'Neill to the American stage in the Fifties and the renewed European interest in his work was a proper occasion for reëxamining his reputation. It had been examined about ten years before, when investigation was apparently concerned with demolishing O'Neill's fame. A new generation seemed to want to denigrate O'Neill, even if it had no new culture-hero to substitute. In the face of the onslaught his friends and admirers could only reflect that these young critics had few opportunities to see O'Neill's plays in adequate stage productions and that nothing charged against his work was really new.

With the Circle in the Square off-Broadway revival of *The Iceman Cometh* in 1956 and the impressive Broadway success of the long-deferred *Long Day's Journey into Night* during the same year* O'Neill's return to favor and the discovery of his power by new audiences became apparent. In the season of 1956-57 he was represented on the New York stage alone by no less than four productions. Before 1960 two other O'Neill plays were on view in the New York theatre as well as abroad: *A Moon for the Misbegotten*, staged in the spring of 1957, and *A Touch of the Poet*, given a star-studded Broadway production in the 1958-59 season.

There can be no doubt that O'Neill represents virtually everything that is fundamentally modern about the American theatre. He reflects also all that has been modern about the European theatre in his restless experimentation, his avid cultivation of new ideas, his assertive individualism, and his intense unease. In many plays, he is most modern when his writing is most personal, and both his success and defeat parallel the course of our modernity. The success was that of a restless spirit honest enough to refuse to feel or think by rote, and the effect is often as provocative as a leading question and as exciting (if also as precarious) as a plunge down a waterfall. The defect of his talent may be summed up as a case of nearly continual straining for a negativeness or sense of desolation not always well founded and more conducive to darkness than to light, liberation, and final purgation.

O'Neill dignified the craft of playwriting in America. He made it a calling rather than a trade, and he gave playwrights, hitherto mostly hacks or entertainers but never oracles, a position of some importance in our cultural life. Winner of the Nobel Prize and author of plays staged in virtually all the capitals of Europe, he was our first dramatist of international standing. Though his power exceeded his skill on many an occasion, his craftsmanship was still sufficient to carry him through some of the most ambitious projects attempted in the Western theatre since Aeschylus wrote his trilogies twenty-four hundred years ago. O'Neill represented the avant-garde both in our country and in Europe in the Twenties, and his banner may still be seen fluttering in the vanguard. It is not too much to say that even our most venturesome living playwrights are

---

* This autobiographical play was written in 1940, but withheld from the public until Mrs. O'Neill allowed the Yale University Press to publish it in 1956.

generally discreet technicians in comparison with him. A leader of the experimental Little Theatre movement, led by his own play-producing organization, the Provincetown Players of Greenwich Village, and after 1920 the leading playwright also of the progressive wing of Broadway professionalism, O'Neill sparked a revolt of great moment against commonplace realism.

O'Neill also expressed a general reaction against Victorian mores, especially against the Puritanism and Protestant ethic associated with American Victorianism, ranging himself in this respect on the side of the rebels of his generation led by Van Wyck Brooks and Randolph Bourne. Combined with a deeply felt (if also fashionably Bohemian) rejection of middle-class complacencies, machine-worship, dollar-idolatry, and the entire cult of go-getting opportunism, O'Neill's lofty individualism placed him in the forefront of those who began to modernize the content of American drama no less than its form. Both dramatic form and content were further modernized by his response to the spread of Freudianism or depth psychology that led to his attempting to dramatize subconscious pressures. The means he adopted for this purpose alone carried him into areas of experimentation which only venturesome playwrights dared enter and where only exceptionally adept ones could survive.

O'Neill's career allows us to conclude that we should not take him less seriously than we do, for his struggles with form and content were singularly intense and imaginative. More than any other writer in the American theatre he endeavored to give range and significance to the drama, which had previously been mostly a narrowly commercial enterprise. This endeavor alone would justify our sense of indebtedness to him and our readiness to place him in the company of the European theatrical pioneers. But there is another, less easily definable, quality that distinguishes O'Neill. Almost alone among our professional playwrights, he possessed a sense of integrity and self-immolating artistry that he never betrayed or even rationed.

Moving darkly through the maze of the modern world, O'Neill, in his maturity, refused to be comforted by the material enticements of modern society. He accepted no solace from Marxist movements that powerfully attracted many of his fellow writers and attracted him briefly, too, in his youth. He accepted no assurances from the status quo either.

Another way of describing O'Neill's compulsion to wrestle with the angel—and O'Neill was one of the most compelled of modern playwrights

—is to say that he was loyal to a tragic sense of life. He was a natural tragedian, though it is possible to question whether any particular play of his quite lived up to traditional high standards of tragedy, and though his forte was more tragicality than tragedy. But even if we agree with critics who believe his work, in lacking poetry and elevation, falls short of tragedy, we cannot legitimately deny his work tragic ambience. Above all, we must grant the integrity of his despair.

Although a frequently amiable person whose sense of humor (and it was often sturdy, even raffish) has been insufficiently acknowledged, O'Neill could never abide complacency. In the interview he gave to the press on the eve of the première of *The Iceman Cometh,* produced by the Theatre Guild in September, 1946, he reaffirmed his position by calling the United States the "greatest failure" in the world. The reason was "the everlasting game of trying to possess your own soul by possessing something outside of it, too," and America with its immense resources had been especially tempted to play that game. "This was really said in the Bible much better," he added. "We are the greatest example of 'For what shall it profit a man if he shall gain the whole world and lose his own soul?' We had so much and could have gone either way. . . ." O'Neill proceeded to enlarge his indictment to include the whole human race, concluding that, "if humanity failed to appreciate the secret of happiness contained in that simple sentence," it was time to "dump" the human race "down the nearest drain and let the ants have a chance."

O'Neill produced an impression of greatness by virtue of the absolute demands he made upon life and by an acute awareness of humanity's failures. His aim was to make the theatre express a Luciferian aspiration exceeded in some of his plays only by his sense of calamity that amounted to a Satanic sense of damnation. O'Neill is one of the few Faustians of modern literature—others are Dostoevski, Strindberg, and Kafka—for whom damnation is a psychological reality rather than a convenient religious fiction.

It is true that O'Neill sometimes appears to be aiming too consciously at greatness. In the pursuit of magnitude he falls into some errors of taste and tact and tends to pile up his catastrophic situations and to schematize his dramatic conceptions—witness such ambitiously conceived pieces as *Strange Interlude* and *Mourning Becomes Electra.* But apparently the labor in his work had to *show* before the work could be impressive at all. He is not the man for finesse; his temperament appears to have had little use for it. Whenever there is truth or depth of experience in the plays it is futile to wish that he had composed them less repetitively and insistently. Their emotional power is bound up with their massiveness.

O'Neill's raw talent may embarrass his admirers, but it tends to reduce his detractors to impotence once they leave the library. In recent decades he presented the English-speaking commercial theatre with extreme challenges offered by only one other playwright, Sean O'Casey. O'Neill made the theatre rise to both his reasonable and unreasonable expectations. Intent upon having his say regardless of consequences to dramatic form or length, O'Neill became one of those rare playwrights with whom the practical theatre has been compelled to come to terms. There have been such writers in every theatrical period that has had some claim to significance.

Of O'Neill's modern matter not much remains to be said; it has already been touched upon by my reference to Freudian psychology and social thought. The rest of the substance of modernism to which O'Neill gave attention consists of the now shopworn ideas of naturalism and scientism, the mechanistic and deterministic substitutes for faith in divine providence. But one major qualification must be added on O'Neill's behalf. Modernism was not in his case a sign of complacency. He was not content in unbelief. Modernism did not solve any fundamental problems for him, nor did it unriddle the world for him as it supposedly did for shallower men.

It is apparent that in O'Neill's search for values, a term that would be ostentatious when applied to most of his fellow playwrights, he had in view the magnitude of theme and treatment present in the past great ages of the theatre, especially in the age of Attic tragedy. Its masterpieces had left a strong imprint on his imagination. He sought that magnitude not as an imitator but as a strenuously creative artist. The Orestean trilogy furnishes the basis of *Mourning Becomes Electra*, and it is possible to detect the Hippolytus theme in *Desire Under the Elms*. But the classic manner is barely visible in O'Neill's plays; psychological pressures take the place of the classic Fate, and the dialogue of the characters is generally plain. Yet he attained dramatic expansiveness and frequent elevation in his plays.

We do not come close enough to O'Neill's particular genius until we realize that it is obsessed with damnation. The anguish of alienation so

pronounced in his work is far less conspicuous in the tragedies of Sophocles, Shakespeare, and Racine. They possessed the inestimable balm of
great poetry, but this undeniably great gift is not the sole reason for their
power to radiate light as well as heat and to attain a healing power rarely
discernible in O'Neill. The point is that, unlike O'Neill, they were profoundly affirmative. After the 1920 production of *Beyond the Horizon*
the elder O'Neill said to his son, "Are you trying to send your audience
home to commit suicide?" There was a basis to the question.

Pessimism and the tragic spirit (which is ultimately affirmative) are
at war in the works of O'Neill. In the canon there are plays, such as *The
Iceman Cometh*, in which the playwright seems to put a premium on
desperation, or, as in *A Moon for the Misbegotten,* to become prodigal
with misery. But though he appears to have the Jacobean playwrights'
taste for morbidity, he was usually more inclined to be mordant than
morbid in his commentary on life, and his manner was chiefly one of a
determined reaction against the optimism of shallow people breezily at
ease in Zion. "Sure I'll write about happiness," he declared in an interview in 1922, "if I can happen to meet up with that luxury," and he went
on to maintain that he found a compensating exaltation in writing tragedy.
"A work of art," he said, "is always happy; all else is unhappy." But all
these qualifications cannot quite remove an impression of incompleteness
produced by much of his work. It is an incompleteness of tragedy, reflect-
ing an incompleteness in the playwright himself.

O'Neill expresses a keen sense of loss quite aside from the usual tragic
awareness of the misery of human life. It is hardly a secret that his special sense of desolation was associated with the loss of faith on the part
of an introspective man who was born and reared a Catholic. A determined individualist unable to attach himself to the social causes that won
the allegiance of many intellectuals in his time, he did not discover compensatory convictions. O'Neill gave continual evidence of traumatic experience in his youth, and the loss of religious faith was an important part
of it; he makes much of the problem in *Dynamo* and *Days Without End*.
We find in his work a keen sense of loss of connection—of connection
with God, nature, society, family, father.

O'Neill's ambivalence is certainly no longer a secret. He set it down,
dramatizing its source in the family situation with rough tenderness and
candor when he wrote *Long Day's Journey into Night*. This play, written
late in his career, is explicit about ambivalences projected and symbolized

in earlier plays. Here he was a characteristically modern dramatist, a divided man who was acutely aware of the division not only in himself but in his fellow men. Like his favorite modern playwright Strindberg, O'Neill made division itself the subject of his plays. In them he tried to master the division he found in human nature and in the human condition, and because this was no easy enterprise he was doomed to repeat the effort constantly.

Had O'Neill been a shallow man he might have settled for small satisfactions, had he been an essentially irreligious man he might not have been concerned with lack of faith, had he been an unloving man he might have been content with the gregariousness that passes for love among low-voltage individuals. The tensions in his work are nearly always connected with his struggle against alienation. The secret of his dramatic intensity is to be found not in his theatricality but in his rebellion and anger, in an inability to resign himself to an arid view and way of life. He could not be at ease in a world without God, without love, and without trust in life.

It rests with the critic to test these generalizations by considering O'Neill's plays individually. In a rapid review it is apparent that the theme of division was constantly present in his theatrical imagination. O'Neill is apt to split his characters frequently. Thus the artist-hero, surely a projected image of the author himself, appears as a divided man in *The Great God Brown*. Dion Anthony is as schizoid as the name would suggest; one part of him belongs to Dionysus and is life-loving, lustful, and creative, while the other part of him belongs to St. Anthony and is inhibitive, pervaded by a sense of sin, and inclined to denial of the flesh. In *Days Without End*, the man-of-the-world John Loving has two selves intended to be played by separate actors. He has both a sophisticated, cynical self and a suppressed personality that is loving and longs for and elects goodness. Since one self can survive only through the elimination of the other, the spiritual self rises beside the cross only when its Mephistophelian double falls dead.

Divided personalities also appear in contrasted forms in such earlier plays as *The Emperor Jones, The Hairy Ape,* and *Strange Interlude,* but never before so specifically as separate characters in an explicit conflict between belief and unbelief. *Days Without End,* presented by the Theatre Guild early in 1934, was the last new play of O'Neill's that Broadway was to see until a dozen years later when *The Iceman Cometh* opened in New York in September, 1946.

The season of 1933-34 marks the end of O'Neill's trauma of division. It appears to resolve as well his protracted conflict with the actual and symbolic fathers, a conflict directly represented in *Desire Under the Elms, Dynamo, Strange Interlude,* and *Mourning Becomes Electra.* In *Days Without End* the reconciliation is with God. In *Ah, Wilderness!,* the genial period comedy of O'Neill's boyhood that appeared earlier in the same theatrical season, the reconciliation is with a worldly father, the small-town editor Nat Miller who watches over his son's adolescence with amused tolerance. It seemed as if the playwright's twenty-year war with the fathers was terminated. But the war resumed in the plays written subsequently, and the rift between O'Neill and the world appeared to have actually grown wider. He is at odds with life once more in *The Iceman Cometh,* in which he contends that only illusions can make existence endurable. He shows its hopelessness with both sentimental and ironic overtones in *A Moon for the Misbegotten;* and he makes disillusionment with parents and an elder brother the primal family drama in *Long Day's Journey into Night.*

These plays make it plain that O'Neill remained the dramatist of failure and alienation to the very end of his career. It is as if he himself were the center of dramatic conflicts that could be allayed perhaps but never resolved without some visitation—some experience on the road to Damascus—that never came to him. Peace of the spirit had come briefly after great turbulence to his favorite modern author, Strindberg; it is possible that O'Neill once expected peace for himself, too. But it is evident that once O'Neill saw the world going from bad to worse in the Thirties he found justification for the very worst construction he had put on human nature and the destiny of the species.

Still, the source of the anguish in the late plays as in the early ones is personal, not political. If his plays have a larger reference than personal grief the credit belongs to his creative imagination. He had the true artist's power of imaginative projection necessary for the creation of significant drama. He also had the egocentricity of men of romantic sensibility (such as Byron and Goethe), who make the world a reflection of their own spiritual condition. He perceived the world primarily through

his temperament and mood; division in himself became division in the
rest of the world. When angry with the world he could have borrowed
Othello's words about Desdemona:

> ... when I love thee not,
> Chaos is come again.

Should we consider O'Neill overwrought it would be well to remember
that his emotional power lies largely in his sense of significant torment.
If he strains so much it is partly because his subject matter has more than
surface reality for him; his dramatic material invariably acquires poetic
and, at times, even metaphysical connotations. The loneliness of sailors
in the SS *Glencairn* sea pieces, for example, becomes the loneliness of
man in the universe, and the disorientation of Yank, the hairy ape who
tries so desperately to belong, is a symbol of man's severance from the
world of nature. Yank, O'Neill declared, is "the symbol of man who has
lost his old harmony with nature, the harmony he used to have as an
animal and has not yet acquired in a spiritual way." Unable to move
forward toward complete humanity Yank dies in his attempt to return
to the animal state.

In a play filled with naturalistic dialogue as primitive as the mentality
of Yank and his fellow stokers, O'Neill still had in mind only the larger
meaning. "The subject," he said, "is the same one that always was and
always will be the one subject for drama, and that is man and his struggle with his fate. The struggle used to be with the gods, but is now with
himself, his own past, his attempt to belong." Anna Christie's father is
continually conscious of the irony of fate and of a malevolence in the
nature of things that the old sailor associates with the "old davil sea."
And in succumbing to primal fears in the jungle, Emperor Jones reënacts
the whole drama of atavism, the drama of humanity's inability to abolish
the ghosts of the racial past.

Play after play reflects O'Neill's disinterest in literalness and dissatisfaction with the naturalism he scorned as "holding the family Kodak up
to ill-nature" and favoring "the banality of surfaces." It was the deep
experience and the large frame of reference that interested him. It is
true enough that his effort to use symbolism and attain emotional resonance contrasts noticeably with the low condition of most of his heroes
and with the commonplaceness of their dialogue. The familiar O'Neill
characters such as Chris Christopherson, Yank, Orin, and Hickey are

anything but Promethean figures. But they are frequently involved in situations that transcend their actual condition or environment. They rise in stature with their awareness of irony and of crass casualty in the universe, with their sense of being lost in the cosmos, with the intensity of their fateful love and hate. It is impossible to forget that O'Neill himself is speaking through them; it is *his* largeness of tragic feeling that gives them their magnitude.

An amplitude of tragic perception appears even in so intimate a family drama as *Long Day's Journey into Night*. As family drama alone it is patently repetitive and labored; those who respond to it solely as a naturalistic slice-of-life are well entitled to their reservations. But there is more to *Long Day's Journey into Night*. The line of development in the play is young O'Neill's introduction to a tragic view of life through disenchantment with his family. The family is the *microcosm* through which the artist gets his first hard look at the *macrocosm*. This first look is also romantic, recalling the doldrums of the lost generation of the eighteen-nineties; the young O'Neill broods on the lachrymose poetry of Ernest Dowson. But we know that the look grew harder in the course of O'Neill's career.

The tragic sense of isolation announced in this play (but actually expressed in most of the plays that preceded it for more than two decades) is the final clue to O'Neill's course as a modern dramatist. The rift in the formative period of his life is reflected by the rifts in his playwriting. O'Neill's divided artistry has long been apparent and it will have to count importantly in any final appraisal: a discrepancy between vaulting intentions and lagging execution, between intense action and prosy dialogue, between a penchant for the austerities of high tragedy and an addiction to commonplace psychopathology, and the many fluctuations in dramatic style.

O'Neill was programmatically opposed to realism or naturalism, and aside from favoring symbolism resorted to the expressionist technique of fantastic distortion in such plays as *The Emperor Jones* and *The Hairy Ape*. Nevertheless, these and other means of stylization do not reveal him in the fullness of his power and apparently left him unsatisfied. He turned away from them, and some of his most powerful writing appears in the invigorated naturalistic vein of *Desire Under the Elms, Mourning Becomes Electra, The Iceman Cometh, Long Day's Journey into Night,* and *A Touch of the Poet*. O'Neill's dramatic writing is divided between imaginative flights and traffic with humanity on the gritty ground. Just as his feeling for sailors, derelicts, and commoners is generally preferable to his dealings with educated and highly placed characters, so is his realism to his fancies, his earthiness to his literary ambitions.

O'Neill was not what we would call an integrated artist. On the contrary, his interest and power in the theatre were derived from his dividedness. (The one exception is the sunny comic artistry of *Ah, Wilderness!*) The alienation in his dramatic talent commands respect for a writer who had the courage of his discontent. This talent fails to carry him to the eminence of the indisputably great playwrights of the past, and it leaves room for very mixed reactions to his work. But alienation was the cross O'Neill had to bear, proudly chose to bear, and he carried it further into the theatre than any other modern playwright after Strindberg. No other dramatist of our century has thus far attained his dark and disturbing impressiveness, and no degree of astute criticism has yet invalidated at least this much claim for his labors—the labors of a modern Sisyphus in Tartarus.

7 TENNESSEE WILLIAMS: 1940–60

In an addendum written in March, 1944, for the published text of *Battle of Angels,* Tennessee Williams affirmed his allegiance to the plastic medium of the theatre. "I have never for a moment doubted that there are people—millions!—to say things to," he concluded. "We come to each other, gradually, but with love. It is the short reach of my arms that hinders, not the length and multiplicity of theirs. With love and honesty, the embrace is inevitable."

When *The Glass Menagerie* reached Broadway one year later, on March 31, 1945, the embrace was consummated. The thirty-one-year-old Southern playwright met and won his audience, and the country's most formidable band of critics awarded him the New York Drama Critics Circle Award for the best American play of the 1944-45 season. In the fall of 1945 his earlier dramatization of a D.H. Lawrence story under the title *You Touched Me,* written in collaboration with Donald Windham, was presented. If this second occasion for an embrace proved less ardent it was still an encounter with a well-disposed public that patronized the play for several months. Two years later, on December 3, 1947, *A Streetcar Named Desire* opened and took its place as the outstanding American drama of several seasons. The play held its own even against so attractive a rival as *Mister Roberts* and won a second Drama Critics Circle Award as well as the Pulitzer Prize. By common consent Williams was the foremost new playwright to have appeared on the American scene in a decade. (Arthur Miller was as yet only at the foothills of his ascent with *All My Sons.*) Broadway eagerly awaited *Summer and Smoke* which received glowing reports when Margo Jones presented it in her little Dallas theatre in the round during the summer of 1947.

All was not well when Tennessee Williams predicted an inevitable

77

embrace between himself and the theatre public. A group of his one-acters aptly entitled *American Blues,* since their scene was the depression period, had won a small cash award from the Group Theater in 1939. He had received a Rockefeller Foundation fellowship and had been given a scholarship to an advanced playwrights' seminar at the New School for Social Research in February, 1940. The class was conducted by Theresa Helburn and me, both of us associates of the Theatre Guild. When our student showed us a draft of *Battle of Angels* at the end of the semester, it was natural that we should submit it to the Guild. The play went into rehearsal under excellent auspices: Margaret Webster was the director and Miriam Hopkins the leading lady. It opened in Boston in the fall of 1940, but the results were catastrophic.

The play concluded melodramatically with a conflagration. The stage manager, having previously been warned that he was weakening the effect by his chary use of the smokepots, decided to make the scene as thoroughly realistic as possible. An audience already outraged by the unsparing presentation of repressed sexuality in a Southern community was literally smoked out of the theatre. Miss Hopkins had to brush away waves of smoke in order to respond to the trickle of polite applause that greeted her when she took her curtain call. The reviewers were luke-warm at best, and soon Boston's Watch and Ward Society began to make itself heard. The Theatre Guild withdrew the production and sent a letter of apology to its subscribers. (But it also assured them that they had been introduced to an uncommonly promising new talent.) The author, who had lost an unusual opportunity in the theater, became once more, as he put it, that "most common American phenomenon: the root-less wandering writer," who ekes out a living by doing odd jobs.

He was ushering in a movie theatre for a weekly wage of seventeen dollars when Metro-Goldwyn-Mayer took him out to Culver City along with other young hopefuls. The studio promptly forgot about him after he submitted a screenplay outline that contained the germ of *The Glass Menagerie.* They wrote him off as just another bad penny in Hollywood's expensive slot machine, and dismissed him at the end of his first six month contractual period.

If his prospects seemed bleak in the early months of 1944 Tennessee Williams nevertheless had a few reasons for self-confidence. He had been sufficiently inured to straitened circumstances during his youth, especially while pursuing his studies at the University of Missouri, Washington

University, and the University of Iowa. His education had even been interrupted by two years of depressing clerkship for a shoe company. His later apprenticeship to the writing profession had included desultory work as an elevator operator in a New Orleans hotel, as a teletype operator for engineers in Jacksonville, Florida, and as a waiter and reciter of verses in a Greenwich Village night club. He also knew the direction he was taking and had, in fact, already covered some of the road, having absorbed and poured out considerable experience in the remarkable one-act plays later collected under the title of 27 *Wagons Full of Cotton.*

Williams was developing a precise naturalism, compounded of compassion and sharp observation; his plays were filled with some of those unsavory details that Boston first nighters had found offensive but that the author considered a necessary part of the truth he had set out to tell. But he felt a need for expression that he could not satisfy with anything less than the full visual and aural complement of the theatrical arts. Although he was also writing poetry and short stories Williams was certain that his métier was the theatre because he found himself continually thinking in terms of sound, color, and stage movement. He had grasped the fact that the theatre was something more than written language. "The turbulent business of my nerves," he declared, "demanded something more animate than written language could be." He was also moving toward a fusion of naturalistic detail with symbolism and poetic sensibility rare in American playwriting.

Williams was ready to carve out plays that would be as singular as their author. Although one could surmise that he was much affected by Chekhov, D.H. Lawrence, and Faulkner, he drew too much upon his own observation to be actually imitative except when he was obviously striving to be literary. He did not fall neatly into the category of social and polemical dramatists who dominated the theatre of the Thirties, even if his experience of the depression period inclined him toward revolt against the Old South and toward themes of defeat or stalemate that were economic as well as psychological. His interest was primarily in individuals rather than in social conditions. His background alone would have distinguished him from urban playwrights such as Odets, Arthur Miller, and Lillian Hellman, who were attuned to sociological analysis and regarded personal problems in the light of social conditioning and economic conflict. By comparison with the writers of social drama this Mississippi-born descendant of Tennessee pioneers was insular. He had been conventionally reared and educated. His father, formerly a salesman in the delta region, was the sales manager of a shoe company in St. Louis, and his maternal grandfather was an Episcopalian clergyman. Cities appal Williams. He disliked St. Louis, where he spent his boyhood, and he has never felt acclimated to New York. Once he felt free to wander his inclinations took him to Florida, Taos, Mexico, the Latin Quarter of New Orleans, and more recently to Italy and other parts of Europe and America. The pattern of his behavior established itself early in his life, and it has been marked by a tendency to isolate himself, to keep his individuality inviolate, and to resort to flight whenever he feels hard pressed. But his most habitual flight is not merely *from* something, but *toward* something—toward creation, the one escape that is also a way of being found.

The one-act plays which first drew attention to Williams foreshadow his later work thematically and stylistically. *Moony's Kid Don't Cry* presents a factory worker who longs to swing an ax in the Canadian woods. A carefree youth, he doesn't hesitate to buy his month-old baby a ten-dollar hobbyhorse when he still owes money to the maternity hospital. Moony, whose escape is effectively scotched by a practical wife, is the prototype of the restive young heroes of *Battle of Angels* and *The Glass Menagerie*.

One naturalistic one-acter, *27 Wagons Full of Cotton*, gives a foretaste of the rowdy humor that was to flavor *A Streetcar Named Desire* with an authentic environment and provide some counterpoint to the oppressive material. The naturalism of Erskine Caldwell and William Faulkner is very much in evidence in *27 Wagons Full of Cotton*. The play concerns a cotton-gin owner, hard pressed by the depression, who loses his childish wife to a business rival whose cotton gin he burned down. This raffish play, combined with other dramatic material, subsequently became the grotesquely comic film *Baby Doll*.

Another, rather literary, little play, *The Purification*, was a tragedy of incest and Spanish honor. Williams' poetic power and theatrical imagination were conspicuously present in this early work. Finally, *The Long Goodbye* anticipated *The Glass Menagerie*, with its efficient use of a retrospective technique of playwriting.

Most noteworthy in these one-acters are evidences of a rare compassion for life's misfits and a general ability to transcend crude reality. Pity glows in the baleful red-light district atmosphere of *Hello from Bertha,* in which an ailing harlot loses her mind. Pity assumes a quiet persuasiveness in a vignette, *Lord Byron's Love Letter,* in which two women's pathetic poverty is revealed in their effort to subsist on donations by Mardi Gras tourists to whom they display a letter from Byron. Williams is particularly affecting in his early treatment of battered characters who try to retain shreds of their former respectability. Self-delusion, he realizes, is the last refuge of the hopelessly defeated. He studies its manifestations in *The Portrait of a Madonna* with such clinical precision that this one-acter would be appalling if it were less beautifully written. Its desiccated heroine, who imagines herself being violated by an invisible former admirer and plays the young Southern belle by bandying charming talk with imaginary beaux, could have become almost as memorable a character as Blanche Du Bois in *A Streetcar Named Desire* if Williams had built a full-length play around her.

Williams would like to grant these unfortunates the shelter of illusions, but is pained that the world is less likely to be tender toward them. Mrs. Hardwick-Moore of *The Lady of Larkspur Lotion* is the butt of her landlady, who jibes at the poor woman's social pretensions and at her invention of a Brazilian rubber plantation, from which her income is incomprehensibly delayed. Only a fellow boarder, a writer nearly as impoverished as Mrs. Hardwick-Moore, is charitable enough to realize that "there are no lies but the lies that are stuffed in the mouth by the hard-knuckled hand of need." He alone is willing to indulge her increasingly reckless fabrication as she locates the plantation only a short distance from the Mediterranean but near enough to the Channel for her to distinguish the cliffs of Dover on a clear morning. . . .

It is quite apparent that Williams was nearly fully formed in these short plays as a painter of a segment of the American scene, a dramatist of desire and frustration, and a poet of the human compensatory mechanism. It is a curious side light on American playwriting that, like O'Neill, Paul Green, Odets, and Wilder, Williams started unfolding his dramatic talent in the one-act form.

When he wrote *Battle of Angels,* the first of the full-length plays to attract a Broadway management, Williams was on less securely charted territory. He did not yet know his way through a plot maze sustained for an entire evening. He was so poorly guided in the revisions made for the Theatre Guild that the produced play was inferior to the accepted script;

he also appears at this stage to have been influenced somewhat too strongly by D.H. Lawrence. *Battle of Angels* was unsatisfactory even in the revision published in 1945, which differs from the Boston failure in that it lacks the climactic conflagration, stresses the note of social protest in one scene, and employs a prologue and epilogue. Williams plainly tried to throw together too many of the elements he had dramatized separately in his best one-acters. He brought his vagabond hero, Val Xavier, into a decayed town, involved him with a frenzied aristocratic girl, grouped an assorted number of repressed matrons and unsympathetic townsmen around him, and made him fall in love with the frustrated wife of a storekeeper dying of cancer. He not only made the mistake of multiplying dramatic elements instead of fusing them but piled up fortuitous situations (*i.e.* the arrival of an avenging fury in the shape of a woman from whom he had escaped and the killing of the wife, Myra, by the jealous storekeeper, a murder for which Val is then innocently lynched). Moreover, the playwright made the mistake of creating a character who is a cross between a provincial vagrant and a D.H. Lawrence primitive, presented here as an example of pure natural man who is bound to be destroyed by contact with society.

Williams has been unwilling to relinquish this early work, for which I, too, formed an attachment. He returned to it more than fifteen years later and brought it to New York in the spring of 1957 under the title of *Orpheus Descending.** The new version contains improvements over the unpublished 1940 Theatre Guild and the published 1945 versions, but the important fact is that this revision gives the work a symbolic extension of meaning. Val Xavier became Orpheus and a symbol of the eternal artist who is trapped and destroyed in the sorry world; Val arriving in a bigoted Southern town was Orpheus descending into the Underworld. *Orpheus Descending* did not succeed on Broadway, although the direction was entrusted to Harold Clurman, one of the most reliable and brilliant of American stage directors. (An off-Broadway production in the 1959-60 season was more successful.) But no one could mistake the play for the work of a mediocre playwright, for it had profound imaginativeness. It simply failed to exist naturally and convincingly on the level of surface reality (Val Xavier is a bore even if Orpheus is a culture-hero), before ascending to "higher" levels of meaning. Such levels can be successfully sustained on the stage only while firmly established on the ground level of experience.

* For further comment on *Orpheus Descending* see Part II.

In its symbolism *Orpheus Descending*, along with *Camino Real*, represents Williams' most characteristic tendency next to his naturalistic leanings: he grew fond of the poetry of French symbolism and decadence, apparently liked Hart Crane especially, and early developed a penchant for using symbols, large and small.

In *Orpheus Descending* and *Camino Real* Williams also reveals two characteristic faults. One of these, intrinsic to his estheticism, is an excessive reliance on fairly transparent symbolism; for example, Williams made the husband in the first-mentioned play become Pluto incarnate in a decidedly obvious way in the last act. The other fault, intrinsic to Williams' flair for the dramatic, is a tendency toward sensational violence. The realities of the drama market being what they are, it inevitably follows that the symbolism would weaken Williams' popularity, and that the sensationalism would enhance it. The ultrasymbolist dramas, *Orpheus Descending* and *Camino Real*, were financial failures, despite the fact that the author had prestige and a following in the Fifties that were not his in the winter of 1940.

Williams' career was stalemated for close to five years; he did not become a successful playwright until the production of *The Glass Menagerie* in 1945. *Battle of Angels*, nevertheless, contains some of his most imaginative dialogue and memorable character drawing. Myra, the heroine (renamed Lady in *Orpheus Descending*), is a rounded portrait; and Williams could barely improve upon his sexually inflamed secondary character, the ultrareligious woman Vee Talbot, who paints the figure of Christ only to discover in amazement that she has drawn a picture of Val Xavier.

Williams achieved a quiet order and simplification absent in *Battle of Angels* with his next work, *You Touched Me*. This is a comedy in which a Canadian soldier liberates a girl from her musty British environment and the mummifying influence of a spinster. But here he was working with another writer's material, paying an overdue debt to D.H. Lawrence. The lack of personal observation was apparent in this competent dramatization; the play did not bear his own special signature of anguish. Even simplification has to become a highly personal achievement in Williams' case.

It became so profoundly personal and so notably sensitive in *The Glass Menagerie* that there was no longer any doubt that the American theatre had acquired a new dramatist. When *A Streetcar Named Desire* reached

Broadway two years later his success was even greater. If his artistry was less exquisite, his dramatic drive had measurably increased. He was in command of a large and turbulent action, and he extended the range of his characterization and the variety of his dialogue.

The plays that first thrust Tennessee Williams into the front rank have much in common besides their clear focus and economical construction. Both *The Glass Menagerie* and *A Streetcar Named Desire* transmute the base metal of reality into theatrical and, frequently, verbal poetry. Both supplement the action with symbolic elements of mood and music. A major theme is Southern womanhood helpless in the grip of the new world, while its old world of social position and financial security is a Paradise Lost. But differences of emphasis and style make the two dramas distinct.

The Glass Menagerie is a memory play in which crucial episodes from family history are evoked in the comments of a narrator, the poet Tom, who is now in the merchant marine. The form departs from the fourth-wall convention of realistic dramaturgy and suggests the Japanese Noh drama, in which story consists mostly of remembered fragments of experience. If Williams had had his way with the Broadway production *The Glass Menagerie* would have struck the public as even more unconventional, since his text calls for the use of a screen on which pictures and legends are to be projected. Disregarded by the producer-director Eddie Dowling, these stage directions nevertheless appear in the published play. They may strike us as redundant and rather precious; the young playwright was straining for effect, perhaps without realizing how well he had succeeded in making his simple tale hauntingly self-sufficient. At the same time the original stage directions confirm the impression that Williams, for better and worse, was committed from the start to experimentation with poetic or theatricalist form.

As plainly stated by Tom, the background of the action of *The Glass Menagerie* is a crisis in society, for the depression decade is teetering on the brink of World War II. His tale belongs to a time "when the huge middle-class of America was matriculating in a school for the blind," when "their eyes had failed them, or they had failed their eyes, and so they were having their fingers pressed forcibly down on the fiery Braille alphabet of a dissolving economy." But Tom's memory takes him back to his straitened home life and the need to revolt that finally sent him to sea. In episodes softened by the patina of time he recalls the painful shyness of his lovable crippled sister, Laura, and the tragicomic efforts of his mother, Amanda, to marry her off, as well as his own desperation as an underpaid shoe company clerk who dreams of escaping from his drab life. The climax comes when, nagged by the desperate mother, Tom brings Laura a gentleman caller, who turns out to be engaged to another girl.

Without much more story than this Williams achieves a delicate synthesis of sympathy and objectivity by making three-dimensional characters out of Tom's family and the young Gentleman Caller, who is trying to pull himself out of the rut of a routine position and to recover the self-esteem he once had as a schoolboy success. The carping mother could easily become a caricature, especially when she remembers herself as a Southern belle. In reality she is an impoverished middle-aged woman deserted by her husband, a telephone man who "fell in love with long distances" and who probably found an incitement in his wife's pretensions. Amanda is redeemed by solicitude for her children, her laughable but touching effort to sell a magazine subscription over the telephone at dawn, and her admission that Laura must get a husband if she is to escape the fate of the "little birdlike women without any nest" Amanda has known in the South. Laura, too shy even to take a course in typewriting, behaves with sweet dignity and becoming stoicism when she is let down by her first and only gentleman caller; as impersonated by Julie Haydon, Laura was, in her air of delicate lostness, an unforgettable Marie Laurencin portrait. Yet Williams makes it plain that pity for the lost should not be allowed to destroy the instinct for self-preservation that made Tom leave home; the compassionate soul must try to save itself as best it can. Although Tom will never forget Laura and the candles she blew out he is now part of the larger world that must find a common salvation in action, "for nowadays the world is lit by lightning."

In *A Streetcar Named Desire* health and disease are again at war, but more openly and more sensationally. The lines of conflict are sharply drawn in this naturalistic drama whose story, unlike that of *The Glass Menagerie*, is not revealed impressionistically through a mist of memory. Nothing is circuitous in *Streetcar*, and the dramatic action drives directly to its fateful conclusion as the plebeian Stan Kowalski and patrician Blanche Du Bois confront each other. Like Williams' other Southern heroines, who invariably suggest Picasso's dehydrated "Demoiselles d'Avignon," Blanche Du Bois is not only a recognizable human being but also an expressive abstraction. She is decadence, pretension, hysteria, charm faded, sensibility misapplied, sensitivity rudely jolted by the world, hope deferred, life wasted. It is her final tragedy that the life she encounters in her married sister's home becomes a hell of humiliation precisely when she is most desperately in need of sympathy. Her plantation lost, the teaching profession closed to her, her reputation gone, her nerves stretched to the snapping point, Blanche comes to her sister Stella in the French Quarter. She finds her married to a lusty ex-sergeant of Polish extraction. He discovers Blanche's lurid past and, though he may be momentarily touched by her fate on learning of the unhappy marriage that drove her to moral turpitude, his standards do not call for charity. With her superior airs and queasiness she has interfered with Stanley's married happiness, and she must go. Loyal to his friend, who served in the same military outfit with him, he feels obliged to forewarn Mitch, who is about to propose to her, that Blanche was a harlot. Having sensed a challenge to his robust manhood from the moment he met Blanche, he must even violate her while his wife is giving birth in the city hospital. It is his awesome, earthy health, which will defend itself at any cost, that destroys Blanche. Stella must send the hapless woman to a state institution if she is to protect her marriage and preserve her faith in Stanley once Blanche's accusations against him can no longer be ignored.

As in *The Glass Menagerie* and the one-acters, the private drama is pyramided on a social base. Blanche is the last descendant to cling to the family plantation of "Belle Reve," sold acre by acre by improvident male relatives "for their epic fornications, to put it plainly," as she says. Simplehearted Stella has lost caste by her earthy marriage to Kowalski, but has saved herself in the process. Blanche tried to stand firm on a quicksand marriage to a sensitive boy who turned out to be a homosexual and committed suicide. Then Blanche also declassed herself—right into a house of ill-fame. The substructure of the story has some resemblance to *The Cherry Orchard,* whose aristocrats were also unable to adjust to reality and were crushed by it. But Williams limits himself to allusions to social reality; *Streetcar* is not a social drama. He also subordinates his ambivalent feelings, that Stanley and the denizens of the New Orleans slum street ironically called Elysian Fields represent health and survival, to a poet's pity for Blanche. For him she is not only an individual woman, but a symbol of the many shorn lambs for whom no wind is ever tempered except in men's hearts and in the understanding of writers like Williams himself. It is undoubtedly for this reason that the author called his play a "tragedy of incomprehension." In the words of his quotation from Hart Crane, the play "entered the broken world to trace the visionary company of love, its voice an instant in the wind (I know not whither hurled)." It is largely compassion that sublimated the naturalism of Williams' writing in *Streetcar* and produced its most memorable lines, such as Blanche's cry when she finds herself loved for a moment, "Sometimes there's God so quickly."

With *The Glass Menagerie* and *A Streetcar Named Desire*, both plays of the Forties, Tennessee Williams unquestionably reached the climax of his early career. The plays he turned out in the Fifties may be said to represent a middle period, for they did not so much advance his artistry as broaden it. However, the broadening process was already discernible in the Forties in *Summer and Smoke*. The play failed on Broadway in the fall of 1948 only to be revived in the next decade with extraordinary success in the off-Broadway theatre.* It is a play which could be criticized as too sprawling; it was a letdown for reviewers and playgoers who had been enthralled by the spiraling turbulence of *Streetcar*. The author himself knew that he was employing a horizontal line of development. In his production notes he relied on changes of lighting rather than dropping the curtain to indicate the divisions of the play. He requested that, "Everything possible should be done to give an unbroken fluid quality to the sequence of scenes." This indispensable requirement was first met by the Circle in the Square revival. Williams' characters do not come into focus at once, except in the most obvious manner of a conflict of flesh and spirit. The heroine, Alma, represents spirit and the hero John (later Doctor John) flesh. As fully realized individuals they acquire definition slowly in the mist of their confusions, evoking the late George Jean Nathan's acute criticism that the author employed "a scrim treatment of character . . . hiding his real delineation behind pseudo-poetical gauze which blurs his audience's vision." In the Circle in the Square production the scrim treatment was turned into an advantage and proved to be poetically expressive. The play, as Brooks Atkinson rightly sensed, is in some respects more genuinely compelling than *Streetcar*; it seems closer to life and further from contrivance.

* See Part II for a review of this production.

If *Summer and Smoke* is the less effective play one thing is certainly apparent: Williams did not intend to repeat the tight, near-melodramatic, action-drama pattern of *Streetcar* simply because it worked so well for him and his audiences. Elia Kazan called that play, in his Director's Notebook*, a "poetic tragedy, not a realistic or a naturalistic one." In "physicalizing" the action Kazan realized the active character of a *Streetcar* and neither the author nor the regular playgoer is likely to forget the naturalistic effectiveness of the work. But for the author, *Summer and Smoke* represented artistic independence. In returning to the poetic, impressionistic manner of *The Glass Menagerie*—though with a broadening of the action—Williams remained unfettered to any success formula.

Concerning the plays that followed *Summer and Smoke* in the Fifties,** it is worth observing how differently their author worked in each case. *The Rose Tattoo,* which reached Broadway early in 1951, was written as a *comedy.* This alone is a departure. (Williams' one-act comedies were not Broadway productions and *Baby Doll* had not yet been filmed.) But in addition, Williams makes his central heroine a full-blooded woman quite unlike the more or less wilted Southern ladies he had hitherto favored.

An earthy lyricism appears in his portrait of Serafina delle Rose and in sketches of her neighbors. "Out of the lives of some simple human beings Mr. Williams has composed a song of earth," wrote Brooks Atkinson. Praise for the writer could accompany even less exalted opinions of *The Rose Tattoo,* views more impatient with the author's attentiveness to the widowed Serafina's overimaginative if recently underactive libido. Praise is definitely in order for a remarkably comic portrait of Serafina's suitor, Alvaro Mangiacavallo; for a delicate treatment of Serafina's daughter's love affair with a young sailor; and for Serafina's old-world reaction to this relationship. For though Serafina is tempestuous, she is not licentious and brings a highly moral attitude to love and marriage. There is also much vivid reality in the background, in the village located "somewhere along the Gulf Coast between New Orleans and Mobile." These merits in the play add up to one achievement: the comic utilization of a sensibility that hitherto had painted with a much darker palette.

Still, *The Rose Tattoo* is a minor accomplishment for the author. Its

* Published in Toby Cole and Helen Krich Chinoy's *Directing the Play,* The Bobbs-Merrill Company, Inc., 1953.
** Comments on some of these will be found in Part II of the book.

box-office success did not tether him to comedy of sex which could easily have become the permanent output of a less independent and ambitious writer. Instead, Williams' ambition next led him into the quicksands of ultrasymbolist and surrealist drama in *Camino Real,* a work theatricalized, perhaps overtheatricalized, by both the author and director in the 1953 Broadway production. Louis Kronenberger charged the play with "that feverish excess that is the foe of true intensity." Yet Williams intended it as a comment on the state of the world. The nightmare of corruption, tyranny, and sadism in *Camino Real* is more than equaled by the world we have known since the emergence of Stalin and Hitler. Perhaps the author's imagination is too engrossed with surrealist pictures of decadence. But what true artist is not—except that he usually opposes a strong Apollonian wholeness to the destructive element in his imagination?

It is to Williams' credit that he showed himself in possession of a will to health along with his fascination with the underworld of the id. In *Camino Real* historical characters have escaped from the infernal world of his imagining. Byron escapes when he goes out to die for Greek liberty, as does Don Quixote when he recklessly follows the call of his delusionary idealism. But these escapes are not worked out dramatically; they are an ill-fitting, if deeply intended, coda. It is not so much that the author's matter or idea is obscure as that his manner is choppy and his story diffuse. If anything, his ideas suffer as mere ideas or symbols and literary allusions. The play is at once too baldly abstruse and too strenuously theatrical.

Despite the criticism I have just summarized, it is evident that only a man of exceptional dramatic talent could have written *Camino Real.* No one else would have dared to write it; no one else could have written it in so snarled a manner, attempting to say so much about human life and the state of the world. Though *Camino Real* looks like a deliberate literary exercise (chiefly because of its literary allusiveness), it was wrung out of its author's consciousness. It is a *compelled* piece of work even while appearing to be a contrived one. External evidence for such a deduction appeared when Williams painted another Hell in *Orpheus Descending.*[*]

The author is in more control here even if less encouraging about the possibilities of escape. As if he simply could not banish his nightmare view of the world, he brought it to the foreground once more in

[*] See Part II for discussions of *Orpheus Descending* and *Garden District.*

Suddenly Last Summer. This less than full-length drama shared an off-Broadway theatre with an inconsequential one-acter under the collective title of *Garden District.** With its appalling report of the death of a homosexual esthete and of strange cannibalistic fantasy, this play is Williams' most thoroughly pessimistic reckoning with life. Had he written it about a dozen years earlier and presented it in Paris, he would undoubtedly have qualified as a culture-hero of the postwar existentialist movement.

During the Fifties Tennessee Williams moved in various directions with different degrees of range and intensity in *Camino Real, Orpheus Descending,* and *Suddenly Last Summer.* These plays represent the most intensive use of the dramatic imagination in a single decade by any American playwright since O'Neill. At the same time Williams continued to make profitable use of his flair for naturalistic drama in two great box-office successes: *Cat on a Hot Tin Roof* and *Sweet Bird of Youth. Cat* enthralled most playgoers in 1955 with its extraordinarily vivid characterizations and its driving action. Even Londoners apparently agreed that Williams' treatment of the struggle for truth and life that takes place in a Southern family constituted powerful if ugly drama. Ugly or not, the play presents as strong a struggle against failure as one could expect from any playwriting of the Fifties.

But it was perfectly evident that Williams was not moving in the direction of sweetness and light when he gave playgoers *Sweet Bird of Youth* in 1959.** It would be difficult to find a more unsavory report on the monstrous behavior of men and women than this exposé of a movie star, her gigolo, a demagogic Southern senator, and his semifascist supporters led by his sadistic son. But whatever criticism one can direct at this extremely successful play (and like other sensational Williams plays it mingles melodrama with character creation, and a taste for Grand Guignol with a feeling for poetry), it is plain that Williams has a grip of iron once he lights upon real characters in recognizable, if extreme, situations.

It is fair to say that Williams is the mid-century theatre's most impressive, though not necessarily most gratifying, American playwright. Whether he fails with fantasy or succeeds with reality, he makes indifference to the theatre virtually impossible. Since he is still considerably

* See Part II for discussions of *Orpheus Descending* and *Garden District.*
** For a review see Part II.

under fifty it is too soon to form a conclusive estimate of his career. But to judge from the last twenty years one can surmise that instinctive dramatic feeling will remain his forte and that want of control will be his chief defect. He will probably have to continue to indulge his taste for literature, melodrama, and strenous theatricality, unless he is brought back to the delicate artistry of *The Glass Menagerie*. He will have a problem in finding proper balance between dramatic excitement and dramatic reality. When the balance is more or less attained it will still be necessary to determine whether the play is serving an idea or whether an idea is being forcibly attached to the runaway theatricality of the play. In *Cat on a Hot Tin Roof*, for example, it is difficult to discern any unity of theme (and therefore any point worth the labor of the action), despite constant and rhetorical insistence on facing the truth.

We might ask some disconcerting questions about Williams' entire career of the Fifties. Are its affirmations particularly compelling or rewarding? Obviously they are not. If this is true, are the negations particularly stirring and significant? I think it is easier to say that they are stirring *rather than* significant. What is most stirring in the plays is partly character drama, partly the pressure of generally explosive action, and partly the stabbing power of individual lines and conversations. Williams has proved himself capable of producing remarkable scenes, as in the first act of *Sweet Bird of Youth* or the showdown scene between father and son in *Cat on a Hot Tin Roof*.

Like all effective *play*wrights, Tennessee Williams has been virtually from the start of his career a vivid and exciting *scene*wright. But in composing a balance sheet of credits and debits we must take one final matter into consideration: Williams' consuming theatricality. This theatricality is partly the poet's and partly the showman's. It is truly difficult to know, as it is not in the case of the indisputably great dramatists before him, to what degree theatricality in his work has sensationalized life instead of illuminating it.

8 JEAN GIRAUDOUX
AS VIRTUOSO

I discovered Giraudoux in the late Twenties when his *Siegfried,* introduced to New York by Eva Le Gallienne's Civic Repertory Theatre, impressed me as an intelligent contrivance. His comment on the evils of nationalism was not exactly startling in its originality or passion, but he had an engaging way of projecting a point of view. He was suave, aloof, and ironic while other European pacifist playwrights of the period usually sputtered with anguish and worked themselves into expressionistic frenzies of protest. He was as articulate as they were inarticulate, and as urbane as they were hysterical. The Giraudoux of this first encounter was an exquisitely civilized writer. In contriving a tale of amnesia and mistaken identities as a result of which a French soldier becomes a German after World War I, Giraudoux was plainly a fabulist. His favorite strategy, that of inventing or adapting a fable or myth, was already in evidence; since he had first written *Siegfried* as a novel, under another title, this tendency to use a literary underpinning antedates his theatrical career. Only one reservation marred my awareness of the new playwright: he seemed self-conscious in his ingenuity and more taken with his clever plot than with the human drama latent in the work.

The shadow of this clever trickster, man of the world, and littérateur has always stood between me and my inclination to accept Giraudoux as a major dramatist. It would be obtuseness on my part not to acknowledge him as an extremely attractive writer for the stage, but it is my ambivalence toward him that concerns me here. While the French have been somewhat reserved in their estimate of him, my impulse has been a typically American one: to turn him into a master figure of modern theatre.

My doubts came to a climax when I got to know his *Electre* in the late Thirties; my mixed feelings toward this notable work have never left me. I have had divided feelings about his other plays, most of which I admired, but the discomfort of my division has usually been less pronounced. His *Judith* has troubled me more; I almost dislike it. His *Electre* epitomizes the possession of positive and negative characteristics which, in my opinion, will keep Giraudoux in the honorable limbo of distinguished playwrights who have just missed greatness.

One aspect of Giraudoux' artistry, his comic leverage, has never given me pause. Whenever he is consistently light of heart or fancy, he is thoroughly enchanting. His success is then complete, within the bounds of his favorite mixed genre of comedy and fancy. *Intermezzo*, unsuccessfully and awkwardly presented on Broadway as *The Enchanted*, seems to me his most charming, if hardly his most incisive, play. I can also accept his entertaining one-acter, *The Apollo of Bellac*, as a refreshing farce, although its oversimplifications have been a trifle too strenuous in most productions. I have not found *The Apollo* as remarkable as some reviewers, but this little comedy is captivating, and nobody has written anything as charming in English since Synge and Lady Gregory.

Giraudoux' *Amphitryon 38* is an entrancing comedy. It is equally satisfactory as a literary tour de force and as bedroom comedy, although it would be difficult to notice any marked distinction between the two in this instance. But my high estimation of the author's poetic-comic vein is not a recent opinion conveniently formed for the purpose of withholding any other kind of approbation from the author. My liking for *Amphitryon 38* dates back to the Thirties. I recommended it enthusiastically to the Theatre Guild, which produced it with Alfred Lunt and Lynn Fontanne, giving the author his first and probably greatest success on Broadway.

One cannot acclaim Giraudoux as a minor writer to avoid considering him a major one. His claims to that status were fully evident to me the moment I read *Electre* for the Theatre Guild in 1937 or 1938. Although we did not undertake to produce it on Broadway because we felt the chances of presenting it successfully were slim, the play deserved high regard; *Electre* shows an unusual largesse of mind and spirit.

La Guerre de Troie n'aura pas lieu (in Christopher Fry's translation, *Tiger at the Gates*), *Ondine, Judith,* and *The Madwoman of Chaillot* also advanced various claims to Giraudoux' importance one would like to endorse. (I can cite only a few titles because Giraudoux, a prolific author as well as a busy man of affairs, did not bring his talent to the theatre until he was forty-six years old.) But when the spell of this master stylist lifts, one is holding quicksilver. No one in France, except Claudel, has more right to be regarded as an important playwright, and no one else, who has written for the modern French stage, except Giraudoux' successor Anouilh, leaves me with a more uneasy feeling of having been deluded by literary and theatrical witchcraft.

In view of Giraudoux' unquestioned talent—his intelligence, verve, and mastery of language—this conclusion seems grossly unfair. Yet such is my verdict. *Electre* has continued to fluctuate in my estimate between profundity and arty sophistication. It is alternately tragic and arch; now devastatingly ironic, now merely clever; now penetrating and now boulevardishly bedroomy; now dedicated to dramatic truth and now to dramatic legerdemain.

La Guerre de Troie n'aura pas lieu, another example, is a brilliant conceit and a sardonically moving drama. This play is somewhat artificial and skittish, as well as wordy in commentary without being wholly convincing in content. In pricking the vanity of warmongers the author draws blood only from the epidermis. Certainly when World War II broke out less than five years after the play was written, Giraudoux' commentary on the causes of war seemed generally superficial. To take the final measure of this play it is necessary only to turn to *The Trojan Women* of Euripides and *The Plough and the Stars* of O'Casey. The comparison is invidious, and perhaps shouldn't be made at all if we merely want to determine whether Giraudoux' play has merit—which indubitably it has. Yet the total still does not amount to a great dramatic experience.

Ondine is a beautifully composed fairy tale, rich in poetic pathos and despair. But the very character of the fable about the love of a water sprite and a knight attenuates tragic conflict and favors atmospheric not dramatic pressure. *Judith* seems to me too greatly entangled in motivation and countermotivation, too much involved in analytical complexities to deliver the dramatic power promised by the tone and substance of the play. We derive more smoke than light from it, and regardless of the considerable interest in Judith's fluctuating attitude toward herself and

Holofernes, our interest remains moderate. We feel forced to attend to her complexities (and Giraudoux' literary virtuosity) rather than to become truly absorbed in her humanity. Although *Judith* is psychological drama, it is circumscribed, like *Ondine* and *La Guerre de Troie*, by a seemingly congenital fondness for playing with notions.

Not even *The Madwoman of Chaillot* is exempt. We can cherish the play as a delightful fugue of bizarre improvisations and poetic moods, but its theme, annihilation of the predators of modern society, promises more than it delivers. Wholly adult statement on the rapacious society that aroused Giraudoux' distaste is withheld; instead a fairy-tale resolution—the lurid old Countess relegates the entrepreneurs to Paris sewers—is offered. We should be grateful that Giraudoux has spared us a dull anticapitalistic disquisition. The result is a mad and rueful dramatic statement in the modes of comedy, satire, and poetry—a work that is as indefinable as it is ingratiating. One cannot, however, put *The Madwoman of Chaillot* on a par with *Major Barbara, John Gabriel Borkman,* or *Heartbreak House*. Giraudoux' play is only a brilliant display of fireworks in comparison with some modern playwrights' heavy artillery. The author runs head-on to confront an issue, then sprints away from it with equal brio. He vacillates between poetry and vaudeville (though it is superb vaudeville); between saturnine seriousness and frolicsome triviality.

The Madwoman of Chaillot brought Giraudoux closest to a wrangle with the contemporary world that ruffled his aplomb as a gentleman, diplomat, and man of letters. But it is his spirited *Electre* that carries him to the heights of tragic art, and it is in this work that we may best observe the distractions, discrepancies, and divided aims of his artistry—the qualities that make him so fascinating a playwright but that have also left him stranded midway in his dramatic ascent. *Electre* may be described as a perfect example of the dilemma of the modern playwright who wants to be tragic yet urbane, passionate yet detached, emotional yet intellectual, vigorous yet literary all at the same time. The contrast with a writer like O'Neill who was decidedly *not* urbane is familiar enough.* But the postwar literary generation has not been eager to

* The reader may be interested in my comparison, "The Electras of Giraudoux and O'Neill" in *The Theatre in Our Times*. Crown Publishers, Inc., 1954, pp. 257–266.

approve a playwright whose sense of tragedy lacks the finesse required by their literary training.)

Giraudoux' success in writing sardonic tragedy imaginatively in both literary and theatrical terms has been of greater moment to the postwar generation. But how successful has he been? My mixed feelings about his *Electre* have been shared by many of my graduate students who are dedicated to the theatre and to the search for new avenues of dramatic art. One must conclude that Giraudoux won only an inconclusive success with a play that should have qualified him for the select company of great modern playwrights. Tragedy and urbanity do not mix well in his *Electre,* at least not well enough.

To say that Giraudoux did not write *Electre* with conviction would be to ignore his entire political career and to be insensitive to the pressure of his irony. With this play he followed a tradition. The classics have been rewritten periodically in France ever since the Renaissance. But far from being a literary exercise, *Electre* expresses its author's continuous concern over the hatred that has poisoned relations between France and Germany ever since the Franco-Prussian War. Two ruinous wars apparently had not sated the chauvinistic lust for vengeance. Giraudoux, the German-educated French diplomat, dedicated both his diplomatic and literary career to its extinction. Adopting the Euripidean rather than the Sophoclean view of the Oresteian legend, Giraudoux sees no liberating glory in the vengeance of Agamemnon's children. He credits Clytemnestra with remorse and Aegisthus with some nobility. His vengeance-bent Electra is obsessively neurotic. She is an unlovely heroine. Horror attends her steps and at the end she causes the death of her mother and Aegisthus. More than this, Electra brings ruin to her country and death to many of its inhabitants who might have lived out their lives in peace. The symbolic Furies, who are nasty little girls in the first scene of the play, are full-grown at the end; they are exactly as tall as Electra herself, for the Furies and Electra have become identical. As flames consume the city Giraudoux' frantic heroine is left clinging only to her belief in the rightness of her position, and to the dubious comfort that her country will be reëstablished on new foundations of truth.

A mordant power informs Giraudoux' tragedy. His abhorrence of violence, even in the name of justice, inspires an especially effective exchange of speeches between Electra and the Furies. One of them, observing the conflagration in the city, declares that this is the light

Electra wanted with her demand for truth. Electra can only reply with desperate futility, "I have my conscience. . . . I have justice, I have everything."

The thrust of dramatic warning is greatly strengthened by the tensions between mother and daughter, mother and son (the avenger-son, Orestes), and between Electra and Aegisthus. The latter comes to admire her after undergoing an ironic transformation from lecherous poltroon to a person capable of appreciating nobility (Electra is, alas, relentlessly noble). A fierce quarrel between Clytemnestra and Electra on the question of sibling rivalry—did the infant Orestes fall or was he jealously pushed by Electra—is poignant in its absurdity. Now and again brief bursts of irony brighten the sultry atmosphere of the work. The huge irony of Aegisthus' transformation into a hero capable of saving his country just before he is annihilated by Electra's righteousness is immensely effective. This change draws Electra's bitter protest against the gods' hypocrisy and malice. They can't do this to her, she cries out. Why should they redeem her mother's lover and collaborator in the murder of Agamemnon. The gods have made "a parasite into a just man" and "a usurper into a king."

A symbolist imagination also courses through the play and deepens its hues. Giraudoux' vision of a sanguinary reckoning in ancient Greece was a close parallel to the Nazi program of revenge for Germany's defeat in 1918. The effect of the little Furies is as eerie as the sense of ripening doom is oppressive. The nasty children who call themselves "the little Eumenides" grow and "get fat" as one looks at them; one can even watch their eyelashes growing, says one of Giraudoux' characters. A vulture hovers over Aegisthus when Orestes appears; when the reformed Aegisthus behaves humanely, injudiciously releasing Orestes from his chains, the bird of death begins to descend. No less grim is the preternatural figure of Zeus in the role of The Beggar as he follows the folly of human action with supercilious indifference to human suffering.

What is it that essentially limits Giraudoux' achievement in this play? The fact that *Electre* is overinsistent in its wit; Giraudoux cannot resist delivering himself of bright sallies of words or a clover leaf turn of events. This inclination carries him so far from the swirl of conflict engulfing Clytemnestra, her lover, and her children that lengthy discursive passages impede the action or swerve it from its direction. The diversionary tendency almost becomes a technique in itself, and it crops up not merely when characters discuss the pertinent issues but also when their concerns are merely peripheral.

One portion of the play is virtually indistinguishable from Parisian boulevard comedy or farce. The President of the Council, who is being betrayed by a flighty wife, is personally connected with Electra solely as cousin of The Gardener who has been selected to marry Electra to prevent her from causing mischief. This comedy of adultery lightens the work and constitutes a subplot in the Elizabethan manner. It is actually woven into the play so deftly that it does not block the traffic of the central action, and yet it is obtrusive enough to call attention to itself as the superimposed by-play of a witty writer. The author seems to invite the audience to observe how adept he is at playing the Parisian modernizer of myth.

Giraudoux' attitude of sophisticated detachment is even more pronounced when he weaves his airy way in and out of stage illusion. The playwright seems to flaunt both his ingenuity and his detachment from the reality of the work with which he expects to engage the spectator's interest. In two instances he actually interrupts the action in order to inform the spectators that he is contriving a play to beguile an audience. He goes out of his way to establish the author and the spectator in the theatre rather than in the midst of life. This is apparent when The Gardener, relieved of his obligation to marry Electra, steps up to the front of the stage and harangues the audience: "I'm no longer in the running. That's why I'm free to come and tell you what the play can't tell you."

Wit will out, and "The Gardener's Lament," as this interlude is called, is a truly marvelous passage of verbal pyrotechnics. But it is also telling the audience that the author, anxiously guarding his claim to urbanity, is not involved in his play, which is not the case at all. The other deliberate violation of stage illusion occurs at the end of the first act, when The Beggar, now recognizably Zeus, comments on Electra while she lies asleep near her brother Orestes. The Beggar's long speech, a virtuoso's display of rhetoric, clearly is directed at the audience, for the fluent god departs with an admonition to the spectators: "But all you who remain here, be quiet now: This is Electra's first rest and the last rest of Orestes." Once more the audience is reminded that the author does not intend to lose himself in an illusion of reality or expect that the playgoer will. But Giraudoux contradicts himself; some of the scenes that follow, like some of the scenes that have come before, have the dramatic power to produce as much illusion of reality as any realist could possibly intend. By comparison with their intense immediacy the monologues of The Gardener and The Beggar seem pretentious and academically labored. The device of intrusion, while theatrically arresting, is dramatically questionable.

Such obtrusive cleverness calls attention to the author's self-conscious and exhibitionistic virtuosity. Wit has, in these instances, become ostentatious theatricality, and it almost casts doubt on the truth of the play and the sincerity of the author. Theatricality has both enriched the play's external action and undercut the validity of its claims as an engrossing audience experience. *Electre* thus becomes an amalgam of absorbing drama and a facile lecture-demonstration. It advertises itself as a display piece of dramatic fabrication. The play contains an episode toward the end where The Beggar describes the murder of Aegisthus *before* Orestes kills him. It is a brilliant piece of imaginative theatricality, it is a trick in the best sense of a Cocteau *truc,* it is a convenient condensation of action at that point in the play; but it is also a transparently gratuitous contrivance.

The conspicuous intrusions of the playwright into the dramatic development comprise the crux of Giraudoux' self-advertising playwriting. The total effect of this supererogatory display of author's independence from story, this superfluous assurance that he is contriving theatre makes *Electre* labored and precious. A potential masterpiece was botched by the modernism of a writer whose wit, imagination, and dramatic talent wrought intriguing rather than great drama.

We owe Giraudoux much admiration, but it is decidedly risky to make a leader of him and try to follow him into a new Canaan of dramaturgy and dramatic style. He was distinctly Parisian, and worked in a decorative literary tradition that impresses French critics less than it impresses us, to whom it has seemed entirely fresh. He also followed the theatre-for-theatre's sake tradition of the disciples of Jacques Copeau, among whom the most successful practitioner was Giraudoux' friend and producer, Louis Jouvet. Giraudoux brought literary grace and intelligence to that tradition. He did not, however, overcome its pitfalls of cultivated artifice when he succumbed to the seductions of baroque rhetoric and arch dramaturgy, at which he was supremely adept. Although the results were delightful so long as he confined himself to comic improvisation and genial fancy, they also fixed the bounds beyond which he could not move without peril.

A characteristic saying of Giraudoux', quoted in the *Columbia Dictionary of Modern European Literature,* reads: *"La Mort est si ancienne qu'on lui parle latin."* But if Death is so ancient that one speaks Latin to her, the wit of Giraudoux is so familiar to Europeans and bilingual Americans that they may expect it to speak French to them. In French, Giraudoux' discourse flows with an unceasing abundance, so that Broadway producers have usually considered it imperative to curtail the baroque stream of his sentences. The lavishly decorated wit, which often becomes an approximation of poetry, seems to flow less from conviction than from pleasure. Artifice in dialogues and dramaturgy did not serve him unequivocally. This moderate diplomat-dramatist and wit was a man at ease in his milieu, rather than a pioneer to be followed into new pathways.

Giraudoux came to the theatre as a middle-aged man with a number of graceful and polished impressionistic novels to his credit. He began publishing in 1909, and it was as a stylist, rich in imagery and amusing extravaganza, that he first won a reputation. He was by then a gentleman of settled taste, which had been formed at the turn of the century (he was born in Bellac, Haute-Vienne, in 1882), and he remained a congenial belletrist somewhat on the level of Anatole France. Giraudoux did not undergo any shattering experience on some new road to Damascus even during the cataclysmic last decade before his death in 1944. He remained a career-diplomat of the Quai d'Orsay to the end and was Chief of Information in the compromising Daladier government briefly in power before France surrendered to Germany in 1940. Though he published essays in 1939 in which he insisted on the importance of France's remaining a great power, rational compromise was Giraudoux' most cherished principle and his policy.

Compared with the unimaginative realists who still rule the commercial stage, Giraudoux will probably always qualify as a progressive writer. But it would be more correct to honor him as a writer who *closed,* rather than opened, an era in the theatre. In our eagerness to crawl out of realism's peephole we should not follow him blindly into his forest of words.

9 FOUNDATION

OR NO FOUNDATION

"Unhappy are the playhouses that have no history."

—ARSÈNE HOUSSAYE

As a youngster associated with the stage I decided that both the theatre and I would do very well to forget about Aristotle. This innocent symbol of the constraints of rule and sensibleness without sensibility is the butt of ignorance compounded by infantile revolt. The burgeoning American theatre of the Twenties represented challenge in the work of O'Neill and liveliness in the debunking junkets of the Kaufman school precisely because it struck out recklessly in any direction away from Main Street.

In my own by no means singular case there was experimentation in verse; I was a verse-librist and imagist, and at one time even found myself listed somewhere as an Objectivist poet. Only one of the poems I managed to publish in a variety of periodicals for several years had a strict metric pattern and for that I had the excuse that the effect was satirical, since the subject was suburbia. I also recall becoming a poetry critic for *Books: Herald Tribune* at the ripe age of twenty-two and reviewing the verse of Masters, Aiken, and others without benefit of poetic theory or concern with levels of meaning, synaesthesia, types of ambiguity, intentional fallacy, and affective fallacy. Yet I published literary criticism of a sort, got paid the customary pittance for it, and even collected compliments from elder statesmen. I also wrote a novel about this time, just as I had had the temerity to write a book-length study of the novel several years earlier, without knowing anything about the principles of fiction. The gospel of art as expression or self-expression sustained me, and criticism

101

was truly the impressionistic adventure of my soul among masterpieces, near-masterpieces, and trash. Needless to say I was not alone in this respect, but the story of my insouciant generation—the early Twenties—has been rendered too often and too well for me to expand upon it.

Art was undoubtedly our objective even when social protest was present, and we were not yet apologetic about believing in Beauty—perhaps because the pursuit of beauty was itself a revolt from the philistine milieu whose comforts some of us were enjoying. It would not have been difficult to catch us in paradoxical attitudes. It seemed as if we believed that we could serve art best by serving it casually. (The Theatre Guild's busiest and best director, the late Philip Moeller, remained a brilliant amateur right up to the time he abandoned the theatre for good, in 1938, twenty years before his demise.) I suppose we could be logically accused of favoring the seductive paradox of artistry without control, or of wanting to be thoroughly creative and thoroughly free at the same time. Even T.S. Eliot, who was later bent on correcting this notion, put this paradox into brilliant practice in *The Waste Land* in 1922.

But when we moved into the theatre with an amateur's fervor it was not always art we sought so much as the release of being occupied with something nonutilitarian and unconventional. When I followed and lamely tried to participate in the adventure of the Provincetown Players on MacDougal Street, the Neighborhood Playhouse, and the young Theatre Guild, mostly as a sort of hanger-on, it was less art than liberation I sought. As in the case of so many of us, I wanted to be free from a moderately well-to-do middle-class home. The theatre, for all the labor involved, was an especially attractive means of escape; its very discipline was, by contrast with the Main Street decorum, an exercise in indiscipline. Art was important, but freedom was even more important.

I recall from my earliest associations as a translator, adapter, and play-editor with the Theatre Guild that the important consideration was our feeling about the work, our spontaneous discovery of some challenge or excitement in it, our unprompted belief that we had been stimulated or invigorated. We were miles away from the kind of marriage to explication that might have made us favor a work and have confidence in its success because so much about it could be explained. We rarely stuck to a position, committing ourselves neither to realism nor to the nonrealistic styles of Rice's *The Adding Machine* or Lawson's jazz-symphony, *Processional*. The Guild was utterly eclectic in play selection, and decisions were made by majority vote at board of directors meetings that sizzled with repartee. The directors had no program except perhaps of producing plays that fascinated them and were often sure to lose money. Some members of the Guild looked upon the nascent social-minded Group Theatre of the early Thirties with misgivings. It seemed too susceptible to dogmatism. Members of the Group deplored the Guild's "lack of a sense of direction."

The Guild's brilliant stage director, Philip Moeller, worked mostly by instinct. He intoxicated himself by banging out Wagnerian music on the piano in the rehearsal room when he wasn't engaged in affectionate badinage with the superb actress Helen Westley. She was magnificent in temper and in acting ability, and had unbounded enthusiasm for unconventional drama. Moeller was far more interested in Balzac, music, and Greece than in cogitation about any theory of theatre. Lee Simonson, wit and artist, made a contribution to American scenic design second only to that of Robert Edmond Jones, yet Simonson expressed nothing but scepticism concerning the esthetics of Gordon Craig.

The voice of Lawrence Langner was often decisive at the Theatre Guild. Patent-lawyer, playwright, man of the world, he flitted back and forth from Europe to America, and mediated diplomatically between the Guild and O'Neill and between the Guild and Shaw. He was the last man in the world to prefer an analysis to a venture or a passion. His vigor and resourcefulness were amazing, and his creative impulses came with incalculable speed.

Watching over the Guild's contentious divinities like a Demeter with an antique smile stood untiring Theresa Helburn, the resourceful heroine of many a crisis. She died on August 18, 1959, in her seventy-second year, after having given half a century of determined exertion to the theatre. But this cultivated woman was impatient with any abstract consideration of principles of art, the direction of modern drama, and the style of a play or production. She, too, created productions—*Oklahoma!* originated in her fertile mind—by impulse.

From many years of association with the early Theatre Guild I can recall frequent attempts to develop various kinds of theatre (including musical comedy and something called ballet-drama), but extremely few words concerning dramatic theory. It is the adjective *contrived* that was most frequently and lethally applied to unworthy plays in the days when the Guild belonged to the avant-garde. Contrivance was considered tanta-

mount to the death of art. So was any close formulation of aims. A program was something to be tossed up like a ball in the air, a paper hat
to be worn for a gala occasion, a Chinese lantern to be hung up in a
garden of delights. Hedonists, individualists, improvisers, and artists, the
Guild's leaders, made a turbulent family. Until 1939 they were showmen
as intellectuals and intellectuals as showmen. No wonder they impressed
the younger generation of the depression period as dilettantes without
moorings in social and artistic conviction. But one might have wondered
how dilettantes could give the theatre so many brilliant productions.

I remember an experience that chastened my own puritanical conscience and should refute those who hold that good theatre must be
planned, organized, and meticulously developed. We were rehearsing
O'Neill's *Ah, Wilderness!* with George M. Cohan in the role of the
small-town editor. Day followed day while the great Cohan sat idly on
the stage or went through the motions of rehearsal with bland insouciance,
causing confusion while he fluffed his lines or called for prompting with
a snap of the finger. When I couldn't bear to see another rehearsal go to
pieces I turned to Theresa Helburn and unburdened my despair. She
smiled soberly at me and assured me that "it would be all right." And
it *was* all right once a performance had to be delivered. Cohan had been
easing himself into the role in his own free, easy, and unanalytical way,
and he ultimately gave the greatest performance of his long career.

Many years later the whole character of the great success *Oklahoma!*
began to crystallize in form as a result of a casual conversation I had
with Miss Helburn. I primly suggested the need of a spine, a special
justification, at a time when all we could see in this musical were beautiful fragments. At her request I gave Miss Helburn a memorandum. Somehow between then and the out-of-town tryouts in New Haven and Boston
the musical play absorbed my stiff formulations through her mediacy.
They were absorbed so inconspicuously, so unintellectually that Lawrence Langner in later writing about the development (reflected in the
change of title from *Away We Go* to *Oklahoma!*) was understandably
vague. In *The Magic Curtain* Langner simply reports the following:
"Terry and John Gassner suggested some kind of rousing song of the
earth would be helpful in the second act, and one day Dick and Oscar
appeared at the theatre, sat at the piano . . . while they played for us
the rousing melody of the song *Oklahoma!*"

By comparison with the ardent proponents of the social theatre that developed in New York after 1931, those of us who remained associated with the Theatre Guild during the Thirties were likely to be considered frivolous. It became fashionable to be serious and responsible about art and society. A theatre undeviatingly concerned with social questions was regarded as an absolute necessity during the lingering depression period. And the picture darkened after 1933 with the rise of Hitler, the Spanish civil war, and the fearful expectation of World War II. Only a segment of the American theatre was responsive by design and dedication to the issues of the times and tried to form itself into a movement, to formulate and follow programs. This was the leftist theatre which I, as well as other critics, observed with sympathetic interest, hoping that its fervor would prove fruitful. Admiring its passionate involvement with imme-diate questions of the depression and Nazi era, we were also embar-rassed by its frequently intemperate dogmatism. As a Theatre Guild associate I was often the recipient of slurs on the Guild's bumbling ivory tower, on its art for art's sake, softheaded ("hang your clothes on a hickory tree but don't go near the water") type of liberalism.

Still, even the leftism of the Thirties was more wayward and impro-visatory than one might have imagined. For one thing, it was a mélange of liberalism and radicalism united only by opposition to fascism and a general worry over the imminence of war. Even New Dealism was no real cement for this Left of conflicting liberal, socialist, and communist wings. The very term Left was ambiguous, and those associated with it were as diverse politically as they were esthetically. The one thing they had in common was contempt for commercialism in the theatre; even so there were *degrees* of contempt, since job-hunters in the theatre could not usually afford to be particularly selective. In the exercise of their pro-fession the playwrights and producing groups combined realism with stylization and naturalism with expressionism. The vaguely defined movement drew together realists and maverick poets, practical individuals and artistic perfectionists, opportunists and idealists, sociologists and esthetes.

It was plain that American theatre still had no aptitude for consistency and singleness of purpose. The Group Theatre, famous for social realism, commendably tried to produce stylized drama. It presented Paul Green's *Johnny Johnson* and an epic theatre version of *An American Tragedy* entitled *The Case of Clyde Griffiths,* as well as many plays in which Group Theatre realism was the sole or dominant style. Eclecticism in policy and poetic sensibility in practice resulted in the lovely production of Saroyan's *My Heart's in the Highlands* which Robert Lewis staged for the Group Theatre in 1939. The production will be remembered by those who saw it for its symbolic, surrealistic mise en scène, for Art Smith's bugle-playing refugee from an old people's home, and for the quick-spirited Philip Loeb's Ben Alexander, the laureate of all talentless poets.

Perhaps the one new wrinkle in dramatic criticism during the Thirties (new for America but not for Europe) was a tendency to accuse play-wrights of escaping from reality and of being confused in their thinking. Shaw had made a similar charge in the 1890's, especially in reviews of Pinero's *The Second Mrs. Tanqueray* and *The Notorious Mrs. Ebbsmith.* But the new sociological criticism tended to be rather inflexible and righteous. It was also distinctly naïve in its assumption that a writer could create without temperament and without indulging his preformed private taste, feeling, and thought. The clamor was often for the clarity of a writer of tracts and for the conclusions of a trained sociologist.

It is doubtful that the militant dramatic criticism of the Thirties greatly affected the writing of talented playwrights, unless they were of a very impressionable age. It was usually the talentless who could be most easily persuaded to lean heavily on a crutch of class-struggle dogma. Whatever the authors' political affiliations, the living dramatic work of the period emerged not from any watertight compartment of ideas but mainly from irritations and sympathies, ardors and intuitions. It can be safely claimed that nowhere did the theatre rest less on a theoretical base than in America—and this continues to be the case.

Should this state of affairs be accounted a virtue of our theatre? To a degree, yes, since a theatre without variety and spontaneity is likely to be a very dull affair. But the hedge-hopping and improvisatory behavior of the American theatre has its dangers, too. The Theatre Guild began to show the effects of being foot-loose after 1930, and ran into much difficulty toward the end of that decade. It nearly collapsed in 1938 after a long string of financial failures. Its amorphousness kept it from becoming the great institutional theatre that America needed. Whether the Guild could have been anything but amorphous and whether it could have nourished itself at all without opportunistic extension in several directions is debatable. The unsubsidized Guild, like any other producing organization, had to cope with economic problems and to face Broadway audiences that were willing to pay only for entertainment, audiences that had no consistency of view. Also the Guild was in special difficulties because it was committed to producing a certain number of plays—generally six—every season. All that one could predict with certainty was that Guild plays would be well written and that the productions would be well polished. They were invariably said to be in good taste, a sure indication of the absence of any real understanding of art.

Good taste, if the phrase is allowable at all, is not a constant but a variable; one thing in a Philip Barry play and an altogether different thing in *Awake and Sing!, Death of a Salesman,* or *Murder in the Cathedral.* The Guild's production of the realistic small-town drama *Come Back, Little Sheba* was faultlessly tasteful. Nevertheless, the habit of applying good taste as a kind of shellac dies hard. It was applied in a successful but much too pretty and arch *As You Like It* starring Katharine Hepburn, and in productions by various other managements.

We are still suffering, both in production and playwriting, from a want of focus. The majority of playwrights have given slight thought to anything but the grinding out of plays. They have been too often content with aperçus and expedients. I doubt that any artist sees his problems from every angle or fully understands the infinitely complex essence of his creativity. Even such singularly lucid playwrights as Shaw and Bertolt Brecht have not always understood their creative processes or realized the possibilities or limitations of their procedures. Yet the effort to understand one's own aims must continue, and such effort must focus, as a small number of playwrights like Brecht and Arthur Miller realized, on the whole character and point of modern playwriting. Neither critic nor playwright can afford to operate solely by instinct in our confounding and dismaying age. After having participated in some seventy-five stage productions and struggling with a great many more (between nine and ten thousand!) unproduced play-scripts I have become convinced that the mindless and passionless flux in our theatre is egregiously wasteful, even if I don't know how to correct this condition.

In the early Forties there was common ground in the aggravation of crisis, the preservation of freedom, and the simple problem of national survival. But little of this got itself translated into effective dramatic art. We experienced brief release from dramaturgic controls and collective

anxiety through the pure-in-heart, trust-in-the-little-people plays of William Saroyan, beginning with *My Heart's in the Highlands*. We tried,
rather unsuccessfully, to respond to the war's call for heroic drama. It
is true that Sidney Kingsley's *The Patriots*, a lesson in national unity,
treated Hamilton and Jefferson with appreciative intelligence. But a program of historical drama was successfully initiated in America only in
outdoor pageant theatre, chiefly in the South under the inspired leadership of Paul Green, who started it with *The Lost Colony* several years
before World War II.

The outstanding Broadway play of this period of crisis was undoubtedly
The Skin of Our Teeth. But Thornton Wilder's chronicle of man's precarious survival since the Ice Age and the Deluge, with its wonderful
Finnegan's Wake kind of synthesis of time past and time present, won
little support in New York after it succeeded in confusing its tryout
audiences.

After World War II we had a brief flurry of liberal problem plays.
But no special kind of theatre arose in the early postwar years. A transformation of our theatre was not apparent even when the new playwrights—Williams, Miller, and Inge—started emerging after 1945. It was
characteristic of the times that Williams in the Fifties moved ahead with
a free-wheeling eclecticism to become the new period's most thriving
playwright.

Arthur Miller impressed both the critics and the playgoing multitude
as a young man with a purpose. But until 1959, when *A Raisin in the Sun*
reached Broadway, Miller was an isolated figure. The American theatre
had experienced neither a vigorous movement toward realism nor an
esthetic development toward a special style to sustain Miller's efforts or
encourage other playwrights. Whether Miller's work is favored or dis-
favored in this quarter or that, there has been no discernible attempt to
locate his plays in a larger frame of reference. The plays have simply come
and gone so far as the Broadway theatre is concerned. But neither the
casualness of presentation nor the absence of cohesive theatre effort alters
the fact that toward the end of the Fifties there were decidedly successful
off-Broadway productions of *The Crucible* and of Miller's adaptation of
Ibsen's polemic, *An Enemy of the People*.

In the postwar period, we have returned to the habitual haphazardness
of our theatre. The New York City Center, under the courageous guidance of indefatigable Jean Dalrymple, bravely continues its short theatri-

cal seasons, but is dependent upon improvisation and expediency. The Phoenix Theatre, situated between Broadway and off-Broadway, has made costly efforts to present meaningful productions. But the management of Norris Houghton and T.E. Hambleton has been under constant economic pressure to resort to expedients and modify policy. The Phoenix was not given an opportunity in the Fifties to organize its own company and create a repertory of classics and recent works of merit and significance. Dreams of establishing repertory theatres and creating a National Theatre failed to materialize despite the labors of many admir able persons at ANTA, especially Robert Breen and Robert Whitehead.

A new college-trained generation of the Fifties has taken an exalted view of tradition and a dim one of the loose ideal, self-expression. But its ablest representatives are interested primarily in close criticism, symbolist interpretation, lyric poetry, and literary drama. This generation has been understandably repelled by our disorderly theatre, scornful of its playwrights, and disdainful even of O'Neill. Very little, however, has occurred in the American theatre to alter its character as a haphazard enterprise. Even off-Broadway production has operated in a generally opportunistic manner.

The anarchy of show business, the lack of a national theatre, and the generally inchoate condition of American cultural life makes exalted demands upon the professional stage quixotic. To hanker for unity or a unified sensibility, society, and culture can lead to nothing but withdrawal from the theatre as a vulgar occupation. It is apparent, at the beginning of the precarious decade of the Sixties, that this anarchy is bound to continue. Neither a new art theatre reminiscent of the Twenties nor a new theatre of social consciousness recalling the Thirties has sent out any tap roots during the fifteen year post-World War II period. We have encountered only the isolated careers of several talented new writers. Few theatrical developments of international import have come to our attention from other countries in the Fifties, although Anouilh, Beckett, Ionesco, and Duerrenmatt have impressed us with individual plays. The important thing at this juncture is the persistence of individual effort and the incandescence of some particular play or production. Such liveliness of spirit and intelligence restores confidence in the theatre just when all confidence seems to have vanished.

10 THE PRACTICALITY OF
IMPRACTICAL CRITICISM

Trust not yourself, but your defects to know
Make use of ev'ry friend—and ev'ry foe.—ALEXANDER POPE

Neutralism is the great seduction of our age. Objections to a criticism that exposes defects with scorn and indignation come from such antithetical sources as the practical world of management and the impractical world of academic learning. Having worked in the theatre on both sides of the fence, as both producer and reviewer of plays, I am doubly sympathetic to critical neutralism. As a member of a producing organization I could hardly fail to hope that the productions with which I was associated would receive favorable press; without it we had no prospects of financial success or of critical esteem. As a producer I winced when our work was attacked. It did not matter much whether the assault was justified or unjustified, or whether it was made courteously or discourteously. I do not recall ever being severely jolted by undeserved public praise or an undeserved long run on Broadway, especially if the Theatre Guild or I received the windfall. The critic in me, the person who reviewed plays for periodicals and on radio, wished he could be kinder whenever a fine intention, a noble fire, or a glimmering promise (or even the friendship or admiration of a producer, author, or principal) was involved in a Broadway failure.

The proposal of those who periodically suggest that reviewers confine themselves to reporting instead of reviewing is impractical. A report also reflects an attitude (it is possible to summarize even *Hamlet*, as Voltaire once did, and make it seem pretty dreadful). The reader of the neutral report is unlikely to be sufficiently impelled to rush to the box office. He may even construe mere reporting as a patent warning to stay away, for how could a reviewer remain neutral in encountering excellence? One solution, a producer's and press agent's dream, is that the drama critic contribute not neutrality but a contagious enthusiasm for dramatic art that will send readers pell-mell to the theatre. But the critic whose praise is indiscriminate will not hold his followers either, for no reader is likely to be subservient enough to take guidance for long from a reviewer who persistently overrates productions.

So much for mundane play reviewing!

Academic neutralism is motivated by other considerations. The academician seeks a reputation for scholarly objectivity; he has his sense of history to serve, his obligation to maintain perspectives, his honorable passion to put order into the untidy palace of art. I can respect the desire to organize the data of art. (Possibly I am here confusing respect with self-respect, since I once wrote a longish history of world drama, evidently the longest in the language.)

But I am shaken by the obvious impossibility of excluding subjectivity from intellect. *Parti pris* cannot even be excluded from the critic's selection or categorizing texts which he will judge. The scholar faces the problem of determining which plays are tragedies and which are not. He must certainly have qualms of critical conscience about putting *Hamlet, Ghosts, The Cherry Orchard,* and *Death of a Salesman* into the same pigeonhole.

A genuine scholar-neutralist is usually miles removed by temperament from the dramatic impulse and the theatrical world. His views on dramatic art are likely to be as unreliable as a blind man's appreciation of a Matisse canvas, for the sense of theatre which makes criticism valuable is almost always absent. Whatever advantages may be claimed for hypothetical objectivity in literary criticism, the result is usually sterility in dramatic criticism. The phenomena to be observed in the theatre are invariably the *interaction* of a play, a production, and an audience.

Northrop Frye, in his impressive *Anatomy of Criticism*, writes that, "There are no definite positions to be taken in chemistry or philology, and if there are any to be taken in criticism, criticism is not a field of genuine learning." Professor Frye goes on to say, "One's 'definite position' is one's weakness, the source of one's liability to error and prejudice, and to gain adherents to a definite position is only to multiply one's weakness like an infection."

I have seen this rigidity too. It happened to the left-wing criticism of the Thirties when persons I could only consider dolts tried to stretch works of art on an egregiously procrustean bed of Marxist ideology, invariably misapplying dialectical materialism in matters to which the theory was irrelevant. A decade or so later it happened again when academic persons, who were by no means dolts tried to squeeze art into the vise of some category of myth, ritualism, Anglican Church mysticism, or sophomorically crude there-ain't-no-God type of existentialism. The pitfalls against which Northrop Frye warns us have opened for many. Yet he leaves me uneasy. His viewpoint tends to reduce the important function of theatrical criticism, which serves to drive the theatre out of one rut after another. Mr. Frye could not have been thinking of the theatre when he wrote: "This is the real level of culture and of liberal education . . . On this level there is no itch to make weighty judgment, and none of the ill effects which follow the debauchery of judiciousness and made the word critic a synonym for an educated shrew." It was surely overestimation of criticism when the executive editor of the intellectual Readers' Subscription club could state approvingly that the ideas in Fry's book are "disinterested," "do not incite to action," and "refer to literature, and yet they are completely independent." His conclusion was that "criticism must first of all refer to itself."

Dramatic criticism that refers first of all to itself, rather than to the reality of a production (or at least the reality of a play) is a patent absurdity. Instead of drawing conclusions from theatrical practice it imposes rules. If there is one thing that experience teaches, it is that the theatre can do very well without a priori critical theory.

Having disposed of the indiscriminately enthusiastic reviewer and the neutral academician, let us speak up for the critic. In praising him I speak up not merely for the scholar-critic or critic specialist, but for the play reviewer's alter ego too. I mean the true critic who lurks (often somewhat apologetically) in the lines of a newspaper review, or who now and then takes charge of the customary Sunday article. The impractical critic I am writing about is a composite character for the purposes of this argument. He is the person show business least fancies in any guise. If he writes for a small weekly, monthly, or quarterly periodical, he is usually ignored; there is little concern for his opinion because his effect on the box-office receipts is negligible. If this disinterested critic appears in the guise of a newspaper reviewer, he is regarded as a veritable wolf in sheep's clothing and resented as a kill-joy intruder. Nothing is more disconcerting to the guardians of show business than the intrusion of a critic into the preserves of popular play reviewing. But the critic who does not concern himself with the practicality of his criticism, who does not care about keeping the season's productions solvent, is extremely important to the theatre. He performs a distinct service.

The only really practical criticism in the long run is impractical criticism, concerned with standards of excellence rather than box-office receipts. These standards cannot be absolute and considerable flexibility accompanied by resistance is needed for the practice of criticism. Only by maintaining standards of worth can the critic prevent the professional theatre from disappearing for want of merit; only by *raising* his sights can he promote progress.

Independence of judgment obviously does not prevent the true critic from commending worthy work with considerable enthusiasm. The good critic can be as instructive in his appreciations as in his depreciations, even if the commendations sometimes fail to satisfy the producer who wants a rave notice. The genuine critic serves the theatre in the long run by praising with qualification, by making comparisons between one work and another, and by raising questions altogether irrelevant to the prosperity of a particular show. Whether or not the critic reaches a large public, he certainly reaches the playwright, the producer, the director, and the actors. He penetrates to the very heart of the theatre by speaking to its creators.

An effective critic ultimately commands the respect of these creators even when his criticism is negative. He earns the right to be listened to by the closeness of his reasoning, the scrupulousness of his analysis, and the interest and originality of what he has to say. It must be evident that his condemnation is not born of mere whim, prejudice, or obtuseness. If his comments are astringent it is more than probable that those he hurts will be in no mood to appreciate his uninvited censure. Its salutary effects are never immediately apparent; if his criticism has any value it will be recognized only after the wound has closed. If the critic is not heeded by those who have some vested interests in the theatre of the present, he may instruct those who have none—a new generation pressing close upon the heels of the old.

The generalization that the best criticism is often destructive draws support from the example of such worthies as Lessing, Shaw, and Nathan. Imposing service is performed by gadfly criticism which prevents the stage from becoming smug and stale, or by the bulldozer school that topples unwholesome edifices and helps to clear away the rubbish. Such criticism often contains the best writing because it requires wit, color, verve, and imagination to be effective. There cannot be any handmaidenly meekness about it, for the negations of good criticism must come from conviction. Consequently there is sometimes more liveliness in the criticism than in the play or production being discussed—no small factor in creating interest in the art about which the commentator is writing.

If the good critic isn't always fair, he is nevertheless creatively one-sided; this is more important than a mere judiciousness that leaves nothing corrected and nobody stimulated. Anybody can be fair, but not everybody can be creative. What does the theatre need most: fairness or creativeness? Consider how constructive the ultimate results of Shaw's critical destructiveness were when he routed Victorian compromise and Nice-Nellyism from the British stage. It was equally important for George Jean Nathan to discredit the backward Victorianism of the American stage. In the case of Shaw's dramatic criticism, to be destructive toward Pinero was to be constructive toward Ibsen. To be destructive toward Belasco or Owen Davis was to be constructive toward the struggling Eugene O'Neill and O'Casey, for whom Nathan fought bravely and intelligently.

Seen in proper perspective the useful critic will be *against* one thing precisely because he is *for* something else—against the old because he is for the new, against the bad because he is for the good as he sees it. Shaw was against Pinero in the 1890's because he was for Ibsen, against "Sardoodle-dom" of the empty, thrill-contriving, well-made play because he was for Ibsenite drama, infused with perception and pervaded by the modern critical spirit. The complaisant constructive Victorian criticism of the theatre was soon buried along with the plays it approved. Shaw's criticism remains alive along with the anti-Victorian drama to which his destructiveness gave encouragement and justification.

Ultimately the true critic, whether constructive or destructive, is involved with the two most fundamental elements of theatre, its sensibility and intelligence. Perhaps they are simply two different aspects of the same thing. Stark Young, for example, could teach the theatre and its public how to *see*; Shaw, how to *think*. When this kind of criticism comes into being the line between criticism and creation becomes exceedingly thin. Important men of the theatre, such as Shaw, Otto Brahm, Antoine, and others have overstepped the line from either side, turning from reviewing to staging or writing plays. But criticism cannot constitute or approximate creation without possessing critical integrity.

Criticism of high order may have very practical effects on show business. Nathan, for example, helped to make it impossible for a new *Pollyanna* to be a hit in 1954 on Broadway and possible for *The Glass Menagerie* and *The Madwoman of Chaillot* to become hits (although he himself was unenthusiastic about Williams and derogatory toward the adaptation of the French play). These effects were the result of criticism that did not care whether it was practical or a producer had box-office success.

The importance of establishing an area of intelligent discourse about the theatre cannot be discounted. If discussion is one-sidedly favorable it ceases to be criticism and becomes mere gush; the more provocative and keen the discourse the better the criticism. Only free, assertive, and well-aimed opinion can aerate our thinking about the theatre that is so likely to slump into a slough of commonplace imitation or mesmeric sensation. Criticism is the re-creation of feeling into thought. Criticism is essential to the health of the modern theatre. It is at its best when it is not trying to please and when it is least like public relations. To fight over the theatre is to care about the theatre. Unfortunately, most people are merely indifferent.

11 OFF-BROADWAY, PAST AND PRESENT

There has been an off-Broadway since the second decade of our century, just as there has been a succession of new playwrights and new critics. Fortunately, each generation always considers itself unique and prevents its elders from being blasé about it by being invulnerably blasé about its elders. I am confident, therefore, that nothing I am going to say in the role of Father Time will diminish the current enthusiasm of this era for off-Broadway production.

There were two off-Broadway movements before the present one. The first lasted approximately from 1912 to 1927 and came to be variously known as the little theatre movement and the tributary theatre, the latter an absurd term favored by the old *Theatre Arts* magazine. The reverse was the case; Broadway productions had become tributary to university and community theatre production. The second period, loosely called the New Theatre movement, gained momentum in the early years of the depression and was virtually over by 1939 except for flurries of usually less distinctive production activity during and immediately after the war period.

Each movement was more or less a reflection of the time spirit; each brought a creative ferment to the American stage along with the non-theatrical interests—social, political, or cultural—that sparked the neo-phytes. Among these were an impressive number of talented new actors, directors, and designers. But the discovery of new playwrights was the most noteworthy facet of previous off-Broadway movements. The first group of writers, not all of whom managed to thrive in the theatre, included O'Neill, Susan Glaspell, Paul Green, E.P. Conkle, John Howard

Lawson, John Dos Passos, Francis Faragoh, Dan Totheroh, Lynn Riggs, and Virgil Geddes. The second group comprised, among others, Clifford Odets, John Wexley, Irwin Shaw, George Sklar, Albert Maltz, Paul Peters, Marc Blitzstein, Robert Ardrey, Albert Bein, and Victor Wolfson. It is highly probable that other playwrights who made their professional debut directly on Broadway were either influenced or encouraged by the off-Broadway movements.

The first off-Broadway period promoted the rise of satiric and tragic folk drama, and simultaneous ventures in naturalism, symbolism, and expressionism. Off-Broadway insurgency in the Thirties not only sharpened the social focus of some writers and invigorated realism in general, but promoted imaginative, expressionistic, and epic theatre techniques and styles as represented by *Waiting for Lefty, Bury the Dead, The Cradle Will Rock,* and the living newspapers of the Federal theatre.

New writers were among the leaders of each of these off-Broadway movements and determined the spirit and appeal that gave them much of their importance. The most stimulating events were premières of new American plays. There has certainly been no excitement in the Fifties comparable to the production of such new plays as *The Emperor Jones* (1920), *The Hairy Ape* (1922), *All God's Chillun Got Wings* (1924), *In Abraham's Bosom* (1927), *Waiting for Lefty* (1935), *Bury the Dead* (1936), and *The Cradle Will Rock* (1937).

Even the writers who did not start with a program or principle acquired a sense of justification and direction from their association with off-Broadway, came to share ideals with it, and helped to shape its character. After the first O'Neill productions, between 1916 and 1918, the Province-town Players came to be identified with new modes of American playwriting. Many a regional theatre south and west of Manhattan was identified with several species of native folk drama, from which were derived such plays as *Porgy* and *Green Grow the Lilacs,* as well as the musical versions, *Porgy and Bess* and *Oklahoma!*

The playwrights of these off-Broadway movements became a sort of vanguard. Many of them seethed with convictions about nearly everything during their alliance with the pioneering groups. They and their more casual associates (lawyers, judges, sociologists, educators, and such poets as Edna St. Vincent Millay and Alfred Kreymborg) were the palace guards or janizaries and defended their circle with fierce partisanship. Many of the productions of these groups were one-act plays, for the new

groups were favorable to embryonic writers who were not always prepared to develop an extensive dramatic action.

As an eager observer and a more or less active participant in the Twenties and Thirties I have come to expect that an off-Broadway movement
should produce new playwrights and lead the way to vital dramatic forms
and styles. From the earlier avant-gardes I have come to expect revivals
of plays neglected or mismanaged on Broadway. The first off-Broadway
movement was rich in these, as the current movement is; but off-Broadway
in the Thirties gave scant attention to plays of the past until the Federal
Theatre (if it may be counted with off-Broadway productions) swung
into action temporarily. It should be noted that revivals by such groups
as the Provincetown and Washington Square Players and the Neighborhood Playhouse after 1914 were intended to introduce new styles of
dramatic art to the American public and to induce new attitudes and
interest in psychological and social truths. The current off-Broadway
movement has not advanced much further in this direction or followed
it with the same consistency. What was new style then is new style
today; the same works are now being discovered for the present off-
Broadway public: the plays of Ibsen, Strindberg, Chekhov, Wedekind,
Synge, Andreev, and Shaw. There were no Sartre, Brecht, Giraudoux,
Beckett, and O'Casey plays to discover in 1916, but many of the last-
mentioned were first produced on, not off, Broadway. A new generation
should be granted the right to repeat the discoveries of its predecessors,
but it should also make its own discoveries. In the Fifties off-Broadway
discovered the bizarries of Adamov, Genet, Beckett, and Ionesco. Perhaps
the results cannot yet be fully assessed, but it is obvious that these special
off-Broadway discoveries did not galvanize the American theatre of the
decade into even a semblance of new life.

The previous movements aroused the expectation that off-Broadway
enterprise would produce or at least assimilate advances in acting, theatrical design, and styles of stage production. Such expectation has been
realized in the work of José Quintero in his three-sided arena theatre,
Circle in the Square. His finely ground productions of *Summer and
Smoke, The Iceman Cometh, The Children of Darkness,* and *Our
Town* have been widely appreciated. But nowhere else has production
art shown much progress or stylistic distinction. I do not mean to slight
merely competent productions, but even competence is not often found
among cubbyhole and basement producers. Having encountered poor

off-Broadway productions in the Twenties and Thirties, I am disinclined to make an issue of the matter of competence. (I recall with a particular shudder a 1925 production of *The Cenci* in which it was almost impossible to discover whether the actors were speaking the same language.)

That the main explorations should have been undertaken between about 1915 and 1925 was historically inevitable. Early off-Broadway movements involved intensive experimentation in both production and playwrighting. There were so many things then for the off-Broadway groups to learn as virtually new dispensations in dramatic art. The various lessons imparted by Craig, Copeau, Reinhardt, and other leaders were just becoming available to Americans. New techniques were also learned and developed in the embattled off-Broadway New Theatre League groups of the Thirties. They concerned themselves with motion-picture montage as applied to such now virtually forgotten propaganda pieces as *Newsboy*; with quasi-expressionist experiments in the manner of Odets' one-act strike drama *Waiting for Lefty* and Irwin Shaw's antiwar fantasy *Bury the Dead*; with learning-play demonstrations accompanied by modern dances or mass chants (the Brecht dramatization of Gorki's novel, *Mother*, with Hanns Eisler's music staged by the Theatre Union was a prime example); with brilliant ventures in musical revues such as the *Grand Street Follies* and *Pins and Needles*, intimate opera, and the minstrel-show technique in *The Cradle Will Rock*; and with theatricalist-journalistic techniques culminating in the Federal Theatre's living newspaper unit that made a powerful impression with its slum-clearance documentary, *One-Third of a Nation*.

Several groups in New York also managed for a few seasons to maintain their identity and pursue their intellectual and esthetic interests. (It was more possible to do so in periods of lower theatre rentals and production costs.) The Neighborhood Playhouse on Grand Street, endowed by the Misses Alice and Irene Lewisohn in 1915, continued to present variously stylized productions for a dozen years. The range of play selection, from the Hindu theatre classic, *The Little Clay Cart*, to a complex symbolist play by Yeats, or from Sheridan's brittle theatre satire, *The Critic*, to the famous Jewish folk play, *The Dybbuk*, afforded constant stimulation. The Provincetown Players, who presented their first bill in Provincetown, Cape Cod, in 1915, continued to present plays in New York for a period of fourteen years to further their aim of giving "American playwrights a chance to work out their ideas in freedom."

In observing the off-Broadway theatres of the Fifties one discovers much earnest application, literary interest, and appreciation of the power of imaginative staging, but it is rarely possible to come across an implemented and sustained plan or program to develop dramatic art and thought in some significant respect. It is a curious and meaningful fact that the most vital and financially most successful off-Broadway production has been Marc Blitzstein's version of *The Threepenny Opera* by Brecht and Weill. This work is a product of the avant-garde of the Twenties in Central Europe, freely translated by an American author-composer who was eminent in the avant-garde of the Thirties.*

Off-Broadway activity in the Fifties has been primarily an inexpensive way of learning the producing and directing business and of displaying new or neglected acting talent. There is nothing wrong with any of these motivations. They are admirable, especially since the revival of many good plays and a few masterpieces has given the repertory-poor metropolitan area the equivalent of a repertory theatre. But it is plain that except for some country-wide developments in arena staging (actually started two decades before by Glenn Hughes at his University of Washington Penthouse Theatre) off-Broadway enterprise of this period has not blazed any trails. Off-Broadway has only produced for the sake of producing, acted for the sake of acting, designed for the sake of designing, and written for the sake of writing. In the Fifties this motivation has been considered sufficient, and it often has seemed as if dedication to a private belief or intention, let alone a public conviction, is no longer considered necessary or possible.

The new generation is either resolved to be as unromantic as possible and to concentrate on the work rather than the vision, or else it is prematurely old. Some have argued and many agreed that the fault is not in themselves but in their stars. As the Fifties closed there appeared to be no change in this situation, despite the fact that off-Broadway groups are beginning to outproduce Broadway managements in number and sometimes even in efficiency. There is almost as much lingering as there is bustle at the crossroads. (There are exceptions in the Circle in the

---

* *The Threepenny Opera* was staged with great success in Berlin in 1928. The composer, Kurt Weill, died in 1950, but his colleague, Bertolt Brecht, survived until 1956. Marc Blitzstein, born in 1905, won acclaim in 1937 with an improvised production of *The Cradle Will Rock,* a musical satire played without scenery and with the author-composer at the piano (the production could not afford an orchestra).

Square revivals, the Capalbo and Chase revival of *The Threepenny Opera* in Greenwich Village, a valiant Second Avenue loft presentation of Brecht's *The Private Life of the Master Race* in Eric Bentley's effective translation, the Living Theatre's experimental productions—especially of Jack Gelber's *The Connection*—the Rooftop Theatre productions of *Ulysses in Nighttown* and *Clérambard,* and a few other regrettably sporadic efforts.) In view of the difficulties of the decade this may seem to be a churlish observation, but it is hard to define the character of the most important development of mid-century play production in New York in any other way.

Once the limits of the movement are recognized it is apparent that we have had much cause to be grateful. We can count our blessings in the excellent work of the Circle in the Square group that made its official debut in February, 1951, with a revival of Howard Richardson and William Berney's folk-musical, *Dark of the Moon.* The particular specialty of this group has been to make former failures bloom after Broadway has fatalistically consigned them to Cain's warehouse. We can also recall the many seasons of the Shakespearewrights' lively platform productions at Jan Hus house. We can applaud a few productions at the old Cherry Lane Theatre such as Beckett's *Endgame** and O'Casey's *Purple Dust,* and at the Provincetown where it was possible to attend Jeffers' poetic drama, *The Cretan Woman.* We can be grateful for David Ross's enterprise in reviving *The Dybbuk* and Chekhov's four major plays (three were excellently produced), and for such individual productions at the Theatre de Lys as Leslie Stevens' new play, *Bullfight,* and David Z. Goodman's new family drama, *High Named Today.* High praise was earned by the Actors' Playhouse production of James Lee's *Career,* in the productions of *Me, Candido* by Walt Anderson and *A Land Beyond the River* by Loften Mitchell at the Greenwich Mews Theatre, by revivals of Miller's *The Crucible* and his adaptation of *An Enemy of the People.*

Tennessee Williams' *Garden District* was given very successfully in 1957 at the York Theatre as an off-Broadway production, though its author did not need to be discovered. Chekhov did not need discovery either, but the Greenwich Village production of his first play, *Ivanov,* was a discovery for most New Yorkers. A good production of Shaw's discursive comedy, *In Good King Charles's Golden Days,* staged at an east Fourth Street playhouse by Day Tuttle and a production of Shaw's very

* See the review in Part II.

last play, *Buoyant Billions*, staged by Philip Burton at the Provincetown increase our debt to off-Broadway. We can claim at least partial off-Broadway status for Equity Library productions, for the short-lived New Stages coöperative enterprise that produced Barry Stavis' *Galileo* and Sartre's *The Respectful Prostitute* and *The Victors* in 1948-49, for the New York City Center that has revived plays and musicals year after year as a quasi-subsidized municipal institution, and especially for the Phoenix Theatre.

It can be argued that we are stretching a point in calling these off-Broadway productions; the Phoenix, for example, has been giving costly ultraprofessional productions in Maurice Schwartz's former Yiddish Art theatre seating 1,186 spectators.* All these ventures *are* off-Broadway by location, by virtue of receiving concessions from the theatrical unions, by not operating for profit, and (excepting City Center) by not favoring popular plays and musicals.

New York has found a typically American way of solving some problems of our theatre: the way of multiple enterprise. This has resulted in a welter of short-lived and inadequately produced plays, but it has also yielded theatrical abundance. The results have been neither revolutionary (in the sense of achieving new styles of playwriting and production, expressing new convictions or philosophies of dramatic art, or enforcing new perspectives) nor conservative, in the sense of ensuring the preservation of a cultural heritage with a repertory of national and international masterpieces. Due largely to individual and a few institutional efforts, off-Broadway playgoing in the Fifties became a busy, varied, and even occasionally rewarding experience. Off-Broadway enterprise has helped to make New York City one of the chief centers and sources of mid-century theatre. That it has not initiated or developed a new dispensation in dramatic art is the result not of any special apathy on the part of producers but of such factors as the general failure of vision and nerve after World War II.

The economic realities of New York production are beginning to become oppressive even to the off-Broadway movement. We shall be fortunate if professional off-Broadway activity does not become a severely

---

* The reader will find reviews of a number of Phoenix productions in the second part of this book. An excellent, detailed account of the Phoenix Theatre's recent producing career is the article, "The Phoenix Has Two Heads," by Albert Bermel in the Autumn, 1959, issue of *The Tulane Review*, edited by Robert W. Corrigan.

curtailed in the oncoming Sixties as Broadway activity already is. Within half a decade costs of production have doubled while the incidence of profitable stage production has been about five per cent. Though its shortcomings in the Fifties cannot be overlooked, it is distressing to contemplate the future of New York production *without* off-Broadway theatre.

Signs of enervation have continued to appear ever since, as if a law of entropy were operative in a period of uncertainty and disillusionment. In 1958-59, the last complete season under review here, the Pulitzer Prize poetic drama, *J.B.*, moved toward a tame conclusion, after hurling the challenge of Job against the miseries of the modern world. The appealing Drama Critics Circle Award play *A Raisin in the Sun* followed a conventional dramatic pattern, wavering between domestic comedy and drama of protest. Nevertheless, one simply cannot turn criticism into dismissal or indulge impatience or disappointment implacably without placing nearly all playwriting under a theatre-destroying interdict. One way to insure the continuation of entropy is to use it as a reason or excuse for summarily invalidating all the dramatic work of the period. Another way is to refuse to recognize defect or insufficiency in any dramatic work that has earned respect. Let us examine some of the plays in question.

The Country Girl: Odets in the Fifties

At first it seems that one would only carp at this excellently constructed and generally affecting drama because it is by Clifford Odets, the *Sturm und Drang* poet of the theatre of the Thirties. If expectations were modestly scaled one could be pleased to note the author's progress after his less satisfactory anti-Hollywood diatribe, *The Big Knife*, for *The Country Girl* was a distinct improvement in character creation, action, and argument. But it was not an improvement upon *Awake and Sing!*, produced fifteen years earlier; it represented a contraction of interest and vision.

It is not fair to make esteem for the work of a writer's ardent youth a lien on his entire life. Nor is it right to use past accomplishment as a stick with which to beat a perfectly competent contemporary play. Still, excellence is not easily forgotten, and a descent from eminence is not likely to be observed without a pang. My own sense of disappointment, in spite of the solid workmanship of *The Country Girl*, was a measure of esteem for the author, as well as for the kind of theatre his early work represented, a theatre of passionate sympathies. I persist in believing that Odets was more gifted than all but two or three of the playwrights who accumulated more impressive records than he in the Fifties.

The Country Girl is entirely satisfactory as a vivid triangle. A want of originality may be charged against this backstage drama, for the play deals with an alcoholic actor's return to the theatre under the spur of a hardy wife and an admiring young director. Even so, Odets wrote and staged a familiar story with such vitality that the theatrical power of the experience made originality a secondary matter. One could also argue with the conventionality of the denouement: the long-suffering wife's decision to give up the director who has fallen in love with her and to remain with her husband. But the conventional conclusion is reached unconventionally after much preliminary tension, and with distinctly character-based reality.

The gist of the author's conception is the remarkable fortitude of the country girl type of woman. I don't know whether Odets intended to pay a tribute to a certain kind of woman, but that is the effect of his play—though balanced (and for some playgoers no doubt overshadowed) by the drama of the actor-husband whose weakness and anxiety try her endurance. She appears to have even been drawn with the same ambivalence that Shaw brought to his Candida; consequently she has a special fascination that may account for her collecting the kind of enthusiasts whom Shaw angrily called Candidamaniacs. But perhaps this portrait of a corn-fed madonna owed much to Uta Hagen, who has distinguished herself repeatedly ever since playing Nina in *The Sea Gull* in 1938. Miss Hagen gave the impression of having drawn the portrait no less than Odets did. Here was one of those utterly authentic pieces of characterization that can be a source of genuine pride. Along with Mildred Dunnock, Mildred Natwick, and Judith Anderson, Miss Hagen can be relied upon to create indelible characterizations.

Yet *The Country Girl* seemed a rather strained work; its narrow scope made the pressure of feeling seem excessive. The play could leave one wondering why its author tried to engage our interest so weightily. But to make these reservations public is to carry us back to the original problem of enervation in the case of a significant number of playwrights who established themselves before 1940.

Barry and Sherwood: *Second Threshold*

With the death of Philip Barry in 1949, the American theatre lost one of its most attractive writers. With the death of Robert Sherwood in 1955, the loss was decidedly compounded, for Sherwood had gained much distinction not only in comedy but in dramatic journalism. The two men usually went their separate ways as writers, Barry to success in the diminishing genre of American comedy of manners and to disappointment in most of his endeavors at writing symbolic morality plays. Sherwood, forsaking the ingenuities of comic writing that had proved immensely rewarding in *The Road to Rome* and *Reunion in Vienna*, soberly plunged into politics on behalf of liberal causes. He even sacrificed his playwriting to convictions he last expressed effectively in 1940 with *There Shall Be No Night*. But nothing he wrote for the stage after 1940 brought him back to the theatre until he took an interest in a friend's comedy.

Only friendship could join Sherwood and Barry. But friendship did, and the results appeared in Sherwood's completion of Barry's *Second Threshold* after his death. A sensitively composed work, it was a testimonial to the decent feelings of both good men. As it happened, neither writer was fated to have anything on the Broadway stage after *Second Threshold* that could make a better bid for an appreciative reception. Yet an ebb in the dramatic energy at their command was plainly discernible, and the play, which falls somewhere between comedy and serious drama, lacks both the deceased playwright's comic verve and the surviving friend's zest for political assault. The work is overcast with a weariness of soul that makes it singularly appealing to a minority, but there is too little verve in this work of intelligence and good taste.

Second Threshold suffers from a divided interest and spirit. It is ostensibly a comedy, but an elegiac intention overshadows its cultivated atmosphere and fluent dialogue. The play starts with the disillusion and suicidal thoughts of a former American statesman, and the quiet desperation he displays does not mix well with the authors' efforts to produce humor. Barry's story, freed from the leading character's state of depression in the first act, might have been distilled into a Barry comic brew. But neither Barry, writing at the top of his bent, nor Robert Sherwood, working sympathetically with the script the playwright left unfinished, went much beyond mingling the statesman's anguish with an adolescent's antics and adding a happy ending in which the statesman's depression is dissipated. A divided intention is further evident in the fact that the desperation, at first assumed to be that of a statesman whose talents are allowed to rust unused, is soon transformed into the misery of a father distressed by his daughter's engagement to an elderly man. The resolution of the play shows the daughter drawing closer to the statesman-father and turning her affections to a suitable young man.

Then why the cashiered-diplomat theme at all? The statesman is not functionally in the play. It is as if the Cheshire cat turned out to be an Angora and his grin belonged to a Siamese. I do not intend to be niggling, since I have a considerable affection for *Second Threshold* and thought the play exceptionally well staged and performed. But I also wanted it to succeed. It did not, and I would like to ascertain why the work failed to exert effectively its literate and intelligent playwriting. To blame the audience is absurd; it has often generously supported comedies just as sensitive and just as intellectual. It is also worth observing that all successful Barry comedies, from *Holiday* to *The Philadelphia Story*, presented a unified attitude and development. But there is not much point in blaming the authors for the divided attitude I ascribe to them; I merely cite their case as an example of starting a theme and implying it repeatedly, yet actually veering away from it. This tendency to wander from subject to subject is characteristic of much contemporary writing in which no central impulse—not to mention vision or conviction—seems to be present.

Lillian Hellman: *The Autumn Garden*

I

Lillian Hellman's reputation for formidable writing, established over more than fifteen years, took some of her public and nearly all the New York reviewers by surprise in 1951. The play with which she inaugurated the new decade was not of the same wrought-iron construction as the celebrated *The Children's Hour* (1934), *Watch on the Rhine* (1941), and *Another Part of the Forest* (1946). On the surface the new work was a different kind of play. But far from crediting her with an advance in technique and style, many reviewers looked askance at the work. We did not feel at ease with it, as if it called for self-appraisals we are usually reluctant to make. The author could not be absolved from all blame for failure to absorb us completely in the world she had created. Though I liked it well enough to cast a minority vote in its favor at the Drama Critics Circle Awards meeting in 1952, I was insufficiently drawn to the play.

The Autumn Garden, which possessed a generous measure of Lillian Hellman's ablest writing, was vigorously directed by Harold Clurman, and was favored with some of the best acting of Fredric March, Florence Eldridge, and Kent Smith. Miss Hellman presented the hard doctrine that our little weaknesses pile up like calcium in the body and end in a bursitis of character. She made her points deftly and surely. At the same time she found a way of relieving the sour taste with a commendable variety of characterization and some leavening of humor and pathos. At first glance it would appear that the play did not prevail because Miss Hellman tried to write like Chekhov and, plainly lacking Chekhov's oblique style and bizarre humor, failed. If true at all, it is so only very superficially. It *is* true that she attempted a more contrapuntal and less plotty technique than had been her wont, but the style and the judiciary intention were Hellman's and not Chekhov's.

Critics who had previously demurred at the tight structure of her earlier plays began to long for it. Critics who had felt qualified enthusiasm for *The Little Foxes* and *Watch on the Rhine* (on the grounds of its allegedly outdated well-made play construction and melodrama) found her reformation as a playwright less to their taste than might have been expected. Evidently audiences, too, were lukewarm. The reason is, I believe, quite simple: they didn't quite know where Miss Hellman stood. Like the old-fashioned preacher, she was against sin—specifically the sin of apathy or accidie. But what was she *for*? This could be made plain in a play only in its ascending dramatic line, and what did that consist of? A young girl from Europe blackmails one of Miss Hellman's decadents and returns to her people with the loot. Since neither the girl nor her people represent any vision or any ideal in the play other than that of keeping financially solvent, what gratification did the playwright provide? Miss Hellman, perhaps striving for a symbolic representation of the failures of society, made her indictment too general to be wholly effective, and her tough-fibred resolution too dubious to be gratifying.

2

It is worth noting that the dramatic problem which Lillian Hellman had some difficulty in resolving in *The Autumn Garden* first arose during the war period, when she found it necessary to break the iron ring of well-wrought dramaturgy to consider lives in flux rather than in a single driving action. When Miss Hellman dealt with her favorite theme of moral failure in *The Searching Wind*, produced and directed by Herman Shumlin in 1944, she faced the problem of combining her practised emotional concentration and her largely untried distribution of interest. Miss Hellman's problem has also been our mid-century theatre's problem. At that time I wrote in *The Forum*:

Miss Hellman is the possessor of the most masculine mind among our native playwrights. She concerns herself clearly, as well as intensely, with the issues of our day and she never lets sentimentality or poetic vagaries stand in her way as she moves relentlessly to the center of a problem. She plans her approach, never swerving from the logic and inevitability of her plotting. She has been charged with a certain dry and cold deliberateness, with writing well-made plays that have the attributes of a demonstration and lack the desiderata of charm, poetry, imaginativeness. It has been charged that she has written thinly disguised melodrama in *The Children's Hour, Days to Come, The Little Foxes,* and *Watch On the Rhine.*

As Miss Hellman is hardly . . . a placid person, . . . she has known how to defend herself. She has confounded her critics by offering the first intelligent definition of melodrama since the days when critics began to give plays which hew close to their theme or dramatize violence or elemental evil the brushoff by means of the two derogatory epithets of well-made play and melodrama. There is nothing dishonorable about a play that happens to be scrupulously planned and constructed or tightly-knit. If lucidity and power happen to be achieved by these means, only a queasy stomach will complain. The only thing wrong with writing the well-made play, at the time when Bernard Shaw was blasting away at it in the 1890's, was that it had become writing according to formula, and that it used situations without credibility. Anything was acceptable to the tricky dramatist so long as it created suspense, and this kind of contrivance has been rightly relegated to Grade B motion pictures. Since Miss Hellman never employs unmotivated action, she has no need to apologize for her technique. And she herself has said the final word on melodrama in writing that "melodrama uses violence for no purpose, to point no moral, to say nothing in say-nothing's worst sense." Her own plays, on the contrary, invariably employ violence to exemplify and underline her subject, which is the struggle between good and evil in society. Always, contrary to the practice of most writers on social themes, Miss Hellman is a strong believer in personal responsibility. She never allows her

characters to plead Not guilty by transferring all the blame to society
and claiming that they could not help themselves. Like a Calvinist
she probes into the soul of her culprits for a personal indictment. Men
and women have been endowed with reason, they have had the examples of history to guide them, and there have been many good and
stalwart people who defied the corruption of an age, who saw clearly,
who fought bravely. All of Miss Hellman's social plays are also character dramas.

In *The Searching Wind* Miss Hellman broke through the barriers
of the well-made play, possibly because she wanted to experiment with
a more fluid type of drama, and probably because her subject—the
appeasements that brought us to the verge of disaster—had international scope, filled two decades, and appeared in both public and
private life. The appeasements represented a way of living, of thinking, and of acting. Ignoring, for the present, the malevolent schemers
who had had an economic stake in fascism, as well as the unscrupulous
diplomats playing at balance-of-power politics, Miss Hellman turned
to the question of what was psychologically and morally wrong with
the men and women of good will, intelligence, and breeding. Paren-
thetically, let us observe that she has often been most relentless toward
those who knew or should have known better; she pays less attention
to mere vermin, since it is to be expected that vermin will behave like
vermin. . . . She is hardest, for instance, in her war-time film *The
North Star* on the cultivated surgeon who despises the Nazis yet lends
his intelligence and competence to their nefarious purposes.

The Searching Wind reveals Miss Hellman looking for the tragic
flaw in the relatively decent people upon whom she lays the onus of
responsibility. She finds this flaw unerringly. Her characters turn
away from reality, avoid taking a stand, give up too easily. A prominent
family searches its heart on the occasion of the discovery that the
wounded soldier son is about to have his leg amputated. The family
has failed on two planes—the public and the private—in politics and
in love. Disappointed in the trend of events beginning with Mussolini's march on Rome in 1922, the liberal publisher Moses Taney
(admirably played by the veteran Dudley Digges) gives up his newspaper and retires from the political arena. As attaché to the American
embassy in Rome and later as ambassador, his son-in-law Alexander
Hazen fiddles while Mussolini and Hitler rise to power. . . . Hazen's

domestic life parallels his failure of foresight, integrity, and nerve. He married Taney's daughter, the predatory Emily Hazen, instead of the high-minded girl, Catherine Bowman, whose lover he had been. Catherine constantly goaded him into taking a political stand while he was inclined to shift with the wind. But he found no happiness with Emily, tried to hold on to Catherine clandestinely, yet never broke forthrightly with his wife, and so stood betwixt and between as a husband and lover, just as he did as a citizen.

All this comes out in tense retrospective episodes, framed by the showdown and stock-taking of the first and last scenes of the play. Dennis King as Hazen and Barbara O'Neill and Cornelia Otis Skinner, as mistress and wife respectively, conveyed this sorry tale with authenticity and dignity. The final word is had by the wounded son, arrestingly played by Montgomery Clift, who wants to be sure that his generation will not have fought in vain. If *The Searching Wind* was one of Miss Hellman's weaker plays, if it never quite fused the political and the private stories, and if the triangle seemed labored and the showdown forced, no serious drama of the season had so much intensity of heart-searching and so much challenge for the future. The play is suffused with moral passion, the passion this playwright expresses with the greatest effect. The flaws of *The Searching Wind* are inherent in the problem of writing a contemporary chronicle play. Perhaps the cumbersomeness is rooted in the one limitation that her playwriting has revealed consistently; she expressed it well herself in writing that the drama "is a tight, unbending, unfluid, meager form."

Miss Hellman may overcome this limitation without surrendering her integrity of judgment, and the vigor and vitality with which she always writes will continue to make her a major force in the American theatre.

The question I did not consider in forming these opinions in 1944 was how well the time-spirit of another decade would sustain her broadening talent. Comprehensiveness did not lessen her power and a compassionate viewpoint would not blunt the edge of her writing. *The Autumn Garden,* in 1951, spoke better for her than for the decade. The power and edge of her writing remained generally intact, this time without the possibility of provoking the charge of melodrama that *The Children's Hour* and *Watch on the Rhine* aroused. But the elements compounded in *The*

Autumn Garden, especially the contribution of the refugee girl, may have produced a listlessness in the spectator that neither the writing nor the staging of the play could quite overcome except in the excellent leading-character part filled with genuine distinction by Florence Eldridge.

It is the measure of Lillian Hellman's superiority to most American playwrights that nine years after *The Autumn Garden* she could return to Broadway with an original play that gave no sign of diminished energy. *Toys in the Attic,* which opened on Broadway toward the close of the 1959-60 season, proved to be one of her most hard-driving plays. Among her earlier works only *The Little Foxes,* her masterpiece of the strenuous Thirties, had possessed as much penetration and dramatic vitality, and rarely before had Miss Hellman written dialogue with such vigor and virtuosity. It was possible to realize at the end of the decade that at least one American playwright had kept her sword of judgment—or rather her "knife of truth," as the neurotic child-wife of the play would have said— unblunted in the damp mental climate.

She had brought to the task of adapting Emmanuel Robles' *Monserrat* earlier in the decade an existentialist concern with decisions that test men's stamina; and in adapting Anouilh's Joan of Arc drama, *The Lark,* she had invigorated the play by counteracting the French author's rather facile skepticism. If a loss of dramatic voltage was apparent in *The Autumn Garden* at the beginning of the decade it could be attributed to her experimentation with a relatively loose form of dramaturgy for the purpose of securing amplitude of characterization and giving a rueful account of enervation and failure in society.

In *Toys in the Attic* Miss Hellman picked up the sword of judgment many playwrights of the Fifties had laid aside and wielded it with re- newed vigor. But this time, compassion guided her hand so that she per- formed surgery on her characters instead of summarily decapitating them. In *Toys in the Attic* a young man's life is ruined by his well-meaning spinster sisters—one has desired him incestuously, and both have weak- ened him with excessive protectiveness—and the catastrophe that results in his disfigurement and in the extinction of self-confidence is brought about by his frantically jealous child-wife, who also wrecks her mother's life. Miss Hellman's play was distinctly superior to the other new plays of the 1959-60 theatrical season by virtue of its controlled but vigorous artistry, excellent dialogue, revealing and varied characterization, absorbing action, and mature comprehension of human attitudes, relationships, and drives. Even the seeming faults of the play were contributive to its powerful effect. The first act was somewhat slow and meandering, but Miss Hellman prepared us suspensively with this act for the mounting passions and the tightly coiled spring of doom in the rest of the play.

It was the special merit of Lillian Hellman's work that its painful story unfolded "naturally;" dreadful things are done by the onstage characters out of anxiety and loss of control rather than out of ingrained villainy. The author's corresponding view of life is ironic and is trenchantly expressed, but there is no gloating over human misery, no horror-mongering, no traffic with sensationalism in *Toys in the Attic*. And, unlike some well-known contemporary playwrights here and abroad, Miss Hellman proved again that she could deal with human failure without falling in love with it herself. She remained admirably sane in the midst of the ugliness and confusion she so unerringly exposed. Although she looked at life unsentimentally, she combined sympathy with her judgment of the characters. She was especially understanding in her treatment of the scapegrace brother's affectionate and awkwardly expressed feelings for his sisters, and a Negro lover's manly attachment to the wealthy white woman so attractively played by Irene Worth. We were shown that for people to behave monstrously it is not even necessary for them to be monstrous, it is sufficient only to be unthinkingly possessive and "loving." In fine, *Toys in the Attic* was mordant rather than morbid drama. Since Miss Hellman's dialogue was little short of brilliant and her sense of dramatic structure sure enough to sustain her story and theme, her work could command our respect and many playgoers' only slightly qualified enthusiasm.

The Broadway production directed with distinction by Arthur Penn proved itself entirely worthy of Miss Hellman's craft. But it was altogether apparent that the playwright was directly responsible for the excellence of the presentation. For one thing, Miss Hellman contributed an absorbing story that could be translated into vivid stage action. For another, she supplied the actors with multidimensional characters. Maureen Stapleton especially had a full range of emotions to convey as the younger spinster who is in love with her brother and jealous of his child-wife. The appealing British actress Irene Worth also had a role of some substance when called upon to play a woman who has been burdened with a chronically troublesome immature daughter. And the im-

mensely rich role of Julian, the spinsters' well-intentioned but ill-starred
brother, was as beneficial to the superb acting of Jason Robards, Jr., as
his talent was to the role. Not the least of Miss Hellman's perdurable
gifts is her ability to write for actors. Her art of characterization is insight
exercised in the theatre that completes itself in performance. With such
talent at her disposal and a vigorous mind and temperament as her natural
endowments, Miss Hellman was one of the very few playwrights who
could be expected to stop the escape of energy from the decade's theatre.
But there were unfortunately too few playwrights in America who could
follow her example of mastering melancholy views and visions instead
of being mastered by them.

Allegory: Coxe and Chapman's *Billy Budd*

The dramatization of Melville's famous short novel of the sea was
partly a tribute to the inspiration of Professor Willard Thorpe, Princeton
specialist in American literature and a Melville enthusiast under whom
both Coxe and Chapman had studied. Another stimulus must have come
directly from the sea and from wartime service; Louis O. Coxe and Robert
Chapman both served in the Navy during World War II. They first
wrought a spare, verse version of the Melville story and saw it staged
under the title of *Uniform of Flesh* in January, 1949, by the Experimental Theatre of the American National Theatre and Academy. Then
they amplified the work and, seizing on the imaginative moral features
of the story, composed a play that could be regarded as a fairly independent creation. As Brooks Atkinson put it *Billy Budd* was "a fully wrought
play in its own right." Certainly the authors saw the story in the light of
its philosophical idea that absolutes of good and evil could not survive
in the world. This viewpoint would have justified an epigraph recalled by
Mr. Atkinson from Melville himself:

> *Yea and Nay—*
> *Each hath his say;*
> *But God, He keeps the middle way.*

In the authors' own words, "Melville's story of good, evil, and the way
the world takes to such absolutes" naturally produced a "morality play."
  The fate of the play was rather curious. No effort was spared to make

it succeed. Norris Houghton staged it with regard for the dignity of the work and an attentive eye for the late eighteenth-century background set on a sailing vessel. The cast was headed by the gifted Dennis King, who gave a brilliant performance as Captain Vere of the Royal British Navy. The work commanded respect, not merely as a morality play (for as such it had specific limitations) but as a poetic drama of some stature. For this reason the producers, Chandler Cowles and Anthony B. Farrell, kept the play running though it lost money week after week. The plot elements stir tremendous interest: a basic conflict between good and evil, a grossly maligned innocent, a trial (and trials rarely fail to be dramatic), and a flagrant miscarriage of justice when Billy Budd is hanged. The special significance of the event could hardly escape us so soon after World War II, for the action takes place during the age of the French Revolution, when an inflexible Mutiny Act suppressed insubordination in the British fleet. "For us, as inchoate playwrights, in January of 1947," said the authors, "Melville's story was material enough for the veterans of a war, a depression, and the moving cold war."

Yet I unwillingly shared the tepid reaction around me when I saw *Billy Budd* at New York's Biltmore Theatre. I felt frustrated and slightly battered rather than fulfilled, and I overheard similar sentiments from the audience. The dissatisfaction seemed to me important because I knew this was no ordinary play to be brusquely dismissed when it displeased us in some particulars. I believe in a double standard for play reviewing, though not the way some reviewers practice it. They are unforgiving when a distinguished effort misses by a yard but indulgent when a mindless entertainment misses by a mile. I am inclined to cheer the distinguished failure, to be forgiving toward a noble, if only half-successful, effort. But shortcomings and flaws must be noted as such if values are to be respected and if criticism is to rise above the state of cheerleading.

One way of defining the central flaw is to say that *Billy Budd* promised tragedy but provided only pathos. It was an undischarged pathos at that, weighed down by speeches that seemed labored and that slowed down the action at points when a protest against injustice was taking form in the play or was being aroused in the spectator. I was more ready to resent the speechmaking of Captain Vere as arrant sophism than to be moved by it or to appreciate its logic and philosophical irony. Good writing therefore gave the impression of being turgid.

It seemed also as if the plight of the sailor-hero, Billy, could not produce tragedy because his half-symbolic character was unfortunately infantile. This might have been alleviated by better casting or a different interpretation on the part of the young actor Charles Nolte. It was important to point up the relentlessness of totalitarian law, here represented by wartime naval law; the point was made in one closely reasoned and extremely effective scene in the Captain's cabin. But the inhuman machine must destroy real men if we are to be fully stirred, whereas the inarticulate Billy remained an allegorical wraith or an overgrown child. Worse still, the innocent sailor boy going to his death with a blessing for the dear old ship's captain, who has reasoned him into a noose, was as intolerable to my sense of humor as to my morality. The almost wholly childlike, passive character of Billy tended to abort this noteworthy play's effectiveness.

On the stage an allegorical character is embodied in a breathing actor, seen in the round. Billy's fate necessarily involves us with a *person* rather than with an idea. His acceptance of his sentence and execution (he climbs the rigging of the ship to hang himself) is humanly intolerable. A character in a realistically staged production, out of the covers of a book, will be felt and appraised entirely as a man. Thus this most competent Broadway production left something to be desired. A bolder, more stylized treatment, a production with some sort of frame could have made us see the play as a fable and dissolve the pain of the staged events. But it would be a mistake to ascribe the major defects to the production rather than to the subject itself.

Kingsley's *Darkness at Noon* and Political Drama

Sidney Kingsley has been one of the hardiest of the playwrights brought into the American theatre in the Thirties. The 1933 Group Theatre production of his medical drama, *Men in White,* was his eventful introduction; the play was superbly staged by Lee Strasberg, brilliantly designed by Mordecai Gorelik. It received a Pulitzer Prize in 1934. Mr. Kingsley gave Broadway his powerful slum drama, *Dead End,* two years later. Three years after that he presented a moving, insufficiently appreciated dramatization of a Millen Brand novel under the title of *The World We Make.* During World War II he produced a highly creditable historical drama, *The Patriots,* in which the political opponents, Jefferson and Hamilton, proved themselves equally devoted to the formative American nation—a necessary reminder that patriotism can soar with both the left wing and the right. Then, in 1949, Kingsley wrote his *Measure for Measure* drama, *Detective Story*, in which his Angelo, the overzealous Detective McLeod, suffered moral bankruptcy and emotional collapse. With this play Kingsley came close to turning adult melodrama into naturalistic tragedy.

With this background Kingsley, still bent upon exposing self-righteousness as the root of much evil, turned to Soviet Russia, which in his estimation had become the graveyard of humanitarian ideals. Lacking first-hand information about Stalin's Russia but thoroughly disenchanted with communism, Kingsley proceeded to dramatize a novel. Arthur Koestler's *Darkness at Noon* is based on the Moscow trials and the degradation of Marxist dogma. The result, which won Kingsley a Drama Critics Circle Award, was worth observing as a venture in political drama, at which the playwrights of the Fifties were unskillful. Still, Kingsley's success was ambiguous enough to be questioned. Critical opinion reflected a divided impression and the public gave the play less support than might have been expected considering the timeliness of the subject, the excellence of the staging, and the affecting performance of Claude Rains as the disenchanted old Bolshevik, Rubashov.

Kingsley converted the novel to a play without losing the advantages of unified drama or sacrificing of tension. Any loss sustained in the dramatization involved the psychological subtleties of Koestler's treatment. Kingsley sacrificed these values partly as a necessity of craft and partly as a consequence of launching the fiercest possible attack against Stalinism. Koestler's objective was to explain how a courageous revolutionist, a victim of the Moscow trial purges, could bring himself to the point of confessing to crimes of which he was innocent, even though he knew the confession would not save his life. For Kingsley this was a matter of secondary interest. His main concern was with the evils of Communist dictatorship and with the moral failure of Rubashov. Originally supporting the revolution out of the noblest of motives he comes to realize, as he reviews his life while awaiting execution, how hazardous it is to follow the principle that the end justifies the means.

Perhaps Kingsley was remembering a statement by his favorite hero, Thomas Jefferson: "Sometimes it is said that man cannot be trusted with the government of himself. Can he then be trusted with the government of others?" *Darkness at Noon* was a technical feat and a fervid protest. For all the playwright's efficiency and liberal's conviction, however, the play proved to be more workmanlike than inspired, more melodramatic than tragic, more denunciatory than psychologically and intellectually explorative.

The play Kingsley put together was a network of short scenes in the present and past. Like Koestler's novel the play dealt mainly with Rubashov's emotional crisis and remorse. But Kingsley's apparent reluctance to develop sufficiently Rubashov's tortured process, that leads to a false confession made in the interests of Soviet security and world revolution, missed the profundity of the novel. Kingsley's character was too greatly worn down by gnawing reminiscences to be anything but an essentially passive victim. He flickered out instead of undergoing a tragic explosion and illumination. The flicker of the man, not the flame, was consecrated in what was only potentially tragic drama.

2 POINTS OF RETURN

Van Druten's *I am a Camera* and the Chekhov Myth

Walter Kerr in his lively book, *How Not to Write a Play*, must have startled some of his admirers by saying that the example of Chekhov was bad for American playwrights. It is problematic whether most of them ever really followed that example; my own impression is that even *Awake and Sing!* and *The Autumn Garden* represented deviation more than sedulous imitation. But I agree that Chekhov's style and technique *can* set a bad example, if only in imitating the inimitable. One can extend Mr. Kerr's statement to the playwrights of every other nation including Russia itself. Leonid Andreev was unable, for instance, to move into Chekhov's territory of bizarre frustration and depressed desperation with such pieces as *Katerina Ivanovna* and *The Waltz of the Dogs*. An apparent exception recently was the English theatre's *The Chalk Garden*. But Enid Bagnold's drama actually moved with a most un-Chekhovian stiffness in the joints. Other recent English plays such as *The Entertainer* and *Epitaph for George Dillon* were too harsh in exposure and too poor in poetic atmosphere to be identified with Chekhov's dramatic style. Nevertheless, British writers have some affinity for Chekhov, partly because England has a decaying upper class.

It is not surprising therefore that John Van Druten, a former distinguished subject of Britain, should have consciously identified himself with Chekhov in dramatizing *The Berlin Stories* by Christopher Isherwood. The latter was much concerned with social deterioration during the Thirties, a period that constantly tested the intelligence and stamina of educated Britons. *I am a Camera*, sensitively written and staged by Van Druten, provided proof of his Chekhovian inclinations. The play-

144

wright displayed the happy faculty of sympathizing with his disoriented characters yet observing them with detached objectivity. He even succeeded in giving his dramatization an appropriately melancholy atmosphere by presenting the action through the memory of his narrator. This character called "Christopher Isherwood" is an English writer who fritters away part of his youth in the belief that he is advancing his literary ambitions by living abroad in Berlin. He proposes to do this by turning himself into a camera and fixing in his mind photographs of expatriated Anglo-Saxons and confused Germans immediately prior to the outbreak of World War II.

John Van Druten made it quite evident that the I-am-a-camera attitude of young Isherwood was essentially as unproductive as it was egotistical, and that the irresponsible behavior of the other expatriates on whom the would-be writer trained his camera was no less deplorable. At the play's end it is apparent that Isherwood is about to liberate himself from the long trance into which he has fallen and that a rude awakening is in store for all who had nursed delusions during the prewar period. I am a Camera failed to realize fully its major theme of moral sloth in the midst of the gathering storm of nazism. The fictional Christopher Isherwood tries to absorb life by osmosis and strikes up a platonic relationship with an extraordinarily unstable English girl who makes a pretence of earning her living as a night-club entertainer while fiddling close harmonics on the strings of sensualism. The picture of prewar Europe is amplified by portraits of an American playboy, of a young German Jew who wins his way out of the trap of assimilationist self-deception with some difficulty, and of a landlady who echoes anti-Semitic canards idiotically. Van Druten's picture of social decadence had revealing moments, and the well-directed principal performances were excellent. Broadway justly rang the praises of Julie Harris, who created the role of the fancy-free, desperately arid English girl. But the play was insufficiently alive as a whole; the dramatic movement was stalemated by a caressing interest in the impasse of the principals. This defect could not be passed off as a commendable superiority to plot entitling the author to recognition as a Chekhovian playwright.

Van Druten followed every twist and turn of his heroine's disorientation, devoting the major part of the play to her, when actually this expatriated Lorelei is of secondary importance to the drama of people's failure to face the social crises of the Thirties. There is reason to suspect that Miss Harris' lady would have been a tramp in any society; certainly as a hopeless egocentric she would have been ineffectual even if her morals had been above suspicion. The same stalemate in the dramatic treatment was inherent in Van Druten's Christopher Isherwood. He is required to concentrate too long on the one personal relationship, his friendship with the English girl, that can least illuminate the social scene he is photographing. Nor does he emerge from the role of camera as we have a right to require from his intelligence. Van Druten allows him to leave for England at the end of the play with no achieved point of view and with no resolve that would represent any true development. The real Christopher Isherwood, on the contrary, did learn something important about the crisis of his time, took action as a matured author, and composed several challenging works, including *The Berlin Stories*.

My purpose has been to show how an interesting play by a literate playwright fails for want of strenuous application of mind and spirit to his matter. But something else is apparent: the difference between Chekhovian variants of drama and Chekhov's own plays. In Chekhov, we find either a distinct development, as in *The Sea Gull* and *The Cherry Orchard*, in which a stalemate leads to a catastrophe, and one way of life is displaced by another; or we observe characters staging an intense struggle against an impasse before suffering defeat, as in *Uncle Vanya* and *The Three Sisters*. Stanislavski was quite correct in opposing the notion that Chekhov's characters were utterly passive, and absolutely right in attributing an invigorating quality to their discontent, their explosions of rage at their torpid way of life, and their dreams of a better world. The pseudo-Chekhovians make much of the possibility of writing plotless plays (as Mr. Van Druten did in a New York *Times* article published in advance of *I am a Camera*), but they tend to overlook the presence of essential conflict and progression in Chekhov's dramaturgy. They try to be artfully passive; he succeeded in being artfully active.

Marquand and Osborn: *Point of No Return*

Point of No Return was a Broadway offering that held up dramatically in all respects. The colloquial term, held up, emphasizes this play's ambiguous success. The invariably scrupulous Paul Osborn fashioned it out of the novel by invariably scrupulous J.P. Marquand. It was an honest and at the same time skillful dramatization. Osborn managed to say much of what Marquand said and to retain the scope of the novel by composing a series of second-act reminiscences of a New England youth. A play that changes style midstream and then returns to its original matter and style is apt to disintegrate, but this was not true of Osborn's dramatization. The theme, a struggle between nonmaterialistic and materialistic values in our society, unified the play, and the conflict was as apparent in the main character's youthful experiences as in the immediate issue of whether he is to win the coveted vice-presidency of a bank. The dramatic theme also gains dimension from the fact that it is mirrored in the character's New England boyhood and in his love for a girl socially and economically above him. The parallel is carried further in the difficulties of the hero's erratic father. Divided between ideal aims and desire for wealth the remembered father casts a shadow on his son's discontent in the beginning and anticipates his acceptance of the vice-presidency in the end. *Point of No Return* is a lesson in play construction in a theatre that teems with examples of elementary incompetence. Osborn's competence in dramatizing fiction is the result of considerable experience, and it was applied here to the work of an observant and efficient novelist.

Point of No Return can hardly be acclaimed as a miracle of creative originality. But lest we assume that competence in the difficult medium of drama is a mere matter of play-carpentry, it is worth noting that the dramatization was so well constructed because it was organized around a core of significant experience. So conscious of purpose was Osborn that he made ingenious use of an anthropologist, a field worker who is studying American values and mores and who first encounters the hero in his small-town environment. It is this investigator who gives us a repeated cue to the meaning of the hero's problem of finding an acceptable way of life. It was made easy for the audience to pick up the cue, not only to understand the future vice-president's situation, but to sympathize with him and to recognize a significant representation. The middle-class public could leave the play with a shared experience, made utterly real by Henry Fonda, and with a realization that life is like that. The play disturbed a widely attained and recognized equilibrium, then restored it and moved dynamically toward a comfortable resolution. The result was what is known in the commercial theatre as a good play.

To the dismay of many playgoers, provocative new plays are often destructive. They fail to make a connection with a Broadway audience that has enjoyed a relatively settled life. It is worth noting that equilibrium-destroying theatre has aroused interest on a large scale, as a rule, only in periods of severe crisis. Thus we had the vogue of expressionistic drama in Germany after 1916 and of militant leftist drama in the United States after 1929. Violence in the staging of plays in these periods paralleled the violence of the dramatic text. But since the aesthetic drive is constructive rather than disintegrative, and since the human impulse is to arrive at points of comparative rest, audiences as well as playwrights and theatrical artists wearied of disintegrative drama and theatre. By 1924 German expressionism was virtually exhausted and by 1939, after only nine or ten years of activity, the American left-wing theatre had become a bore. Playwrights, however, still do not achieve equilibrium often enough for their middle-class audiences. They fail for two simple reasons: plays are ineptly put together and are not erected on a base of recognizable reality. Paul Osborn avoided both defects.

Nevertheless, the limitations of *Point of No Return* should have been quite apparent even to its friends. The equilibrium with which both novelist and dramatist started is a commonplace reality of the times, and the equilibrium to which they return is equally commonplace. It amounts to little more than saying, "I'll take the vice-presidency of the bank, but I won't belong to your country club." This questionable ambivalence appears somewhat earlier in the attitude of the hero's wife, which might be stated as, "I want you to get that vice-presidency at any cost, but I'll love you even without it." Earlier in the play she has urged him to scramble for the job with the unmistakable argument that their children must have the best opportunities, that is, an exclusive schooling. In returning to his home town the man reviews his past life and finds it so unsatisfactory that he no longer wants the vice-presidency, although he knows that the alternative to winning it is to look for a new position. But the demands of suburban success philosophy remain supreme in the play, and so the vice-presidency has to come to the dissident hero anyhow. The commonplace American dream comes true, though first it must go through the wringer of a somewhat skeptical mind. Equilibrium in *Point of No Return* makes a sort of moral, as well as artistic, stalemate.

There are different degrees and kinds of stasis. In *Point of No Return* it is not so banal as to constitute a total acceptance of Babbittry, but neither does it truly reject Babbitt's values. A picture of a way of life altogether familiar, the play, like the novel, represents an attempt to make the best of both possible worlds: the real world of material success and the ideal world of spiritual integrity. Osborn's treatment, while mature enough to view this effort with some scepticism, is sympathetic toward it. The work stands on a base of opportunistic realism. That is the extent of its success and also the source of its limitation.

The Grass Harp: Capote versus Saroyan

As Truman Capote's play *The Grass Harp* unfolded its tale we expected none of the clever dramaturgy of the Broadway specialists. We expected spontaneity, oddity, nuance, and poetry, and were ready to be grateful for these qualities. Unfortunately these qualities were insufficiently sustained in *The Grass Harp,* and the play moved toward a routine resolution in which everybody returned to drab normality. The play was beautiful in the sense that its sentiments were delicate. Its central situation, of the escape of a spinster and other appealing small-town misfits who take up temporary residence in a tree house in the woods, was an attractive notion. And this loveliness of conception was exquisitely augmented by Virgil Thompson's music and Cecil Beaton's beautiful outdoor setting. But delicacy of sentiment and quaint local color could not give *The Grass Harp* sufficient voltage to galvanize it into theatrical vitality, and so the potentially most valuable play of the 1952-53 season went to waste. Most post mortems of the play were sympathetic, though few were just to the direction of Robert Lewis. He had previously accumulated well-deserved praise for his staging of *My Heart's in the Highlands* and *Brigadoon.* In this case he was accused of having overproduced a gentle little play. However, when the off-Broadway Circle in the Square theatre revived *The Grass Harp* with moderate means the results were still the same; the fragile play continued to look fragile.

The weaknesses of the script cannot be written out; at best, they can be merely concealed. Post mortems that stressed individual faults in the play or the production could not quite explain a defect that seems characteristic of this genre. I should call this a defect of intellect. It is not a lack of either learning or information, but a want of acuity that may be quite untutored, as it was in Saroyan's early plays. *The Grass Harp* has been unfavorably compared with these. Everybody referred to

Saroyan's spontaneity. I wish that more attention had been paid to the vivacity of his affirmations and even his sentimentalities. Saroyan's characters maintained their integrity in a humdrum, practical world that Saroyan took delight in turning topsy-turvy. He was acute enough to know how to confound the workaday, philistine world in such pieces as *My Heart's in the Highlands, The Time of Your Life,* and *The Beautiful People.* A sharp gamin's intelligence played behind the mask of his naïveté and behind the sentimentality of his protestations of brotherly love. In those days Saroyan conquered the commonplace world with a perverse kind of reasoning; he used even his own commonplaces for that purpose. There was a measure of provocative impudence in his gospel of brotherly love which pulled down the mighty. His sentimentality, the element in his work most frequently deplored, sometimes concealed and sometimes flaunted a cutting edge that both his admirers and detractors tended to overlook.

The author of *The Grass Harp* never seriously jolted the conventional world from which his main characters—the fey sister of a hard-driving, sexually frustrated woman; an adolescent lad; and an erratic family servant—temporarily retreated. It was characteristic of Saroyan's rebels that, however bizarre their conduct, they thought fast and ingeniously. Above all, they were not easily suppressed. By comparison, Truman Capote's rebels were almost listless. Except for a superannuated judge's support of the refugees and a bit of bluster on the part of the Negro servant, who insisted that she was of Indian extraction, they displayed little energy of spirit. When the rebels renounced their retreat and returned to the house of the imperious sister they came back to a community they had never disavowed. *The Grass Harp* was ostensibly a play about an escape that terminated with some victory for primal innocence. But the mildly lyrical escape never had much significance; in mind and spirit the characters had never left home, yet their return to the village was largely an anticlimax.

It is reasonable to doubt that the theatre of the Fifties could be invigorated by the mild dissents and tentative rebellions of *The Grass Harp.* It is briefly poignant rather than compelling and moderately amusing rather than distinctively satirical or farcical. The imaginative treatment of rebellion, a privilege vested in the drama ever since Aeschylus dramatized the Prometheus myth, seemed to have disappeared in our mid-century theatre. For a variety of reasons—among which may be listed cold-war politics, congressional inquisitions, disenchantment with revolutionary zeal, and general complacency—the American theatre is no longer likely to thrive on the ferment of discontent. Certainly discontent is not very likely to produce the lively, satirical Kaufman-school farces of the Twenties or the vigorous satires, protests, and acclamations of the Thirties. Our theatre seems to have been extravagantly attached to adolescents, retarded individuals, and naïve eccentrics ever since the brief reign of Saroyan between 1939 and 1941. This was followed by the vogue for wartime sentimental comedies of the calibre of *Kiss and Tell*.

American society has been described as a children's paradise. The same description would fit the mid-century American theatre, including dramatizations of Capote's *The Grass Harp* and Eudora Welty's *The Ponder Heart*. The Capote refugees, although originally invented for the novel, belong to a familiar tribe of American stage simpletons. By American custom they are likely to be identified with the pure in heart, the salt of the earth, and the democratic majority.

The Cave Dwellers: Saroyan's Return

An old clown, still harboring pride in his profession, and an elderly unemployed actress have taken refuge in an abandoned theatre soon to be razed by a wrecking crew. They have been joined by an elderly ex-pugilist, as gentle as he is strong, who lost his title because of his uncustomary kindness to his opponent. The fighter gives entry to a homeless girl who soon thinks she is in love with him. But a few hours later she falls in love with an equally gentle milkman, a graceful young man who has the attractive impediment of being dumb. On the turbulent night before the playhouse is to be razed, this refuge is invaded by a woman in labor, her husband, and the trained bear who has long been a part of their theatrical act. The woman has her child there, the pugilist steals milk for her (the milkman pursues him and falls in love with the girl), and the theatre building gets a few days' reprieve from the benevolent foreman of the wrecking company. The bizarre refugees ultimately leave their shabby Eden and there is an end to *The Cave Dwellers*, Saroyan's symbolist-surrealist fantasy on the unity and love of mankind.

Carmen Capalbo produced and staged this new Saroyan love affair with humanity in 1957, and it was thanks largely to him that it was

possible to see a work of rare loveliness. Capalbo and Chase, the successful producers of *The Threepenny Opera* revival, had leased a small house
on the fringe of Broadway to present unusual plays. (Other items on
their agenda were *A Moon for the Misbegotten* and *The Potting Shed*.)
But *The Cave Dwellers* failed to acquire enough patronage to keep it
running.

For once it was not possible to blame the critics for the failure of the
play; *The Cave Dwellers* had received an excellent press. If anything
the press (I include myself) erred on the side of generosity. We might
have pointed out that Saroyan's shelterless innocents in the center of
town were not contemporaries; their unrelieved poverty identified them
as wraiths from the depression period of the Thirties. Their author dealt
with them as if he had never heard of unemployment insurance and
municipal housing. The pity the audience might have felt for Saroyan's
waifs was qualified by disbelief in their situation. But some of us, and
again I include myself, refused to make an issue of the anachronistic
nature of the situation. Without a doubt we were eager to submit to the
author's old enchantment which has usually offered us either likely people in unlikely situations or unlikely people in likely situations.

The same eagerness to be pleased made us overlook the dark lighting
and emphasis on drabness in the Bijou Theatre production. The unin-
viting, almost uniformly depressing atmosphere could have been enliv-
ened to advantage with the tattered tinsel of an abandoned show-place;
instead, the environment repressed Saroyan's buoyant sentimentality.
Though our rapport with the play and the production was not fatally
affected, we would have been in a happier frame of mind if there had
been more color and gaiety on stage. There were banal moments in the
play, too, but we were usually given some assistance by the actors, especially Eugenie Leontovich and Barry Jones, in these transitions from
one high point to another.

Once public apathy for *The Cave Dwellers* was apparent it was not
difficult to understand it. In my original review of the production I
suspected that my partiality for the play would not be sustained everywhere. Its failure was a keen disappointment to those who missed
Saroyan's élan ever since its quiescence in the mid-Forties. An early fall
production of the 1957-58 season, *The Cave Dwellers* was Saroyan's first
stage production in the Times Square area for some fifteen years. (The

less said about an earlier Greenwich Village production the better; it was a painfully dreary affair.)

There is no need to reach for reasons why we have not had a revival of the Saroyan vogue of the early Forties. It is regrettable that this spirited man has not acquired more than one string to his beggarman's fiddle after his success with *My Heart's in the Highland* and *The Time of Your Life.* But surely not all the frustrations of his later playwriting career can be assigned to Saroyan's own limitations. Perhaps the heavy artillery to which Williams and Miller accustomed playgoers after 1945 accounts for the impression of datedness and futility that Saroyan's lighter tones and insouciance now make. In this respect his situation is not unlike that of the comedy authors whose work seemed unusually brisk and barbed in the Twenties but seem listless and old-fashioned today. *Eheu fugaces!*

The Flowering Peach: Odets, Yea-and-Nay

The Flowering Peach was an allegory developed in such simple terms that it did not look like an artifice at all. The great folk-comedian Menasha Skulnik gave the part of Noah such authenticity that he became as vivid an Everyman as one could desire. Large portions of *The Flowering Peach*, produced in the 1954-55 season, proved to be delightful theatre, thanks largely to Skulnik. To observe the shrug of the shoulder, the folding of the hands following a rising inflection, or a sudden glance adroitly mixing the glare of a lion and the blank patience of a sheep was to watch real artistry. Skulnik *was* world-weary but trusting humanity, vacillating but stubborn humanity, angry but loving humanity. Above all he was *learning* humanity: man discovering that his keenest wounds are suffered in private reality where his love of wife and family lie.

The material for this remarkably plastic performance was present in Odets' text. Some were tempted to comment, with perhaps a touch of philistine complacency, how plainly the rebel of the Thirties had acquired humility. He was inclined to take humanity as it is, which was quite a change for a man who began his career with the explosive *Waiting for Lefty.* In *The Flowering Peach* the ways of God and man were examined and accepted without much hope and without much protest. Odets seemed to be disinclined to justify either God's ways to man or man's ways to God; he regarded them ruefully and displayed them somewhat enigmatically.

Still, *The Flowering Peach* left some of the author's old admirers disturbed. Odets diffused the central section of the play with a domestic imbroglio solved only when two of Noah's sons exchanged wives. It was a structural weakness of the play that this triangle occupied so much of the early foreground of the action. The problem had to be solved before the play as a whole arrived at a climax. As a result, a major line of development dropped out of the play. I assume that the affair was intended to educate the Old Testament patriarch in the ways of tolerance, but this motif was out-of-focus and had dwindled by the last act. The triangle episode did enable Odets romantically to assert the rights of the individual against convention and puritanical morality, as he had done in *Awake and Sing!* written some twenty years before *The Flowering Peach*. (One of Odets' most durable concerns is for the integrity of romantic attachments and for the freedom to make them.)

A far more serious fault was the dramatic void that followed the subplot. The play was kept going with another conflict: the efforts of one brother to establish a profitable monopoly on the ark. There were other details, in themselves very good, but they were conducive to diffuseness. Nowhere was a single focus in evidence, and the basis for a dramatically developed conclusion was never successfully established. This defect probably could not have been overcome even if detected before the Broadway opening, because it was the nature of Odets' method here not to move toward a strong conclusion. Such a conclusion would have required taking a stand *for* or *against* something, while Odets was apparently in no frame of mind to take a stand on anything except the advisability of not taking one.

An Odets, Yea-and-nay, was indeed at the steering wheel of his dramatic contrivance, so that it is little wonder that the play drifted about almost as much as Noah's ark. Inconclusiveness could also be found in the sometimes provocative, sometimes merely provoking, ambiguities of the play. The rebel Odets was present in the play, but so was the anti-rebel.

Odets is still himself in important respects, still the romanticist who hurls himself at large questions with little prospect of answers or even of complete definitions. He is a born folk-dramatist, capable of creating vivid characters and writing richly flavored colloquial speech. Odets must also be credited as the director of *The Flowering Peach*. He showed great astuteness in choosing his Broadway collaborators: Mordecai Gorelik, who designed two excellent sets, and A.H. Feder, who lit the production superbly. All of the performances were satisfactory, some more than satisfactory. That which was flawed in Odets' dramaturgy was altogether mended while Menasha Skulnik was on the stage. *The Flowering Peach* was a generally rewarding, though often frustrating, experience. But it lacked an intellect commensurate with the challenge of the subject and a consistency of viewpoint without which the play was left in a limbo of indeterminate feelings about man and history. The play, one of Odets' most attractive and mature works, was a casualty of the divided mind of the times.

With the subject matter, nuances, and intimations of *The Flowering Peach* we might have expected Odets to crystallize the opinion of an age. Instead we get the author's doubts and vacillations. Different ages of the theatre have precipitated different viewpoints which brought them to some revelation and finality of statement. But there does not seem much probability of our creating a contemporary *Oedipus at Colonus, Everyman,* or *Faust.* Odets may not have even considered aiming so high. *The Flowering Peach* appeared to be the personal testament of a rueful man content to accept contradictions and shortcomings in man and the world. In the first act the pious are left to perish in the Flood, and at the conclusion of the play, Noah pathetically chooses to spend his feeble old age at the home of his monopolistic, well-to-do son because he will be more comfortable there. It seemed as if Odets, with the example of generations of men before him, had given up hopes for a better world and is ready to accept humanity on its own second-best terms.

Religion and Graham Greene's *The Potting Shed*

Nothing in dramaturgy is quite free from dangers, and so it is not at all certain that even a spiritual myth invented by an expert writer will yield a true and full harvest. Graham Greene's religious drama, *The Potting Shed*, won high praise in the 1956-57 season, but the grounds for praise seemed to me highly dubious. Certainly the skillful playwright evolved a story rich with imaginative elements and spiritual implications, but the play was wholly satisfactory only on the level of a mystery story. Mr. Greene achieved an amazing degree of dramatic efficiency, but produced a fable that was decidedly more exciting than illuminating. The play was easier to accept as a literate contrivance than as the kind of spiritual experience that T.S. Eliot had provided in *Murder in the Cathedral* and that Paul Claudel had attempted in half-a-dozen weighty poetic plays.

The Potting Shed established Graham Greene with New York reviewers as an expert playwright. The presentation at the Bijou Theatre, the headquarters of a regrettably short-lived venture in experimental stage production, was an excellent one, proving that Mr. Greene could create character and plot for the theatre as well as for the novel. In the cast were Dame Sybil Thorndike, Sir Lewis Casson, Robert Flemyng, Leueen MacGrath, and Frank Conroy, playing the part of an insecure priest. The play concerns a young man who is a serious problem to his family. His marriage is breaking up because of a peculiar deadness in his character and conduct. There is mystery in this, and in his mother's peculiar attitude toward him. She seems almost unwilling to acknowledge his existence; and she has kept him away from his father, a distinguished Victorian free-thinker, around whom she has long built a protective screen. The truth is gradually bared. It is discovered that the emotionally dead son had once been *physically* dead. Feeling unloved and neglected as a child, he had hanged himself. Brought back to life by a miracle, his mother had kept him away from his father to whom the family's acceptance of a miracle would have been a crushing blow.

The miracle has been bought with the faith of the boy's devout uncle, by now an utterly depraved priest, who had offered God his dearest possession, his faith, in exchange for the boy's life. God apparently had agreed to the bargain; the boy was brought back to life and the priest lost his faith. The strange truth is at last brought out of the family closet, largely through the agency of an inquisitive ingenue! The priest recovers his faith and happiness and, understanding the reason for his own unnatural apathy, the unhappy young man is drawing closer to his wife as the curtain descends.

The very quality that insured continued interest in the plot, the unraveling of the mystery, almost consistently detracted from concern with any deeper values of the work. The detective-story pattern, which baits the trap for the playgoer who would normally avoid a religious drama, is also a trap for the playwright. It leaves little room for those explorations of character conflict through which spiritual struggles can be brought to full life.

Only in Frank Conroy's scene of anguish as the priest deprived of faith did the author convey real force and conviction. In the rest of the play the revelations seemed elusive and even a little spurious. Having made the point that miracles occur despite the agnosticism of the intellectual, a point insisted upon with rather arbitrary transparency, the author left us in the dark on other matters: the validity of anyone's making a bargain with God, the hero's discovery that he has once been dead. It was the machinery of the play rather than the ambiguous product that reviewers admired in *The Potting Shed*.

It is a pity that the most valuable content in the play is least dramatic. The author depended on implications that might or might not be drawn by the audience. That we could all be saved from spiritual emptiness or deadness if only we realized that we were dead and are now alive because of divine intervention is material for the most exalted poetic treatment. A more profound treatment was needed to supplement professional skill. It is regrettable that *The Potting Shed* could be praised, as it was by one newspaper reviewer, only as "brilliantly wrought entertainment."

Had I covered *The Potting Shed* for a newspaper I, too, might have classed the play as entertainment—though not as a compliment to Greene except on the ground that he has learned to contrive plays. But there is more to be said. Paradoxically, I also felt put upon. Mr. Greene was sugar-watering a pill of religion for me, and I've always preferred to take my medicine straight. Regardless of its intent *The Potting Shed* is part potboiler and part propaganda.

It is doubtful that modern religious drama can be created except with absolute integrity. Otherwise its proponents waste their breath and their efforts are labor in the wind of unbelief. My prejudice is quite apparent, but I don't mind making it even plainer: I bridle at religious salesman-ship. I have as little use for the soft sell in religion as for a sequestered virtue in morals, especially when the method used involves an art form.

3 LOW MEN ON A TOTEM POLE

Low Tragedy in Macken's *Home Is the Hero*

Home Is the Hero by the Irish novelist Walter Macken came to our shores in the season of 1954-55. It had a considerable reputation as the best Irish play since Paul Vincent Carroll wrote his *Shadow and Substance* and *The White Steed* in the late Thirties. But New York turned the play down without mercy; I may be the one practicing critic who found himself approving the play and applauding its sponsors, the Theatre Guild and Worthington Miner.

Why should *Home Is the Hero* have misfired on Broadway in spite of excellent performances by Glenda Farrell, Pat O'Malley, Art Smith, and Walter Macken himself in the leading role? The play presents the emotional impasse created by the return of a strong-willed father, Paddo O'Reilly, to his family after a period of imprisonment for manslaughter. His self-torment is genuine, but the moment it becomes mingled with self-will, the moment he resumes his tyrannical ways, he becomes intolerable to his family. Since Macken's characterization apparently affected his audience no less unpleasantly this intensely felt play was summarily dismissed as depressing and pointless. For the public in Ireland, which recognized the autocrat-father as a type, Paddo was apparently a tragic character. He was that for me, too, because his aspirations for himself and his family are high and because he owes his downfall to a tragic flaw of almost classical hubris; he is righteous and highhanded in support of unquestionably honorable intentions.

Broadway has manifested increasing impatience with those exhibitions of human error and suffering that seem intrinsically insoluble, as well as with those presented as soluble by social action. This attitude virtually rules out the entire field of modern serious drama unless the production on stage provides extraordinary compensations. Broadway's present unresponsiveness is not due to high critical acumen. It is merely a sign of indifference both to fate and social responsibility which have invigorated much of the dramatic work of the past.

Another, related, explanation is that Macken's play is austere without being beautiful, a failing in realistic tragedy since the beginning of modern theatre. High tragedy transmutes pain into poetry. Low tragedy often leaves the pain untranslated into universality and unsublimated by verbal music. The very realistic Broadway production, with its lack of atmosphere and its concentration on the surface facts of family drama, made all too evident the desiccated character of low tragedy in *Home Is the Hero*. The limitation is in the genre itself. The music of Irish speech that must have contributed to the success of the original Dublin production was absent. It is unlikely, however, that Macken was opposed to the realistic New York production since he had constructed his play and drawn his characters along realistic lines. It is probable only that the Irish in him felt and *heard* the play more poetically.

Only fitfully in some minor characterization, as in Art Smith's Trapper, did some element of loveliness come to a brief glow. The raw nerves of the drama lay exposed too long and too conspicuously. This defect is characteristic of our realistic theatre, and it was particularly detrimental to the work of an author who did not command O'Casey's high key dialogue.

Gazzo's *A Hatful of Rain*: The Real and the Grotesque

At the other extreme of the spectrum ranging from pure theatricality to pure life Michael Gazzo's *A Hatful of Rain* provided the extremes of naturalistic playwriting. The subject of a former soldier's drug addiction is painful enough without a direct representation of his dependency on relentless dope peddlers. The naturalism was intensified rather than mitigated by the surrounding circumstances of penurious life in a tenement, the wife's pregnancy, a brother's clownish craving for her, and an egotistic father's angry incomprehension of his son's condition. Naturalism dominated the direction by Frank Corsaro and the forceful performances of Shelley Winters and Ben Gazzara in the lead roles. Gazzara played the drug addict, Johnny Pope, with remarkable authenticity and convincing anguish. One would have thought that Miss Winters, who had previously played in twenty-two motion pictures, had never been closer to Hollywood's glamor factories than New York's Lower East Side.

Naturalism, we are told continually, is passé. Evidently neither the author nor the producer, Jay Julien, had ever heard this. The quality of many contemporary plays tends to support the dire hypothesis that naturalism is dead, but *A Hatful of Rain* simply refused to lie down and die. It was brimful of life. Its clinical reality provided a grotesque kind of fascination. The three bizarre dope peddlers gave the play ghoulish humor, confirming my belief that extreme naturalism is as apt to be grotesque as real. (A good example of this tendency is *Tobacco Road*. Naturalism is closer to extreme romanticism than we generally think it is.) The ringleader of the pushers, a decadent dandy and sadist called Mother (he mothered drug addicts when he wasn't beating them into pulp), was played as a double-breasted, well-tailored figure out of hell. There was something bizarre in virtually all the other roles except that played by Shelley Winters.

No doubt sensing something preternatural as well as natural in *A Hatful of Rain*, Mordecai Gorelik, whose understanding of plays he designs is probably unexcelled in America, made his naturalistic, imaginative, and intensely dramatic setting a veritable symbol of the inferno that is the situation and state of mind of Johnny Pope. Gorelik's East Side upper-story apartment stood seemingly suspended in dead space against a background of tenements and their fire escapes. At the same time the apartment was held as if in a vise by unyielding, sharply outlined areas to the left and right, with a ladder at one side leading to the roof from which the dope peddlers menacingly descended.

Noteworthy, too, were such macabre accents in the stage production as the weird white-soled sneakers of one of Mother's subordinates, who negotiated the ladder leading to the roof with the noiseless speed of a hep hobgoblin. And there was something positively eery in Mother's meticulously professional air while dispensing dope to a victim. He had the air of an executioner-surgeon in his businesslike way of putting on and taking off his gloves, in the briskness of his walk, and in the uncanny quality of his laughter, especially his strangely shrill giggle when he himself was exhilarated by dope.

I call attention to these matters to remind us that it is absurd to dismiss all manifestation of naturalism as the antithesis of "art." The contrary view—"the compatibility of the worst of life with the best of art," as the critic W.C. Brownell put it—has much to be said for it. Naturalism can quite easily blend or flare up into imaginative drama. The real pursued to its extreme can become unreal. That which seems photographically true can become strange; mere factual detail can become imaginatively compelling, even symbolic. As an example, observe the close relationship between naturalistic detail and great poetry in the *Inferno,* or between ultranaturalistic detail and extravagant fantasy in the medieval art of a Brueghel or Bosch.

A Hatful of Rain had obvious weaknesses and limitations. The author overmotivated the drug addiction with an entire family history that tended to encumber the play. But these faults derived not from naturalism but from dramatic prodigality. Other productions of the 1955-56 season tended to substantiate the view that naturalistic drama brought to its proper pitch could still sound a compelling note. The most genuine poetic effects in the Broadway version of Miller's *A View from the Bridge,* for example, were to be found not in the narrative frame (with the reflective Brooklyn waterfront lawyer's literary language and references to Greek tragedy), but in the explosive conduct of a simple longshoreman obsessed with near-incestuous desire and blind jealousy. In *A Hatful of Rain* no such contrast was to be found between frame and story or between two styles of dramatic art. Yet most playgoers were moved and troubled; absorbed by a painfully distressing theatrical experience.

Clinic and Symbol
in Wishengrad's *The Rope Dancers*

It is often hard to pinpoint the flaws in some of the raw case histories of the realistic theatre. They enforce such respect that we are embarrassed by our acceptance of the many pleasant and polished entertainments. Clarity is often lost in some of these slice of life situations, and inevitably tragic power vanishes as blow after blow of human misery deadens our sensibility. For these reasons Morton Wishengrad's painful but absorbing drama *The Rope Dancers* is difficult to describe and to assay.

The environment of the play is the New York slums at the turn of the century; the protagonists are Irish immigrants. The plot concerns a puritanical young woman who interprets the birth of her six-fingered child as a punishment for her husband's light-hearted behavior and for her own secret enjoyment of sexual experience. The child, whom the mother's shame and solicitude have turned into a clinical case, dies after an operation for the removal of her deformity. Death brings her estranged parents together, her mother realizing belatedly that love is a more reliable defense than pride.

The Rope Dancers is not only a bleak drama but a bewildering one. The ending is especially unsatisfactory, for the child's death is an arbitrary event (as wantonly arbitrary as life proves to be at times, the author might maintain in his defense) and the reconciliation of the parents neither resolves their protracted conflict nor clarifies it. But, though as a meaningful work the play was strained, the performances of Siobhán McKenna and Art Carney as the parents and of Beverly Lunsford as the deformed little girl made several scenes overpowering. Though the argument remained obscure or forced, the emotion of the characters was consistently affecting. In this play the parts were greater than the whole, as is so often the case when playwrights try to write about real life. Nevertheless, the scene-by-scene effect had a high voltage, and the talented author would have produced a totally engrossing play if only he had sustained a clear and compelling idea.

Perhaps the idea was there, for Wishengrad certainly demonstrated the evils of a puritanical view of sexual attraction. He was also concerned with the error of egotism which treats virtue as a private possession and that sets the individual above the rest of mankind. But it was not possible to come away from *The Rope Dancers* without feeling that one had been thrust into the morass of a very special situation rather than a representative one. There was also a lack of tragic elevation in the extremely irritating woman, played by Siobhán McKenna, the weak husband whose appealing qualities cannot make him impressive, and the neurotic little girl with six fingers on one hand, whose plight evokes our sympathy rather than admiration.

The hand with six fingers represents a differentiation from normality that can prove extravagantly troublesome to the mind that dwells on it. The puritanical mother's interpretation of her child's abnormality as heaven's punishment for sexual desire is more than simply the decisive cause of the failure of her marriage. It represents a familiar tendency to attribute misfortune to guilt. It is a tendency with which the Jewish author of the play must have been familiar; it has been endemic among the people of "the Book" ever since Old Testament prophets attributed the misfortunes of a tiny nation to moral guilt rather than to geographical location.

But the mother's behavior also illustrates the morbid exaggeration of accidental abnormalities to be found everywhere. The neurotic little girl, who has been compelled to wear a glove on her hand since childhood, tells the doctor who has come to see her, ". . . my name is Elizabeth Pamela Ursula Hyland and I have six fingers." The doctor replies, "My name is Isaac Jacobson. I am a Jew." The father says, "We have kept her covered for eleven years." Dr. Jacobson replies, "What a waste of life! We all wear a glove over something." The mother declares, "Evil is on her hand." Dr. Jacobson gives the only intelligent reply in this case by saying, "Evil is in the mind."

Though hardly profound, dialogue like this could be written only by a playwright whose creative purpose and imagination extended beyond clinical case histories. But for all its intelligence, its fitting symbolism, and its universality of motivation, the writing could not counteract the oppressively clinical character of the play. Exactly why this should be the case was a troublesome question to one who found merit in the work and wished that it had stood up better and longer on Broadway. The only answer I could give is that the miserable principals of the play were not intrinsically interesting; they were merely miserable. This was particularly true of the woman whose attitude and conduct were central and decisive. Although she was abundantly motivated in all her misjudgment and aberrations she remained a case-history figure rather than an interesting or even endurable person. She seemed to have been born in the author's head instead of having been observed and felt as a character possessed of independent reality.

It has become increasingly necessary to remind ourselves that explanations and motivations do not bring characters to life in the theatre. Psychology cannot provide character creation. We should also disabuse ourselves of the notion that a sick character is more interesting than a healthy one. The assumption that perversion or mental disturbance automatically qualifies a character for rapt attention has virtually become an article of faith.

I do not attribute so crude an assumption to the author of *The Rope*

Dancers because he clearly disapproves of his confused heroine. But the fact is that I wearied of her long before the author did. A whole human being is more interesting than a half one, and a character is far more engrossing as a character than as a case history.

Laurents: A *Clearing in the Woods*

Failure of the ego is a recurrent and troubling theme of serious drama, and the subject is no less disturbing when the author endeavors to explain it with modern psychological terminology and refuses to doom his characters to failure. A commendable effort in this direction was made by Arthur Laurents, the talented playwright whose first Broadway play, *Home of the Brave,* combined psychological and social interests. *A Clearing in the Woods* deserved a much longer run than it got in 1957 (the injustice was somewhat repaired by an off-Broadway revival in the season of 1958-59). The play had some scenes that were vastly superior to the work we generally get from even more successful writers; and several talented performers in a cast headed by Kim Stanley labored energetically, though not always successfully, to give credibility to the drama.

In his worthy attempt Mr. Laurents encountered difficulties which are apparently endemic in the theatre. Like other playwrights who deserve our regard, Laurents tried to break with humdrum realistic dramaturgy without shelving realism of characterization. He resorted to an imaginative method of representing the neurotic young woman who creates present tensions through past traumas. Taking his cue apparently from both psychoanalytical procedure and expressionistic flash-back technique, he described his heroine's situation and traced the course of her cure by means of encounters between the grown woman and three younger selves representing earlier stages in her life. He healed the rift between these various incarnations of her developing personality, attaining reconciliation on the premise (if I understood the author) that mental health is attainable only when we have assimilated our various selves instead of rejecting them (as the disturbed heroine had done throughout the greater part of the play).

In ingeniously disintegrating his heroine before integrating her, Mr. Laurents became involved with four complicated persons, whereas even one of these would have given enough trouble to a playwright. The exposition of the play had to repeat itself several times and the author had to attend to four plot and character developments instead of one. The play had a disconcerting way of initiating an action and then starting up another one. Perhaps the author's logic could be proved quite acceptable, but the validity of his argument could not by itself prevent playgoers from forming only fragmentary impressions. In trying to overcome diffuseness Mr. Laurents struggled manfully for lean action and taut relationships. It is a tribute to his talent and resourcefulness that he nearly succeeded; just as one's interest dropped, the action or the problem took a turn that restored attention or recovered concern.

Fundamentally, *A Clearing in the Woods* was a case of all the king's horses and all the king's men being unable to put Humpty-Dumpty together again. We came to know the parts of the heroine's personality rather than the person herself. Her past, distributed at the various levels of her case history, overshadowed her present, which had to be glimpsed mainly at the beginning and the end of the drama. Yet the heroine's struggle for health could have a clear significance only if the total person mattered to us *in the present*. The dramatic worth of the partitioned heroine needed to be established; and here is where the question of values arises. Dramatic worth was simply assumed. The play was an excellent example of the modern tendency to interest ourselves overwhelmingly in character as a social or psychological problem until the problem overshadows the person.

The failure of the Broadway production distressed me not only because *A Clearing in the Woods* had intrinsic merits, but because I had invested much hope in the author's career ever since *Home of the Brave*. Fortunately, the author more than retrieved his fortunes after *A Clearing in the Woods* as the librettist of the successful musicals *West Side Story* and *Gypsy*, both of which he supplied with story elements that helped to give American musicals respectable status as a form of drama. But because of my regard for the author I very much hope that he will write a play before long that shows his stature as an independent author. Dramatic talent and intelligence such as his have been anything but abundant in our mid-century theatre.

Faulkner: *Requiem for a Nun*

The constant playgoer assesses Broadway theatre norms by the productions he supports. Faulkner's *Requiem for a Nun* and Williams' *Sweet*

Bird of Youth recommended themselves to playgoers of the 1958-59 season chiefly because of their morbid intensity. The best way to counteract
the bland healthiness that characterizes domestic and liberal drama of
the commercial theatre is by an open concern with *unhealthiness*. Unfortunately the risks of flying in the face of playgoing habits are considerable; unless sensationalism runs amok on the stage—in which case public
taste rises manfully to the challenge and swells the box-office receipts—
unpleasantness simply does not pay off.

Normally a play like *A Raisin in the Sun* wins abundant support for
its simple realism while a putrescent production arriving in New York
after a flourishing tour in the outlands is quickly snuffed out by a bad
press and public indifference. But though the New York theatre audience may be puritanical and high-minded, it is usually willing to be
seduced under accredited intellectual auspices. Decently mediocre work
may be overrated because its sentiments are approvable, but plays of
honorable intent and acrid matter can be too quickly dismissed in this
sanctimonious milieu.

It was easy to underrate the Broadway production of Faulkner's
Requiem for a Nun. It was a bleak and oppressive play despite the efforts
of an energetic cast headed by Ruth Ford in the role of the sordid heroine,
Temple Drake. Miss Ford appeared to have gone out of her way to convey a personality whose salvation or damnation was a matter of complete
indifference to the spectator. Faulkner demands our attention to this cold-
hearted and lecherous woman, to her weakling of a husband, and to a
half-witted Negro servant, Nancy, who has been Temple's companion
in a brothel. For all the alleged nobility of her soul Nancy was really
too witless to draw more than momentary pity from us when she is sen-
tenced to death. She is guilty of infanticide, having murdered Temple's
child in order to dissuade the mother from committing adultery. Characters for whom a novelist can make valid claims of interest are apt to look
painfully barren on the stage under the merciless spotlights.

The logic of *Requiem for a Nun* was shaky, and whatever motivation
it had was largely invalidated by the worthlessness of the central stage
character. In the novel from which the play was adapted, she is the
Temple Drake of *Sanctuary* who becomes Mrs. Gowan Stevens. In playing Temple, who is supposed to be only twenty-five years old, Miss Ford
lacked the volatility and grace of youth, and she seemed too hardened
in sensibility to arouse our sympathy or concern. The action that finally

forces her to confess her evil past seemed imposed, and it muddled the play instead of giving it a consistent motivation. Temple's dreadful past in a Southern bordello, where she had been placed by an impotent pervert for voyeuristic gratification, is dredged up apparently to save Nancy from execution as a self-confessed murderess. The expiatory act of confession supposedly saves Temple's own soul. But the effect is only one of maladroit sensationalism.

There is little point in dwelling upon the defects of the play or production. No matter how poorly adapted for Broadway success *Requiem for a Nun* could command more respect than most productions of the 1958-59 Broadway season. It had impressive severity and a dissolving and suggestive atmosphere. Mr. Faulkner and Miss Ford, who evidently helped to adapt the play, required concentration from the playgoer even though ultimately they did not succeed in rewarding it. Some playgoers felt complimented or challenged by the hard substance of this unattractive work. Many were also irritated at the elusive ugliness of the theme, but at least they were not drugged by banality or fed a nursing bottle of sugared water. With a younger and more appealing heroine it is even possible that *Requiem for a Nun* might have provided some poetry of compassion and salvation in the febrile night of Faulkner's Gothic nightmare.

William Inge and the Subtragic Muse:
The Dark at the Top of the Stairs

The high place William Inge has occupied in the American theatre of the Fifties has been gratifying to me. I believe I was among the first to take an interest in his work before Broadway embraced him, and I have a deep personal regard for him. For the public his success has posed no problems, for he is an observant and sympathetic playwright who has not made extravagant demands upon his audience. He has provided the gratifications of recognition rather than discovery. But to me—and, I suspect, to him, too—his success since the production of *Come Back, Little Sheba* in 1950 has been somewhat ambiguous. It was especially so to me in the case of the Broadway production of *The Dark at the Top of the Stairs* during the 1957-58 season. Whereas Williams and Miller had failures as well as triumphs, play after play of Inge's succeeded; he did not have a single failure on Broadway until the production of *Loss of Roses* during the 1959-60 season, and he did not win a single meretricious success. Nevertheless, he has rarely been considered the equal of Williams and Miller even by his warmest admirers.

In play after play Inge has brought the lives of ordinary American men, women, and children alive on the stage, and he has moved and amused us with their fortunes. Frequently he has fallen just short of achieving a shattering experience. His technique and style of writing have been limited in range, depth, and challenge, and his demands on stagecraft have not exceeded the resources of familiar realism. But he has avoided playing a larger and more serious gambit with his characters. Both in *Picnic* and *The Dark at the Top of the Stairs* it seemed as if he were about to cross over into a more challenging terrain of playwriting, only to allow himself to be pulled back at the barrier. Our usual disinclination to produce tragic drama is also revealed in an Inge production, and especially so by *The Dark at the Top of the Stairs*. Judgment is not easily rendered against a playwright and his collaborators in any deviation from tragic art. But judgment is necessary, and explanations must be sought in the case of this play which captivated large audiences and was memorable for Elia Kazan's vigorous yet sensitive direction.

I

Like the mitigating mildness and leniency of the last acts of most successful American satirical comedies, the evasion of tragedy has long been an observed shortcoming of our drama. Our playwrights and stage directors are often too easily satisfied with surface realism to be aware of the necessity of carrying potentially tragic or satiric plays to their proper conclusion. Sometimes a writer, producer, or director is conscious of his compromise or even deliberate in employing it in behalf of bigger box-office receipts. (George S. Kaufman once explained that he didn't really write satire for Broadway because "Satire is what closes Saturday night.")

Sometimes there is complicity in the material itself, in characters difficult to dignify and situations impossible to present as tragically inevitable or insoluble. Even the playwright's integrity may impede the movement toward tragic climax; he may reject a tragic interpretation on the grounds that it would falsify his observations. William Inge is one of the most talented playwrights of our mid-century theatre, and those of us who have known him ever since he began his career in the mid-Forties would not hesitate to testify under oath that his probity as a writer is unquestionable. But it has been suggested that he is more susceptible to the changes requested by producers or directors than he should be. That question arose when he put aside one ending in favor of another, less corrosive one urged upon him by Director Joshua Logan during the production of *Picnic*; it rose again with *The Dark at the Top of the Stairs*. But it would be rash to assume that the ending favored by the director of *Picnic* was the wrong one or that the original conclusion would have turned the play into a tragedy. The problem was whether the heroine, a pretty, nubile but otherwise unremarkable girl, should run away with an athletic young vagrant after he has been forced to leave town.

In the original version the girl stayed home in a Midwestern town with her mother and faced the possibility of a life of frustration similar to her neighbors'. In the Broadway version the heroine allows the young man to depart alone, and then, rejecting warnings and seeing her mother's arid life as a warning, follows him to the city.

Picnic is within obvious limits a vivid and moving play. It undoubtedly owed some of its popularity to the effective staging, and it is possible that the upbeat ending increased its appeal. The author himself was clearly of two minds, as almost any playwright might be under the pressure of tense rehearsal and try-out periods. He continued to be of two minds long after the premiére. He sanctioned a Midwestern production that restored his original ending and contemplated the restoration of this ending with some further underpinning for a Random House collection of his plays. In preparing the fifth volume of my *Best American Plays* series I offerred Inge an opportunity to restore the ending or to print it side-by-side with the Broadway version. He appeared to welcome the opportunity, but ultimately preferred to have me reprint the Broadway version because a restoration of the original would have required other alterations earlier in the play. He hoped to be able to make these for the Random House edition of his collected plays, but when this volume appeared, *Picnic* still had only the Broadway ending.

Inge was entitled to these vacillations because of the nature of his material, and his notable honesty would not allow him to take an absolute stand on so delicate a mater. I have recited these details in order to make several points. It is as unjust as it is obtuse to attack a genuinely creative director such as Joshua Logan or Elia Kazan because he has persuaded a playwright out of one treatment into another. It is equally unjust and obtuse to attack a playwright for having allowed himself to be persuaded. The playwright cannot always be certain that one treatment is better than another, and sometimes cannot even be firmly in favor of one ending rather than another.

2

The question of whether William Inge should or should not have written *Picnic* as a tragedy may seem pointless, but some commentators were disappointed that the play did not attain sharper definition and a more drastic conclusion. This was a well-etched genre painting of small town life, reaching a verdict on the frustrations of provincial women and the stalemate of men in a dreary environment. Yet it was inadequate and some critical playgoers questioned the validity and even the integrity of the ending. According to them the happy conclusion of the girl's escape evaded tragic consequences. Without entirely agreeing, I did feel a want of passionate playwriting in the play; and *The Dark at the Top of the Stairs* proved equally frustrating, despite its good reviews and box-office popularity. It was a moving play with excellently drawn characters, and in a world where masterpieces are scarce it was entitled to its success. But much of the effect was the result of arresting fragments combined without emotional or logical necessity, fragments that point to a devastating resolution. But both author and director elected another conclusion that is possible, since nearly everything in life is possible, yet hardly probable and certainly less compelling.

The play concerns the fear of the dark at the top of the stairs, the unknown, that haunts Inge's Midwestern family. The dark, fear of the future in general and of sex in particular, could be anxiety in almost any form from almost any source. The specific problem, explored with noteworthy sensitivity, concerns incomprehension or failure of communication among people. Children are caught up in their parents' marital complications; a father is incapable of admitting defeat to his wife (he is a harness salesman in the dawning age of the automobile in Oklahoma); a mother is overprotective toward her little boy and overinsistent in trying to steer her husband into another business; a daughter's extreme shyness results indirectly in the suicide of a lonely Jewish schoolboy; an excessively animated but sexually starved aunt crushes her mild-mannered husband with her domineering personality. Like much of the author's work, it is a group play and is excellently orchestrated.

In the first act of *The Dark at the Top of the Stairs* a baseless quarrel between husband and wife results in his departure. The tension arises from the husband's inability to communicate his anxieties to his wife and from the latter's failure to realize how frightened of the future this superficially confident man is. The rift in their relations serves to expose the children's unhappiness in their suddenly broken home: the ingrown character of the little boy, and the adolescent problems of the teen-age daughter and her sense of guilt over the Jewish schoolboy's suicide. But a curious thing happens: the harness salesman returns home, quickly becomes reconciled to his wife, tries to get the children out of the house by sending them to a movie, and draws his wife upstairs. Love, it is implied, will master the dark at the top of the stairs.

Although they felt some uneasiness with the solution playgoers in general were not dissatisfied. (A minority did find the suicide of the Jewish cadet out of place, and others complained of the patchiness of the work.) Though usually rated the best of Inge's plays, this well-received drama failed to make as profound an impression as the main matter and several moving scenes would lead one to expect. I felt that we had been fobbed off with a facile resolution and that, while individual scenes rang true, the play as a whole was synthetic. The Jewish cadet's drama was dragged in, and the play, sometimes veering toward comedy and sometimes toward tragedy, was inconsistent in tone.

Whether by original design or later calculation the final form was polished as a *show* rather than as a completed drama; it offered something for everybody rather than a consistent reality for somebody. I did not believe for a moment that the children, upon whom much of the attention was focused, would have their problems resolved by the father's return. They seemed doomed to neurosis; their father's return, especially *this* father's return, could not save them. The last scene of the play, the prodigal lummox beckoning his wife upstairs to bed while trying to get the kids out of the house, struck me as forcibly and inharmoniously comic. I had little stomach for comedy after observing the suffering of the children and experiencing the penumbral mood of the scenes just past. It was impossible for me to put them out of mind in watching the facile resolution.

The elision of tragedy in *The Dark at the Top of the Stairs* was understandable. The principal characters were two children and four second-rate adults who hardly qualified for high-tragic status. To force tragedy on them might well have been extreme. But the attempt to offer *The Dark at the Top of the Stairs* as a comedy was also unconvincing after the first domestic quarrel scene. Only the playgoer with very modest expectations and little regard for the author's talent could be satisfied with the "happy ending" resolution. Surely the frustrations and guilts of the characters and the suicide of the cadet show that the author's deepest emotions lay elsewhere than in a comedy of domestic relations.

It appeared to me that William Inge's rare talent had once more had its potential strength diminished and diverted by his material, by his otherwise admirably moderate and considerate temperament, and possibly by the pressures of the Broadway super-market. On a subtragic level the play proved arresting. The playgoer could be satisfied by a succession of almost Chekhovian scenes of observation, conflict, and recognition, so long as one desisted from trying to put them together. There were wonderful things to remember in addition to the convincing performances of Theresa Wright, as the abandoned wife, Pat Hingle, as the temporarily absconding husband, and the defensively breezy aunt played by the vibrant actress Eileen Heckart. Charles Saari played the disordered family's unhappy little son with poignant conviction; and Timmy Everett as Sammy Goldenbaum, son of a broken home who is kept at a military school by his irresponsible mother, was responsible for the most unforgettable scene of the production when he calls on the daughter to take her to a dance.

The Dark at the Top of the Stairs, considered both as a play and a production, had all the ingredients of the masterpiece which its author has repeatedly been on the verge of writing. But these ingredients were not blended by a sufficiently determined intent. Whatever his actual intention in *The Dark at the Top of the Stairs,* he appears to have been most deeply concerned with traumatic family rifts and their devastating effect on children. But his group play technique tends to dissolve this central drama in favor of peripheral themes, chiefly the mistakes that women make in trying to run men's lives. Everything Inge shows us here seems to be authentic, but his several truths weaken the one truth. A play about family trauma would have produced a more gripping and fully realized drama, a successful or unsuccessful *major* drama rather than a successful minor play. As it stands, *The Dark at the Top of the Stairs* is successful because it is many things to its audience. It moves the public without shattering it, and provokes middle-aged relief when the errant husband returns, is reconciled with his wife, and comically beckons her upstairs.

In the last Inge play of the decade, the unfortunate *A Loss of Roses* (unfortunate, especially, because the Broadway production was very inadequate), a solution to a potentially tragic or at least desperate situation is also reached with more optimism than conviction and less struggle than wishful thinking. The mother-fixated young hero goes to bed once with his mother's friend, a stranded tent-show actress, and this single experience is apparently enough to emancipate him from incestuous desires.

From the author's own account in *Esquire,* we learn that Inge wanted to write "a Venus-Adonis story, an older-woman-and-younger-man story." He further defines his intention by declaring, "I wanted to show how incest exists in everyday lives, and show how I have observed it in everyday life." The two statements make me wonder whether Inge has not been an easy mark for two current trends: the tendency to psychologize relationships by placing undue emphasis on the Oedipus complex and the assumption that with this hypothesis we are creating and conveying character in depth, whereas we are only standardizing it with modish analyses.

William Inge needs a larger and more original vision than psychotherapy affords if his fine symphonic gifts are to come completely into focus. Even when the psychoanalytical motivations on which he relies are absorbing and compelling in the dramatic action, he does not carry them to the ultimate tragic conclusion. Instead he contents himself with such questionable solutions as the return of the father in *The Dark at the Top of the Stairs* or the successful exorcism of a fixation by one night of love in *A Loss of Roses.*

Whatever psychiatry can do, it cannot take the place of *dramatic* logic and *tragic* vision.

John Osborne's *Look Back in Anger*

John Osborne's *Look Back in Anger* won considerable support on Broadway for its pungent realism. The work was unmistakable evidence of new talent, and both its merits and limitations are significant. The play came to us strongly, and not altogether correctly, recommended as the first serious effort of the younger generation in England. New York critics were pleased to discover that England could still produce a work of passion and protest instead of its customary drawing-room amenities and acerbities. But some of us thought of this drama as the conclusion rather than the beginning of an era of playwriting, as a blind alley rather than as a vision of promise and advance.

The subject of the play is the despair of a generation that has only bitter memories of past betrayals of ideals. The rancorous young hero's father had fought in the Spanish civil war on the Republican side. The son, who operates a sweets stall in London, can only look back in anger and toward a void in the future. He lashes out at those who are closest to him, especially his long-suffering, upper-class wife, in a vain effort to assuage his sense of futility and stalemate. His wife leaves him at last, but with a woman's tenderness for her suffering man she returns to care for him and to try to fill the void in her own life, left by the loss of her baby.

Whatever the merits of the writing, and they are considerable, Look Back in Anger is limited by the nihilism of its author and the crackle and sputter of fireworks in a mist. For a play characterized by admirably sustained dialogue and taut, fragmentary conflicts Look Back in Anger was curiously unsatisfying. The irritation, even outrage, that I noted in the audience during the intermissions was unique in my playgoing experience. Most Broadway playgoers were fascinated by the superb performances of Mary Ure as the wife and Kenneth Haigh as the angry husband, and by the passion and expressive power of the writing. But they left the theatre desolated rather than purged.

The realism of seedy settings, vibrant acting, forthright staging, the sordid story, and the pungent dialogue was altogether appropriate here. But in the context of the play the realistic refinements are only arid achievements. There was a time, not so very long ago, when it was possible to associate realistic art with a positive attitude rather than with the negations of a Look Back in Anger. Positive realism is rare today, and as often as not it is indirect and ambiguous; it is a glow in the dark rather than a spacious sunburst. Only the nihilism of a Williams or Osborne releases the full voltage of realism on our stage, and the effect of the work as a whole is likely to be less gratifying than the effect of individual scenes. Direct affirmativeness produces mainly the torpid flow of such mildly optimistic liberal writings as The Prescott Proposals.

Equally symptomatic is the inconclusiveness present in the literature of protest. The energy of even so intense a work as *Look Back in Anger* begins to run out after the first act, and the wife's return at the end leads to no particular conclusion. John Osborne's vigorous writing cannot move ahead full steam when he presumably believes he has nowhere to go. The weakening of *Look Back in Anger* after the first act is perhaps the most conclusive evidence we have that modern drama is in a state of crisis. Modern stage realism was the product of both anger and hope. Now only the anger provides energy; the hope, producing mostly mild problem plays and liberal tracts in dialogue, only debilitates. While Ibsen and his school led the theatre modern realism was a mark of health. Outraged Victorian moralists characterized it as decadence then and, ironically now that our professional moralists no longer trouble themselves over the state of the theatre, they may yet be proved right.

I cannot join those who consider every sign of subsiding realism a mark of progress or those who exult over this state of affairs in the contemporary theatre. We are not yet ready to dismiss realism categorically. The fact is that *Look Back in Anger* begins with the jet propulsion of stripped emotion and makes most flights of fancy and poetry in our theatre seem unexciting.

Epitaph for George Dillon and *The Entertainer*

A play easy to underrate in America is *Epitaph for George Dillion*, written by England's angry young man, John Osborne, with Anthony Creighton, an English actor. The theme of the play is surrender, specifically the submission of a playwright and actor of some talent to the seedy lower middle-class life he has always scorned. When he resigns himself to grinding out trash for a broker of cheap but successful plays and to marrying a crude young girl he made pregnant in a moment of desperation his self-styled epitaph reads, "Here lies George Dillon . . . who hoped he was that mysterious ridiculous being called an artist."

It was miraculous that the authors and actor Robert Stephens, who played the title role of both the Broadway and London productions, could command the interest and sympathy of some reviewers, for George Dillon is a decidedly irritating person. Credit for surmounting this obstacle must go to the force of the writing and the acting. (There was also an espe-

cially fine performance by Eileen Herlie as the one person who understands and bears with Dillon's unpleasant traits until he allows himself
to be trapped into professional and domestic mediocrity.) Perhaps the
most effective aspect of the play was the depiction of the arid lower
middle-class world upon which Dillon sponges before his defeat. It was
the authors' ability to capture a pervasive wasteland emotion, with its
attendant feelings of scorn and indignation, rather than any sympathy
for Dillon as a character that won adherents for the play.

By showing George Dillon in a relentlessly unheroic light Osborne
and Creighton refused to indulge the public in its customary idealization
of artists as nobly starving geniuses. Instead of relying on this romantic
tradition which might have made Dillon lovable, they tried to win
approval with the realistic approach that most would-be artists are men
of only moderate talent and will.

In comparison with the star actress of *Sweet Bird of Youth,* young
Dillon is a mild character. His restiveness is understandable, his mockery
of others is patently a form of self-flagellation, and the collapse of his
resistance to the seductions and encroachments of the commonplace is
curiously moving. We may feel that he deserves a dressing down, but we
are unwilling to ratify his defeat as a good thing. His airs of superiority
are his defense against the desiccation that he fears in himself and in
the surrounding world. The purpose of the authors of *Epitaph* was to
expose. They exposed a truth capable of disturbing and stirring us, for
Dillon, the figure of the floundering demiurge in our society, is unfortunately representative. Our world is full of Dillons who gradually sink
into a morass of hack professionalism and barren respectability, and who
become discontented providers for families they frequently didn't want.
The fierce mask of their youth and aspiration disappears; a drowsy numb-
ness overpowers them until they become as pitiable as they were once
unendurable. In its insight into such characters *Epitaph* is disturbingly
revealing and ultimately compassionate.

Osborne's previous Broadway production, *The Entertainer,* had one
advantage that *Epitaph* lacked: a star personality that could attract the
public even when play and role did not. Sir Laurence Olivier's characterization of a seedy English music-hall comedian was nothing short of
brilliant, and he received unfailing support from Brenda da Banzie in
the role of the long-suffering wife.

This play struck reviewers as a drab showpiece that was only an excuse for displaying the chameleon talent of Olivier. Broadway's judgment may have had some basis, but we should also have remembered that it takes talent for a playwright to draw common characters as uncommonly as Osborne did. To make a vulgar smart-alecky vaudevillian, Archie Rice, win our sympathy without dissolving our judgment requires insight and skill. Though Archie is aware that he is a crashing failure in show business, music-hall entertainment is all the business he knows or cares to know and he rejects an opportunity to leave the scene of his failures. He will not renounce his claim to being a very special insolvent, rather than an ordinary, solvent individual. He is a music-hall Willie Loman in a tight, untragic spot. Yet he meant more than that to his author; there is a suggestion that Osborne's hoofer may represent Britannia groggy from the blows she has sustained in the postwar winter of her discontent. But chiefly Archie is the whole of tawdry, bumbling, and persistent humanity; this slouching, slithering, grimly merrymaking comic's apologetic eyes and hunched-up shoulders spoke for all bankrupt mankind.

Though it had a richer dramatic structure there was less opportunity for bravura acting in *Epitaph for George Dillon,* yet it won avid supporters. Undoubtedly the two depressed plays which followed Osborne's first angry one will have longer careers than their life on Broadway suggests (particularly *Epitaph* since it is not only a better sustained play than *Look Back in Anger* but one less dependent upon star casting).

It is probably true that the drama of nontragic failure will have to be translated into more familiar terms for the popular theatre in America. This may not be an easy thing to do without a firmer grasp of social reality than has been shown in the Fifties. Miller's *Death of a Salesman,* produced on Broadway in 1949, did not have a single worthy successor during the next decade except possibly his own social tragedy, *The Crucible.*

Too Late the Phalarope:
Alternatives in Social Drama

Broadway is sufficiently discouraged from risking investments in weighty dramas for us to wonder how a play such as *Too Late the Phalarope* manages to get produced. It is greatly to the credit of the managements that they stage plays of this character more often than do producers in London and Paris. Unfortunately, the credit frequently goes more to laudable intentions than to achievement.

In the dramatization of Alan Paton's South African novel the producer's aims were particularly high. This is a story of race relations that culminates in the tragic isolation of a Transvaal police officer who has fallen honorably in love with a Kaffir girl. When Mary K. Frank decided to produce *Too Late the Phalarope* in 1956 she knew that it would be difficult to win an audience. It was too balanced and too circumspect a play to attract the public with sensationalism or with political partisanship, but Miss Frank obviously spared neither effort nor expense in its support. The tragic role of the officer was filled by the appealing actor Barry Sullivan. The officer hero's elderly father was played superbly by Finlay Currie, a seventy-eight-year-old Scot actor who made his American debut in this production. There was not a poor performance in the entire production staged by John Stix, who had made his own Broadway directorial debut only a few years before with *Take a Giant Step*. Settings and lighting by George Jenkins deserved all the praise they received. Every detail of the production was indeed commendable, and an especially gratifying feature was a score by the South African composer Josef Marais.

Because of the attention lavished on Robert Yale Libott's dramatization the work earned respect for everyone associated with it. But *Too Late the Phalarope* could not win its bout with the Broadway public. To do so it would have had to be a stronger play in every respect. Even the third and most powerful act, in which the emphasis rested on the intolerant Transvaal father who rejected and abandoned his son, Lieutenant Pieter van Vlaanderen, left a curious out-of-focus impression. The author should have concentrated his light on the young man himself if the play was to be charged with dramatic meaning. The old man's problem by comparison with his son's was quite secondary, and his inflexible attitude could hold no surprises for anyone. The play was Pieter's drama rather than his father's. Pieter's collapse as a character comes after the discovery of his affair with the native girl. The play is unfortunately too concerned with the theme of white intolerance in South Africa which has been obvious from the beginning and has been hammered into our consciousness in several previous episodes. The personal tragedy of Pieter, a decent man torn between a cold wife and a seductive native girl, is itself rather blunted by the fact that he feels thoroughly guilty in violating the racial code.

One of the limitations of Broadway criticism is that it places too much reliance on craft. It assumes that skill can effect what only conviction actually can. In *Too Late the Phalarope* the belief that racial intolerance is an evil was presented half-heartedly. This was evident particularly in the third act when Lieutenant Pieter drops out of the play without either insight or protest, and all that is asked for him by the sympathetic police captain is *forgiveness* after due punishment. This resolution of the play might have had sensational impact in South Africa, but hardly in New York. The flaw in conception is also observable in the constant attribution of Pieter's fall from grace to the coldness of his Caucasian wife—as unattractive a woman as anyone could present in a poor sinner's defense before the Judgment Seat. The play structure was made soggy by obscurely symbolic talk about a bird that had no function whatsoever in the play. Altogether it was evident that the playwright was directing attention to peripheral considerations.

The dramatization of *Too Late the Phalarope* vividly illustrates the dilemma that faces writers of social drama today. They either demonstrate a point of view by composing a work vitiated by flat characters, one-sided attitudes, and one-dimensional writing, or else they attend to characterization in the round and lose their sense of direction. There is another alternative: to write a genuine drama of social conflict. But nobody in the American theatre except Arthur Miller has recently brought much mind or passion to it. There is a fourth alternative: to create the kind of poetically conclusive drama about inconclusiveness that Chekhov created and that unfortunately only he had the genius to write.

There is a final alternative. It is to make tragedy out of life's impossibilities and out of the impasses that men seem fated to encounter in a given time or place, impasses to which they tragically succumb or through which they must hew a path of tragic self-sacrifice. Sartre has pointed to this alternative as Ibsen pointed to it somewhat differently in the nineteenth century. Arthur Miller also has looked in this direction.

It is this final alternative that the dramatist of *Too Late the Phalarope* seemed to be seeking. If so, his was an honorable search made too infrequently by his contemporaries. But in this play it was apparent that the search for tragedy was hobbled by sociological considerations and sidetracked by psychological ones: a father-son conflict only tenuously related to the racial issue. Tragic force made itself felt to some degree in the last act, but unfortunately it tended to obscure rather than to clarify the play. It was even doubtful whether the tragic flaw and tragic stature were assigned to the right person; both qualities seemed to belong less to the young hero of the play than to the obdurate old Transvaal father who locked his heart against him.

Obviously these reflections have been aired at length more for the sake of examining the plight of serious social drama than for the limited purpose of criticizing an incompletely realized play.

Nash: A Handful of Fire

The dangers of providing the commercial stage with big plays are most apparent when the alternative of producing small ones is attractive. *A Handful of Fire* by N. Richard Nash, who was more fortunate earlier in the Fifties with his folksy comedy *The Rainmaker,* was an outstanding example of a potentially delicate play converted into a labored spectacle. The temptation to theatrical largesse which seemed to mesmerize author, producers, and director lay in the esoteric nature of the characters and their environment. In electing to write an allegory the author chose an excellent plot with which to represent the conflict between absolute good and evil. He then proceeded consciously to undermine his whole premise.

The play is set in a Mexican border town. Pepe, a naïvely innocent Mexican youth living in an age of large and small dictators, has no inkling of the way of the world. He comes into contact with arbitrary power as represented by Manuel, the owner of a gambling casino as well as nearly everything else in the town. Pepe tries valiantly to shed his innocence and to become one of Manuel's henchmen, and he might succeed in his ambitions if he does not make the mistake of falling in love. Complications multiply because his loved one has been the mistress of the town's racketeer-boss; Pepe discovers that Maria is not as innocent as she seems, and Manuel tries to get rid of Pepe. Nothing goes well for Pepe and Maria until the end of the play, when love teaches them to forgive each other. Nothing goes well for Manuel either. He could have won an easy victory over his hapless rival, but love for Maria has made him irresolute in the clinches.

This fable, told ruefully and with a sprinkling of humor, could have made a pleasant little comedy. The mistake lay in trying to make it a pleasant *big* one. The production assumed musical comedy and big-time melodrama proportions, though the author tried to maintain the fragility of the Pepe-Maria romance and the director undertook to keep the local color and folk poetry intact.

A Handful of Fire is an example of how show business strives to make the best of both worlds. The drama became overweighted with intrigue, comic and sinister gangsterism, and even bordello drama (including such old chestnuts as the sentimental middle-aged madam and the soul-pure, love-stricken teen-age inmate). Nothing was left to the imagination after the promising first quarter of an hour. In Pepe's self-conscious and self-pitying awareness of the precarious status of innocence in a venal world the play had the makings of a lyrical little piece spiced with pathos and irony. It also had the ingredients for a sardonic view of love, for the infatuated Manuel loses his bearings as soon as he abandons the consistency of villainy. But in the whirl of action and counteraction the potentialities of *A Handful of Fire* rapidly lost their advantage. The play was neither delicate enough for poetic romance nor sharp enough for satire. As a result the acting and direction, altogether excellent at the beginning, deteriorated during the course of the play.

The theatre being what it is, *A Handful of Fire* closed just as quickly as many a worse play, losing its investors a tidy $150,000. There is irony and a kind of rough justice in the probability that it would have been one-half as unsatisfactory if it had cost only half as much. At least there would have been the considerable gain of only half as much monotony caused by the elaboration of the obvious. Moral: There are times and occasions when the theatre can satisfy most by daring to be little.

4 PAST AND PRESENT

American Shakespeare: *Othello, Much Ado About Nothing,* and *The Merchant of Venice*

Nothing on Broadway during the end of the 1956-57 season was comparable in interest or importance to what transpired on the periphery that extends to Stratford, Connecticut, during the summer. For better or worse, the American Shakespeare Festival Theatre acquired a Broadway professionalism in nearly every sense of the term, and only with this standard in mind can an assessment of its work be made. The one thing Stratford did not have in its second and third seasons was a reverential, ritualistic, or academic attitude. The first season, which was both ritualistic and academic, was a disastrous failure. But subsequently, under the guidance of the distinguished producer-director John Houseman, who resigned his post at the close of the 1959 season, the American Shakespeare Festival Theatre became a generally successful enterprise. Its third season was especially gratifying to large audiences and to most reviewers, leaving only scholar-critics in a state ranging from polite perturbation to a keen sense of outrage.

The selection of plays for the 1957 season was excellent. *Othello, The Merchant of Venice,* and *Much Ado about Nothing* represent Shakespeare's mastery of tragedy, romantic drama, and comedy of manners. The cast, headed by Katharine Hepburn, Alfred Drake, Earle Hyman, and Morris Carnovsky, was the best since the Festival Theatre had opened. Though the casting was not ideal in every production John Houseman managed to collect the best repertory company we have had in the United States since the short-lived Theatre Guild Acting Company in 1926. It became evident after the third production, *Much Ado about Nothing,* that repertory *suited* the performers, something that cannot be said about other hastily assembled and briefly sustained American repertory companies within recent memory.

Alfred Drake never gave better performances than his Iago and Benedick; and Katharine Hepburn's Portia and Beatrice surpassed every performance of hers since her portrayal of Tracy in *The Philadelphia Story* nearly twenty years before. Only in the grandfather role of *Awake and Sing!* had that deep and noble actor Morris Carnovsky equaled the performance he gave as Shylock. If there has been a better balanced and more fully realized Shylock than Carnovsky's in the entire stage history of *The Merchant of Venice* it is not apparent to me from my personal experience or reading.

Only Earle Hyman failed to rise sufficiently to his major assignment, the coveted role of Othello. He was a lightweight in the role; whereas only a heavyweight can make the Moor tragic and credible rather than pathetic and fatuous in the eyes of the twentieth-century nonoperatic public. Actually Hyman gave more of an acting performance than did Paul Robeson, the most memorable Moor of our times. But despite an impressive physical appearance, Hyman's appealing personality seemed frail, whereas Robeson had brought to the role a monolithic grandeur that was sufficient for tragedy even when he did very little acting.

Many people tried to *explain* Hyman's Othello, but nobody tried to explain Robeson's—nobody had to. The playing of the part should not lead us into too close a search for psychological motivation. It is a search that may have interesting results for the scholar-critic but that tends to weaken Shakespeare's tragedy: the story of the fall of a lofty man. We read Shakespeare amiss and we play his tragic heroes unsatisfactorily when we have to resort to psychological explanations. Nowadays we often tend to confuse character creation and psychology. If a character in a play is sufficiently rounded and alive he does not have to be explained; it is enough to *experience* him and temporarily join our life with his. In *The Merchant of Venice*, however, Earle Hyman gave a delightfully comic performance as the Prince of Morocco, in which his acting intelligence and vivid personality gave the role a stylized flamboyance.

The playing of many minor parts in the three plays was an especially encouraging aspect of the productions. Richard Waring's melancholy Antonio in *The Merchant*, Sada Thompson's Emilia in *Othello*, Lois Nettleton's Nerissa in *The Merchant*, and Richard Easton's excellent

Claudio and John Colicos' Leonato in *Much Ado* were all commendable. It is always heartening to see a good acting company come into being and it was a pity that such valuable actors of the previous season as Nina Foch and Arnold Moss had disappeared from the roster.

The difficulties of maintaining a permanent professional company for only a three-months' season each year are enormous. When the results prove as good as they did during the summer of 1957, one's appetite for a permanent repertory theatre is whetted. But probably only a year-round commitment could prevent continual defections from a repertory company, and with the seductions of Hollywood and star salaries even that might not be enough. We can only be grateful that so good a cast was assembled and made to harmonize its performances so well in so little time. The company was a credit to Houseman and to Jack Landau, the associate director. Their joint staging of *Much Ado* and Landau's direction of *The Merchant* were full of brilliantly theatrical details.

Particularly gratifying was the deft use of the classic eccyclema for representing interior scenes. Like the Germans, we have usually over-produced our plays on Broadway with the use of stage machinery. In two Stratford productions the scenery, far from lumbering forward, seemed to dance and twinkle into position. The same expressive lightness, combined with an effortless economy in the use of space, appeared in other scenic elements—notably a Venetian bridge used for several effects in *The Merchant* and the gates and balcony of the *Much Ado* setting. The locale of *Much Ado* was our own Spanish-colonial Southwest, a director's conceit to which exception could be taken. Yet all the settings contributed by Rouben ter-Arutunian with help from Jean Rosenthal and Tharon Musser avoided arty extremism as much as strict regionalism. Even in the case of *Much Ado* the directors avoided travesty in making their Texan locale a gay mélange of styles. There was a lively mingling of Spanish grandees, Mexican peóns, American cowboys, and Western sheriffs (Dogberry and his watchmen) on the stage. Except for a few wild pistol shots the spirit of this production was more Viennese than Southwestern.

But praise for the productions cannot be unqualified, for each had its special limitations. *Othello* managed to be passably tragic only because the antagonist rather than the protagonist provided the essence of tragedy. Earle Hyman conveyed a harassed Othello, but as Iago, Alfred Drake provided a melancholy obsessiveness and somber malice that had tragic grandeur. Drake made attendance at this *Othello* rewarding, but he could not compensate for the absence of a true "fall from an eminence" in the case of "the noble Moor" by arrogating tragic qualities to himself.

The *Merchant* production had many splendors, among them the superb casket scene with Miss Hepburn coaching Donald Harron's excellent Bassanio from the side lines. But the celebrated trial scene, Shakespeare's pièce de résistance, lost conviction in Miss Hepburn's choppily nervous reading of the "quality of mercy" speech. (This interpretation may have been deliberately adopted for comic effect, but it made the speech ineffectual.) And the garden scene never had the final magic needed to dissolve the play into poetry. Despite the unity that kindly disposed scholar-critics find in it, *The Merchant* is a play composed of disparate elements. There is only one solvent for Shylock's anger, Antonio's melancholia, Bassanio's and Lorenzo's romances, Portia's and Nerissa's playfulness, the other suitor's foibles, and the two Gobbos' farce. That solvent is Shakespeare's poetry of language and of theatre, here an unimpeded flow of moods, sensations, and sympathies.

The *Much Ado about Nothing* production raises some questions about the objectives of Shakespearian theatre in the United States. Are we going to Americanize Shakespeare in institutionalizing him? How far can modernization go and still be Shakespeare? Early in the *Much Ado* proceedings, I was infuriated by the unnecessary sacrilege. But as the production evolved I was pleased, though not altogether reconciled to the treatment, by the beauty of the staging and decor, the charm of many of the performances, and the anachronistically amusing fresh treatment of Dogberry and the watch as a Western posse. For once Dogberry and his low-comic associates were more than merely tolerable, and Don John, playing a nineteenth-century melodramatic villain in black costume, became a delightful figure of farce rather than the egregious bore he so often is.

From a conventional point of view a Southwestern *Much Ado About Nothing* was outrageous, a priori. Yet the effect was entertaining and novel. Katharine Hepburn and Alfred Drake would not have made a more charming Beatrice and Benedick in scrupulously Elizabethan or Renaissance settings and costumes. Miss Hepburn was light, bright, beautiful, and tart, at once all-hoyden and all-girl in one prancing and entrancingly gowned body. Alfred Drake, handsome in a Spanish grandee's embroidered costume, had a suitable zest as the invincible bachelor Benedick, and he registered an appealing wistfulness when trapped into impending matrimony. The universality of Shakespeare's playwriting was not betrayed by the novelty of the presentation, once the initial shock wore off; grudgingly I had to concede that there was actually some gain in the insouciance and piquancy of the treatment.

Where but in the United States would a more or less official Shakespearian organization stage a Southwestern *Much Ado about Nothing*? Why do the directors of the American Shakespeare Festival Theatre in Connecticut suffer this unorthodox approach to the plays? Certainly not to instruct us in Shakespearian dramatic art as literature and certainly not to preserve Shakespeare as a national institution. The aim of the Broadway-oriented Festival Theatre is solely to make Shakespeare lively theatre.

Nevertheless, we become aware of serious limitations in the carefree American Festival style when a major work of Shakespeare is to be served. A tragic masterpiece such as *Othello* does not yield to ingenious exploitations of theatricality, and John Houseman commendably exercised restraint, even if he was not otherwise altogether successful. The Shakespeare of romance, comedy, farce, and fanciful theatricality responds to modern and American coaxing; the Shakespeare of high tragedy, of the works in which the play is the poem and the poem is the play does not submit to theatrical ministrations. This is equally true of the great lyrical moments in Shakespeare which require true music, and of the immortal characters such as Shylock. And it is this major work that justifies a Shakespearian theatre as a permanent institution rather than as a mere extension of commercial Broadway production in Connecticut's green and pleasant fields.

No stage production can exhaust the riches of an *Othello*; the verbal imagery particularly is likely to race past the playgoer too swiftly. There are nuances that we are much more apt to observe and appreciate in the printed play. In the theatre we can actually get along without full consciousness of the individual lines and images because the actor adds another dimension to the text. However it is important that the *actor* should be fully aware of all this and that it should influence his reading of the lines, his gestures, his stage movement, and his characterization. This constant awareness is rarely possible in a mode of staging that depends upon production conceits or gimmicks introduced by director-virtuosi rather than upon the actors' and directors' thorough and profound familiarity with the play as a poem.

Such familiarity can come only after many years of Shakespearian acting and staging. But most American actors as yet give the impression of knowing these great plays *only* as plays, and thus only half-knowing them at best. They experience them only on the transparent level of action, not on the translucent levels of sensibility, subconscious motivation, and verbal subtleties—as when Othello's speech becomes infiltrated with Iago's sensual and sadistic imagery. In this connection I wish that every actor playing Othello and every producer of the play would read Coleridge's sentences on *Othello* in his *Table Talk*:

> Jealousy does not strike me as the point in his passion; I take it to be rather an agony that the creature whom he had believed angelic, with whom he had garnered up his heart, and whom he could not help still loving, should be proved impure and worthless. It was the struggle *not* to love her. It was a moral indignation and regret that virtue should so fall:—'But yet the *pity* of it, Iago!—O Iago! the *pity* of it, Iago!' In addition to this, his honour was concerned: Iago would not have succeeded but by hinting that his honour was compromised. There is no ferocity in Othello; his mind is majestic and composed . . . I do not think there is any jealousy, properly so called, in the character of Othello. There is no predisposition to suspicion, which I take to be an essential term in the definition of the word.

To give us more of the poem should be the goal of every Shakespearian enterprise in America that is already capable of giving everything else. This is a reasonable request, but it calls for tremendous exertion. It requires the development of a permanent acting company with a reliable reserve of replacements. It requires year-round performances, which presentations on Broadway, off-Broadway, and on tour should make possible. And it requires general improvement in the training of our actors as speakers and as mimes; mere declamation is not enough, for Shakespeare, like every other playwright, leaves a great deal *between* the words.

Happily the leaders of the still very young American Shakespeare Festival Theatre appear to be aware of this problem. The reason that they are still far from their goal is that there is so little precedent for Shakespearian production in the recent American theatre. In their contemporary performances there is also the danger of succumbing to the seductions of a production idea, of being strenuous when there is nothing essential to be strenuous about, of relying on American tempo at the expense of language, and of straining for a bright new look just for the novelty of the impression. This is dangerous ground; we can give the impression that we are feeling superior to Shakespeare or that we are apologizing and compensating for the fact that he wrote some three hundred and fifty years ago.

It is easy and obvious to say that with Shakespeare the text should take precedence over production and acting notions. But stage directors, designers, and actors should also bear in mind Robert B. Heilman's admonition, "A play written in poetic form is simply not the same kind of literary work as a play written in prose." Even more useful is the caveat of a good contemporary journeyman in the world of which Shakespeare is the master. A verse play, according to Christopher Fry, is not a prose play which happens to be written in verse: "The poetry and the construction are inseparate. Who understands the poetry understands the construction, who understands the construction understands the poetry, for the poetry is the action and the action—even apart from the words— is the figure of the poetry."

Producing Miss Julie and Uncle Vanya

Supporters of truthfulness in the theatre discovered much about its possibilities and limitations in the modern drama from two off-Broadway productions of the 1955-56 season: Chekhov's Uncle Vanya and Strindberg's Miss Julie. Both authors took for their subject the theme of failure, but their methods were as different as their results; Chekhov veered toward comedy and Strindberg toward melodrama. It was also instructive and a little disturbing to observe how production difficulties can vary from play to play regardless of the historical importance or intrinsic strength of the work. Strindberg's Miss Julie is one of the important classics of modern naturalism. It was acknowledged as nothing less than that when the advanced theatres, led by Antoine's Théâtre Libre in 1892, began presenting the play to their audiences as a prime example of modernism. In a famous preface the author himself presented it to his reading public as the ideal modern drama. Yet *Miss Julie* seemed rather arid when revived by the Phoenix management.

Uncle Vanya, a work of considerably less importance in the history of the stage, a play in which Chekhov denounced or challenged nothing and nobody, glowed with life on a cramped and poorly situated stage. From the *Uncle Vanya* production it was possible to learn how naturalness and truth can be integrated into one consuming experience that is as poetic as it is real. It is too late in the day to elaborate upon the merits of Chekhovian naturalism (a more suitable term might be poetic naturalism), but David Ross gave New York the best *Uncle Vanya* in more than a quarter of a century. It was done in an excellent complete translation by Stark Young, rather than in an adaptation, such as the Rose Caylor version staged in the Thirties by Jed Harris with Osgood Perkins as a memorable Astroff. The Young translation was deftly produced at the tiny Fourth Street Theatre on a stage so small and so awkwardly placed between two banks of seats that performing on it was a considerable feat and making an act change on it a small miracle. It was to the credit of the director and his actors that the performance was generally so lively and moving. Although George Voskovec's Vanya seemed too vivacious, as if he were enjoying himself instead of being unintentionally comic, Signe Hasso, a refugee from the celluloid capital, was an entrancing Elena; the late Clarence Derwent a genuinely comic Professor Serebriakoff; and Franchot Tone a superb Dr. Astroff.

It is hard to say what engrossed me most in Chekhov's quite familiar play. There is no obvious comedy except for a little irreverent humor now and then at the expense of Vanya's pedantic brother-in-law. Vanya is an object of only the gentlest of smiles, and ordinary definitions of comedy are inadequate for gauging the quality of the play. Vanya himself is to be understood only in the light of sympathy; he is not a bit more ridiculous than pathetic in his infatuation with the Professor's beautiful and bored new wife. Chekhov's special quality in *Uncle Vanya* lay in his ability to turn absurdity into pathos, a feat impossible to any writer lacking Chekhov's rueful detachment and ironic compassion.

Another remarkable and truly poetic quality appears in *Uncle Vanya* more than in any other Chekhov play. Perhaps it is best described as chiaroscuro, a term borrowed from painting. The stalemate of Vanya and of other characters on the Professor's estate, Vanya's growing infatuation and his mounting realization that he has been cheated out of life, and above all the absurd act of trying to shoot the Professor, his former brother-in-law for whom he is still slavishly running the estate in the provinces, are some of the many little strokes that Chekhov uses to form a soft texture of half-tones. But I must shift to still another medium to describe the effect of *Uncle Vanya*. The affection we have for this play is really affection for a poem called *Uncle Vanya*.

The poem is the result of compassion; the chiaroscuro arises from a disposition too kind to excoriate life's absurdly shorn sheep. Where the author's kindness ends, the chiaroscuro ends too. When Chekhov found it justifiable to expose the Professor-egotist, who has been subsisting ungratefully on the devotion and labor of Vanya, he produced a vivid and scathing portrait of a pedant who expects everyone to cater to him. The late Clarence Derwent's impersonation of this man had the hard glitter of an educated parasite. There may be other ways of impersonating the Professor but a cool and lofty parasitism belongs to the character. Chekhov brought tenderness to his comic failures but no compassion toward those who ride roughshod over others. His portrait of another such character, the righteous young doctor in his earliest full-length play, *Ivanov*, is also an example of Chekhov's tough-mindedness.

I think we are attracted to *Uncle Vanya* because Chekhov gave us a play almost entirely composed of individuals living together in isolation (the isolation of their egotism, their ennui, or their frustration), yet also managed to relate them as fellow prisoners of life and make them matter beyond their personal situation. Living as they do on a provincial estate in Russia, disintegrating a little day by day, they even represent a social situation. Time, space, and lack of communication between people (distance from person to person, not simply the distance from the cosmopolitan centers of Europe) are the great corroders of self-realization and happiness in this play. The corrosion is present in the work not only as pathos but as comedy, and not only as a realistic picture of provincial life but as a poetry of unfulfilled longings and dreams.

To stage a play possessed of these varied qualities is a gratifying experience. Whether or not he is aware of it the author of such a work is constantly working for the actors and the director. For this reason I have never yet seen a bad professional production of *Uncle Vanya*. (The only one that failed to satisfy me, the *Uncle Vanya* the Old Vic brought here in 1946, was not badly done; it was simply lost in the vast auditorium of the old Century Theatre.) How important assistance from the dramatist is in the revival of masterpieces and landmarks in modern drama is apparent when we try to match formidable galleons, such as Ibsen's late play *The Master Builder* or Strindberg's early and powerful plays, against Chekhov's lighter and decidedly more maneuverable craft. With help from David Ross, audiences got a voyage through life out of a simple production of *Uncle Vanya.*

Audiences received less from the more elaborate Phoenix Theatre production of *Miss Julie.* It was preceded by Strindberg's dramatic monologue, *The Stronger,* a tour de force in the realistic theatre which I thought was crudely interpreted. A two-character play in which only one of the two women speaks, it is deceptively simple. It is a test for an actress who plays Mrs. X, the wife who has recovered her husband and holds on to him by subordinating herself to him, because she must win our support and retain our sympathy. Playing the mute Miss Y is almost as difficult because she must take punishment without defense. Ruth Ford and Viveca Lindfors, as directed by George Tabori, may not have failed Strindberg, the henpecked Bluebeard who was undoubtedly the world's most articulate male chauvinist. Probably they behaved exactly as their author would have wanted them to behave; he drew Mrs. X as deservedly triumphant and manifestly stronger than her romantic rival Miss Y. One reacts with distaste to Mrs. X as the epitome of all the strained yet smug, insecure yet complacent matrons who flourish in all corners of the world. Only the sick egotist and conscious antifeminist in Strindberg could have tolerated this woman, for his genius drove him to take up in his personal life with independent women who would give him a fight.

In taking the egotist, Strindberg, at his word, the Phoenix production of *The Stronger* was an arid experience. In Strindberg's dramas of sex the interpretation should be based not on his extravagantly bourgeois views on marriage, but on his dramatic sense and power to characterize. This was especially apparent in the staging of George Tabori's free adaptation of *Miss Julie* with James Daly as the valet Jean, Ruth Ford as the cook Kristin, and Viveca Lindfors as the hapless Miss Julie. The first act was excellent, but the second was generally mechanical and strained. The play, which Strindberg wrote for continuous performance, was broken up into two parts—an error of considerable magnitude because the mood of the play is one of mounting hysteria. Miss Julie is driven to give herself to her father's valet and then to cut her throat in desperation.

The *Miss Julie* production had one value above all others for Broadway's sentimentalists: it gave them a lesson in complete and relentless integrity. For all their addiction to realism, Broadway's playwrights and audiences still must learn that the *promise* of telling the truth implicit in the verisimilitude of a play and production entails the *obligation* of telling it. The satanic Strindberg was more ethical both as an artist and moralist than the pliant realists he and Ibsen spawned in the theatre. Yet it is apparent that Strindberg is *using* people, certainly using Julie, instead of being used by the characters he has brought to life. One gets the opposite impression from the plastic dramatic art of Chekhov despite the clear evidence of his amused objectivity and ironic detachment.

Strindberg is sadistic and unlovable in *Miss Julie.* At the end it is possible to feel that he has immolated Miss Julie to his antifeminist obsession. In anything but a richly dimensioned performance of the neurotic girl's role (which one did not get from the Phoenix production), there is no other way one can feel. The probability is that Miss Lindfors was interpreting Strindberg accurately, but the difference between a correct interpretation and a great performance in this role is simply one of transcendence. The great actress would have first assimilated and then transcended the limitations predicated for her. Miss Julie is an aristocratic girl who succumbs to the sexual allure of her father's servant, reluctantly agrees to run away with him, and kills herself under his hypnotizing influence after he has cut the throat of the pet bird she hated to leave behind. A great actress would have given Strindberg the fierce fight he always looked for from a woman who attracted him. A great actress would have immolated the stupid male who tried to immolate her; to a woman of genius almost any male must appear stupid when he is reckless enough to tangle with her. Such an actress would have surmounted the clinical barriers set up for her; she would have used Strindberg at least as much as Strindberg intended to use her.

In concentrating on the *conflict* of the sexes in his plays Strindberg excluded a good deal of the *life* of the sexes. That life must be put back into the plays by the performers. The raw material is there, but it is there often only by implication; it lies beneath the surface of the roles in greatly condensed form and must be discovered by the actors before it can be brought to the surface and made theatrically explicit. There have been some perverse giants among the playwrights of the modern stage (O'Casey, Pirandello, and Strindberg, and the latter-day symbolist Ibsen) whose bizarrely intense creativity cannot be matched by merely good performers. In these cases genius in playwriting requires genius in performance.

Oddly enough Chekhov, who has long been credited with formidable subtlety, presents fewer difficulties for performers and audience than Strindberg or Claudel. Chekhov helps the interpreting artist, and actors should be grateful to him for giving them such winning personalities to play. He expands roles that a more single-minded playwright—and who could be more single-tracked than Strindberg—would be apt to condense. Chekhov also reveals the great tact of a supremely civilized and balanced person. It led him to modulate feelings, moderate extremes of emotion with sane humor, and use chiaroscuro in portraying characters who would be pilloried in cruel daylight by more strident authors. Though it is possible to admire some of his formidable colleagues it is delightfully easy to love Chekhov.

Reviving Turgenev's A Month in the Country

Another example of how showmanship sometimes makes short shrift of difficulties with gratifying results was the Phoenix Theatre production of *A Month in the Country*. When the novelist, Ivan Turgenev, wrote the play in 1849 he did not consider it stageworthy. But sixty years later the Moscow Art Theatre had no difficulty in making a success of the work after reducing it to manageable proportion. In 1930 the Theatre Guild also disproved Turgenev's self-criticism with a production for which Rouben Mamoulian, the director, made a playing version.

The Phoenix Theatre dispelled the difficulties in the text even more thoroughly. Michael Redgrave, the director, had an understandable affinity for the Emlyn Williams' adaptation, in which he had starred at the St. James's Theatre in London in 1943. The text had been brought to a high polish; it is an excellent version and carries the dramatic action flowingly from scene to scene. Mr. Redgrave gave every evidence of knowing how to navigate in the intricate but pellucid stream of this pre-Chekhovian tragi-comedy. The play concerns a woman's ennui while on a country estate and the unhappy results of her falling in love with her child's tutor. The casting of the production was excellent, especially in the choice of Uta Hagen. Her playing of the heroine, Natalia Petrovna, was brilliantly projected and compellingly sensitive. Though everybody praised this performance it received less recognition than it merited, partly because Miss Hagen was playing off-Broadway and partly because the role is an unsensational one. But I have seldom seen a performance to equal Miss Hagen's in authority, depth, and sheer beauty since the days of my youthful enthusiasm for Emily Stevens, Nazimova, Pauline Lord, and Lynn Fontanne.

A Month in the Country presents most of the difficulties of Chekhov without Chekhov's compensating skill. Turgenev's original work (which may be read in my book, A Treasury of the Theatre: From Aeschylus to Turgenev) is a long and cumbersome drama as well as a penetrating work of realism. The Phoenix production employed stylized scenery combining interior and exterior scenes that could be viewed simultaneously. As a result there was no need to cramp or slow down action, no need to drop curtains and shift scenery, and the play became a supremely fluid work.

The results of this surgery and stylization were so gratifying that there was no point in protesting that a great modern piece had been shrunk from orchestral to chamber music version. The fact is that Broadway and its environs are not always up to the full orchestra. For various practical reasons—the limited span of the spectator's attention and the increased costs of stage production, for instance—the commercial theatre prefers a trim play. Not much harm was done in the case of A Month in the Country, in which Turgenev's hobbled provincial lives have fairly exhausted their dramatic potentialities by the end. Their various kinds of sensibility, so important in this play, have been sufficiently exposed. The revolt of the wife against provincial ennui, which does not really have dramatically drastic results, before she subsides into quiescent wifehood requires little elaboration of plot and hardly any conflict of ideas. All that might be said for the full-length version, which Turgenev never saw staged, is that it has the density of observation we associate with modern fiction.

The trimming down of epic as opposed to domestic plays, the abbreviation of a Shakespearian drama, for example, is decidedly less excusable. We do not really see Hamlet and King Lear at all in two-hour versions. Fortunately the habit of perpetrating mayhem on Shakespeare's plays has passed out of favor since the days of Irving's abbreviated and rearranged versions. The Victorian actor-managers had had to make changes in order to allow for shifting the heavy scenery.

A more exigent problem in contemporary playwriting is the producers' discouragement of any efforts that require epic breadth or novel-like richness. The young playwright is apt to create with a stop watch in his brain when he sees one successful play after another run the same neat course of two hours and twenty minutes, with time out for one or two intermissions. Length should not be confused with merit—the Greek masters, assisted by economy of verse, myth, and a community of interests, did very well with short plays—but an extensive treatment may be the best one for some subjects.

Looking back upon my own involvement with Broadway production for several decades I am amazed at the number of times well-intentioned producers took an interest in a play because of its rich texture, only to eliminate much of the texture in favor of structure. Broadway has long suffered from a tendency to option a play for production because of the abundance of life in it only to destroy most of that life in order to show an audience a play that will look as smooth as a well-kept lawn. When I remember my unhappy experiences with this currycombing of scripts, of starting with a superabundant play and ending with a tame one indistinguishable in quality with dozens of other trim plays, when I think of all the money spent on taking options on plays that are finally relinquished by the producers after the property has been improved at the expense of its life, I am angry with the entire professional theatre business. No self-respecting publisher of novels with a twitching blue pencil would dare to do what play producers do as a matter of course. This mania for major surgery is not confined to producers; some play agents and many directors have it, and I even know scene designers who caught the habit.

The more I think of this tendency, the more I respect Shaw's obstinacy in rejecting suggestions that he reduce his disquisitory abundance, and the less patient I become with those whose nearly automatic response to a long play is to wish to cut it. A notable example was O'Neill's lengthy drama *The Iceman Cometh*. When the Broadway Theatre Guild production, staged by Eddie Dowling, lagged at the box office it was difficult to find anyone in the profession who didn't think the play needed cutting. But there was hardly a whisper to this effect when *The Iceman Cometh* at the Circle in the Square proved exciting because of dynamic stage direction by José Quintero and electrifying acting by Jason Robards, Jr.

The Doctor's Dilemma and
Saint Joan: Shaw Half-Revived

Perhaps all that actually matters for the continuity of the theatre is that it continue to provide excursions out of a workaday existence. For that purpose a great play is not indispensable, provided good stage productions are available. We look for the good play, that needle in the haystack, mainly because we assume that it will yield a better production than a bad play will (this is an assumption more comforting than valid). In theatrical practice *Hamlet* may provide a miserable evening and *Private Lives* a delightful one. And no play at all, but a mere exhibition of performing talent may prove more gratifying than either. That was my own experience, for example, at the joint appearance of Ruth and Paul Draper on Broadway in 1954. Paul Draper was particularly admirable; there was a compelling vitality in his expressive footwork, in the noble and mobile simplicity of his face, and in the contrasting hesitancy of a bravely mastered stammer in his speech.

Paul Draper's pantomimed "Satire on a Political Speech" and Ruth Draper's monologue, "Opening a Bazaar," demonstrated the potency of satire, that genre which nearly everybody has been avoiding in the recent theatre. We have been hearing a great deal about the disappointing lack of tragedy in contemporary drama. It is time we heard more about the disappointing lack of satire. Tragedy and satiric comedy have invariably been found in conjunction in the great ages of the theatre: in the classic Athens of Euripides and Aristophanes, in the London of Shakespeare and Jonson, in the Paris of Racine and Molière. In mixed forms of modern drama, just as in Elizabethan dark comedy, we may even discern an illustration of Socrates' conclusion that the genius of comedy is the same as that of tragedy. Satiric comedy is perhaps even more indicative of command of the reality of an age than is tragedy. In the contemporary American theatre only virtuoso performers like the Drapers, Menasha Skulnik, and musical clown-artists (Carol Haney in *The*

Pajama Game, for instance) appear to understand the use of the armed comic approach. This is a pity, for it is difficult to think of a single recent play of American origin that wouldn't have been more stimulating if satire had been one of its components.

The Phoenix Theatre production of *The Doctor's Dilemma* in the 1954-55 season illustrated our general inadequacy in deploying satire with any degree of success in the mid-century theatre. The production was more than merely adequate only when heavy underscoring of the satire was present in Shaw's own text. Sir Ralph Bloomfield Bonington, the bumbling medico who wants to "stimulate the phagocytes," was energetically and entertainingly played by Frederic Worlock. Shepperd Strudwick was an able, if somewhat stiff, Sir Colenso Ridgeon. Sidney Lumet's direction had him reading his lines in the last scene with a crisp strenuousness which is funny only if you happen to believe that a physician boasting to a widow that he killed her husband is funny.

Shaw was an intellectual ruffian, but he also had taste. In Dubedat's dying scene Lumet made conspicuous use of a faceless figure of death placed, for good measure, on the chair where the painter Dubedat used to place his models. Perhaps he was partial to effects no one is likely to miss because of his successful command of television technique. No doubt Lumet could motivate the presence of this prop, since Dubedat, who knows that he is dying, might have been painting a picture for which he needed the allegorical figure. But not everything that can be motivated is necessary, and in the context of this particular scene Death was a distracting redundancy.

Even so fine an actress as Geraldine Fitzgerald was a vulgarized Jennifer Dubedat, busily and fussily insistent in the early scenes and devoid of radiance in the last ones. In 1941 Katherine Cornell managed this role beautifully with far less strain and far less acting. Miss Fitzgerald's Jennifer was truly motivated and better acted, but would have been more at home in an Actors' Studio character drama than in the comic world of Shaw. Uncertainly applied Method acting seemed to weigh down several of the performances and nearly all of the direction.

Roddy McDowall's gaminlike Louis Dubedat was likeable and very real, yet lacked the distinction one may reasonably expect from this combination of genius and rascality. It is true that Dubedat is supposed to be very young, but Shaw never characterized him as callow and adolescent. When we Stanislavski-ize youth on Broadway we somehow confuse a

lack of years with a lack of grace and manners. Although young Mc-
Dowall performed with earnestness and skill he was the director's Dube-
dat, not Shaw's; he belonged in his two big scenes to a good Group
Theater drama rather than to Shavian high comedy.

It is as much within the province of art to know when reality should
not intrude as when it should be highlighted, for reality in art is relative
to the ruling style. But the substitution of realistic representation for
style should not be laid exclusively to Broadway's door or to the Phoenix
Theatre. The same tendency, without the accompanying skill of professionalism, may be frequently observed in the noncommercial theatre.
Moreover, the Phoenix Theatre deserved a salute for its production. In
giving New York *The Doctor's Dilemma*, Norris Houghton and T.
Edward Hambleton gave us the one play of the season that possessed
stature as well as interest, consummation as well as stimulation. One
might say that the play expresses the marriage of Molière's comedy of
good sense with the fin de siècle antiphilistinism associated with Wilde
and Whistler. (It is sometimes useful to remember that Shaw, along
with other moderns such as Yeats and Gide, was close to the esthetic
movement of the Nineties. But the product of the aforementioned marriage is a unique creation, a Shavian comedy of ideas.)

The Doctor's Dilemma resolves nothing. But after seeing this production, a playgoer could understand why dramatic modernism at the turn
of the century made the theatre an influential force with a public that
read modern fiction and belles-lettres and that adopted modern views in
philosophy and sociology. The strongest point in favor of the Phoenix
Theatre was that one could, after all, *see* the play, even if one saw it
somewhat divested of glitter, glow, and edge.

While the American theatre has continued to manifest a strong reliance upon Shaw—the Fifties had little nourishment from modern drama
except the staples of the New York stage: Shaw and O'Neill—there is
evidence of an emphasis on the substance rather than the fire and sparkle
of his work. By substance I mean those qualities that Shaw's Victorian
critics before and after World War I prized most in a play and took the
greatest pleasure in denying to him: force of sentiment and truth of
character. The wheel has swung full circle and it is becoming fashionable
to attribute decent sentiments and generous feelings to the once dreaded
monster of marble intelligence. We also have begun to credit him with

the ability to create living characters. A previous generation denied this, alleging that he created only mouthpieces and peopled his stage with multiple reflections of a heretic familiarly called G.B.S.

This once prevailing view granted Shaw nearly every talent except the ability to present a believable world. It is the view that A.B. Walkley expressed even about so conservative a play in the Shavian canon as *Candida*. Unable to grant it any marked quality of reality Walkley wrote in 1904 that:

> Fantasy has its place in the theatre, as well as realism, and that is one reason why the theatre has room for Mr. Bernard Shaw. His method of travestying life is to eliminate from it everything but the pure intelligence. Just as Mr. H.G. Wells amuses us by supposing a world where the laws of gravity are suspended, or where there is no such thing as time, or where space is of x dimensions, so Mr. Shaw amuses us by representing a world where conduct is regulated by thought, and men love women, as the civil servant in *Pickwick* ate crumpets, on principle.

Walkley found *Candida* "capital sport" and noted that its chief delight, "the chief delight of every one of Mr. Shaw's plays," was "its brilliant dialectic."

But the voice of Walkley is no longer heard—if indeed it ever was—in the egalitarian land of the free and its no less egalitarian theatre. Like the late Huey Long we are bent upon making every Shavian character a king, or at least upon giving him a life insurance policy. Actors seem equally resolved to tack on fringe benefits in the form of detailed and scrupulously observed traits. Fortunately there are exceptions to this tendency to perform Shaw loaded down with the ball and chain of realism. Maurice Evans' 1947 production of *Man and Superman*, his playing of John Tanner, preserved the Shaw who laughed his way through the theatre. It was possible to applaud Albert Marre's 1953 staging of *Misalliance* for the New York City Drama Company. The play was performed as a farce of ideas in which the mental acrobatics of each Shavian marionette were carefully coached to avoid any tendency to turn a show into a sermon and an entertainment into a portrait gallery. It was wisdom on Katharine Hepburn's part to play the heroine of *The Millionairess* in 1952 with tongue-in-cheek abandon rather than pump that effervescent jade of Shaw's imagining full of motivation. (Conversely, it was right for Charles Laughton and his associates of the *Don Juan in Hell* reading that toured the country in 1951-52 to keep a tight rein on harlequinade histrionics. The work was a pyrotechnical display of fancy and discourse from the start.) But our tendency to tame Shaw while favoring him, to domesticate or housebreak Shaw while adopting him is growing noticeably. We draw his sting, as if we are resolved to deprive him of his right to be considered one of the world's great satirists, and we subdue his buoyancy as if it is a quality unbecoming a writer whom we are bent upon investing with the respectability of a classic. We give him character creation instead, even when Shaw had other and (heresy!) more appropriate intentions.

Shaw, I fear, may yet be turned into a respectably solid playwright, if Broadway producers have their way. The attempt to give him these solid qualities appeared in productions of *Saint Joan,* with Uta Hagen trying very hard to be a real Joan—and succeeding, *The Apple Cart,* and *Major Barbara,* despite a thoroughly playful theatrical opening styled by Laughton's staging and Oenslager's designing. But the tendency was particularly marked, I thought, in the Phoenix revival of *The Doctor's Dilemma.* In this production Louis and Jennifer Dubedat were painstakingly real, therefore imaginatively unreal, and a couple of physicians were so lifelike that they might have been respected members of any British medical society. I had hoped for considerably more stimulation than that afforded by this meticulous revival.

There was even more striking evidence of our uncertain way with Shaw when the Phoenix Theatre once more gave him a hearing in the 1956-57 season with Siobhán McKenna playing The Maid in *Saint Joan.* Whether we agreed with Atkinson, who found her performance insufficiently spirtual, or with the party of enthusiasts who found her uplifting (I am suspicious of the uplift in *Saint Joan* without being satisfied with a purely realistic, peasant version of Joan), it is doubtful that the production did justice to Bernard Shaw. Miss McKenna had her moments of impressive passion but provided a studied rather than an inspired performance. It was easier to appreciate the peasant than the saint in her playing. Matter and spirit rarely fused in the performance; they existed in separate compartments to be taken out for display on separate occasions. On the whole, the production was earthbound. This is not to say that it would have been necessarily better to sentimentalize Joan into an entirely spiritual creature, which would have gone counter to

Shaw's intentions. But it was essential to safeguard the wit and fire of *Shaw*, his lively sense of human contradictions, his scorn of such chauvinism as John de Stogumber's, his regard for intelligence, his fine irony, and his pluck. The Phoenix production of *Saint Joan* needed not spirituality but spirit.

Shaw, tiring of the adulation lavished upon his Candida as the perfect woman, brushed off his admirers and hers as Candidamaniacs. What would he say to those of us who have insisted on taking him more seriously in the Fifties than he has ever been taken before? Would he remind us that though his contemporaries persisted in shrugging him off as an amusing buffoon he had always wanted to be taken seriously? Perhaps. But would he be pleased to find himself so sober, so tame, and so unsparkling a playwright as some productions make him out to be? It is also doubtful that he would be happy to be treated as a "solid" playwright or as a reliable creator of "real" characters. A solid Shaw stands a good chance of petrifying if he becomes any more solid, whereas the mercurial Shaw may continue to be lively for a long time to come. Nevertheless, our frequently lukewarm theatre will find it difficult to stave off the tendency to only half-revive Shaw while trying to keep him alive.

5 THE COMIC MUSE

American Musical Comedy

By the Beautiful Sea, produced in the spring of 1954, had pleasant music by Arthur Schwartz, gay costuming by Irene Sharaff, lavish decor by Jo Mielziner, and vivacious choreography by Helen Tamiris. In short, it was entertainment with the usual genuine ingredients supplied by showmen. Only the ingredients called book and lyrics (here supplied by Herbert and Dorothy Fields) expose themselves at once in routine musicals as something less than divinely inspired. It is customary for the clan of critics to make snide remarks to the effect that the show was fine but that the book was weak. There is surely a contradiction in such statements, for how can the show be good if the book and lyrics are not? The answer is simple enough. Standard Broadway musicals are mostly patchwork; busy critic and paying spectator alike flutter from patch to patch and alight on this or that one. The fact that the parts do not agree makes little difference; on the contrary, it is this diversity, a fundamental disharmony, that makes a show rather than a music-drama.

There is a tacit understanding on Broadway that the authors of the book and lyrics are usually the whipping boys of the play reviewers' and discriminating playgoers' critical consciences. You will notice, if you stay close to the market place long enough, that such excoriated authors return the next season with a whole skin, ready to be struck again and never the worse for the recurring experience. The bad notices they received the previous season will not prevent the authors from being called upon to do the book and lyrics of still another musical. The reason we play this sort of game year in and year out is that we do not really want a good book and good lyrics (of the calibre of *Regina* and *Candide,* for

202

example). The former would be too unified for pleasure and the latter too difficult for apprehension. Musical comedy is the kind of show that cannot survive on the patronage of the art lover, the intellectual, and the man of specially developed taste.

I have stressed this point for two reasons. One is that we ought to do away with the hypocrisy of crying out against the sins of the authors while praising almost everyone else's wares in the musical theatre. The fact is that we don't want authors to be consistent and richly imaginative artists; we want them only to service an entertainment. Otherwise we may get (the Lord forbid) little works of art like the *Ballet Ballads* of John Latouche and Jerome Moross of several seasons ago. The rhapsodies of the best reviewers could not secure it a profitable run.

My other reason for discoursing on the subject of the musical stage is that I think we ought to begin to evince a little scepticism of the bromide that the American theatre's greatest achievements, its justification and glory, have been musical comedy and music-drama. This has been a favorite of American dramatic criticism since *Oklahoma!* opened about two decades ago. Neither musical comedy nor music-drama has actually developed since then, though *Carousel, South Pacific,* and other pieces suggest that the Broadway musical theatre is not in danger of rapid deterioration. With few exceptions the later musicals have not been better, they have been inferior. The form has not been made more satisfactory. Agnes De Mille's integration of ballet into dramatic action is not even being retained in most musical productions. The fact is that Broadway musicals are and must remain a makeshift species of showmanship under present conditions of inflated production costs and the need to please a public that brings only its own flabby spirit of accommodation to the theatre. If standards presumably set by *Oklahoma!* and *Carousel* actually prevailed, would *By the Beautiful Sea, Kismet, Wish You Were Here, Miss Liberty,* and numerous other recent exhibitions have been produced at all?

By the Beautiful Sea was a vehicle for Shirley Booth. There were rumors that she was unhappy with the show and critics commented that much of the material was unworthy of her. Such reports and comments only support my contention that all the talk of our giving rise to an art of musical theatre is poppycock. The show had a good run despite the dissatisfaction of the star and critics. We can only conclude that the standards for musical theatre are inviolably those of show business. The big-city public is perfectly content with a conglomeration of skits, songs, dances independent of purpose, provided the proceedings are sprightly and the performances appealing by their standards. It is characteristic of the prevailing view, shared by many critics and the public (as well as by the producers and the performing artists), that one talks of good and bad material. That is the way show business operates; it assumes the primacy of the performer (as an Ibsen or Chekhov play does not) and then worries about giving him something with which to demonstrate his skill, as if he were the trapeze artist or the bareback rider in a circus. I don't object to this kind of show at all, but, no matter how new-fangled, it is the most elementary kind of theatre we have now that vaudeville is gone. It cannot be considered the summum bonum of American art unless it is assumed that the American drama cannot amount to anything.

Judging *By the Beautiful Sea* as typical musical comedy is easy. But it is the overvaluation of our musical genre that is the real subject of this chapter. Given half an occasion or opportunity many persons will make extravagant claims for American musical comedy. When *The Golden Apple,* produced in March, 1954, as an experiment of the Phoenix Theatre, was transferred to Broadway and when *The Pajama Game,* a musical by George Abbott and Richard Bissell with music and lyrics by Richard Adler and Jerry Ross and based on Bissell's novel *7½ Cents,* opened in May, 1954, there was much enthusiasm about the genre. Confidence in Broadway rose again, as if another Ibsen or at least another Tennessee Williams had come to the commercial theatre.

In the first instance Broadway proved itself capable of playing host to a folk-play version of Homer by such highbrows as John Latouche and Jerome Moross. Gratification over the success of *The Golden Apple* was entirely in order. But we succumb to a confusion of values if we fail to realize that a folksy adulteration of the *Iliad* and *Odyssey* (quite apart from a treatment that runs downhill in the second act) does not offer salvation for the theatre. It cannot thrive on collegiate or varsity popularizations of the classics, no matter how good. Pseudosophistication is not a foundation for vital art.

In the second instance, *The Pajama Game,* old and new sophisticated acting personnel (John Raitt, Eddie Foy, Jr., Carol Haney, and others) actually *created* a musical comedy out of such unusual ingredients as a sit-down strike in a pajama factory. The plain, down-to-earth subject of management-labor conflict and the unromantic picture of factory life were effectively translated into theatre by lean writing, exuberant dancing (especially by Carol Haney), and fine songs, three of which ("Steam Heat," "Hey There," "Hernando's Hideaway") won instant success. Watching this musical account of the struggle over a seven-and-a-half-cents-per-hour raise in wages, one found oneself thrust back two decades into the class-struggle theatre of the mid-Thirties. But one does not have to be cynical about proletarian ideals to doubt that our theatrical maturity is assured by *The Pajama Game*. Here, as in most other musical comedies, it is essentially the variety show, with its frequently dazzling tidbits of virtuosity in performance, that engages us.

Since diversified virtuosity has rarely failed the theatre since the dawn of mime in the ancient world success of this order should not be described as the birth of a new heaven and earth. It should not even be confused with the achievement of a *Gesamtkunstswerk,* that is of the arts *in fusion* rather than of art *in diffusion.* Even *Oklahoma!* was more art in diffusion than art in complete fusion. It was a composite of musical numbers—including the inevitable waltz—complete integration appearing only in the Agnes De Mille ballet that closed the first half of the entertainment. Although our musicals should not be deprived of variety there is in them a dissipation of feeling, point, and purpose that must be set down as a limitation.

A viewpoint in our musicals is usually indistinct or nonexistent, something that cannot be said about *The Beggar's Opera* or its Brecht-Weill version, *The Threepenny Opera.* At best we encounter a sentiment in our native musicals, not the hard core nor the crystalline reality of a consistent attitude. The commendable vigor cannot quite conceal or compensate for a frequent inertness of mind and flabbiness of spirit in the work.

I do not demand that there shall be no cakes and ale in the world of entertainment. But I do not like to be made to feel that I am getting steak when I am actually getting smörgåsbord. A work supposedly as involved with the real world of wages and factory life as *The Pajama Game* neatly evades dramatic realism and genuine satire, which is always a form of dramatic realism whether the whiplash is applied by Jonson, Molière, Shaw, or Brecht. Musicals seem to be created under some unwritten (though not at all unspoken) interdict against integrity of realism, penetration of mind, concentration of satire, and consistency of style. Like most Americans I have a weakness for musicals and enjoy about one-third of many of them extravagantly (one out of three is about par for any season), but I fear that we claim too much for them. If our claims had some basis in the Forties (actually beginning with the Rodgers and Hart *Pal Joey*, rather than with the Rodgers and Hammerstein *Oklahoma!* which arrived several years later), we should have become wary of making too much of them in the Fifties. There has been no extended musical-comedy renaissance in the last ten years; there have been merely successful musicals and unsuccessful ones.

Musicals of scattered merit flourished like the green bay tree throughout the Fifties. But not even *Guys and Dolls,* the most vivacious of them, *The Music Man,* with its expansive spirit, *West Side Story,* with its vivid immediacy, or *My Fair Lady* shake my opinion: neither individually nor collectively have they provided a fresh dispensation or opened new vistas for our theatre. *My Fair Lady,* for all its musical expansion of Shaw's story, really amounts to a contraction of Shaw's mind and spirit. We need only compare the unregenerate Doolittle's brilliant speeches in *Pygmalion* with the rousing but less than provocative popular numbers assigned to him in *My Fair Lady* or compare Shaw's ending with the mineral oil of the musical's denouement, however spiked it was by the exquisite tartness that Rex Harrison and Julie Andrews brought to the roles of Professor Higgins and Eliza. A few of Broadway's failures, especially *Regina* and *Candide,* actually had a keener edge and were more distinctly fused and integrated works, but they passed quickly out of the theatre's province into opera.

Menasha Skulnik in *The Fifth Season*

Concerning Sylvia Regan's genre comedy, *The Fifth Season,* produced in 1953, one had to make the obvious comment that regardless of how greatly the playwrights may fail us the clowns of the theatre never let us down. Miss Regan's little comedy concerns the tribulations of two dress manufacturers in Manhattan's famed garment center. Johnny Goodwin, one of the partners, has high-flown ideas of business enterprise that could land him either in jail or in bankruptcy proceedings, and the latter, combined with a divorce suit, are indeed imminent. But the infinitely humble Max Pincus, the other partner, salvages both the business and Goodwin's marriage. Since the playwright's cup runneth over,

Pincus, played by Skulnik, is rewarded with marriage to a lovable immigrant girl.

Normally this sort of play would find Broadway hard-hearted, in spite of efficient stage direction by Gregory Ratoff and a good cast in which Richard Whorf excelled as Mr. Goodwin. But *The Fifth Season* was saved by a little gentleman, Menasha Skulnik, who wore motley on the Yiddish-speaking stage for quite a while and who now wears it on the English-speaking stage with equal grace. It is undoubtedly the best-tailored garment turned out in New York City in any season. Woebegone but keen-witted, self-deprecating but reliable in every ridiculous crisis, the little man raises his eyebrows to heaven, flutters his hands, and performs miracles of hair-breadth escape with a modesty that is as touching as it is amusing. He has the kind of self-deprecation that is characteristic only of life's stepchildren who expect nothing more than calamity on earth and are genuinely surprised when anything good comes their way. "As goes Skulnik, so goes the play," wrote *Variety*. The point is that Skulnik goes much further than any ordinary play. Even sentimentality is endurable while he is on the stage, though it is not the sentimentality but the skill that we admire in his performance. This skill consists of the art of surprising himself continually and of using his entire body to register a comic or pathetic response. His timing is that of the whole man, and so it *is* the whole man, representative of the lostness of all men in the mazes of absurd circumstance. He makes all humanity seem vulnerable.

At the performance of *The Fifth Season* I attended, no one seemed more entranced than Professor Oscar James Campbell, the Shakespearian scholar. His delight made me wonder whether he did not sense a kinship between Miss Regan's Max Pincus and Shakespeare's clowns. Perhaps we would have a better theatre if we turned it over to the clowns.

Aymé's Clérambard

The wit of *Clérambard*, the work of the gifted French writer Marcel Aymé, has a sharp edge with no romantic solvent. At first there is a resemblance to sophisticated American humor of the debunking school of the Twenties once associated with George S. Kaufman and his collaborators. Aymé appears to have been satirizing the vanishing French aristocracy, and he has a bland irreverence that recalls George S. Kaufman's flip treatment of fools and philistines. But *Clérambard* leaves the norms of American playwriting far behind after the first fifteen minutes of playing; it is quite different from a comedy or farce of manners.

First staged in Paris in 1950, the play uses the seedy condition of a down-at-heels aristocratic family as a springboard for an extravagant fantasy that turns truth and delusion topsy-turvy. The Comte de Clérambard, who tyrannizes his family and hunts down his neighbors' domestic animals in order to fill his larder, receives a visitation from Saint Francis of Assisi. Since the Saint performs the miracle of restoring the life of a dog the Comte had assassinated, conversion of the overawed aristocrat is inevitable. But contrary to expectation, this development does not yield sweetness and salvation. After the visitation Aymé's tone is more mocking and scornful than before, for the Comte becomes even more unbearable *after* his conversion. His unctuousness as he defends the life of a spider in the living room and calls it "my little sister" is intolerable. In his repulsive idealism he forces his half-witted son to marry the local prostitute, and finally he sets off to emulate Saint Francis by embarking upon a life devoted to sacrifice (mainly that of others), poverty, and the making of pilgrimages.

Here is the reversal of values that has been so difficult for American playwrights to effect with wit and ease. But Aymé turns an even more daring somersault. Having shown the Comte as a worse rather than better man after the religious visitation (which turns out to have been an illusion), the author perpetrates a real miracle. Everybody on stage apparently sees it except for the local priest, and Clérambard and his family, having upset the life of their community, ecstatically depart on their pilgrimage in a ramshackle vehicle. The miracle comes after the Comte has himself despaired of his mission and has been logically convinced that the appearance of St. Francis was an hallucination. Are we to conclude, then, that the real miracle is a reward for the Comte's consuming longing for saintliness? It is impossible to guess at Aymé's purpose beyond his intention of unbalancing the spectator's mind by piling irony upon irony.

Like other exercises of its kind, *Clérambard* works directly upon the theatrical sensibility of the spectator and leaves little residue of meaning or experience. This fact hardly dismays the devout theatrician and it was particularly fitting here, for the dramatic action of the play could not survive the scrutiny of reason. At the Rooftop Theatre such scrutiny was never undertaken while the Comte, brilliantly played by Claude Dauphin, was on stage. Alvin Epstein, an excellent mime, played the idiot son, and other experts of comic acting such as Ruth McDevitt and Will Kuluva gave Dauphin able support. It was difficult to ask pertinent questions without being impertinent. However, in France the infectiousness of the play was even more in evidence, and although the adaptation at the Rooftop was satisfactory the play needed the fluency of the original French.

Considering *Clérambard* solely as an entertainment may be sufficient; it requires no special analysis for our playgoers. But what is really hard for Americans to understand is the *character* of the play. We have nothing like it except in some musical comedies—and considering the moral fervor of most Rodgers and Hammerstein musicals I use the word *some* advisedly. *Theatre for theatre's sake,* especially in a comedy of ideas, is simply not our strong point. When we are in the theatre we are apt to yield to momentary enchantment because nothing is required of us except to sit back and enjoy ourselves. But we have no aptitude for theatricality carried as far as Aymé carried it in *Clérambard,* an exotic plant in our comparatively plain garden. I am not so sure that I don't prefer our own garden to be more or less plain, but looking into other people's can be a stimulating pastime.

The Lesson of the *Comédie Française*

If both New York and Paris had run true to form we might have been inclined to underrate the *Comédie Française* during its 1955-56 visit. There was time when the *Comédie* was looked upon from both sides of the Atlantic as a stodgy institution. I remember that in the early career of the Theatre Guild there was great reluctance to entertain the idea of seeking a subsidy lest the Guild suffer the fate of the French national theatre. I also recall how Lee Simonson used to warn us that if we weren't careful we would become as stodgy an institution as the *Comédie Française.* (This brilliant artist and man of the theatre sounded his warning in the same spirit of devotion to a living stage that made him write me, when I recommended a Goldoni comedy for production in the Thirties, that we were "off the Goldoni standard.")

But there have been changes on both sides of the ocean in the past two decades. The *Comédie* has been reinvigorated while the institutional theatres of New York, forced to become virtually self-supporting, have died out or have suffered a change that makes them indistinguishable from other competent managements. Lacking a vital institution of its own in the Fifties, New York was not disposed to look down on the *Comédie*; the latter in turn genuinely merited admiration for its exquisite taste in décor and stage direction and for its seemingly effortless command of acting style.

The *Comédie* productions reflected a sense of security in grace and control rarely discoverable in our own theatre. Too often we behave like oversized bulls in china shops, and this is unfortunately the case both in commercial and experimental productions. We rarely stand still long enough for discourse, as the *Comédie* actors do. We constantly underscore a speech, a line, a word, a syllable, whereas the *Comédie* actors maintain a steady flow of balanced syllables and clauses. This rhythm of speech is interrupted only by some characters of eccentric speech who are to be made the object of punitive ridicule.

A less expected grace was present in the *Comédie's* productions on this visit. There was a delightful freshness of invention in them. An example is the transformation of the two hobgoblins of Marivaux' *Arlequin Poli par l'Amour* into two garden statues. They danced and mimed whatever dramatic action was required of them, but no sooner was their task ended than they were amusingly back on their pedestal in the park, inanimate and frozen into imperturbable marble, while the queen of the fairies suffered the all too human anguish of a love-tormented woman. From a large repertory of long and short plays the French national company brought us this mellowed yet still lively one-acter; as well as Musset's short piece, *Un Caprice*; and the three full-bodied comedies, *Le Bourgeois Gentilhomme*, *Le Barbier de Séville*, and *Le Jeu de l'Amour et du Hasard*.

To describe the merits of these productions—the completely theatrical feats of speech, pose, gesture, and movement—is no more satisfactory than to reduce a poem to its prose content. The experience was pure theatre precisely because there can be no descriptive equivalent for it. Yet one was constantly aware of a ruling intelligence and an operative critical mind.

The visit of the *Comédie* under Sol Hurok's management was an experience in total theatre. When encountered in productions as good as those presented in Manhattan by the *Comédie* these plays could make playgoers feel *civilized,* which is, perhaps the greatest achievement of all.

Two for the Seesaw and The Seesaw Log

I

Competence in playwrighting and play production is never a guarantee of financial success or artistic acclaim. Our university theatre departments exalt and endeavor to teach this competence, but as far as the contemporary theatre is concerned, mere ability has been increasingly unimportant except in the area of stage mechanics. There are instances when the disregard of every procedure once associated with competence becomes a cachet of distinction. Saroyan comes easily to mind, and so do Ionesco and Beckett. Inspired amateurism has come increasingly into vogue, often for better, sometimes for worse.

The stage productions that command the greatest interest in New York vary from downright defiance of conventional theatre to marriages of convenience, whether fusions of common matter with uncommon sensibility (*The Dark at the Top of the Stairs*) or mixtures of ordinary action with bizarre details, as in *Two for the Seesaw*. Both techniques can become suspect, the former in effects of desperation or sensationalism and the latter in acts of marketable compromise. Together these two schools of playwriting make metropolitan playgoing a varied, stimulating, and irritating venture. They comprise nearly all the theatre that commands any regard today or has any sort of future.

Where one stands with respect to the two schools is a different matter, and a long essay could not exhaust their critical, artistic, and practical implications. Everyone can determine for himself whether his fundamental loyalty belongs to a play like Samuel Beckett's *Endgame* presented in Greenwich Village or to one like William Gibson's *Two for the Seesaw* uptown at the Booth. Though some people cannot favor the one without loathing the other there are metropolitan playgoers who are eclectic in their tastes and can enjoy each play. They pride themselves on their tolerance. It is undoubtedly thanks to their catholicity that a cosmopolitan theatre survives at all.

Unfortunately we blunt our judgment and give no help to creative

effort when we endorse the esoteric uncritically or accept the pragmatic
without reservation. This eclectic minority, of which I am a part, pursues
a random kind of play patronage that never corrects its perspective. Perhaps this catchall urbanity is the only possible approach in an age of
transition, but even the best of our New York seasons is a monument to
the reign of flabby Alexandrianism rather than to true vitality in taste
and creation. I do not think well of myself, either, for enjoying plays as
antipodal as *Two for the Seesaw* and *Endgame* instead of being enraged
by one or the other. I am ashamed to find myself raising only a mild protest against the nihilism of the artistic left or the philistinism of the right.

It is a bitter fact of life that the theatre has this weakening effect after
decades of playgoing or professional participation upon even reasonably
resistant individuals. It is essential to correct our sights even if this means
contradicting our original feeling when we were merely reacting as a
member of the audience. It is not dishonest to be honest with ourselves
and to distrust our original responses. We are not uncorrupted when we
we are in the auditorium; we are susceptible to seduction from the stage.
The fallacy that we are on the side of the angels when we are with the
majority is equalled only by the fallacy that the seduction of the audience
is the ultimate in theatrical achievement.

Two for the Seesaw is a prime example of the type of playwriting and
production that prevails with metropolitan audiences by clever accommodation to their standards of taste, interest, and value. It is clever rather
than profound playwriting but it also exudes an air of wisdom, kindli-
ness, and truth of character that makes friends at the box office. This
two-act play was a tour de force both in construction and in the performances of Henry Fonda and Anne Bancroft, who made her Broadway
debut in the play. Interest never flags in this comedy of sentiment until
we are being prepared for the anticlimactic resolution. The continuously
moving action, varied with many a reversal of mood, feeling, and situation, never gives the *impression* of thinness (though I think it *is* thin).

Two for the Seesaw starts with the meeting in New York of a cultivated Midwestern attorney, Jerry Ryan, who is about to get a divorce
from his wife, and a footloose and fancy-free girl from the Bronx named
Gittel Mosca, who is pursuing a doubtful career as a dancer. Jerry has
a bad conscience about the wife from whom he is seeking independence,
and Gittel has bleeding ulcers and a fiery but uncommonly sympathetic
and yielding nature. Loneliness brings them together, and they surmount

differences of religion and manners with wonderful ease. (Liberals cannot help but approve this effortless tolerance, and it is well known that Broadway audiences are unfailingly liberal!) Jerry and Gittel live together for months; they separate at last after she discovers and he admits that he still loves his wife. But the author tells us that they are both the better for their experience. They have matured; he has recovered confidence in himself while she has learned to defend herself against a too yielding heart. (Presumably she will become less promiscuous than she used to be; she may even insist on monogamy and a marriage certificate.)

A closer look at *Two for the Seesaw* is somewhat disenchanting. The ingenuity of the playwriting is beyond question; its genuineness as a study of character and as a comment on life is very much in question. At first the two characters on stage may give us an impression of reality, for Henry Fonda lent the hero his own sincerity and Anne Bancroft created a wonderfully fresh and energetic personality for the heroine. But their nebulous association with other characters is puzzling. Why Jerry left his wife and why he returns to her is fully explained, yet the character of the wife is extremely vague; she is only a voice at the other end of a telephone connection. Although she is described as a rich man's beautiful daughter who has coddled her husband, this is a postulate rather than a reality in the play. It cannot make Jerry's presence in Manhattan carry much conviction; flight from overprotection in the case of a grown man is a rather tenuous premise.

Even when providing amusing and appealing scenes *Two for the Seesaw* gives strong indications of contrivance under its surface verisimilitude. The telephone is in constant use, connecting the characters, promoting the plot, and calling attention to the two settings in which all of the action alternates. The play calls for two actors and thirteen or more stagehands! Thanks to the latter the sets are often in motion, but insight into character is hardly advanced by an army of scene shifters. The play strains to achieve an ardent rapprochement between the two characters, wins our sympathy for them with its comedy and sentiment, and then, shortly after we are satisfied that this oddly mismatched pair have overcome the social barriers, we are told that Jerry still loves his invisible wife. He returns to her after exacting her promise that she will not coddle him any longer, a stipulation which should be funny but is apparently intended to be taken with perfect seriousness. The gentleman and the Bronx street brawler (the author's dubious term for Gittel) separate before liberalism can take hold and give the lovers anything more than a fleeting relationship.

With *Two for the Seesaw* we are back to the pseudo-Ibsenism of Pinero, about whom Shaw said that, "he has no idea beyond that of doing something daring and bringing down the house by running away from the consequences." Gibson could claim to have written a realistic play with an ingenious twist. He sends Jerry home to a palpitating Nebraska wife whose only fault had been to try to make things easy for her husband. The husband suddenly decides that it is time to stop receiving and to start giving. It can be argued that reality is being honestly served when prince and pauper, gentleman and street brawler go their separate ways. But realism can be manipulated by writers who aim to please an audience rather than to disturb it, and I suspect that it is manipulation rather than reality that wins out in the resolution of his romance.

These paragraphs express my minority opinion of an extremely well-performed play. *Two for the Seesaw* was very efficient as entertainment, and as a character Gittel was an admirable creation. Only in promising to be more did the work become less.

2

I realized when I conceived these criticisms of *Two for the Seesaw* that some of them might censure the playwright unjustly. Having been closely involved in numerous professional stage productions I am aware that alterations, deletions, and additions are often made by the playwright at the behest of producers and directors. But I did not think that the author had received enough provocation to want to lodge a public protest or that this particular play had been butchered while the author lay prostrate in an out-of-town hotel. However, along with the text of the play Gibson's detailed report on the vicissitudes of the play was published by Alfred A. Knopf in 1959 under the title of *The Seesaw Log*.

In reading this story of the author's tribulations as he followed his play through production we can sympathize with his annoyance when he writes at one point in the *Log* that while watching the tryout audience laugh, "a dozen trivial changes made in rehearsal for reasons I could guess at—rearrangements of lines to sharpen laughs, synonymous substitutions for immediate clarity, dilutions of the girl's promiscuity and displeasing profanities—stuck in my ear at each performance like pins; but

I was growing too demoralized and too sick in my bones of our incessant conversations to argue every miniscule item."

Gibson got his lumps like many other playwrights and undoubtedly he was not exaggerating in saying, "An alienation from my own work was setting in, and with it a benumbment." He learned that he should not have expected to control his theatrical work in the way that a novelist or poet controls his work when it is being published. The theatre is no place for a fastidious man of letters, which is more the theatre's misfortune than we are apt to think. Gibson learned that there is no time in play production to pause and determine whether revisions made under pressure produce a truer, profounder, and more revealing work than the original version. The sole criterion that determines the changes made in a play before it opens on Broadway is that of theatrical effectiveness. Such absorption with effectiveness means that everybody involved with the production (except possibly the author) will try to tailor the play to the taste of the playgoing multitude.

Although Gibson believes that his play was "improved" only "by becoming poorer," the audience's enjoyment was obviously not lessened by the fact that it did not know what happened behind the scenes. But if the audience does not need to know what has gone on during the course of a particular production, the play reviewer *must* not know. He cannot properly judge the play he sees on stage by waiving blame or credit for the contributions assigned to those normally responsible.

Though one would not have suspected it in the Broadway production it appears from *The Seesaw Log* that Gibson started with the idea that Jerry is very much in love with the wife he left behind in Nebraska. But as a critic who can judge only by what he sees in the theatre and reads in the text this relationship had so little reality for me that Jerry's return was only a Pinerolike compromise allowing him to desert Gittel and return to his milieu. Whether Gibson had Jerry say such lines to his wife as, "*My terms are steep . . . I won't live in Omaha, and all we'll have is what I earn. I'm beginning very—modestly, a desk and a phone and a pencil. And what's in my head*," with or without pressure from others is irrelevant. It is relevant to criticism only that this conclusion is embarrassingly inadequate.

On thinking about the denouement of the play after reading *The Seesaw Log* I sympathized with Fred and Arthur (Fred Coe, the producer

of the play, and Arthur Penn, its director). They labored to get maximum
humor and theatrical effectiveness from the script. Aside from Gibson's
wonderful characterization of Gittel there was little else in *Two for the
Seesaw* to offer the public.

When complaints reach us that a play has been ruined by revisions
forced upon the author we should examine carefully the work on display.
It may turn out that it lost nothing it couldn't spare, acquired nothing it
couldn't assimilate, and underwent no modifications that could possibly
have affected the depth of the work. Many plays have no depth and no
particular meaning to begin with.

3

Less than a year after the publication of *The Seesaw Log* the author
has another successful play on Broadway. *The Miracle Worker* is also
produced by Coe and directed by Penn, and it stars Miss Bancroft. Apparently the author was not at all devastated by his first bout with Broadway.

The Miracle Worker is anything but a masterpiece. Based on the story
of how Helen Keller was liberated as a child from the prison of blindness,
deafness, and speechlessness by a resolute woman, the play has powerful
action and emotion. It is marred for many of us by the use of superfluous
and sentimental off-stage voices, and it is a pity that producer and director
did not prevail upon the author to discard them. This aside, Gibson created a strong and appealing story centered on the character of a tough-
minded woman. The author produced a striking series of conflicts between Miss Bancroft and the savage little girl whom she helped to become
the Helen Keller of history. He added some helpful shadings to the drama
in his characterization of Helen's parents and elder stepbrother. On the
whole Gibson did well by his producer, director, and actors, with a play
of limited range and depth. In turn they did even better by him; there
is superb acting by Anne Bancroft and the remarkable child actress Patty
Duke. The conflict between teacher and pupil is gripping; *The Miracle
Worker* is, for the most part, arresting theatre.

The production is one of many that have made competent playwrights
look like extraordinary ones. Examples like this should remind us that in
the world of professional theatre we are justified in hoping that playwrights will serve the theatre as well as the theatre often serves them.
Being writers themselves critics are naturally sympathetic to playwrights.

If they ever engaged in the intricacies of stage production they might be more in sympathy with producers. If producers can ruin plays, playwrights can ruin productions. Usually producers collaborate in ruining plays just as they collaborate in saving them, and sometimes there is just a hair's breadth between success and failure. One thing we shall never succeed in doing is making the creative enterprise of theatre calculable.

6 TENNESSEE WILLIAMS

Summer and Smoke:
Williams' Shadow and Substance

As if to upbraid Broadway for the ignoble season of 1951-52 the intrepid Greenwich Village group calling itself Circle in the Square revived *Summer and Smoke* shortly after the season was officially closed. The production, in three-sided arena style, proved very successful. As staged by the talented new director, José Quintero, *Summer and Smoke* represented a triumph of atmosphere and theatrical poetry over the mediocre realism that normally gluts the marketplace of tired Broadway showmanship. The freshness of the Circle in the Square production, greatly sparked by the talent of an unknown actress, Geraldine Page, brought to Tennessee Williams' play a Rembrandtlike imagination. If the effect was that of Faulkner and his Southern Gothic rather than that of Rembrandt the reason lay in the play itself: the provincial stalemate, the crude eroticism, and the senseless feeling of doom that Williams took for his subject.

Summer and Smoke proved to be a better play, though still a novelistic one, than it had seemed to be when the 1948 Broadway production introduced it to the New York public. The moving Circle in the Square production succeeded largely because it gave excellent theatrical realization to the shadow rather than to the substance of the play. The work was steeped in an atmosphere of half-lights; emotions transpired in a mist. The action flowed over three areas: the Winemiller home, where Alma lived with her clergyman father and her neurotic mother; the village square with its public fountain and stone figure of Eternity; and the Buchanan combined home and office of John and his doctor-father. The first and third areas constituted environments, although rather shadowy

ones, while the area between them was pictorially neutral but for the
faintly seen fountain and statue.

The center of the stage, the floor level surrounded on three sides by
rows of seats for the spectators, was not an environment as much as a
state of mind. It was a dark void between the respective homes of Alma
and John, between the clerical parlor and the doctor's office. Symbolically
the division was between the spirit and the flesh; between them lay the
dark central areas, the barrier between the heroine and the sensual lad to
whom she could offer nothing but spiritual love. The entire floor-level
stage consisting of the playing areas was framed by a dark border. Townspeople as well as the principal characters would now and then emerge
from this darkness or disappear into it—at times very suggestively, as in
the case of the Mexican femme fatale with whom Dr. John has a sordid
affair.

I do not say that these and other effects were invariably intentional on
the part of the director, who may have tried to make the best of the limited
possibilities of lighting his centrally located stage. But the effect of a production is in no respect invalidated because it results from having to
surmount difficulties of arena staging.

The unsuccessful Broadway production staged by the late Margo Jones
(who had previously produced it very successfully in the round at her
Dallas arena theatre) had given the play a stiff and mechanical objectivity.
The three areas had been so beautifully designed for the proscenium stage
by Jo Mielziner that each was distinct, particularly the central one. The
permanent setting was centered in the village square which was established by platform levels, by the genteel statue of Eternity, and by a fili-
gree screen affording a suggestive sketch of the town. There was nothing
penumbral about the production; the story and its symbolism stood out
clearly at all times. The only blurring of effects was an unintentional one:
most of the action took place in the side areas in which were set the homes
of the clergyman and the doctor. These were pushed toward the wings
to make room for the designer's pièce de résistance, the eye-filling village
square setting. This concentration at the extremities of the stage, and Jo
Mielziner could have had little choice in the matter once it was agreed
that the square was essential to the symbolism of the play, was distracting
rather than expressive.

The Broadway production lacked cohesion. The succession of sharply
outlined fragments provided a blow-by-blow episodic account of the life

history of a lost lamb and prodigal son. José Quintero's Circle in the Square production suppressed the distinctness of the episodes and fused the fragments in a poetic and physical unity. Such cohesion was desperately needed in a play that added up to little more on the surface than a crude novel about the misfortunes of a clergyman's daughter oversupplied with virginal soulfulness.

The play's interest (in the sense in which we speak of the interest of a case history, a sob-sister newspaper story, or a popular novel) resides in the horizontal, scene-by-scene account of Alma's life. The story recounts with mournful seriousness how a small-town Southern girl loves her childhood companion, a wild boy and even wilder youth. Having become a soulful young lady she resists his carnal advances and tries to satisfy him with spiritual companionship. She finally awakens him to a sense of duty after having left it to other girls to satisfy him sexually. But she loses him to a young girl just after he becomes the local hero as a result of a medical discovery, just when she is at last ready to give herself to him body and soul. Plunged into a state of desperation by the irony of her situation she picks up a traveling salesman in the village square and accompanies him to his room. The story also traces the life of her Dr. John, a restive boy in a stagnant town who cannot be content with Alma's spiritual love. He takes up with a Mexican girl, becomes debauched, falls into despair after his father's death for which he is indirectly responsible, and is encouraged by Alma to resume his medical studies. The popular novel in the play is magnified by the implication at the end that Alma has started down the primrose path of prostitution. The symbolic details are obvious appeals to lending-library tastes. For instance, Alma, whose name means *soul* in Spanish, takes up with the traveling salesman at the very foot of the statue of Eternity, the symbol of soulfulness.

Considered alone the story elements show Williams the potential author of banal novels, not Williams the impressive playwright. In fairness to the playwright let us concede at once that many a distinguished play would be a bad novel, just as many a distinguished novel might be turned into a bad play. Nevertheless an elaborate story thrusts itself into the foreground of *Summer and Smoke* with tedious persistence. A strong reason for being grateful to Quintero is that he forced it into the *background,* for the essential worth of *Summer and Smoke* lies in its integrity as a *play*. As such it is a compound of story, plot, characterization, atmosphere, mood, and an attitude of sultry irony. The Quintero production could not abolish the substance—the story, plot, and characterization—of *Summer and Smoke,* but it could and did soften the outlines. Therefore the director could give primacy to the shadow, the mood and poetry, of the work. Because of Quintero's production method, somewhat comparable to out-of-focus photography, and acting nuances (especially in the case of Geraldine Page's Alma), the Quintero production had a penumbral and preternatural poetic quality. It is useless to try to define it further. "Poetry," says Robert Frost, "is what is lost in translation." I would add only that here and there the production had the glow of a phosphorescent fungus, an integrity of decadence. The usual wholesome American production accommodates itself to the smash-hit requirements of costly show business and the special gospel of popular optimism.

The Circle in the Square production was significant in other respects. It brought to our attention a young director of outstanding talent and an off-Broadway group that could hold its own with any Broadway company. In José Quintero we found a director of extraordinary sensitivity, daring, and probity. With his associates of Circle in the Square, Quintero has gone on to present season after season of good plays in generally excellent productions. In staging *The Iceman Cometh,* he repeated his feat of giving a successful revival to a play that had not fared as well on Broadway as might be expected. Once more Quintero's treatment caught both the poetry and the prose of the work and provided cohesion to a composite account of various defeated lives and separate situations. In writing *The Iceman Cometh,* a play with many personal dramas, O'Neill had in view a multiplicity of individual and collective states of damnation from which the Iceman, Death, alone was expected to bring surcease. O'Neill had made things especially difficult for a director in the case of several of his principals with complexities of guilt. There is the murder of a loving woman by a backsliding husband who can no longer bear to see her suffer from his derelictions, the morbid guilt of a jealous son who has betrayed his technically subversive mother to the police, and the nihilism of a former radical who has lost his reason for living when he loses his revolutionary faith. In giving a triumphant revival to O'Neill's *Iceman* (a play that might not be inaccurately described as an American *Lower Depths* with some characters contributed by the author of *The Brothers Karamazov* and *The Possessed*) Quintero and his associates made a great contribution to the revival of O'Neill's reputation in America. Mrs. O'Neill was rightly persuaded to give them the Broadway production rights to O'Neill's most impressive posthumous drama, *Long Day's Journey into Night*. Their success with this production in 1956 climaxed a second career for America's principal playwright, who had concluded his first career with retirement in the mid-Thirties. Without old and new plays by O'Neill, whose return to the Broadway stage started in 1946 with the Theatre Guild production of *The Iceman Cometh*, the theatre of the Fifties would have been decidedly poorer.

At Circle in the Square, Quintero also gave New York its first professional productions of Alfred Hayes' *The Girl on the Via Flaminia*, Schnitzler's *Reigen* or *La Ronde* (the production did very well by Eric Bentley's vivacious version of this naturalistic masterpiece of the 1890's), and Brendan Behan's Irish prison drama *The Quare Fellow*. Excellent revivals of Wilder's *Our Town* and Edwin Justus Mayer's *Children of Darkness* also greatly enriched the off-Broadway theatre. Circle in the Square's off-Broadway stage productions claimed the interest of reviewers who would not have otherwise ventured below Times Square.

At this writing it is evident that Quintero and his associates will have to leave their little playhouse and find new quarters. But their Circle in the Square venture will be remembered with affection and nostalgia long after it passes into history. It is one of the few theatrical enterprises worth remembering in a decade during which dramatic art maintained a tenuous relation to its times and a precarious existence both above and below Times Square. It is worth noting that no other producing company in New York has given such distinction and so much credit to theatre in the round or rather to a modified arena style of theatre, for the audience surrounded the Circle in the Square acting area on three sides only. The arena style was introduced into America in the early Thirties by Professor Glenn Hughes. Margo Jones gave a nationwide impetus to the style when she started her Dallas little theatre in the Forties. Progress on a national scale was furthered in the next decade by other community and university theatres in the round, especially in Washington, D.C. (under Zelda Fichandler's management), but New Yorkers, who had previously viewed arena theatre productions at the Hotel Edison with mixed feelings, had maintained considerable scepticism toward the style before the successful *Summer and Smoke* revival.

What the *Summer and Smoke* production meant for Tennessee Williams is less certain, although it must have confirmed his confidence in a play that had aroused a tremendous amount of interest when originally produced by Margo Jones. But after the Quintero production the gifted playwright may have taken grim satisfaction in the fact that he was no longer accused of repeating himself, accusations that he had heard the morning after the première of the unsuccessful Broadway production. Perhaps, one could hope, he also perceived failings in the play itself now that it had received a successful production. He must have realized that his episodic chronicle was much too leisurely, explosive though it was now and then. Perhaps for this reason he permitted the deletion of the first scene or prologue from his original text, and never since has he shown us so novelistic a play. Nor has he since given us plays in which passiveness was the chief characteristic of his heroine. *The Rose Tattoo* inaugurated instead the reign of the never-say-die female, of Maggie the *Cat on a Hot Tin Roof*, and of the monstrous Hollywood queen played by Geraldine Page in *Sweet Bird of Youth*. The one lesson that may or may not have been realized by anyone at the time of *Summer and Smoke* was that it was important to discriminate between the value of Tennessee Williams' *story*-making and the value of his *play*-making; between the author of lurid plots or sensational situations and the poetic dramatist who made pulsating plays out of his visions of a world of terror, confusion, and perverse beauty. In this respect Williams can be enrolled in the company of the Jacobean dramatists. Like them, he approached but usually failed to hit the target of high tragedy or if he did hit it, it was at the edges rather than dead center.

Williams' Descent: Orpheus Descending

As if to give special emphasis to the lack of direction that characterizes serious theatrical writing today Broadway opened the spring of 1957 with one of the most chaotic contemporary works of genius at its disposal. In the Producers Theatre presentation of *Orpheus Descending*, a rewriting of his early play *Battle of Angels*, Tennessee Williams scattered the largesse of his invention and pessimism all over the stage. More talent for dramatic writing went into this work than will be found in any other living writer in the Fifties if we except Anouilh in France and O'Casey in England.

Harold Clurman's production, with an excellent setting by Boris Aronson and superb lighting by A. Feder, was everything that a playwright could desire. But the play, which held the audience with its violence, communicated its turbulence more frequently than it communicated its meaning. Only two days before the première the Phoenix Theatre had unfolded an uneven but impressive production of *The Duchess of Malfi,* ably staged by Jack Landau. It was very tempting to describe *Orpheus Descending* as a minor Elizabethan drama, that is, as a melodrama aspiring to the status of tragedy or as a tragedy disintegrating into melodrama. In Williams' play there was the same apparent autonomy of the passions, the same explosion of a world, accompanied by the same earnest but unsuccessful effort to be on the side of redemption and life while the author's vision was indentured to corruption and death.

Williams' effort to achieve integration was obscured for some of us by the immediacy of his wild tale of a young man who seeks nothing but peace and finds only disaster in a small Southern town. The tale involves the mentally disturbed sheriff's wife who confuses sexuality with religious feeling (Joanna Roos was superb in the role of this minor character); a wild girl, beautifully played by Lois Smith, whose idealism has degenerated into promiscuity; the heroine's dying husband, who boasts of having had a share in her father's death and who later shoots her down and then accuses her lover of the murder; the wife, stormily played by Maureen Stapleton, who goads her husband into the maniacal conclusion after taking a lover (she had turned on a former lover who had married money and respectability after giving her a child which she allowed to be torn out of her womb); and the young hero, played by Cliff Robertson, who becomes the object of several frustrated women's desire and dies horribly through no fault of his own. This multiplication of griefs, evils, and horrors simultaneously fascinates and bewilders the spectator.

Williams was by no means contriving situations and events irresponsibly. As any modern poet would do, he presented a plot on several levels. His play was by implication the story of the descent of Orpheus, Val Xavier, a guitar-playing and poetic young man, into Hades. Hell here is the Southern town which festers with frustration and boils with violence. Williams made an effort to plant his flowers of evil in the social realities of our time. The play contains references to racial intolerance and the chain gang and presents a devastating picture of a cultural Sahara in the deep South. Williams also presents a built-in hell in the nervous system of several characters. Though he appears to have succumbed to sentimentality in the treatment of his pedestrian hero as a demigod immolated on the altar of avid femininity, the author of *Orpheus Descending* endeavors to present an accurate view of life and to render a true verdict. But the snarled symbolism of the play diffuses the action and obscures realities of environment and character.

Val Xavier becomes attenuated as a real character once the author turns him into the symbol of the artist lost in a wilderness of lusts and rapacities. This self-pitying version of the artist has been familiar ever since the poet-as-hero romanticism of the early nineteenth century. Myth is scrambled in the play when two legends about Orpheus become entangled in the symbolism of the work. The plot runs parallel to one legend of the bard's descent into the underworld; the other analogy is that of his being torn to pieces by the Bacchantes driven to frenzy by orgiastic religion. The equivalent here is the sex-hunger of Williams' frustrated Southern women. Orpheus-Val does not descend into the underworld in order to recover his lost Eurydice. But he does find an ironically seedy Eurydice, the married woman who desires him and costs him his life. She is certainly lost in this town of bigotry and hatred, and the dying man she has married under economic pressure is certainly the Pluto of Greek myth. He is Death, for he murders his wife and brings death to Val with the false accusation of murder.

There is a great deal to grasp at one sitting, especially when the hero is so many personalities and symbols blended together. We have, for instance, Val the poet, Val the idealized male pursued to his destruction by sex-hungry women, and Val the noble savage of Rousseauist romanticism (probably derived by Williams from D.H. Lawrence, one of his favorite authors).

In *Orpheus Descending,* Williams tried to present two of his major themes conjointly: the tragic isolation of the artist in the hell of modern society and the crucifixion of the pure male on the cross of sexuality. He also wrestles with the worthy but extremely difficult experiment of amalgamating realism and imagination, and of transforming literal reality into poetic reality .

The fact that *Orpheus* was a failure on Broadway does not lessen its superiority to most new plays on view in New York and London. Williams was straining to make a refractory medium express the visions of reality that he shares with other negativistic modernists. He can be roughly compared, for example, with Samuel Beckett, but what distinguishes him from the author of *Waiting for Godot* is the romantic expansiveness of his dialogue, characterization, and plot-making. On these and other grounds we cannot relate Williams to Ionesco, either. In our time only Jean Genet, whose grueling and perversely absorbing plays, *The Maids*, *Deathwatch*, and *The Balcony*, which were briefly displayed at tiny off-Broadway theatres, has displayed the same melodramatic imagination and partiality for naturalistic effluvia.

Orpheus Descending was apparently a necessary recapitulation for Williams. An important venture even in failure, it did credit to both the author and his director. Evidently they disagreed on which aspect of the work needed stressing—the realistic or the symbolic—and on where the concentration of the play should come. But though I would have preferred a fuller development of Val as an individual rather than as an Orpheus symbol the important fact is that a theme very close to a greatly gifted playwright's heart continued to resist his dramatic talent while continuing to fire his imagination.

Williams' "Garden"

Tennessee Williams' two play off-Broadway production *Garden District* won some enthusiastic support in New York during the 1957-58 season. It is remarkable how much forbearance audiences often bring to an unusual work which might just as well have outraged them into insensibility to its values. The first of Williams' pieces, *Something Unspoken*, was of no great consequence, although it confirmed the author's uncanny familiarity with the flutterings of the female heart.

But the longer of the two pieces, *Suddenly Last Summer*, was a work of perversely overwhelming power. It was born of a most desperate view of the world and of the bleakest pessimism. Had a European written it, the play would have received detailed notice in the literary quarterlies; it might have even received profound explications that it does not need. *Suddenly Last Summer* concerns the fate of a degenerate poet reported to have suffered a horrible death at the hands of a cannibalistic swarm of hungry and debauched boys on an unidentified beach. He is the second poet in a Tennessee Williams opus to have been torn to pieces; the first was Val Xavier, the unfortunate hero of *Orpheus Descending*. The fantasy of *sparagmos* or Orphic death for artists has lingered a long time with

Williams. The artist and the normal world are ever at war with each other in his *Weltanschauung*.

The report of the poet's death comes from a nerve-frayed female cousin who accompanied him on his last trip as he searched for exotic and homosexual experiences. His purse-proud and ruthless mother, bent upon suppressing the manner of her son's death, has managed to imprison the girl in a mental institution. She is trying to induce a young surgeon to perform a frontal lobotomy which will empty the girl's mind of horrible memories that are anything but complimentary to the poet and his family. The surgeon interrogates the patient with a truth drug, and the appalling account of the poet's degeneracy and cannibalistic death gushes forth from her lips. The physician concludes that even cannibalism may be the truth rather than a fantasy of the girl's disordered mind.

A satanic view of the world is vividly expressed in an incident told in the play. Once the poet and his mother observed birds of prey hovering over newly hatched sea turtles in order to devour them before they reached the sea. The watching poet had exclaimed that in this example of mass murder in the natural world he had at last seen God. At another point the persecuted heroine dismisses the affection between human beings by saying that, "We all use each other and that's what we call love." Symbolically—and literally, too—the story of the poet's life and death is said to be "a true story about the time and the world we live in."

It matters little whether the gruesome details of the poet's death are literally true. The play emanates from the author's mind, and what really matters is the sensational expression of his most nihilistic mood. But no matter how much he is obsessed with morbid pessimism, Williams is not destroyed as an artist; he presses the nettle of neurosis to his bosom and it brings him honor through creative achievement. This is contrary to moralistic expectations, but art has its own peculiar morality. The playwright brings compassion to the tormented girl and to the entire tormented world of man and animal as well.

If there is an old-fashioned romanticism (a Byronic romanticism?) in Williams' rebellion against the satanic element in nature the objectivity of dramatic writing exercises control over him until the final revelation of cannibalism. Objectivity of characterization also keeps him in check. His exposure of such unscrupulous characters as the deceased poet's mother, incisively portrayed by Hortense Alden, is further proof that taking note of evil is not the same thing as accepting it at the expense of judgment. Williams has rarely written dialogue with such intensity of feeling and vividness of imagery as in *Suddenly Last Summer*. He unfolds his situation with compelling interest, and up to the final revelation he commands belief. Perhaps his talent, which has not been remarkable for steadiness of judgment, would be employed more advantageously if it were free of Grand-Guignolism, but Williams is a writer who must follow where his subject and imagination lead, come what may. In many respects he resembles Strindberg; both make demands on our indulgence that only genius is justified in asking.

It does not follow that Williams does justice to his potentialities. If he would but bring half of his mature talent to writing today a play of such simple sympathy and modest loveliness as *The Glass Menagerie* there would be no one alive except O'Casey to rival him.

Williams' Sweet Bird of Youth

In advance of its Broadway opening *Sweet Bird of Youth* was rumored to be a less formidable drama than several of Tennessee Williams' earlier pieces. But anyone who hoped for a milder and less lurid view of the human condition was disappointed. In this 1959 production the playgoer was introduced to some of the theatre's least attractive characters. Among them were an hysterical Hollywood actress, a gigolo who had infected his home-town girl with venereal disease, a racist Southern politician, and the latter's shiftless son who apparently delights in castrating people.

Williams' picture of the deep South was no more inviting than the bleakest of Faulkner's Southern Gothic landscapes. The fact that the Hollywood actress has moments of natural anxiety and pity and that the gigolo feels a pure love for the girl he contaminated and remorsefully awaits castration did nothing to soften the force of the playwright's impeachment. Williams' fluent writing, which continues to be more nuanced and poetic than most American playwrights', only accelerated the power with which his appalling content was hurled at the playgoer. And Elia Kazan's theatrical imagination worked with feverish intensity to heighten the relationship between the characters as well as to take full advantage of the first direct politcal attack that the author has allowed himself to make in his plays.

The public was unable to resist the combined onslaught of Williams and Kazan. Whatever resistance there had been was quickly extinguished by the power of Paul Newman's performance. There was theatrical excitement in his taut flamboyance in the role of a lost and excitable misfit; a flamboyance almost equalled, though different in age and character, by Sidney Blackmer's portrayal of the political Boss Finley. High praise was also due Geraldine Page's remarkable attunement to the aging actress, reduced to drugs in her effort to defeat time and anxiety. She made this monstrous character exciting both as an imperious movie queen and as a pathetically insecure woman and artist. The reality and the charlatanry, the egotism and insecurity, and the fragility and strength of the character were all part of her interpretation. The portrait of this woman was immensely successful, especially while she was anxiously awaiting news of her effort to stage a comeback in films. Two experts, the author and his star actress, were equally responsible for the portrait. Tennessee Williams has rarely created a character so distinctly in the round, so mercurial yet so well defined, and so monstrous yet so appealing; Miss Page had never before turned in so unmistakable a triumph of acting personality and technical skill.

Sweet Bird of Youth became a palpable hit. Part of the reason for its success could be attributed to Cheryl Crawford, the producer of the show, who merits all her rewards. To her persistence in the heartbreaking business of Broadway production she has invariably brought integrity and discrimination, ever since her association with Harold Clurman and Lee Strasberg in founding the Group Theatre in the early Thirties. But despite the talent of playwright, cast, and sponsorship, I had strong reservations about *Sweet Bird of Youth*.

The split dramatic construction divided attention between the personal drama and Williams' comprehensive attack on racist demagoguery. The attempt to focus sympathy on two self-confessed monsters, the actress and the gigolo, was hardly less disturbing. Even the author's noteworthy skill in blending disparate plot elements did not mitigate the impression of overstuffed playmaking. The gigolo had once seduced Boss Finley's daughter, giving her both a child and a venereal disease requiring surgical ministrations. When he compulsively returns home and flaunts his presence in town he invites the vengeance of Boss Finley and his racist supporters, led by the son. They threaten castration as the punishment to fit the crime, a punishment they have recently meted out to a Negro agitator. At the end of the play the gigolo, overwhelmed with a sense of guilt and still longing for the girl whose life he has ruined, his delusions of hoped for Hollywood success gone, awaits his tormentors and the horror of his fate.

The *frissons* in the play can be gauged from this précis, and they were more than sufficient to capture an audience. But such elements are also indicative of strain. The artist *manqué* pitted against a destructive Southern community has long been one of Williams' themes. Williams' actual or imagined conflict with the Southern world of his youth apparently rankles. He drew this world in early plays and symbolized it in *Camino Real* and, entirely to his credit, he simply cannot reconcile himself to it. It is unfair to accuse him of disingenuously adding topicality to his new play, though we can question his mixing of the ingredients; and the strain in the action comes from the author's feelings, not from deliberate sensationalism.

It is more difficult to defend him against another complaint, that of expecting us to care for his fated monsters. *Sweet Bird of Youth* was based on a premise that simply could not support it. A confusion of values was bound to occur when we were asked to sympathize with a Hollywood harridan and her gigolo and to empathize with characters who were more properly objects of satire than of pathos. Perhaps comic detachment was the proper point of view to bring to these characters. Mockery, rather than tragic pity, is what these monsters and the world of cheap values they represent richly deserve. Charlatanry, vainglory, dog-eat-dog motivation, and alternating hypocrisy and cynicism appear constantly in their conduct and confessions.

Williams was certainly drawn to a comic perspective of the actress and her relations with the boy early in the play, and his exposé here was nothing short of brilliant. Comedy was applied with particular success to the Newman role, especially in the scene in which he plants a recording machine under the bed in the hope of blackmailing the actress into starting him on a Hollywood career. Because she proves more than a match for him the humor of the scene is memorable. This duel of intrigue between two shabby characters evoked Elia Kazan's most authoritative direction and best exemplified Geraldine Page's virtuosity.

A great musicologist, Sir Donald Tovey, once said that comedy is often the only dignified means of expressing very deep feeling. Williams' comic attitude toward his principal characters unquestionably arose out of his deepest feelings, and an admirer might wish that the playwright had maintained his comic objectivity. But his attitude wavered; in the later sequences of the play he tried to impose tragedy on his comedy and as a result the boy becomes a factitiously tragic figure. A similar limitation appeared in the unflagging and driving Elia Kazan production; it fluctuated between comic incisiveness and dubious tragicality. After the first act both play and production tended to favor the latter. In a theatre in which effectiveness attained at any cost is virtually the only criterion (it best protects an investment against loss) it may be too much to expect controlled dramatic imagination. The alternative treatment in *Sweet Bird of Youth* would have required a consistently satiric imagination, one not to be diverted by melodramatic political elements and castration fantasies. Admittedly a completely satirical treatment of these materials would have been difficult to achieve and even harder to market. But since it *was* attained in some scenes by the combined talents of Williams, Kazan, Newman, and Page, it is all the more regrettable that their success was not constant.

Perhaps we will have to ripen into a much older civilization before the normal bent of our serious artists becomes predominantly comic. We cannot wait that long for the natural aging process of a society. We might hasten the process slightly by a reëxamination of tragedy and comedy, with a little irreverent thinking about the former and a greater appreciation of the latter. Is tragedy so precious or so necessary that we must risk melodramatic extravagance in order to attain it? Can we hope to achieve it with mean-spirited characters and situations which might better qualify as objects of comic scrutiny? Far too often we identify seriousness with tragicality without first ascertaining the worth of the characters and the quality of their values. Comic intelligence rarely makes false evaluations. If we are to be serious we might do worse than to start being serious about comedy.

7 THE LATTER-DAY O'NEILL

The Iceman Cometh Intact

When *The Iceman Cometh* first appeared under the Guild's auspices many admirers of O'Neill had misgivings. I recall that at the annual session of the Drama Critics Circle Award only George Jean Nathan, Richard Watts, Jr., and I selected it as the best play of the season. Yet everybody agreed that it was an imposing work that seemed to burst the boundaries of the theatre. The production gave some of O'Neill's critics the opportunity to repeat the charge that America's greatest playwright couldn't write prose and that he was not soigné enough to mingle in the civilized company of European playwrights.

The Circle in the Square production directed by José Quintero at the end of the 1956-57 season made nonsense of such charges. It did so by not avoiding the challenges of the dramatic text. Quintero did not attempt to smooth the wrinkles in the writing, nor did he reduce the great quantity of dialogue and monologue. He did not avoid the even more formidable volume of O'Neill's despair.

The result was an overpowering and exhilarating experience. Mustering the full strength of his growing talent José Quintero directed the play as one tremendous flow of life raging and subsiding in a welter of anguish and confusion. Making full use of the three-sided arena stage at Circle in the Square he put O'Neill's action in the midst of the audience by effective use of floor space and the vitality of the acting and direction. In this intimate arena production nobody sought to achieve esthetic distance. Quintero submitted to O'Neill instead of trying to tame and refine him. The director's chief triumph was his preservation of O'Neill's conquest of the pettiness of existence with massive gloom and rage.

232

The director allowed the architecture of *The Iceman Cometh* to remain as cyclopean as the author had left it instead of trying to reshape it and refine it. The lesson to be derived from this procedure is that professionalism proves most rewarding when it takes difficult art at its face value on the right occasion with the right technique, and yields no inch to the playgoers' frailty. This kind of directorial honesty is always rewarding if the actors are good enough, as Mr. Quintero's were in every case from the least important actress playing one of the tarts to Jason Robards, Jr., who played the almost inhumanly exacting part of Hickey.

A Moon for the Misbegotten

On reading O'Neill's posthumously published drama, *A Moon for the Misbegotten*, in 1952 I was at first put off by a laboriousness which appears in much of our modern American literature from Melville, Whitman, Dreiser, and Sinclair Lewis right up to William Faulkner. The stream of American culture appears to have been the natural habitat of powerful primitives. O'Neill was surely one of them. Every new publication or production of his plays since the early Twenties, with the pleasant exception of *Ah, Wilderness!* has tended to strengthen this impression of cumbersome magnificence. My first impression as a reader I set down loftily in the sentences that follow:

> It seemed that *A Moon for the Misbegotten* could only call attention to the lumpishness we must still learn to overcome in ambitious playwriting. The play is most alive when O'Neill conveys the plain reality of the Irish farmer, Phil Hogan, and his oversized daughter, Josie, in a relationship at once amusing and touching. There is much vitality in Hogan's efforts to hold on to his farm and to marry off his daughter to his educated barfly-friend Tyrone. But in writing this play O'Neill was once more absorbed in the larger matters of self-damnation, futility, and ironic fate. And as usual O'Neill made these absolutes swell to huge and vague proportions like a cumulus cloud. Josie's fate is determined by the fact that she is grotesquely large. Her physical size is treated as a fatality of nature. O'Neill is again found grasping for the extraordinary and the grotesque with the object of defining life "tragically." Lest Josie should find fulfillment in love, which would

either annihilate or mitigate the tragic premise, O'Neill presents the
one man who is strongly drawn to her as another kind of freak. A
mother-fixated and self-destroying drunkard and wastrel, he is one
huge Negation; and for all the excellent realistic details that provide
verisimilitude, the portrait of Tyrone is another oversized abstraction.
Since Josie is endowed with the yearnings of a woman, O'Neill's
giantess grows before our eyes into a Positive. But the female Positive
is left stranded by the masculine—and intellectual—Negative. Modern
intellectual despair must be served and the human condition be made
untenable!

The original Theatre Guild try-out production was stranded in the
Midwest in 1947 for want of an oversized actress capable of playing Josie,
but in 1957 New York saw *A Moon for the Misbegotten* as a special art
theatre production. Now the peevishness I registered on first reading the
play was more than balanced by that hammering effect that O'Neill's
work so often has in the theatre and that makes the work of his neater
contemporaries seem picayune. For all my discomfort I included *A Moon
for the Misbegotten* in my next volume of *Best American Plays* (the
Fourth Series). The fact is that the record of my encounter with this
drama of desperation seems to me as important as my eventual surrender.
It tells me, and it may tell others too, what qualities usually make unsuccessful O'Neill drama vastly more compelling than many successful plays
by other American playwrights.

Produced for the first time on Broadway by Carmen Capalbo and
Stanley Chase as Production 2 of an experimental Bijou Theatre series,
A Moon for the Misbegotten proved to be another impressive O'Neill
item. Dour but tender, the love story of an overgrown farm girl and a
spiritually dead Broadway playboy lashed to the wheel of his morbid
memories was a unique work, perhaps best described as a naturalistic
romance. This is an anomalous designation bound to offend the logically
minded, and bound to impress others as a euphemistic way of saying that
the author was simply a concealed sentimentalist in this piece. But O'Neill
was driven and fate-obsessed in treating "the misbegotten." Both his romantic afflatus, present from the start of his career, and his naturalistic
penchant for seedy life and malevolent cosmic determinism were genuine
aspects of his temperament. Even the element of the grotesque, strongly
marked in the play, is a grotesquerie of both romanticism and naturalism.

The production staged by Carmen Capalbo seemed too deliberate but probably could not be substantially lightened or leavened. It was apparent in this drama of ill-fated love that O'Neill had again succumbed to his tendency to magnify every emotion and action. Cyril Cusack played the raffish father with gratifying ease. But Wendy Hiller, while giving a superb performance as the lovelorn slattern, showed the strain of having to play an overemphatic role. And Franchot Tone in the role of the self-damned prodigal, James Tyrone, Jr. (also a character in *Long Day's Journey into Night*), evinced some embarrassment, as if he were uncomfortable with either the egregiousness of his damnation or the pawkiness of his language.

Nevertheless, *A Moon for the Misbegotten* overshadowed every other non-O'Neill play of the season. (Toward the end of the 1956-57 season, which should be known as the O'Neill season, there were four O'Neill productions in New York if we include *New Girl in Town*, the musical version of *Anna Christie*.) I confess to having been held and stirred by the play even while trying to resist its assault on my equanimity. His usual magic of moods and tensions was present in the web of the plot, and his very insistence on the hopelessness of his characters was a form of loving concern for them. He cared so much about them that in the end others could be mesmerized into caring about them too. And caring or not caring with any personal intensity was still a major consideration in a theatre that had lost much of the unapologetic fervor it had once possessed.

Long Day's Journey into Night

José Quintero's staging of O'Neill's long autobiographical drama, *Long Day's Journey into Night*, in the fall of 1956 was a flawless production. It is understandable that playgoers who had never known the full force of the original productions of *Desire Under the Elms*, *Strange Interlude*, and *Mourning Becomes Electra* should have considered O'Neill's last play his greatest. No friend of the author would be inclined to disagree with this judgment. It was fitting that the posthumous triumph should accrue to his name as a result of Mrs. O'Neill's approving the production of a play that might otherwise have been withheld for twenty years after her husband's death.

The professional American theatre had served O'Neill's reputation effectively only three times before in the twenty years since the Theatre Guild production of *Ah, Wilderness!* in 1935. Two of these events, the Harold Clurman revival of *Desire Under the Elms*, staged for the American National Theatre and Academy, and the Quintero revival of *The Iceman Cometh* at Circle in the Square, had not even reached Broadway. In staging *Long Day's Journey into Night*, written about fifteen years earlier, Quintero and his associates brought O'Neill's second mainly posthumous career to an impressive climax. This was less than half a dozen years after it had become customary in intellectual circles to characterize O'Neill's work as being more effort than achievement and almost hopelessly dated. This was the second period of underestimating O'Neill. The first had been in the late Thirties when proponents of left-wing theatre condemned him for not writing Marxist social drama. The critics of the early Fifties condemned O'Neill simply for *not writing*, that is for not writing fine literature.

It took a strong effort to restore balance with the presentation of *Long Day's Journey into Night*. It was one of O'Neill's leviathans, a four-hour play of turbulence and fatefulness. Perhaps the most remarkable feature of the production that reached New York, therefore, was its fluency and freedom from strain. Quintero staged the play with imperturbable relaxation, as if the painful intensities of young O'Neill's life with a drug-addicted mother, an alcoholic brother, and a miserly father were an almost everyday family picture. Some directors might have been overcome by the suffering in *Long Day's Journey* or been overimpressed by its length. But it seemed as if nothing in the author's autobiography could elude this director's quiet strength in dealing with human error and misery. Nothing intense in the play was overpointed or treated with awe by the director, yet nothing painful was actually softened or abated. One got the impression that the director had brought to the play a sort of Apollonian equanimity along with his human sympathy.

The direction and performances were in mutual support. Fredric March as the father-hero who is an insecure matinee idol gave the part all the multidimensioned reality one could desire. Florence Eldridge was deeply moving if unavoidably static in the role of the mother who has plunged into drug addiction. Jason Robards, Jr., grew overpowering as he revealed the depths of love-hate beneath his alcoholism and the ambivalent attitude toward his younger brother. The young brother is

Eugene O'Neill himself, the future dramatist of doom who observed its shadow falling on himself and his family before beginning to postulate it as the universal human condition. Bradford Dillman was genuinely affecting as the incipient young author who makes the dreadful discoveries that his mother is addicted to drugs, his father intensely self-centered and miserly, his brother a hopeless failure filled with sibling hatred, and he himself a tubercular patient.

It seemed as if O'Neill had deliberately set out to contradict Thomas Mann, who wrote in *Tonio Kröger* that, "If you care too much about what you have to say, if your heart is too much in it, you can be pretty sure of making a mess." By the time O'Neill wrote *Long Day's Journey* he was already about a third of a century removed from the experience itself and was able to make drama out of his theme. He was the author-as-young-man refining his tragic sensibility in the cauldron of the family situation. There is so little personal pressure, so little compelled writing in most contemporary plays that O'Neill makes most more polished playwrights seem miniscule beside him.

Long Day's Journey into Night is essentially a simple play. It is almost disconcertingly elementary because its author, though obviously selective, seems to have been disinclined to suppress any detail. But O'Neill's simplicities happened to be human complexities. They needed only to be revealed—though hardly at so great a length as O'Neill considered necessary—to prove oddly compelling on the stage. His play was a long journey of discoveries and recognitions within a brief period of time into which a world of experience was packed, cramped, and confined. For the playgoer it was a long journey too. It brought him into O'Neill's domestic dark night of the soul from which there was no likelihood of emergence into the light of mystic illumination. In confronting the dark with O'Neill it was possible for playgoers to feel fortified, as if they had seen all they needed to see of human failure and could emerge on the other side of despair.

With the publication and production of *Long Day's Journey into Night* it became easier than it had ever been before to see O'Neill's total dramatic work in perspective and to observe the personal nature of his tragic view of life. Limited though that view was, it was impressive because it was truly his own; he had mined it out of his life and family relationships. The first traumatic insights of youth remained, in a variety of sublimated and half-sublimated ways, the insights of mature age. In a time of massive disenchantments and catastrophes they conspired to make him the inconsolable giant of the modern drama. It also became clear why, remembering his brother James, he had to write so desolate a play as *A Moon for the Misbegotten*.

A Touch of the Poet

A Touch of the Poet is our last legacy but one from the period when O'Neill retired to write a formidable cycle he did not live to complete. It must be a dismaying work to idolaters of trim playwriting, and it must be downright painful—though no more so than a dozen other plays by O'Neill—to those who judge the drama by literary standards exclusively. Thanks to the taste and efficiency of English departments, young writers are so well-schooled in moderation these days that Eugene O'Neill's firing power, justifying a verbosity that would have proved fatal to any other American playwright, is not likely to be emulated much in America. One finds qualities of the primitive among great playwrights. The primitiveness that sustained O'Neill on his way to fame also encumbered him, and it will probably never similarly sustain anyone else. By primitiveness I do not mean ineptness, but an unrefined directness, a monumental insistence on feeling or idea. This persistence occasionally makes one uncomfortable. But O'Neill usually had his way with us all the same; he injected his vitriol and glucose into the blood stream, and he hammered his points into the brain.

A Touch of the Poet prevailed upon the Broadway stage in the 1958-59 season not by finesse but by simple power. It piled detail upon detail, and if you were attending to the play instead of trying to be clever at its expense characters came to life, feelings became real, and a trivial theatre briefly became an intense world. To try to explain how O'Neill achieved this effect, not with simple reiteration but with dramatic creativity, would only lead to a lengthy and inconclusive disquisition.

Merely to say that O'Neill wrote for actors does not explain his power, though *A Touch of the Poet* shows its author doing precisely that. The entire premise of the play is based on the fact that the main character is an actor. He is one kind of man by humble birth and humiliating circumstance; he is another, more glamorous kind of man by preference and histrionics. The pretense is not just a matter of common histrionics,

but of men's rising "on the stepping stones/Of their dead selves to higher
things" by some charisma of personality, by some will to believe, and by
some power of the imagination.

The play that reached New York, after a dubious out-of-town reception while the production was still in a formative stage, proved impressive and appealing. Harold Clurman's staging was a triumph of intelligence and sensibility, and the performances of Helen Hayes, Kim Stanley, and Eric Portman in the leading parts justified various degrees of
qualified enthusiasm. Miss Hayes appeared too consciously an actress in
her part, but she rightly suggested the overeagerness of a woman
trying to please her husband and living in a state of continual anxiety.
Though Portman could barely be understood at times this was partly
because he made unintelligibility part of the character, with results as
dramatic as they were sometimes disconcerting.

For an audience in need of a major dramatic experience it was irrelevant that *A Touch of the Poet* is not one of O'Neill's major dramas. Its
central character, the Irish innkeeper Con Melody, is pretentious and
snobbish about his aristocratic origins. He is, in Broadway parlance, a
phony, insufferably heartless in his behavior toward his long-suffering
Irish peasant wife and his daughter, whom he treats as slaves. At the
end of the play he is a deflated man rather than a tragic figure, a fact
which may have tried the patience of the spectator but did not necessarily
invalidate the play. Con Melody was a failure, but his struggle against
his realization and acceptance of failure was little short of heroic. It is a
tribute to O'Neill's power of sympathy that while Con Melody causes
us much irritation we can join his rebellious daughter in regretting that
he has renounced his pretensions at the end of the play.

O'Neill managed to give Con Melody size as well as vanity. The man
has a touch of the poet, and the title characterizes his dreams of vainglory and his reluctance to accept a commonplace life. Melody's effort to
abolish the tawdriness of life by means of a desperately maintained fiction
has an uncommon resonance. Clinging to his brief illusion of glory as an
officer in the British army during the Napoleonic wars, he adapts more
than family and tavern to his fantasy. Melody scorns the young society
of the American republic recently liberated from England and voices
contempt for the rule of the *canaille* in a leveling democracy. He reacts
against America in the same way a poet might react against Yankee
materialism. Trapped in the New England of the early nineteenth cen-

tury he takes to his cups, but for all his bitterness retains a certain gal-
lantry of heart and mind worthy of a former officer of His Majesty's
army. In the course of the play his pretensions are thoroughly deflated
by the Yankee father of another poet, a young man who has taken a fancy
to Melody's daughter. Crushed when the rich merchant refuses to fight
a gentlemen's duel with him and has him jailed instead, Melody renounces his dream of magnificence in the land of the philistines. He
shoots the thoroughbred mare that has symbolized his aspirations and
delusions. The renunciation humanizes him, but it is painful to watch.

Harold Clurman performed a feat in pacing the play for Broadway so
that it was constantly in a state of developing tension. Each actor responded with conspicuous delineations. Even the single appearance of
Betty Field as a woman guarding her distinction in the world of Yankee
merchants (she played the mother of the poet who has fallen in love with
Sara) was an authentic characterization and a tour de force of theatricalization. Kim Stanley was wildly beautiful and stormily dramatic in the
role of the mettlesome daughter who is more like her father than she
realizes.

But for the success of A Touch of the Poet the ultimate credit belongs
to O'Neill. Written in 1942, it is anything but a brilliant play, but a
decidedly compelling, if somewhat trying, one. Once more O'Neill dead
proved to be more alive than most of his living contemporaries and successors. Once again the secret of his magic was an integrity and an intensity rarely found in the theatre at any time.

It is difficult to believe that O'Neill would not have been pleased at
the attribution of much of the play's success to the production and actors.
Although few dramatists were as insistent upon having their full say in
their play manuscripts and although he always wrote as though he had
calculated every detail of stage action, O'Neill always gave actors rich
histrionic opportunities. Himself the son of an actor, he was closely
involved with stage production during his association with the Provincetown Players as their author and, later, one of their three directors. He
had a knowledge of acting and a respect for its contribution that persons
with a purely literary training rarely acquire. He would have agreed
emphatically with Sidney Howard, another playwright well versed in
the collective art of the theatre, who wrote that, "The better, the more
profoundly the dramatist writes, of course, the better he will serve actors,

and that is his *raison d'être*. Audiences do not go to the theatre to hear plays but to see them."

In spite of the gracelessness charged against him, O'Neill was a meticulous writer, and he might have questioned Howard's further statement that playwriting "does not spring from a literary impulse but from a love of the brave, ephemeral, beautiful art of acting." Regardless of his specific intentions O'Neill's plays, with all their verbal freight, usually came out as histrionically shaped material. Lest we lose sight of the author's reliance on the actor in the density of his action and characterization, we should examine the long individual passages in O'Neill's plays that call for a bravura performance. Hickey's immense monologue on death in *The Iceman Cometh* is an example. So is the posthumously released one-act piece, *Hughie*, published by Yale University Press. Virtually a dramatic monologue, *Hughie* would exhaust its content in half a dozen sentences if the multitude of words put into a lonely man's mouth were not fundamentally a scenario for an actor's performance.

I would like to conclude these remarks on O'Neill's posthumous full-length work with the words of one of his most loyal friends and admirers, the late Dudley Nichols, who was also my long-time friend and collaborator. In reply to some reservations I had made about the dialogue in O'Neill's plays he wrote me as follows:

> His [O'Neill's] one passion was to *dig*, into man and himself, and try to understand what man is—and if he heard a ghostly echo of godhead now and again, he wanted to get that in too . . . he was a gifted poet, who put his poetry into perception and architecture rather than into words—satisfied to let his words be as exact and expressive as he could make them. Poetry is simply a "making" power, it is the creative spirit of all the arts—not just an arrangement of words as so many unpoetical people imagine.

8 EUROPEAN VISTAS

Tyrone Guthrie's or Pirandello's *Six Characters*

Perhaps we submit ourselves too wholeheartedly to the allure of theatricality. We should try instead to take theatricality naturally and with the customary ease of the performers of the *Comédie Française*. This organization has long maintained an histrionic tradition to guard against the overstrenuousness of the *parvenu* in theatricality. Tyrone Guthrie's superb direction of the Phoenix Theatre's 1955-56 revival of Pirandello's brilliant play, *Six Characters in Search of an Author,* inspires this reservation. The operation performed on this celebrated play by Dr. Guthrie and by one of the best actors in his cast, Michael Wager, overemphasized the role of the actors as against the characters. But most of the emphasis came from theatrical overproduction. The actors tripped deliberately over the props and there was a general fuss about stage business that tended to overshadow the content (more or less philosophical and tragic) that gives *Six Characters* its impressiveness as a play.

It was to the credit of the play as well as the Guthrie production that this revival of Pirandello's masterpiece was almost continuously fascinating, though almost entirely wrong in my opinion. With all its improvisation it remained a play about people who, in Pirandello's own words, "think what they feel." For playgoers who think what they feel the production managed to hold interest despite the backstage life. Though the actors tended to become too prominent they were vivid stage personalities, due to the thoroughly rehearsed performances of Kurt Kasznar, Natalie Schafer, and others. The characters, Whitfield Connor, Katherine Squire, Betty Lou Holland, and Michael Wager, proved to be histrionic. Histrionic the characters should be, to some degree, for they too

242

are creations of an author writing for the stage, even if he supposedly failed to finish the play he wrote about them. The prime limitation of both the play and the production is one that seems to pervade the modern theatre. *Six Characters,* for all the art, skill, and intelligence that went into its making, fails to resolve an essential conflict between theatrical reality and the illusion of extratheatrical reality.

No such conflict existed for Sophocles and Shakespeare, but it has plagued and fascinated the playwrights of our century. The theatre lacks a settled style for elevated drama. Thus Thornton Wilder could not resolve the conflict of two kinds of reality in *The Skin of Our Teeth,* which suffers at times from skittishness in the midst of a brilliant comic creation. *The Matchmaker* is completely fused in structure, atmosphere, and tone only at the expense of dramatic significance, which it would be pedantically foolish to expect from this carefree farce. The split between life and theatre is apparent in many stimulating modern plays; but it often prevents even the best of them from materializing as unequivocal vision and experience.

No such split existed in classic, renaissance, or neoclassic French drama because the questions of what is theatre and what is life, what is stage convention and what is extratheatrical was not a subject for concern, doubt, or public debate. In *Henry V* Shakespeare disposes of the life-theatre antithesis by telling his audience to "make imaginary puissance" and goes on with his mimic business. Where make-believe is the playwright's subject there is no confusion apparent in the old theatre. Beaumont and Fletcher, for instance, in *The Knight of the Burning Pestle,* evinced no particular concern over any dichotomy between life and theatre or about the possibility of confusing the two as Pirandello, the modern man, did. On the contrary they were amused and expected their public to be entertained by the notion that the earnest middle-class folk of their play should get theatre and life mixed up.

Pirandello, who did deliberately blend theatre and life and expected his audience to follow his concern about the theatricality of reality, presents great difficulties to the producer of a play such as *Six Characters in Search of an Author.* In staging the play for the intrepid Phoenix Theatre management Tyrone Guthrie was forewarned by the failure of two previous Broadway productions of the play. Apparently he was resolved not to allow his production to be caught in any metaphysical trap of Pirandello's devising. He did *not* want to be drawn into discussions of being and nonbeing, of what is real or not real; he wished to make it clear to the audience that the actors, the real persons in the production, were simply making up a lurid story about a broken-up, bitter, and confused family. At the end, after the painful suicide of a young character, we knew that the actors had been merely playing at make-believe. We knew, because at the most distressing point in the climax of the family's drama, the drama of the invented but uncompleted characters who have started looking for an author to round out their lives, the actors grab a stuffed figure from the wings and proceed to toss it about. Guthrie, in short, overcame the difficulties of the play, and the only question concerning his adaptation and production is whether he did not kill the patient by curing him. He unscrambled the play that Pirandello had very deliberately and very provocatively scrambled. He simplified the meaning of an action that Pirandello had intentionally complicated. Since the whole of the play and the very reason for Pirandello's writing it lay precisely in the complications, the adaptation and staging by Tyrone Guthrie. sacrificed this play in favor of a simpler one that Pirandello might have written but most certainly did not. Ultimately we have to decide whether we want *Six Characters* by Pirandello or *Six Characters* by Guthrie. Guthrie's play was funnier as well as clearer on the surface, while Pirandello's is a work of an entirely different calibre, a cerebral drama that is caviar to the general public. But we would be wrong to dismiss it before we have actually seen it on the stage. We certainly did not see it at the Phoenix Theatre in spite of the earnestness of the management and the overwhelming skill of the director.

A churlish playgoer might have concluded that the Guthrie production did not actually simplify the problem much as introduce a new one, making one wonder why the play should be taken seriously at all. One is not really likely to lessen the difficulties of Pirandello's play by compounding its theatricality. The author makes it plain in *Six Characters* that he intends to disqualify the realistic theatre as a mirror of reality.

Perhaps we should set limits to our penchant for theatricalizing what is already theatrical. In our century part of the business of modernism has been to worry about the problem of calling attention to the histrionic character of the stage as the medium of dramatic art. Even where no such concern appears, we are likely to find the playwright somehow hinting to us that he is being daring or bright or ingenious or progressive in violating the simple illusion of reality. Invariably, if we examine the play or the production closely enough, the effect is a weakening of the dramatic action, the dramatic meaning, or the raison d'être of a serious work.

Harlequinade in Anouilh's *Mademoiselle Colombe*

Broadway, once the citadel of topical realism, has been increasingly attracted in recent years to a retheatricalization of the drama. The period of realistic plays seems to be drawing to an end, and we now seem to be favoring again the discovery of theatrical possibilities.

Since our mentors in this enterprise are chiefly the French it may be useful to look at Jean Anouilh's *Mademoiselle Colombe*, as adapted by that keen-minded critic Louis Kronenberger and staged by Harold Clurman. The latter's training under the archtheatricalist Jacques Copeau is often overlooked because of his noteworthy association with the socially oriented Group Theatre of the Thirties. The vogue of Anouilh, both in his native France and in England, is largely the result of his ability to interfuse a disenchanted viewpoint with as much theatricalism as his subject can afford. In this combination of the real and the theatrical, of truth and art there is always considerable fascination. In *Colombe*, Anouilh went further toward making theatre out of the realities of character and environment than in *Thieves' Carnival, Ring Round the Moon,* or *Antigone*. Moreover, in *Colombe* Anouilh made much of the very tension between personal relations and make-believe.

In *Ring Round the Moon* (originally *L'Invitation au Château*) a man hires an actress to draw his brother away from an unpleasant millionairess. In *Antigone* Creon merely "put on an act" for the good of the country by refusing burial to the unidentifiable remains of one of Antigone's brothers. But *Colombe* is, on the surface, a story about the theatre itself. The son of a prominent actress at the turn of the century entrusts his young wife to his mother when he is conscripted into the French army. The young woman is delightfully susceptible to the uninhibited life of the theatrical set. She soon proves unfaithful to her husband with his brother who is a gay bounder loosely attached to the stage. When Colombe leaves her husband toward the end of the play and he is alone on the stage we are treated to a flash-back scene in which he recalls how he first met her in the theatre trying to deliver flowers to his famous mother. Inevitably the play is replete with amusing histrionic outbursts by the celebrated actress and the bizarre philanderings of her leading man, her playwright, and her business manager.

Shrewd characterizations are as abundant in this piece as humor, and the Broadway production was up to all requirements. Julie Harris was superb as she made the transition from a respectable but impressionable young wife to a flamboyant ingenue. She added, for good measure, a fierce forcefulness when she finally told her husband that his moralistic rigor had been sheer egotism. Eli Wallach brought a comic and a pathetic quality to his role as Colombe's husband, although his New York accent bothered me and I didn't understand why his director allowed him to stare continually into the auditorium. Sam Jaffe was excellent in his dual role of prize cuckold and irritated secretary to the leading actress. The formidable Edna Best pulled out all stops as she blustered in the role of Sarah Bernhardt's rival. Within Boris Aronson's ingenious and brilliantly comic settings, particularly the star's quarters, all was theatre.

If not everything was satisfactory in the production, if the effect seemed scattered, the underlying reason may have been the impossibility of establishing a common style or effective ensemble performance under the hurried and haphazard procedures of Broadway production. Edna Best had a way of cracking the seams of the production with her energetic acting. In discussions of a theatrical play such as *Colombe* my complaint may resemble a guest's grumbling against a wedding on the grounds that the bride is too pretty. Edna Best's playing was simply too strong for Broadway, where we are unaccustomed to such forceful histrionics. If her style of acting was also too strong for the play, the reason was that some of the other actors seemed to take her tantrums too seriously instead of with comic knowingness. They should have realized that she was putting on a show for *them* as well as for herself.

On Broadway, indeed, the stress on theatrical life in the story diminished apparent subtleties of characterization and the author's worldly wisdom. Theatre within the theatre undoubtedly added savor to the story; Anouilh, however, intended this background not as an end in itself, but as a means toward his particular kind of ruefully skeptical approach to human nature. He was trying to tell us that human nature abhors a vacuum and that self-righteousness cannot fill it. Undoubtedly the premise of *Colombe* can be worded differently, but the substance of the play is its worldly tolerance, predicated on the belief that life wants *more* life rather than less. That is what the awakened Colombe tells her righteous husband, and that is what he is trying to understand. His reaction to her infidelity is not so much indignation as a sincere desire to find out how she could have been unfaithful. Egotism, the barrier between one person's principles and another person's desires, stands in the way of his comprehension.

Apparently an American drama jury cannot be impressed when the vehicle for this or any other idea carries so much theatrical freight which the audience considers corny. (The French and English public, less dedicated than we are to the cult of experience outside the theatre, has always taken delight in kleig-light experience.) There are gratifications to be found in this not altogether satisfactory and somewhat disturbing play, below the surface interest of show-business comedy. Anouilh is one of the few twentieth-century playwrights after Pirandello who is really adept at deriving comedy, pathos, irony, and sympathy from contrasts of reality and illusion. Though he lacks Pirandello's incisiveness he is a Pirandellian playwright. His Colombe is the eternal Columbine in a harlequinade where even the characters find it difficult to determine what is theatre and what is life. Anouilh provides correctives, here and in perhaps a dozen other plays, to humdrum realistic playwriting.

Regrettably, this particular harlequinade was mired in domestic drama compounded of standard ingredients of boulevard adultery and sentimentality. For all his Gallic scepticism and lightness of touch Anouilh is constantly in danger of lapsing into sentimentality with his usual regrets for the passing of love, youth, beauty, purity, integrity, and what not. The originality of Anouilh—at least for a Broadway-jaded public— lies in his urbane manner and theatricalized technique. Posture takes the place of poetry and profundity in his plays. When the posture loses its aplomb, as it does in Colombe, the magic with which Anouilh expects to master us evaporates.

Anouilh's *The Lark:* The Theatricalist Joan

Even so stirring a work as Anouilh's *The Lark*, in Lillian Hellman's energetic adaptation, jeopardized its potentialities because of the obtrusive theatricality of its structure. Anouilh's treatment of Joan of Arc's story alternates between simple dramatic experience and the pyrotechnics of an author in love with his own inventiveness. Illusion is continually broken, reëstablished, and disestablished until the sincerity of the author and the meaningfulness of his play can be challenged. The results might

have been disastrous on Broadway but for the vigor and direct affirmativeness of Miss Hellman's work on the original version.

We may have been stirred and even stimulated by the Broadway production starring Julie Harris. But looking closely at the work we would
have to confess that we did not really know how the episodes hang together. The early scenes, for example, are supposed to be played at Joan's
trial as reënactments of her past. But the withdrawal of her submission
to the Church (she is in prison then and is receiving a visit from the Earl
of Warwick) and the burning of Joan could not have been reënacted at
her trial since they postdate it. Yet these scenes are followed by the re-
enactment of Joan's crowning of the Dauphin which transpired before
the trial. Indeed this scene closes the play only because one of the characters at the trial has burst on the stage during the execution scene to
declare that the execution must be suspended until the coronation has
been performed. How dubious the device is, even if it brings the play to an
effective close, may be gathered from Christopher Fry's faithfully rendered dialogue for the London production. (The text of the Fry translation
of The Lark has been published by Oxford University Press.) The lines
read:

> Grant a stay of execution. . . . We haven't performed the coronation!
> We said that we were going to play everything! And we haven't at all!
> It isn't justice to her. And she has a right to see the coronation per-
> formed; it's part of her story.
>
> [Since the Bishop who condemned Joan agrees to this change of
> plans, Joan is unchained from the stake and her story is given a happy
> ending.]
>
> . . . an end [says Bishop Cauchon] which will never come to an
> end, which they will always tell, long after they have forgotten our
> names. . . .

Confirmation by the literal Fry translation should exonerate Miss
Hellman of any charge of having falsely theatricalized Anouilh's play.*

* Miss Hellman's adaptation lets illusion take hold of us by withholding the information that actors are putting on a play. Miss Hellman's theatricalization of reality
proved to be quite fascinating. But even an instantly perceived play-within-the-play
technique would not eliminate ambiguities in the work. Even knowing that The
Lark is a play about a play being performed will not necessarily eliminate an uneasy
feeling that reality and stage illusion have become entwined rather disturbingly. In
retrospect I found myself longing for Ibsen's old-fashioned grip on experience or for
Shaw's only slightly less old-fashioned hold on reality in Saint Joan.

The play ends with a picture postcard scene of Joan crowning Charles at Rheims. How inferior such theatrical tightrope walking is in dramatic conviction, though not in sheer histrionic interest, to Shaw's straightforward *Saint Joan!* Even in the Epilogue Shaw's fantasy does not interrupt and alter the representation of Joan's real life. How inferior, too, are Anouilh's theatrics to the tragedies of the Greeks, Shakespeare, and Racine, in which no Pirandellian tricks are played with story and the sequence of events determines the form and style of the work.

That the newspapermen whose reviews send the great public to the box-office were not outraged by *The Lark* is surely a symptom of a relaxation in their critical standards, which until recently were fundamentally realistic. Neither did they protest when Maxwell Anderson's *Joan of Lorraine* was produced about a decade before. In a theatre which does not have a living tradition or classic foundations and in which realism is felt to be old-fashioned anything that breaks the illusionary character of the drama is likely to be welcomed. Yet I too was fascinated by the production of *The Lark* and with the performance of Julie Harris who brought her own theatricality to the role of Joan. The criticism presented in the previous paragraph is merely intended to define the limitations of the play and of all distinguished modern plays that let theatre intrude into life. The old masters let life intrude into theatre.

Within these limits *The Lark* proved to be keenly ironic, swiftly moving, odd, and even stimulating theatre. One might have expected a Joan of Arc play to fail ignominiously after Shaw's *Saint Joan.* That this was not the case was a miracle of sorts for which Julie Harris, Boris Karloff, Christopher Plummer, the other excellent performers, Lillian Hellman, and Jean Anouilh were jointly responsible. But even this talented group of professionals couldn't make as compelling a play as *Saint Joan* out of a work so theatrically oriented and greasepaint conscious as *The Lark.*

The Waltz of the Toreadors: Anouilh's Valse Triste

It was symptomatic of the theatrical season of 1956-57 that it did not bring forth a single work or style of production that could suggest a reliable mode of creativity for the American stage. The introduction to epic theatre by the Phoenix' *The Good Woman of Setzuan* was infelicitous. The Terence Rattigan double-bill, *Separate Tables,* won Broadway's heart with gentle persuasions to tolerance but without furnishing any ferment for American playwriting. Even so home-grown a drama as O'Neill's *Long Day's Journey into Night* was a sport, from which no progeny could be expected. For all its forthrightness of realism and sympathy, this prickly autobiographical drama is a uniquely private experience made public. It is not the sort of work that can be described as seminal.

Among the very few productions of the Fifties from which a more agreeable conclusion could be drawn is Jean Anouilh's rueful farce-comedy, *The Waltz of the Toreadors*. With this play, which arrived in Manhattan while his Joan of Arc drama, *The Lark*, was still successfully touring, Anouilh completed his long-delayed triumph on the American stage. There could no longer be any doubt that the tide of opinion in America had turned in favor of the one French playwright since Giraudoux and Sartre who qualifies for international reputation.

Still, it is questionable whether Anouilh's work leads where American writers can follow with confidence. In this treatment of a retired general's strange domestic life the French author mingled the wildest farce with the deepest pathos allowable to his characters in their provincial aristocratic environment. It should not be difficult to find parallels in the old South, and the play indeed recalls Faulkner's and Williams' work in a variety of details. It is even possible that the enthusiasm of the play-going public and the newspaper reviewers for Anouilh's picture of unsavory domesticity and rancid romanticism could be traced to the preparations they have received from our Southern novelists and playwrights. Actually Anouilh is less provocative in this play than he has been in others such as *Antigone* and *The Lark*. But his concentration on human perversity is more rewarding here because it is less artificially theatrical. He keeps his focus exclusively on human relations and private life, and he takes a more balanced if still bizarre view of the contradictions of the heart. He gives a wry account of the difficulty of renouncing romantic aspirations and resigning oneself to the calm of age; he writes poignantly about the absurd rage of the heart and the folly of the blood. Farcical yet moving, mocking yet sympathetic *The Waltz of the Toreadors* stands between extremes of dramatic experience.

At the time it seemed more likely that *The Waltz of the Toreadors* would appeal to adult playgoers (and it is truly a play for the mature rather than for the nubile) without actually gratifying them. Anouilh's quizzical attitude produced a curious mixture of reality and extravagance. This was especially true in the rivalry of the bemused General and his illegitimate son for the hand of the romantic spinster with whom the father had been infatuated in his cadet days. Perhaps those who favored the play, and favored it extravagantly in my opinion, were a trifle overimpressed because Anouilh's combination of insight and farcicality, of sentimentality with mockery seemed so sophisticated. There may also have been an element of recognition in the reactions of unmarried and too-much-married gentlemen. But theatre does have an insidious way of flattering us into overestimating some of its productions by enabling us to feel urbane. Both Molnar and Noel Coward have been beneficiaries of this ability to make us feel superior and worldly wise.

Perhaps it is ungracious to raise questions of purpose in the case of *The Waltz of the Toreadors,* for if the play had less suggestion of depth and had been received purely as entertainment I should not have been so fastidious. Why, for instance, are we exposed to the contradictions of a woman who hates and despises her husband, but who holds on to him so desperately that she makes a permanent invalid of herself in order to keep him tied to her? Why are we involved with the spectacle of the General's strenuous absurdities as an unfaithful yet apparently cuckolded husband, as a romantic dreamer who must content himself with kitchen maids, and as an absurd roué who cannot capture the one woman whom for decades he has kept quixotically pure? (He loses this love to his naïve young secretary, who turns out to be his illegitimate son by a long-forgotten working girl.) And why is this elderly lover of beauty given parental responsibility for two of the ugliest girls in creation? If the answer is irony it is too pat a quality, adding up to very little that is not inverted romanticism. It may be extravagantly appealing to many playgoers, but it is suspiciously like sado-masochistic *Kitsch.* What we really get from Anouilh here is superficial pessimism compensated by farcicality. There is enough truth in the portrayal of the General's foibles and enough pathos in the absurdity of his situation to win our approval. But we can be misled into overvaluing this play (as we do several other Anouilh pieces such as his hollow *Antigone* and *Eurydice* or *Legend for Lovers*) if we overlook the *artificiality* of the work. Anouilh is for the most part still concerned with the theatricality rather than the reality of his human material. An example of this preoccupation is the sequence in which the General's long admired ideal woman turns up and his secretary-son wins her for himself.

Harold Clurman's production and Ralph Richardson's playing of General St. Pé showed the strain of both farcicality and pathos in the work, but fortunately also contributed moments of incisive characterization. Mildred Natwick created a memorable climax of Strindbergian fury as the invalid wife who turns on her philandering husband, exposing his vanity and assailing him with an hysterical account of her own real or fancied infidelities. Her playing of this pivotal scene brought a terrifying reality to an artificial play. At the end of the scene General St. Pé is goaded into making an attempt to strangle her. He bungles the job as he has bungled all efforts to realize his romantic aspirations. He is reduced to submission to his fate, shackled to a maniacally vindictive wife and fixed to the ludicrous treadmill of one more affair in the rose bushes with one more kitchen girl.

The Waltz of the Toreadors is undeniably fascinating in its twists and turns of action and emotion. But it is also fundamentally deceptive when it wins approbation as a masterpiece rather than as a clever contrivance only now and then galvanized into life. Even Anouilh's pessimism is only half genuine here. It is far from offensive because the highly cultivated author expresses it with attractive whimsicality, but we must not make the mistake of assigning any challenging properties to the author's viewpoint. He is cheerfully hopeless in this play and it is right that he should be. It is obvious that not tragedy but tragicality becomes his largely pinchbeck characters. A good deal of their grief is pose, as is the author's romantic-antiromatic attitude. If there is a *valse triste* in *The Waltz of the Toreadors* it was put there by a showman, not a philosopher.

Beckett: *Waiting for Godot*

To serve the purposes of meaningful drama with showmanship is the greatest art of the theatre. These ingredients were combined in midtown Manhattan when the venturesome Michael Myerberg, calling on seventy thousand intellectuals for support, offered Samuel Beckett's symbolist and static two-act drama, *Waiting for Godot*. This play had long been considered uncommercial and had even closed ignominiously during a Miami tryout run. To my mind *Waiting for Godot* is a touching and beautiful little play that has been blown up beyond all sensible proportions by our recently fashionable obsession with works that invite explication. To a *parvenu* intelligentsia it would seem that a work of art exists not for its own sake but only for the possibilities of interpreting it.

This Alexandrian tendency has appeared in England too, and it is not surprising that the London *Times Literary Supplement* should have devoted its lead article to the symbolism of *Waiting for Godot*. But it is also true that the most intelligent of the champions of ambiguity and one of the ablest of explicators, William Empson, the author of the influential *Seven Types of Ambiguity*, objected vigorously to the *Times* article and pointed out that "not all ambiguity is good."

To all this tohu and bohu about the profundity and difficulty of the play my reply is simply that there is nothing painfully or exhilaratingly ambiguous about *Waiting for Godot* in the first place. It presents the view that man, the hapless wanderer in the universe, brings his quite wonderful humanity—his human capacity for hope, patience, resilience, and, yes, for love of one's kind, too, as well as his animal nature—to the weird journey of existence. He is lost in the universe and found in his own heart and in the hearts of his fellow men. The play also presents the social outlook of the author, an outlook filled with the double-edged disillusionment of a large number of contemporary intellectuals. I call the attitude double-edged because the author impartially cuts down both master and servant, as well as both the past and the present (and probably also the future) social order. Master and servant are inextricably tied to each other in the two most dramatic scenes. In the first of these the master is tyrannical and brash while the servant is obedient; he is vicious only to the man who sympathizes with him and would take his part. In the second scene an indefinite amount of time has elapsed and the social situation has, I presume, evolved: The master who was once so sure of his direction is blind, while the scurvy servant who once had made an attempt to speak, albeit in a rudimentary stream-of-consciousness fashion, is now altogether dumb; and both hapless creatures are so firmly tied to each other that they cannot go anywhere without simply tumbling in a heap together. One may reasonably take this latter scene to be Beckett's comment on social progress.

The details of the relationship between the two tramps, who obviously represent mankind, and the awaited Godot, who never appears, lend themselves to a variety of interpretations. But no matter how we explain the details we cannot stray far from common sense unless we make a determined effort to do so. We cannot stray far from what is more important than a rigorous definition of the play—that is, from a pervasive feeling of tragicomic disenchantment and rueful pride in our persistent humanity. There is a fine sensibility, a delicate vibration to the human

condition in *Waiting for Godot* that can captivate us if we allow ourselves to yield to it. That sensibility is evident in numerous touches of
poetry. It makes *Waiting for Godot* a little masterpiece.

Whatever infidel existentialist or orthodox Christian explanation we
happen to favor, it is not an imposed philosophy but the fragments of
poetry in the dialogue and action that are the reliable touchstones of
the play. An obvious example is the tramp Vladimir's reiterated reply
to the little boy, the angelic messenger or what you will, who brings the
message that Godot isn't coming. The boy asks, "What am I to tell Mr.
Godot, Sir?" The simple human plea for recognition in Vladimir's reply
to this, "Tell him you saw us . . . You did see us, didn't you?" is as moving
as anything to be encountered in the modern drama. Evocative of the
human condition and of the human spirit, this little episode, which occurs
twice in the play, is a direct address to our sensibility and self-respect.
Touches such as the other tramp's cry of animal need, Vladimir's endeavors to teach his primitive friend (or perhaps primitive alter ego)
the rudiments of manners, and Vladimir's shout that the grubby tree
is "covered with leaves" when it actually has put forth only four or five
leaves constitute a rich texture of feeling and implication. Only in terms
of discursive reason, the language of prose argument and of definitions, does *Waiting for Godot* present any difficulties. But common sense
should tell us that no play, whether *Hamlet* or *Waiting for Godot,* succeeds in the theatre because of its difficulties rather than because it trans-
lates itself into experience that one readily feels and understands.

What all this has to do with Broadway showmanship should be evident. It is the business of theatre to bring to light that which is hidden
and make simple that which is complex. This is required by the very
nature of the public medium. Therefore the theatre is a powerful reducing agent (a fact to which intelligent persons ignorant of the theatre or
out of sorts with it apparently cannot reconcile themselves) and everyone who functions in it is also a reducing agent. Thus it happens that
a Broadway producer thinks nothing of sponsoring a play such as *Waiting for Godot* which comes to us under the most formidable intellectual
and esthetic auspices. For the producer it is not a mystery but a show,
not a conundrum but a simple revelation about the conditions of human
existence. Moreover, a Broadway comic such as Bert Lahr (blessings on
his innocence) thought nothing of taking on one of the major roles.
Lahr's playing of the childishly naïve and petulant tramp Estragon was

a work of innocence as well as of standardized clowning at which this veteran of the vaudeville and musical-comedy stages is a supreme master. He actually overcame much that is negative and despairing in Beckett's work. E.G. Marshall, playing the intellectual companion Vladimir, collaborated in winning a victory for an affirmation that is all the more affecting because unaccompanied by pomp, rhetoric, or platitude. (Beckett affirms so little about our humanity and yet so much; this paradox is the heart of the poetry of the play.) Vladimir insists on maintaining human decency despite the indignity of his and Estragon's situation: their awaiting a constantly postponed visit from Godot. This effect, furthered by the rest of the small cast (Kurt Kasznar as the bullying master, Pozzo, and Alvin Epstein as his servant, Lucky) under Herbert Berghof's poignant direction, won my respect and affection for the work.

Still, enthusiasm for this original symbolist drama must allow that Samuel Beckett's play is a self-limiting work with its dour picture of humanity and crude physical details. It drew a heated protest in Joseph Shipley's outraged exclamation in *The New Leader* (May 7, 1956): "But what strange mentality accepts this dungheap agglomeration as representative of the human race? We still know sons of Adam named Einstein and Shakespeare and Mozart." Beckett's description of the situation of humanity is surely not conducive to the range and the elevation we perceive in great drama. The play has been overrated in some quarters precisely because its negativism is so fashionable at present.

A point to be made is that Broadway, in its wizened innocence and insouciance, managed to shake off much of Beckett's negativistic philosophy very much as a dog instinctively shakes water off its back. The reflex action of showmanship was equal to the occasion, as it apparently was not in an earlier tryout in Florida. Good showmanship is always affirmative in its vivacity, and it was at its best while Bert Lahr was on stage giving an abundance of life to Estragon who is half child and half cheat, half world-weary traveler and half resilient clown, half animal and half man. There was no apocalypse indeed in the turbid action or, rather, actively presented nonaction of the play. There was no apocalypse even with Bert Lahr on the stage. But the first Broadway production was generally more affirmative than negative and more tender than severe.

Those who had no imagination to bring to *Waiting for Godot* or those who could not briefly forget that they had heard more plangent music and nobler strains in the theatre were outraged and disappointed. Some

of these latter critics felt that even if Beckett was correct in describing
our primitive state mankind had already transcended it with its Einsteins
and Mozarts, and that the playwright had left out of account civilized—
however precariously civilized—man. But if we glance at the history of
civilization in our own century or if we ask ourselves how often and how
far humanity has lived up to expectations we can find ample justification
for Beckett's point of view.

Two other productions of the play were briefly seen in Manhattan
before 1960; one of these, staged by Herbert Blau, went on to the Brussels World Fair. *Waiting for Godot* spoke for sensitive and intelligent
members of a between wars generation on both sides of the Atlantic.
Some of its audience rejected ascriptions of negativism to the play and
agreed with the anonymous reviewer in the London *Times* who called
Waiting for Godot "one of the most noble and moving plays of our generation . . . a threnody of hope deceived and deferred but never extinguished . . . a play suffused with tenderness for the whole human
perplexity . . . a prolonged and sustained metaphor about the nature of
human life" which made "a particular appeal to the mood of liberal
uncertainty which is the prevailing mood of modern Western Europe."
Other admirers of the play found its negations primary.

But precisely because there has been a tendency to treat *Waiting for
Godot* as a touchstone of modernity and as an expression of the modern
spirit in the West, it is important to separate our appreciation of the
merits of the work from a maudlin self-indulgence in decadent fin de
siècle doldrums. Not all of humanity has failed to meet Godot. Not all
of humanity has felt that it had to wander the earth shiftlessly until it
has met Godot face to face. Perhaps that is the one certain way of never
meeting Him—and of never deserving to be met by Him.

Beckett's *Endgame* and Symbolism

In the enterprise of contemporary unconventional theatre Samuel
Beckett's *Endgame* reveals a singleness of tone and a tenacity of purpose
that commands respect as well as bafflement. It is a more concentrated
work than *Waiting for Godot*, and, for all its negativism and existentialist nausea, a vigorously imaginative one. Though allusive it has no
self-conscious artiness. The movements of *Endgame* are musical rather

than plotty; the familiar Aristotelian dramatic movement of a clearly defined beginning, middle, and end would be less expressive in this ostensibly unregretful account of the dissolution of the world and the hopelessness of the human condition.

In the Cherry Lane Theatre production of the 1957-58 season, as well as in subsequent reading of the text published by the Grove Press, *Endgame* recalled the relentless artistry of Joyce, Beckett's countryman and fellow exile. First written like *Waiting for Godot* in French for the French avant-garde stage, *Fin de Partie* was translated by the author into English under the Joycean title of *Endgame*. The texture of the work in English was therefore entirely authentic, and it is the *texture* rather than the transparent structure (of which there is little) that provides the meaning of the work. Hardly anything happens in the play; nearly everything that might have happened has already transpired: the world has been mysteriously destroyed, perhaps by a nuclear explosion and fallout. What concerns Beckett is the end-of-the-party *feeling* or endgame—not the story nor even the poem, but the poem's musical suggestiveness and imaginative reverberation. The author's feat lay in his ability to make these elusive qualities almost continuously arresting. *Endgame* may go down in the history of the modern theatre as a masterpiece of dramatic decadence. I intend no slur in this designation, for I prefer well-expressed decadence to ill-expressed health.

I also prefer the integrity of despair to optimism by fiat or by accommodation to the requirements of show business. The candor of the honorable damned is superior to the hypocrisy of the dishonorable morale boosters who are legion in an affluent society. Within the ambience of art we should believe only in the redemptive, though limited and temporary, power of art, and on these grounds Beckett's writing deserves our admiration. There is no doubt in my mind that Beckett's plays are the work of a true artist. He is entitled, therefore, to be judged within the environment of art rather than of sociology, religion, or politics insofar as we can divest ourselves of bias.

The yardsticks of dialectical materialism and moralism are equally out of order in appraising the play. Dialectical materialism could only say that *Endgame* is decadent. Moralism and theology would say that the play is sinful, since nothing damns the soul so much as despair of salvation. Neither yardstick could tell us that this hauntingly powerful work of the imagination is art.

There remains in *Endgame* only the problem of communication. There is a large contingent of playgoers incapable of responding to a work of art unless it can be reduced by them to the lowest common denominator of discursive reason. But the production staged by Alan Schneider was so engrossing and the performances of the four actors (Lester Rawlins as Hamm, Alvin Epstein as Clov, P.J. Kelly as Nagg, and Nydia Westman as Nell) so mesmeric that to try to explain the work to those who resisted its magic would have begged the question of the merits of the play. Besides, I felt incompetent to offer explanations at the fall of the curtain on the second night of the off-Broadway production; my first response was simply that of a playgoer. In the following paragraphs I shall do my best to satisfy those who considered my partisanship quixotic.

There is little point in trying to unriddle *Endgame* for you unless you have already responded to its essence without an explanation. How far must we go as playgoers in finding specific and consistent definitions for the two symbolic main characters? Hamm is a tyrannical old despot who sits paralyzed in his wheelchair; his youngest servant, Clov, wheels him around in a curious room with two windows, one affording a view of the land and the other of the ocean. The specific allegorical identity of these two protagonists doesn't really matter. We care more about the immediate stage reality, the end-of-the-world, end-of-the-party reality that they evoke. The *sense* of the work, the sense of impasse, doomsday, and existentialist absurdity is far more real than any discourse can make the play. That is why the good symbolist poem transcends explanation; it is greater than its symbols. If a symbol could be exhausted by definition it would not really be poetic, for it would then have only one fixed or frozen meaning.

There is no formula for ultimate despair, any more than there is for ultimate ecstasy. In this transcendence of formulistic statement *Endgame* is beyond allegory. Any explanation, as in the case of all true poetry, is bound to be only a vague and broken shadow of the thing itself. Coleridge said, "Poetry gives most pleasure when only generally and not perfectly understood."* Nothing happens in *Endgame* and that nothing is what matters. The author's *feeling* about nothing also matters, not because it is true or right but because it is a strongly formed attitude, a felt and

---

* *Notebooks,* 1797.

expressed viewpoint. The *bitterness* matters, as, for example, in the fear expressed by Hamm that mankind, now virtually extinct, might be revived, that evolution might start all over again because of the flea in Clov's trousers (for which reason it must be extirpated at once with insecticide). The *sense of entrapment* matters, as when Hamm says violently, "Use your head, can't you, use your head, you're on earth, there's no cure for that!" The intensity of Hamm's *contempt* matters, as when he shouts sarcastically, "Get out of here" [the shelter, outside of which everything is dead or dying] "and love one another! Lick your neighbor as yourself." The elegiac *mood* matters when Hamm, giving up all resistance to imminent death, sums up his (and mankind's?) situation: "You cried for night; it falls; now cry in darkness." And he reflects, "Moments for nothing, now as always, time was never and time is over, reckoning closed and story ended."

Endgame is not inexplicable, if we must have explication. In an article called "How to Read *Endgame*"* Vivian Mercer has offered an interpretation of the play. I take the liberty of summarizing it here, interpolating a few thoughts of my own.

Everybody and everything outside the shelter, which is the setting, is dead except for a boy standing outside whose chances of survival are slight—although there is just a bare possibility that he will survive. Inside the shelter are the aged legless couple, Nagg and Nell the parents of Hamm, encased in separate ash cans. They still have warm human affection for each other, retaining their pristine simplicity and good will. Being legless they can't go anywhere; they are the discarded past in their ash cans and they are doomed to die. Nell (as sweet a woman as one could want in Nydia Westman's impersonation) does die in the course of the play. The other two characters, Hamm and Clov, are Master and Servant and, vaguely, also Father and Son. Both hope for extinction. Hamm, who is blind and crippled and has to be wheeled about by Clov, longs for death; Clov, tired of him and eager to leave him, thinks of killing him. As mentioned earlier Clov takes such a jaundiced view of life that he quickly destroys the flea in his trousers lest life start all over again. *Hamm*, it might be noted, suggests hammer, and *Clov* suggests *clou*, the French word for nail. The two can be said to be hammer and

* Vivian Mercer, "How to Read *Endgame*," *The Griffin*, June, 1959, The Readers' Subscription, Inc., New York.

nail in their master-slave relationship (a relationship that concerns Beckett also in the earlier *Waiting for Godot*) and in other symbolical relationships as well. While remaining master and servant, Hamm and Clov might also symbolize the two aspects of the human personality, mind and body, or, suggests Professor Mercer, "will" and the "consciousness" in man's mind, for the shelter with its two windows (eyes?) can represent the human skull.

Nagg and Nell to me are simply the ancestors of the human race. But according to Professor Mercer they may represent "the hereditary factors present in character or moral endowment; indeed the two ash cans may represent the gonads, in which the past of the human race lie waiting to become its future." In analyzing Hamm and Clov, Professor Mercer calls attention to parallels with the last phase of a chess game (the endgame). In this interpretation the red-faced Hamm tucked up in his wheelchair is "the red king, who can be moved one square at a time in any direction." The red-faced Clov is another, more mobile red piece, perhaps a knight. Since Nagg and Nell are described as white-faced they are "two immobilized white pieces." Perhaps they represent man's unblemished past when mankind had sweetness, wholesomeness, and creative power. The play is not about a chess game, but the pattern of the endgame in chess may be an analogue to "the end of the party."

Regardless of explanations one thing is certain: *Endgame* is not a play that will endear itself to a large public anywhere as long as it is natural for human beings to resist fatalistic accounts of their condition and prospects. Many will rationalize their dislike for the play by saying it is undramatic. Since there is no possibility of struggle against fate in *Endgame* the pattern of the work cannot follow the pattern of naturally active drama. Music is the natural medium for the expression of moods, and the author himself wrote, "My work is a matter of fundamental sounds." He also warned, "If people want to have headaches among the overtones, let them."

There is surely no conclusively redemptive element in the work; it offers neither the solace we find in *Waiting for Godot,* nor the forbearance that the two tramps have for each other while humbly waiting to meet the Landlord of the world. Vivian Mercer has called *Godot* "a despairing study of hope"; I would go further and say that it is not wholly despairing. No such defense can be offered in behalf of *Endgame*, "a despairing study of despair," to quote Mercer. Ultimately the success of this play as the expression of a twentieth-century state of mind must be accompanied by its failure to please the general public which remains, and probably will always remain, optimistic. It cannot afford the morbid luxury of pessimism. The taste of nothingness may have been felt by almost an entire generation in our time, but a taste *for* nothingness is not widespread even now among playgoers and is not likely to grow.

Obviously, even admirers of *Endgame* hope that history will totally invalidate Beckett's prophetic vision. But regardless of accuracy, Beckett has come close to a state of mind in mid-century civilization. One is reminded of a fragment by Coleridge:

> *Truth I pursued as Fancy sketch'd the way,*
> *And wiser men than I went astray.*

Unimpressed playgoers would say that it was Beckett and not the world that went astray.

Ionesco: *The Lesson* and *The Chairs*

Sometimes the spirit of our age is at home theatrically in a theatre of absurdity. Ionesco's work when well performed is a striking example of how negation can be true, almost pure, theatre. In the 1957-58 season his short plays *The Chairs* and *The Lesson* were staged very competently indeed for the venturesome Phoenix Theatre by Tony Richardson. The small cast could hardly have been improved upon.

The plays require histrionic virtuosity from beginning to end. "Contemporary theatre has been spoiled by the literati," Ionesco insists, "it has become a kind of second-rate literature." For this Romanian-French avant-gardist theatre is "not literature" but simply "what cannot be expressed by any other means." The prevalence of histrionic imagination in his work is only one characteristic of his rampant theatricality, for which he has received much praise and blame. Ionesco is a formidable parodist, a sardonic sceptic, and an almost irrepressibly gay nihilist; he is as effective in comedy as in pathos. He is capable of challenging reflection while outraging sensibility or tickling our funny bone with his clowning, and of depressing and amusing us almost in the same breath. The fact that thus far all his successful plays have been less than full-length pieces only strengthens the impression that in Ionesco we have had a major theatrician but a decidedly minor writer. We may be sure that this opinion, far from perturbing Ionesco, would actually please him. He would be fortified in his opinion that theatre is "what cannot be expressed by writing literature."

The less satisfactory of the two Ionesco plays, *The Lesson*, concerns the homicidal conduct of a professor who is in the habit of stabbing his pupils to death once he has worked himself up to a tantrum in the course of a mad philology lesson. The author's most original achievement is not the Grand Guignol touch, but the perfectly bizarre arithmetic lesson with which the play starts, a scene in which the frenzied rationality of Man and the cool irrationality of Woman are pointedly developed. The scene is wild, poignant, and funny. It exacted theatrical virtuosity from Max Adrian as the professor and from Joan Plowright impersonating a schoolgirl to the last twinkle of her eye and torsion of her figure.

Still, *The Lesson* had too many unblended ingredients and the Grand Guignol touch at the finish, when the professor murders the girl only to receive a new pupil at the fall of the curtain, was a letdown after the glorious farce of the beginning.

The Chairs, the first number on the bill, showed Ionesco's talents to full advantage. Two very old people, wonderfully played by Eli Wallach and the versatile Miss Plowright, are seen in a high octagonal room pierced by many doors and surrounded by endlessly undulating water. The isolated old couple, married perhaps for seventy-five years and constantly absorbed in their recollections, await the arrival of distinguished people who have been invited to hear the aged man's message to mankind. The guests arrive, among them officers and journalists. All of them are *invisible* to the audience; only the chairs hastily assembled by the old couple for the guests are visible. We see only the rapidly multiplying chairs and the frenzied movements of the couple, and we hear their admonitions to the visitors, some of whom have brought children with them. The old man busies himself especially with a lady to whom he had been partial long ago, and his toothless old wife has a hard time warding off a gentleman visitor who is trying to seduce her. At last the guests are all seated in chairs arranged so as to face a speaker. Even the King has arrived and is fulsomely greeted. Everything is ready for the Message, and the formally dressed Orator, the only visible guest, is about to read the man's momentous testament. Their great moment having come, the old couple disappear into the sea outside, presumably because they regard this occasion as a glorious conclusion to their lives. Finally, after many a flourish, the Orator faces the audience of empty chairs and begins to read. The result? The result is *absolute gibberish*.

The implied commentary on the absurdity of the human condition made tolerable only by self-delusion is obvious; there is no need to spell out all the possible symbolism. The negation of the piece is transparent. There is nothing left to the world out of the experience of our lives; we learn nothing from it and we have nothing to impart to others. We try to hold on to shreds of memory, wrap them around our nakedness, and call upon our capacity for self-deception to keep ourselves warm with the remnants. The real meaning is the play, and it reduces itself not to an idea but to a mood and attitude. It is pointless to prove the fallaciousness of Ionesco's idea of the meaninglessness of life or the futility of any effort to make sense out of it. The author is not *arguing*, merely *feeling*. It does not even follow from this work that the author is irrevocably committed to his attitude or to anything else outside the theatre.

Whether we call *The Chairs* decadent or profound there can be no doubt that its *manner* is more original than its matter. A commentary on the vanity of life is turned by Ionesco into a purely theatrical stunt. Except for some scattered minutes of tedium, it proved extremely effective at the Phoenix. The play should prove fascinating in other productions, too, provided it is not staged ponderously. Its negation may even interest playgoers who prefer dramatists with a sanguine disposition, for it conveys the desperate heroism as well as the pathos of men's efforts to give meaning to life.

Despite its pessimism about the human condition *The Chairs* remains a comedy. Man's situation may be desperate, but Ionesco chose to depict it extravagantly and he was justified in calling the play *A Tragic Farce*. The originality of tone and texture suggested by the paradox in the subtitle is fully realized in the play.

In our theatre we rarely maintain contradictory or even simply divergent attitudes in the same dramatic work. Wilder in *The Skin of Our Teeth*, Kaufman and Connelly in *Beggar on Horseback,* and Paul Green in *Johnny Johnson* have done so in the past, but Ionesco's example in the Fifties is not likely to be followed with much zest on our stage. Nevertheless the possibilities of seriocomic theatricality as a way out of the blind alley of our humdrum theatre is inviting.

Brecht's Epic Parable:
The Good Woman of Setzuan at the Phoenix

The Phoenix Theatre presentation of Bertolt Brecht's *The Good Woman of Setzuan,* loyally translated, adapted, and staged by Eric Bentley, was not by inception "Broadway" at all, but it encountered all the vicissitudes, deserved and undeserved, of a Broadway production. The production was poorly received by the press and tepidly supported by the public. Despite my own reservations, which will be duly registered in a subsequent paragraph, I saluted this production as important because the Phoenix was giving the metropolitan public its first view of a major non-musical work by Brecht. *The Good Woman* is one of the two or three greatest morality dramas of the modern stage. It is the imaginative masterpiece of an authentic theatrical genius who tried to say something profoundly true about man and society and to say it with originality. This description of Brecht's place in dramatic history is in no respect invalidated by any dissatisfaction one might charge against the play or this production.

In *The Good Woman of Setzuan,* set in China, supplied with some Chinese theodicy, and stylized in the manner of the Chinese theatre, Brecht wrote a parable on the question: how it is possible to be a decent human being under the pressures and corruptions of a world of exploiters and exploited. In the playwright's quizzical view of the human condition it is not only difficult to be good and to do good in the world, it is incongruous and therefore comic. It is comic in the sense that individuals, such as Brecht's prostitute-heroine who are guided by heart alone, are apt to become the butt of other people's shrewdness and contempt. "The good person as fool" is as original a subject for comedy in this work as the sincere man as fool is an original one in *The Misanthrope.* Brecht's theme is no less difficult for author and audience (and for directors and actors) than Molière's was. *The Misanthrope* was originally a failure on the Parisian stage. Only later was it recognized as a masterpiece in a spuriously romantic interpretation that treated Molière's unreasonable man as a liberal hero rather than as a comic figure of the courtly world of Louis XIV. By the same token *The Good Woman of Setzuan* (literally *The Good Human Being of Setzuan*) was bound to encounter resistance on the Broadway stage, since American optimism would normally reject the "good person as fool" theme as cynical.

In Brecht's case the situation is decidedly more complex. He builds up a brilliant counterpoint without which his meaning would be poorer by half even if it were more tractable to the art of pure comedy. Brecht's comedy is complicated in turning upon itself and enacting the parable of the good man trying to be worldly wise when the kind-hearted prostitute takes measures to defend herself against depredations by the needy and greedy who have swooped down on her. The play's comic complications are multiplied when she assumes the mask of antithesis. The prostitute disappears from time to time and reappears as a fictitious male cousin who can defend her against her dependents and her own loving heart, for the hypothetical cousin is as worldly and hard as she is naïve and gentle. The ironic movement of Brecht's fanciful tragicomedy of ideas, the vulnerability of virtue to exploitation in a dog-eat-dog world, quickly acquires an ironic countermovement. Not only does goodness find itself betrayed by those it is willing to help, but it betrays itself. It does so by becoming *practical,* for its practicality is indistinguishable from ruthlessness. Goodness exploits those who would exploit it, and soon philanthropy allies itself with tyranny and becomes indistinguishable from it.

So goes the world, says Brecht, drawing support for this jaundiced outlook from the long course of human history and not merely from the sectarian Marxism that he favored. Marxist optimism is also tempered here by Calvinist ingredients which add a saturnine quality to the work as a whole. It would seem that the damnation of man is more real in *The Good Woman* than any possible glimmer of salvation through social revolution. Certainly the view enforced at the end of the play leaves Brecht's heroine, as well as the rest of us, in something of a moral dilemma. She will be allowed to reassume the mask of her tough-fibred alter ego, the fictitious cousin, only occasionally under extreme necessity. Whatever Brecht may have thought, the celestial voice that tells her this is hardly the voice of Stalin and his ruthless crew. The dilemma it poses has bruised the souls of good men on many a calvary of policy throughout the ages. Brecht's heroine is left in a state of uncertainty consisting equally of pathos and bewilderment.

Brecht's quizzical view of the moral problem man faces everywhere persists to the end of this work of the modern mind and experience. It makes *The Good Woman* an important experiment in provocative and realistically oriented theatricalism. Although Brecht's experiments were rarely free from irritating features they were full of potentialities for modern playwriting, directing, and acting. They were morganatic marriages of reason and fantasy, and the results were certainly more legitimate than the results of such marriages outside the theatre.

Brecht's genre mediated between comedy and morality drama, between prose and poetry, between realism and fantasy in a truly modern spirit that escaped the confectionary mediations we have long suffered from James M. Barrie and his successors. Brecht's admirers may yet be justified; his style of theatre, with many unforeseeable modifications or variations, has a future if any modern style has. Some of these modifications have, in fact, appeared on the American stage ever since the Thirties, in such works as the "living newspapers," Paul Green's *Johnny Johnson,* and Norman Corwin's recent Lincoln-Douglas drama, *The Rivalry.*

A more modest expectation is that *The Good Woman of Setzuan* will be staged again despite the unlucky Phoenix Theatre production. The Phoenix managers, T. Edward Hambleton and Norris Houghton, deserved more respect from us for their failure than most Broadway managements do for their opulent successes. Praise should be given to Eric Bentley, too, for he was exposed to a great deal of unwarranted abuse as the translator and director of *The Good Woman.* The abuse seems to me to have been based on considerable ignorance; I include here ignorance of Brecht's own limitations and pitfalls, which are considerable. Regardless of shortcomings in the adaptation-translation and production, whether real or fancied (I say fancied because some reviewers obviously only *imagined* what the original was like), the Phoenix Theatre represented Brecht more thoroughly than any other professional or quasi-professional production had done. Too many people have underrated the problems of dealing with a nonmusical Brecht play or with any play written in the style of epic theatre. Epic theatre is associated with Brecht's name and that of Erwin Piscator, the German director whose important contributions have been grossly played down in recent years.

Each play worth producing is a unique entity and every stage production must convey that uniqueness. In spite of possible impressions to the contrary, there is no invariable, routinized epic style for the writing and staging of a play. (There was remarkable variety in Brecht's own work which was composed over a period of a third of a century on two continents and in half a dozen countries.) The Bentley production had considerable fidelity to Brecht as playwright and stage director. Bentley had worked with Brecht, a matter of considerable importance in using the epic style and technique. The routine of epic demonstration, dramaturgy, and didactic theatre stood out more clearly, therefore, than the uniqueness of this particular play. Even the thoroughly expert performances of Uta Hagen, Zero Mostel, Albert Salmi, Nancy Marchand, and others could not remove this impression. An illustration is the insufficiency of comedy whenever Miss Hagen played her alter ego, the fictitious cousin. The situation was intrinsically comic and had many comic twists, but the results were not particularly amusing and I found Miss Hagen's masquerade in the masculine role disconcerting and almost unpleasantly epicene. Yet I also felt I was in the presence of a really great moment of theatre when she imagined herself in the role of a mother leading an imaginary child by the hand.

The overall impression of the production was scattered. A distracting mélange of styles and dissipating of effects has been a constant danger in epic drama ever since its Central European beginnings in the Twenties. Joseph Wood Krutch was adversely affected by these traits when he reported in *The Nation* on Erwin Piscator's impressive production of *The Good Soldier Schweik,* the first nonmusical epic theatre masterpiece in Berlin. The dramatic result of *The Good Woman* also seemed incomplete. The scattered effect has been given a theoretical anti-Aristotelian justification by Brecht's opposition to emotional catharsis which he considered a deterrent to thought and social action on the part of the playgoer. No one will argue that the invariable summum bonum of playwriting is to leave the playgoer emotionally drained, but there is no reason to assume that a technique conducive to social action will invariably yield good drama.

In *The Good Woman* production the progression toward an emotional and intellectual climax seemed desultory. This defect may well not have been due to the direction, but to a play structure of too many short scenes strung together in a horizontal line of action. I sensed a danger in this

epic or horizontal expansiveness some ten years earlier when I read
Brecht's manuscript in German and prevailed upon the Theatre Guild
directorate to option *The Good Woman* for a Broadway production. The
thoughtful playwright Sophie Treadwell who attempted an English
version may have also felt this diffuseness because eventually she abandoned the project after she had been at work for some time. The Phoenix
production can be blamed only theoretically for not sustaining a sufficiently dynamic quality in the action. I say only theoretically because
beyond sharpening the production with an out-of-town tryout the director
could expect to do very little for the play without destroying it. For
better or worse, the main action *is* episodic or horizontal.

The conclusion of the play is a brilliantly conceived denouement.
The hard-pressed employees of the cousin long for the return of the
gentle prostitute, whom they had victimized. When she does not reap-
pear for a while they accuse the cousin of having done away with her.
A trial ensues before three judges. The good prostitute, still disguised as
the cousin, instantly recognizes them as the three little Chinese gods
who, in gratitude for her hospitality when everybody else refused them
shelter, gave her gold. That was the beginning of all her troubles because
it brought the needy to her door. She requests that the court be cleared
and confesses all to the gods, who order her to resume her tender-minded
real self. They relent sufficiently to allow her to assume the disguise of
the tough-minded cousin from time to time, for goodness needs to be
able to take up arms in self-defense if it is to survive.

This conclusion agrees indeed with the political philosophy of Lenin,
who once justified Communist terrorism to Maxim Gorky by expostulat-
ing, "But Maxim, you can't make omelets without cracking eggs!" But
the need of a goodness that can take defensive and corrective measures is
a universal one, and the little gods' recommendation that these measures
be taken moderately and infrequently is the essential point and a wise
one. But the problem that concerns the play itself is how vigorously the
action can be moved toward the denouement and how sharply the trial
scene can be made to attain its climax. If the Phoenix production tended
to flatten out and unfold itself with level coolness its horizontal quality
was intrinsic to the play and its coolness was a desideratum of Brechtian
epic theory and practice. A longer rehearsal period and a company built
into a true ensemble such as Brecht developed in East Berlin would have
enabled Eric Bentley to sharpen his effects. But even the cleverest direc-

tion by remaining faithful to the text is sure to run into difficulties in our professional theatre.

The characteristic of epic theatre that usually proves most troublesome in production is its very epicness. The epic play, made up of such diverse elements as little scenes, narrations, recitations, and songs can become a hodgepodge on the stage, at least on our conventionally static stage. Multiplicity of occurrences rendered in a variety of dramatic, lyrical, and narrative styles can scatter dramatic effect as if the play were a series of ill-assorted fragments. Brecht justified this disunity (it involves deliberate interruptions of mood and feeling and broken, spasmodic action) as a means of preventing immersion in illusion and emotional identification at the expense of critical detachment. This is all very well in theory, but to be thoroughly effective, even on its own terms, an epic production still must *cohere* dramatically and must drive on toward its objective.

The Phoenix production did not cohere or come into focus sufficiently, and no amount of rationalization can remove dissatisfaction on this ground. Perhaps the action needed to be paced differently and a moderately unifying element might have been introduced to advantage. For instance, the Chinese gods who have come down to earth in search of goodness might have been kept in constant view during the action, possibly on a ramp or treadmill. Brecht might not have approved of such an approach to the problem (he probably would have maintained that there was no problem at all), but there is nothing in epic theory to forbid it. There certainly was a problem at the Phoenix due to the irregular play structure and frequent interpolation of recitations and songs. The lyrics in *The Good Woman* are essentially redundant. They are a carryover from Brecht's earlier, quite brilliant, *Lehrstück* technique that subserved his morality play didacticism at the risk of treating the theatre as a kindergarten. A point that should be abundantly evident from the dramatic action gets a second lease on meaning in scattered fragments of lyric and recitative accompanied by an orchestra playing in full view of the audience. (In full view because we mustn't have illusion. We must *know* that we are being addressed and instructed!)

In the Phoenix version of *The Good Woman* the lyrical statements had little dramatic and even less instructive value. Many snatches of verse sounded downright flat, and the Paul Dessau music rendered by vocally limited performers and the faint little orchestra was singularly ineffective. Since Brecht was an excellent poet and Paul Dessau a composer of some distinction New York reviewers were inclined to blame the translator. Without giving any indication that they really knew Brecht's German lyrics they blamed Bentley for spoiling them. The fact is that most of Brecht's lyrics in *The Good Woman* are merely adequate, if not indeed superfluous. Only a free adaptation, which the loyal translator-director did not allow himself, could have given the songs any noteworthy value. The singing could have been improved, but this does not seem to have been one of Dessau's better scores and I suspect that much of it would have impressed us as desultory even in a finer performance.

It is reasonable to conclude that the unsatisfactory features of the Phoenix production were intrinsic to Brecht's theories which have not yet been assimilated into our theatrical practice. There was noticeable crudity in such earlier Brecht productions as *Mother,* presented by the Theatre Union in the Thirties, and *Galileo,* staged by Charles Laughton in the Forties. Many difficulties arise for the translator and director from the fact that Brecht endeavored to re-theatricalize playwriting and stage production on programmatic, esthetic, and sociological foundations. Brecht himself was sometimes victimized by his theoretical aims and seduced into labored playwriting which his keen mind would otherwise have rejected.

Modern theatrical experimentation has often needed release from the strait jacket of theory. Because nonrealistic stylization has been artificially produced in our century, because it started out mainly as art in the head, so to speak, it has lacked organic individuality and flexibility. Brecht was not the only captive of ideas about re-theatricalized and re-formalized theatre. Other captives, many of them greatly gifted men, were as diverse in aim as Meyerhold, who moved forward to machine-age biodynamics, and Yeats, who moved back to Japanese Noh play formalism.

Brecht's death in 1956 brought to an end a fascinating and provocative career in the theatre. In *The Good Woman of Setzuan* and in several other late plays, such as *Mother Courage* and *The Caucasian Chalk Circle,* he was moving in new directions. But he never liberated himself from a rigid didacticism that was as Teutonic as Marxist. In his experiments and theories there were complications and possibilities of error that he rarely overcame after his work with Kurt Weill in *The Threepenny Opera* in the Twenties. He was unable, and perhaps he could not reasonably be expected, to resolve all the problems of twentieth-century theatricalism which he only complicated with his politically committed mind and emotions.

Duerrenmatt: *The Visit*

Friedrich Duerrenmatt's nightmarish drama, *The Visit,* was the climax of the 1958 Broadway season. It had been eighteen years since the Lunts' appearance in Sherwood's war play, *There Shall Be No Night,* eighteen years since they had appeared in a play worthy of their talents. Miss Fontanne's feline portrayal of a vengeance-bent virago and Alfred Lunt's playing of a hunted man in *The Visit* will long be remembered by those who saw the superb Peter Brook production.

The performances of the protagonists were full of significant detail, from the confident swing of Miss Fontanne's gait to the weary slouch of Alfred Lunt's stance, from the fanatical gleam in her eyes to the fear-filmed look he gives his erstwhile friends who shortly will betray him. In this play Miss Fontanne as the relentless heroine is all concentrated purpose, primarily a force and symbol. Lunt as the man whose destruction she encompasses by systematically corrupting his fellow citizens is a humanly simple and defenseless individual.

Only a small town is subverted in the play, but the heroine's conquest is a précis of human history. A millionairess, symbolically only half-human because much of her body maimed by accidents has been replaced by plastic parts, invades a small community to revenge her mistreatment many years before by the townspeople and by one man in particular. At first there is resistance in the village and its moral values are only slightly in jeopardy. Then the Satanic individual asserts her power and corrupts the whole town. Eventually justice is mocked and humanity flouted; a human being is killed—with some show of legality and morality—in a flagrant travesty on justice. The fact that the motivation was originally human enough, that the millionairess had once been grievously wronged, matters little except as a reminder that wrong breeds wrong, that we reap the whirlwind when we sow the wind. Initial injustice is compounded by the millionairess until she infects a whole world.

The dehumanization of men is what concerns Friedrich Duerrenmatt, a Swiss author only lately discovered in America. New Yorkers saw *The Visit* in a Maurice Valency version. The work is stridently Teutonic, but completely absorbing as a dramatic statement. *The Visit* is least satisfactory when judged as a drama of persons. There is little reason to think in terms of rounded characterization; many of the characters are deliberately stock and the plot is developed expressionistically. It is a play of abrupt transitions and symbolic scenes (such as the hunt for an escaped panther, whose death anticipates the fate of the hunted hero). There is a harrowing hallucinatory scene in which the desperate victim tries to board a train out of town but is seized with fear that his fellow townsmen may want to throw him under its wheels. The expressionistic technique of both play and production was its most impressive factor.

The Visit is one of the very few post-World War II plays from Central Europe that expresses any deeply moral conclusions or reveals a clear understanding of what happened to the European soul under Hitler. Usually we have been treated to melodrama rather than to moral probing, and *our* contribution to the subject, the dramatization of *The Diary of Anne Frank,* is an exercise in compassion rather than in analysis. The only Central European World War II play that compares with *The Visit* in power is Carl Zuckmayer's *The Devil's General (Des Teufels General),* a play which has had productions in Europe and England but has not yet been seen on the American stage. We could better afford to emphasize the limitations of *The Visit,* its one-dimensional, extravagant quality and its occasional obviousness, if we had other good plays to set beside it.

But small defects alone don't explain the public's limited enthusiasm despite the popularity of the Lunts and the rapturous newspaper reviews. Symbolism is a kind of stenography to which a key must be found. It is not the first time that both symbolism and expressionism have left American playgoers distantly fascinated rather than absorbed. A public lacking first-hand acquaintance with the nightmare of recent European political history had no key to the heart of *The Visit.* There is always the danger of estrangement in modernistic techniques that attract only intellectual playgoers. Such estrangement is usually a defect unless one tries to turn it into a virtue. Brecht attempted to turn it into a virtue by deliberately cultivating it, and he often succeeded with his stimulating intellectuality and dramatic resourcefulness. *The Visit* escaped abstractness only because Alfred Lunt made such an appealing character of the victim. He was particularly moving in the memorable railroad station scene in which fear masters him until he masters fear and recovers human dignity in a resolve to face his fate.

It must be admitted that *The Visit,* with its vixen-millionairess and retinue of blinded and castrated musicians, was more oppressive than stimulating. Though briskly staged by Peter Brook the action was more conducive to uneasiness and a sense of the macabre than to dramatic fulfillment. Nevertheless the *manner* of the play was undeniably impressive, perhaps because significant social comment has been so rare in the American theatre since the Thirties.

Some perceptive reviewers thought that *The Visit* had less merit than its production and that the script was basically arid. Form and design in the drama (even when O'Neill succumbed to it in *Dynamo, Lazarus Laughed,* and other plays) is of secondary importance to character revelation, and it was plain that the characters of *The Visit* were being pushed about like pawns across a chessboard.

But if *The Visit* was not a great play, it was a superb libretto because it demanded virtuosity from the director and actors. Standardized realistic plays invite only apathy; they ask too little of the actor and at the same time inhibit truly creative staging. *The Visit* said something in the text and then said it again better on the stage.

9 AFFIRMATIONS?

Miller's *The Crucible* as Event and Play

Jed Harris' Broadway production of *The Crucible*, Arthur Miller's drama of the Salem witchcraft trials, was received with qualifications. The play was not fully successful even after the touring version was restaged by the author. Only an off-Broadway production several years later seemed to do full justice to the play.

With the writing and production of *The Crucible* Miller moved in the directions that had already attracted him (he had written an unproduced poetic tragedy on the conquest of Mexico): history and tragedy. History was directly present in *The Crucible,* and tragedy was scaled higher than it had been in *Death of a Salesman.* His independent Colonial farmer, John Proctor, had more tragic stature than the superannuated traveling salesman, Willy Loman. The heroic death of Proctor, who chooses the gallows in preference to submission to unjust authority, is on an obviously higher level of tragic sacrifice than Willy's suicide.

We may surmise that Arthur Miller entertained poetic aspirations. Apparently he was following Maxwell Anderson's example in trying to write poetry in an historical drama before using it in a contemporary context (this came later in *A View from the Bridge*). The poetry in *The Crucible* was a sort of prose-poetry rather than verse, and the seventeenth-century historical context in which it was employed justified a degree of formality and biblical austerity. Miller was not the man to hit upon poetic embellishments accidentally; his playwriting career appears to follow a planned progression from the well-made-play technique of *All My Sons* to the imaginative dramatic construction of *Death of a Salesman* and to the poetic historical writing of *The Crucible.* The

274

author's various introductions to his plays make plain the deliberateness, the strong awareness of objectives, and the self-awareness that characterize his work in the theatre.

The Crucible, then, has importance in the career of a writer whose laudable ambition is to make contemporary American theatre aim high and who also wishes to express the tensions of his own time and place. Taking an exalted view of the theatre's responsibilities and of the artist's function in society as the guardian of its conscience, Miller wrote *The Crucible* in the midst of the McCarthy era. The author's motivation plainly included taking a public stand against authoritarian inquisitions and mass hysteria. These are pompous words perhaps. The play itself has a little too much pomp at times that better dramatic poetry might have transfigured, and too much stiffness that the author might have avoided had he dealt with his own times and been less conscious of period. But the sincerely maintained purpose behind the posture is clear, and it is one of Miller's distinctions that he was one of the very few writers of the period to speak out unequivocally for reason and justice. *The Crucible* will remain alive long after every carping criticism directed at its political implications has been forgotten. (Curiously these criticisms were not by benighted reactionaries but by enlightened intellectuals, and not in the popular press but in literary journals.)

There were some dramatic rewards available to a person of Miller's courage. The topical incitement to passion gave the author a strong impetus in the writing of the climactic scenes. These have since been rarely equalled in strength, and the excitement they provided proved distinctly serviceable when the play was given an off-Broadway revival in 1958, after McCarthyism had subsided as an issue. The later production proved that the play could hold its own without the support of topicality. That it stood up so well was due to the excitement of the action, to the author's underlying passion, and to the character drama and tragic pattern. All this does not mitigate a certain stiffness in the characterization, nor does it remove doubt as to the advisability of making the historical witchcraft trials hinge so much on the perversity of a passionate girl. But the fact remains that Miller built his play with exciting situations and characters rather than puppets.

The Crucible was momentous, if imperfect. I give my own reactions below as a specimen first reaction to the play and its reception. At the second night opening, during the 1952-53 season, the strong impression on the audience was almost the impact of an *event* rather than of just one more serious play. Even while aware of some creakiness in the work, I shared a feeling of grief and anger with others. Writing about the play several weeks later I had some doubts about the quality of the work. Yet I also wrote with some rage directed not only at the historical world of Salem, but at the evil and stupidity in men as well as at the frosty and what seemed to me at the time disingenuous reaction of various intelligent theatregoers:

A history play by virtue of its subject, *The Crucible* is nonetheless a spiraling drama. Miller has once more demonstrated his ability to telescope dramatic material. In writing about the Salem witchcraft trials he has avoided the danger of composing a sprawling chronicle. Moreover, he has made every effort to create a central tragic character in John Proctor, the independent farmer who faces one decision after another and, after some understandable hesitations, makes his choice. It would take too long to prove here the proficiency combined with insight into character that distinguishes *The Crucible*. Even the painstaking Jed Harris production failed to capture the movement toward tragedy and toward unity through character drama Miller developed in his script. This achievement can be observed in the published Viking Press text.

How the contemporary higher criticism can tie itself up in knots when it is confronted by honest, forthright work is well shown in reviews of the play. As usual, the workaday New York newspaper reviewers come off better than the critics who write for recondite publications; the newspapermen report on what they see, whereas esoteric critics see only what they want to discuss. Regardless of Miller's original intentions or later explanations in the Viking book, the play must be assessed simply as a play. If parallels between the past and the present appear, so much the worse for us or for humanity at large rather than for the playwright. If individual lines, such as the question whether the accuser is now always holy, are relevant and probably intentional on Miller's part, the fact remains that a play that holds audiences in its grip as *The Crucible* does, succeeds through the power of its overall dramaturgy rather than through its topical features.

If there are obvious weaknesses in the play they result mainly from the fact that Proctor and his wife are swamped by such a multiplicity of secondary characters that the personal drama of maintaining integrity in the face of compounded evil and folly is often dissipated. It is also unfortunate that the tragedy is started and brought to a climax—and therefore made melodramatic—by the willful action of a demoniacal girl, Abigail. Miller does not succeed in overcoming these defects. But he appears to be aware of them, and his awareness results in adjustments or corrections as the play proceeds. Both Proctor and his wife are made to grow in stature; at the end they are fully developed. Perhaps they grow too rapidly in act four of the text, and the Jed Harris production blurred this growth. By the time the play ends, it is no longer the hit-or-miss chronicle of mass hysteria it tended to become earlier; it is a tragedy and its point is that men, no matter how erring, are capable of enduring everything for their sense of decency. This, too, is more apparent in the published text than it was in the stage production. Those who claim that *The Crucible* is inadequate as a revelation of what happened in Salem are quite correct. It is what transpired in the souls of John and Elizabeth Proctor that finally matters, and to that degree *The Crucible* is neither an exposé nor a merely contemporary protest, but a tragedy. It is regrettable that Jed Harris did not succeed in bringing this out sufficiently in the performances of Arthur Kennedy and Beatrice Straight. They were less commanding on the stage than Walter Hampden's formidable Deputy-Governor Danforth. (A uniformity of excellence in the acting of the principals such as in the off-Broadway 1958-59 Hotel Martinique production would have called more attention to the personal tragedy that Miller came to favor in the play.)

The fact is that good as the Broadway production was it failed to develop fully the wealth of dramatic creativeness that went into the writing of *The Crucible*. Even if Miller did not succeed in drawing his epic material completely together, he created a powerful drama which overshadows current drama here or abroad. It may be sufficient to congratulate ourselves on the presence of Arthur Miller in our theatre. My major regret about this writer is that he is not enough of a poet. I doubt that any post-Shakespearian dramatist could have solved the problems inherent in Miller's material, but a true poet could have transcended them. He could have placed the play beyond time and locality and carried us into the center of tragic vision. A more poetic

playwright could also have economized on those parts of the plot that
are necessarily merely transitional and supplementary and therefore
are relatively flat.

Corwin's The Rivalry

A satisfactory fusion of stylization and truth, of artful construction
and compelling humanity, and of nonrealistic devices and historical
reality is hard to find. Norman Corwin's *The Rivalry*, a stirring play of
the 1958-59 season about the momentous Lincoln-Douglas debates, deserved praise despite its failure to win popular support on Broadway.
Thanks in part to the physical production and to David Amram's musical
score this multiscened drama moved excitingly on the stage with a
dramatic unity that made the historical action a single absorbing experience. The intelligence and loveliness of Nancy Kelly's Adele Douglas,
wife of the little giant, the rough-hewn strength and rueful pathos of
Richard Boone's young Abe Lincoln, and particularly Martin Gabel's
explosive portrayal of Stephen A. Douglas made *The Rivalry* an effective
and very *human* play. All the talent and conviction that went into this
venturesome Cheryl Crawford production yielded a documentary drama
that transcended factual theatre and became a blend of historical tragedy
and folk drama.

The now almost forgotten living newspapers of the Federal Theatre
of the depression era (*Power* and *One-third-of-Nation*, for instance)
introduced a new form of American dramaturgy. But social changes and
the demise of the Federal Theatre closed this chapter of our theatrical
history. It was fitting therefore that Norman Corwin, the most inspired
poetic dramatist and radio writer of the Thirties and Forties, should have
used the dramatic form of the living newspaper for his springboard.
Admittedly *The Rivalry* had distinct limitations as a play. It was unable
to transcend historical fact; it needed some special transfiguration by
tragic poetry to do justice to Corwin's conception of the conflict which
brought Lincoln to the brink of his tragic destiny while testing the moral
worth of his opponent. *The Rivalry* was suspended uneasily between
history and poetry.

Still, Corwin's semidocumentary drama was a noteworthy achievement in a genre that should not be allowed to atrophy. Documentary art suits as pragmatic a nation as ours uncommonly well; our achievements in film documentaries during the Thirties and World War II were remarkable for their vigor. Except in romance about the Civil War we are, alas, notoriously weak in historical memory (justifying Oscar Wilde's quip that America's youth is its oldest tradition). This weakness has been corrected in the South by such gifted and indefatigable writers of pageant drama as Paul Green, who in 1937 created the model for what he calls symphonic dramas with *The Lost Colony*. But except for the rather specious form of historical romance as practised by Maxwell Anderson and a very few others, the sense of history has remained curiously undeveloped on Broadway.

Mary Stuart at the Phoenix: A Future for Poetic Drama?

Salvation of the theatre by a return to the poetic drama of the Elizabethan and romantic periods has been a cherished dream throughout the century. But few playwrights in America except the late Maxwell Anderson have made any strong effort to bring this about. Anderson started a one-man crusade for verse drama in 1930 with *Elizabeth the Queen*, and came to the end of his Elizabethan period with *Anne of the Thousand Days* in 1948. As a result we have had to rely primarily on revivals to set the example. We have had an occasional verse drama from Christopher Fry or T.S. Eliot. But Fry has not been impressive since the romantic production of *The Lady's Not for Burning* in 1949, and Eliot, with *The Cocktail Party* and *The Confidential Clerk*, has been trying to bring his dramatic poetry as close to prose as possible and has succeeded only too well.

In the revivals of poetic drama our main effort has been concentrated on Shakespeare. But Shakespeare is hardly a convincing argument for those who believe that the poetic drama of the past still has a place in the modern theatre; his popularity can be ascribed solely to his private and inimitable genius. Other Elizabethan poets who have had attention on our stage—Marlowe, in Tyrone Guthrie's sumptuous production of *Tamburlaine the Great*; Webster, in an inconclusive *The Duchess of*

Malfi at the Phoenix; and John Ford, whose *'Tis Pity She's a Whore* was ably staged at a small Second Avenue theatre—have made no particular dent in our theatrical world.

If Shakespeare's colleagues, clothed in his reflected glory, cannot prevail with us, what poetic playwright can? Certainly we would not be apt to pick one of the poet-playwrights of the classic German theatre. But in 1957 the Phoenix presented a production of Schiller's *Mary Stuart*, a play that had needed a new English translation and that might have been considered superfluous after Maxwell Anderson's *Mary of Scotland*.

Though *Mary Stuart* became one of the Phoenix Theatre's most admired productions, one wondered who was more mistaken: those who believed that Schiller's verse plays were hopelessly dated for America or those who believed that elevated poetic drama could redeem our theatrical age. The plain facts were that Schiller's play, somewhat cropped and toned down, was not dated, and that there wasn't a glimmer of hope that our times would be redeemed by high romantic tragedy. All that the good reception of *Mary Stuart* really proved is that the taste and thought of our period is eclectic; we don't discriminate strongly among the stage productions that capture our fancy and hold it for a little while. Weren't audiences of the Fifties equally willing to adore both *The Music Man* with its breezy free enterprise American affirmativeness, vintage 1958, and the Greenwich Village production of *The Threepenny Opera* with its anticapitalistic, dadaist nihilism, vintage 1928?

But it was gratifying to have Schiller's play on the boards if for no other reason than for confirmation that the tragic conflict of will and the dignity of language among exalted personages still elevates audiences. In our theatre we are apt to flounder in tepid waters even when we are spared the commonplaceness of ordinary realistic drama. Even our quasi-poetic plays of fantasy and folk-comedy are usually mild in conflict, placid in spirit, and lax in language. Heroic or "high" tragedy such as *Mary Stuart* provides the rare reverse in our theatre. Though historically old-fashioned it is, because of its rarity today, new-fashioned; its contemporary equivalent is not even faintly discernible on the horizon. During the Thirties the tensions of the time favored the rise of intense and far-reaching conflict in social drama. But the war period produced little heroic drama; only French existentialism wrung a certain ambiguous heroism out of despair in such pieces as Anouilh's *Antigone* and Sartre's *The Flies* and *Morts sans Sépulture* (*The Victors*).

If the production of *Mary Stuart* did not force upon us a rueful conclusion that Schiller must be laid in lavender the credit must be distributed among the translator-adapters, the directors, and the actors. Jean Stock Goldstone and John Reich turned out an English version eminently suitable for presentation to the New York public, a drama spare and swift despite its burden of historical matter. The translators also managed to survive their bout with Schiller's language without any flagrant mishaps. Here and there the language sounded stilted, though no more so than Schiller's, but the tone was impressive, the rhythm strong, and the turn of phrase compelling. The original was cut without any noticeable impoverishment of action or banality of line, no small accomplishment under the circumstances.

However, it was the production at the Phoenix that commanded most of our admiration. Tyrone Guthrie's stage direction, the dramatic settings by Donald Oenslager, and the tastefully designed costumes by Alvin Colt were all superb. Dr. Guthrie's remarkably natural treatment of the old play was exemplary; there was neither a pall of academicism on it nor any suggestion of sensationalism or popularization. After his staging of plays by Sophocles, Marlowe, and Shakespeare, Guthrie was just the man to stage *Mary Stuart* without giving the impression that he was doing something extraordinary. Many a Shakespearian or classic production has suffered from being presented either as if the director were walking on eggs or as if he had started throwing them. In contrast to many past poetic and historical productions Guthrie's was atmospheric without being foggy, active without being busy, and dignified without being ceremonious.

It was heartening to discover that our mid-century theatre could manage a classic without making a muddle or a parade of it. The cast was magnificent. No praise is high enough for Irene Worth's Mary Stuart, a faultless, moving, and never maudlin work of characterization. Eva Le Gallienne's Queen Elizabeth was just as impressive a performance. Elizabeth, her eyes outlined by painted circles, was portrayed by Miss Le Gallienne as queen and flirt, statesman and jealous woman, sovereign and virago. So many contradictions could not be encompassed without some conspicuous theatricality, and the marvel was that Miss Le Gallienne, authentically bewigged and overpainted and overdressed, kept her multiple parts under such control. Although the portrayal of Leicester seemed more ponderous than impressive, the rest of the cast was commendable. William Hutt's impressively elongated, ascetical Earl of Shrewsbury, Max

Adrian's saturnine Lord Burleigh, and John Colicos' sinuous and fanatical Mortimer gave sharp definition to the historical picture and the romantic action.

The production of *Mary Stuart* was an encouraging event, and the Phoenix management did the American theatre a far greater service than the successful launching of a normal production can ever do. *Mary Stuart* pointed to the possibility of resuscitating many a seemingly superannuated work for the stage. Though it does not appear likely that such productions will set profitable examples for our playwrights or relate our theatre more vitally to its times they can certainly provide some vivid theatricality, some sense of the past, and perhaps even an expansion of the imagination. They can rescue us from our prose and our provinciality.

Fry: The Firstborn

Prolixity is allowable only to the great playwrights. Shaw could afford to be prolix not only because he had much to say to his audiences, but because he could be intoxicated—and intoxicate us—with the palaver of thought without often falling into romantic or antiromantic platitude. He could be inconclusive *and* stimulating in his comedies of ideas. This is not true of Christopher Fry, who is also restricted by writing verse drama rather than prose. He tends to confuse verse with verbal fireworks intended to enlarge dramatic experience and our mental horizons.

One of the noble deeds of the 1958 New York season was the production of Fry's twelve-year-old Moses drama, *The Firstborn*. Much credit goes to Katharine Cornell and her partner, Roger L. Stevens, for producing it so meticulously. Christopher Fry was writing thoughtfully of conflicting loyalties in times of crisis. The conflict was well realized in Miss Cornell's portrait of the Pharaoh's sister who is Moses' foster mother, in Anthony Quayle's superb Moses, and in Mildred Natwick's Miriam. But this poetic drama of liberation, potentially so meaningful for our own times, was effective only fitfully on the stage. This was no fault of the staging or performances; I did not expect the play to be successful when I read the published version some years ago.

The audience left the theatre more numbed than stimulated. The play bogged down in characterizations, and most of the episodes seemed to be there because the Bible refers to them rather than because they grew naturally out of the situation and attained the intensity of high drama. When he composed *The Firstborn* in 1946 Christopher Fry was still writing as if he had been commissioned by the Canterbury Cathedral Play Festival to supply a pageant drama. His talent is evident again and again, but he did not build a play so much as decorate a tale. His stately manner stands foremost in the play; when he adds his own mite to the Biblical core his matter is mostly platitude.

Not long after *The Firstborn* appeared on Broadway, Yale's School of Drama presented another poetic play with a Biblical background. The world première of the Archibald MacLeish drama of Job, *J.B.*, was received with enthusiasm by Brooks Atkinson and many others who went to New Haven to see Curtis Canfield's vigorous production. An even more enthusiastic press greeted the published text. There can be no mystery about the difference between this work and Fry's play. MacLeish served the dynamics of the stage while Fry was immersed in a flow of tired Victorian blank verse. *The Firstborn* is a slow and turbid play in spite of its potentially exciting subject: the liberation of a nation and its attendant conflicts, including the conflict in the soul of Moses himself.

It is especially trying in standard poetic dramas, usually British in origin, to have the action suspended at some critical point while a character relieves himself of a sermon or lengthy self-analysis. One could wish that the authors of such plays had taken a hint from Edward Lear's limerick on William Gladstone instead of allowing their characters to make bores of themselves at the dramatic crossroads:

> *There was an Old Man at a Station*
> *Who made a promiscuous oration;*
> *But they said, 'Take some snuff!—*
> *You have talked quite enough,*
> *You afflicting Old Man at a Station!'*

The ultimate theatrical power of a play lies in its dramatic progression, no matter how fine the writing and how imaginative the conception or poetic the atmosphere. One of the troubles with English poetic drama for the past sixty years (aside from a profusion of language as an impediment to the action) has been an overabundance of atmosphere. By comparison with the murk of modern poetic writing Sophoclean drama is crystalline and the moodiest of Shakespearian sonnets is opalescent. Humor has helped dispel mist in several of Fry's plays: *A Phoenix Too Frequent, The*

Lady's Not for Burning, and *Venus Observed*. But none of his plays, with the exception of his lovely minor effort *The Boy with a Cart*, has been free of rhetoric that veils rather than reveals the line of dramatic development.

Unfortunately a verse drama in our commercial theatre usually has to be twice as good to get half as far as, for example, a musical comedy. I am puritan enough to feel miserable when I catch myself approving a vaudeville about the making of a musical such as *Say, Darling* while boggling at *The Firstborn*. But, regrettably, *Say, Darling* was on the stage and *The Firstborn* is mostly in a book.

O'Casey: *Pictures in the Hallway*

It is indicative of the general impoverishment of serious theatre in the Fifties that every now and then we found the highest dramatic pitch in a reading rather than in a fully staged play. This was first the case when *Don Juan in Hell* overshadowed virtually every current play in amplitude and depth. *Don Juan in Hell* was at least written in dialogue, an interlude of fantasy and debate in the larger dramatic context of a thoroughly dramatic play, Shaw's *Man and Superman*. The production called *Pictures in the Hallway* was not actually a play at all but a dramatic presentation of selections from O'Casey's autobiographical volume of the same name. Sensitively directed by Stuart Vaughan the readers, led by the well-known actress Aline MacMahon, brought a great glow to the stage. It was O'Casey's love of humanity and perception of human character that produced this glow.

"It was a slap-up surprise to me," wrote O'Casey, "that the Autobiographical books should appear on an American stage, on the stage, anywhere." And well he might say so when his plays had fared so poorly on Broadway. Impressed with a tape recording of the actors' reading, O'Casey concluded with characteristic generosity, "It is all their doing, and it is marvelous in my eyes." But the "play" the actors spoke was first of all O'Casey's creation; and it had to have his genius before *Pictures in the Hallway* could become an event in the theatre rather than simply a stirring book in the library. That the work proved to be successful on the stage is no "slap-up surprise" to anyone who has known O'Casey's autobiographies. These books comprise one of the supreme testaments of the human spirit in English prose, and they are the work of one of the three or four major playwrights the English-speaking world has had since the seventeenth century.

It is one of the marvels of *Pictures in the Hallway* that its compassionately comic account of a Dublin boy's encounters with the injustice of man and the love of woman makes such genuine theatre. It does so with its swirl of melodious language. It is by now a widely known language, for which O'Casey's writings will be cherished long after most contemporary shows are forgotten. The melody changes with the characters and the situation; it becomes gentle or belligerent as the case may require, it rises and falls with the voltage of the experience evoked by the author, it even vibrates at different speeds to different circumstances. The situations vary in tension; some are idyllic while others are lingeringly troubled or briefly tempestuous.

By these and other means a dramatic life is maintained in a work that would normally constitute an exposition and meditation intractable to the theatre. The depressing point brought home by our experience with *Pictures in the Hallway* is how much more dramatic O'Casey is in narrative writing than most contemporary writers have been in playwriting. In his work the experience of life has usually been a *personal* issue, whereas most contemporary playwriting has reflected various degrees of diffidence or standardized opinion.

Since challenge in one direction often draws response from another *Pictures in the Hallway* became the occasion for one of the most creative stage productions we have had in recent seasons. This was surely a reading with a difference, for despite a brief decline of dramatic power here and there, it was engrossing theatre. Each member of the cast was able to develop at least one absorbing characterization, and Aline MacMahon actually developed *two*: a moving portrait of Johnny's tragic mother, Mrs. Casside, and a knowing take-off on a peppery Dublin crone. Without ever leaving their places at lecterns the readers acted out their parts to the life. They made a formal but by no means static grouping as the stage lighting, focusing individually or collectively, softened or sharpened the impression in response to the mood of each scene.

The gratitude that we owe this and later O'Casey readings prepared and directed by Paul Shyre, a dedicated young man of the theatre, does not lessen the one important reservation that must be made about readings. Dialogues and episodes carved out of books should not be considered substitutes for plays written as plays. During the Forties I was myself once a member of a committee to promote dramatic readings and create a Readers' Theatre. We did not propose to supplant theatrical production in New York but merely to supplement it with readings of works for which a fully staged production could not be anticipated. At this writing we do not have any desperate need for Readers' Theatre tactics, for the off-Broadway stage may be counted on to provide a full stage production for works that previously might have been considered only for a reading.

Experiments with readings have been conducted before. But we go too far when we enthusiastically propose readings as replacements for the production of plays or when we assume that every semistaged reading will be a rousing success. Paul Gregory's reading production of *John Brown's Body* with Tyrone Power, Judith Anderson, and other good actors did not match the success of *Don Juan in Hell*. Readings do not comprise a panacea for the stage any more than theatre in the round or arena theatre. A reading cannot make good theatre except by accident unless it becomes good drama first.

More "Readings": O'Casey and Dylan Thomas

In 1957 the vogue of dramatic readings was continued with the presentation of O'Casey's first autobiographical volume *I Knock at the Door* and a solo reading of Dylan Thomas' stories and poems called *A Boy Growing Up*.

The O'Casey reading was especially effective because a vivid group of actors headed by Aline MacMahon gave a varied human dimension and full choir of voices to the narration. The effect was continuously dramatic, and the production had unity despite the diversity of the episodes that established O'Casey's family background and boyhood. The author's ringing language and his sympathy and indignation provided notable passages of narration and even scenes of action. The core of the play provided tension and conflict, attention being concentrated on the struggle against tyrannical authority represented by the Protestant boy's pastor and by the martinet of a Protestant school in Dublin. Presaging the grown man's life-long defiance of inhumanity and constraint, the boy's story had immediacy and significance, and this plot was augmented by reminiscences of O'Casey's greathearted mother and of a charming childhood romance. *I Knock at the Door* was engrossing theatre.

It was a great pity that the production did not appear on a more suitable stage and in a more attractive playhouse. In the somber Belasco theatre the proscenium arch stage was in no way brought forward toward the audience by the lighting. Rapport could have been established more successfully in a smaller and brighter auditorium, and by a reading from a platform or apron stage.

Real estate remains a major deterrent to the multiplication and success of unconventional productions. Our Broadway theatres are essentially opera houses for the projection of emotion by the powerful lungs of singers riddling the audience with tones rather than words. When a conventionally realistic play is staged in these theatres the constant movement of stage action, from actor to actor and from one piece of furniture to another, helps to fix the playgoer's attention. But when the audience has to be reached by words alone, a sense of remoteness can put a pall on the reading. The artistry of the actor-reader behind the proscenium arch is not always sufficient to bridge the gap. In the case of a work such as *I Knock at the Door,* where emotion is everything, it was essential to involve the audience, and the proscenium arch of one of New York's oldest theatres was a tremendous handicap. When reviewers write glowing reports about staged readings in Broadway theatres we may be sure that usually their emotional experience in the tensely festive atmosphere of an opening night is not altogether shared by most playgoers attending later performances and not occupying aisle seats in the first ten rows.

Some imaginative techniques including semi-staged readings have yet to find effective theatrical housing on Broadway. Certainly imaginative presentations require all the help they can get. A trivial drawing-room farce flourished like a green bay tree while *I Knock at the Door* languished at the box office. In the same season Emlyn Williams' superb reading of Dylan Thomas' work closed after a few weeks. In *A Boy Growing Up* Emlyn Williams once more proved his amazing versatility. Himself a Welshman, he appeared to be in complete rapport with Thomas. Playing both the writer and the many characters memorialized in the stories and reminiscences Williams evoked the raffish world which produced the lusty poet and narrator of bizarre fancies and salty recollections. Williams selected the episodes and introduced and concluded them with the sure taste and skill to be expected of a distinguished performer who also happens to be the author of *The Corn Is Green* and other arresting plays. He did invite criticism by occasionally overacting—in one episode, for instance, he simulated flight with an embarrassing flapping of his hands —but it is quite possible that he would not have done so if he had not had to perform behind a proscenium arch. Though some of the smaller scenes tended to dribble out as sketches are wont to do, the Rabelaisian *pièce de résistance*, a full-bodied account of young Dylan's participation in an all-day carouse by his elders, was as richly textured as an O'Casey farce. Equally gratifying was the glorious nonsense of a surrealist segment carved out of the poet's *Adventures in the Skin Trade*.

But readings bring us to a borderline between dramatic and non-dramatic art that cannot be crossed without risk, and *A Boy Growing Up* was only fragmentarily dramatic. Unlike *I Knock at the Door,* the Emlyn Williams recitation was deficient in any unity other than that of the presence of young Dylan Thomas as a character throughout the reading. Dylan was always there, but his growing up was more notably a premise of the title of the show than an organic principle in the development of the episodes. The whole work lacked the beginning, middle, and end Aristotle predicated as the essential rhythm of drama. The evening owed everything to the power of the performance; the literary material seemed to be put together with virtually no dramaturgy at all.

When norms of dramaturgy lose their hold upon the audience we are apt to expect a great deal more of the theatre than is safe. We may come to expect miracles of it and the miracles occasionally materialize, as when Shaw's discussion plays confounded the experts by proving supremely viable on the stage, and when *Don Juan in Hell* toured extensively as a reading. But more often the miracles fail to materialize, as was the case with most surrealistic and expressionist drama during the first quarter of the century.

Robert Anderson:
All Summer Long and *Tea and Sympathy*

I

Many of us in the theatre were made unhappy by Walter Kerr's strictures against the influence of Chekhov on contemporary playwriting. I, for one, was disturbed because it had seemed to me that Chekhov was one of the very few playwrights who could set us a fruitful example, especially since Ibsen's influence had definitely waned and had even come to be considered injurious in the mid-century theatre.

For the present I am discounting the fact that Ibsen's influence has not been invariably injurious. It certainly has done a great deal for Arthur Miller, not only in the obvious case of his problem play and retribution drama, *All My Sons,* but in *Death of a Salesman* (which might be called Miller's *The Master Builder*) and *The Crucible.* But until recently there was no doubt in my mind that we needed Chekhov more than Ibsen or any other modern playwright. The example of Chekhov could assist our playwrights in dissolving the hard argumentative crust of problem plays; at the same time it could wean us away from overplotting and teach us to concentrate on character drama, atmosphere, and nuance.

My confidence, which would not have been broken by patently incompetent playwriting and discountable imitations, was shaken by the 1954 Broadway production of *All Summer Long.* The play revolves around the failure of an American family to save its home, because of listlessness and disorientation. It was written by Robert Anderson and staged in Zelda Fichandler's Washington arena theatre before his success on Broadway with *Tea and Sympathy.* It would have been difficult to find a more intelligent and sensitive playwright for the assignment of dramatizing Donald Wetzel's *A Wreath and a Curse,* the novel upon which *All Summer Long* was based. Nobody familiar with *Tea and Sympathy* could doubt that Robert Anderson would make sensitive drama out of the tensions of these confused young characters who receive little sympathy, guidance, or encouragement from their bumbling elders. Anderson did make sensitive drama out of the substance of the book, and Alan Schneider's production of *All Summer Long,* in the intimacy of a small arena theatre, apparently brought out such appealing qualities in the play that expectations for the success of the dramatization on Broadway ran high. But these were not realized. The play was brought into one of those large Broadway houses in which moods are likely to drift away like smoke, in which attitudes tend to be translated into blatant statement or attitudinizing, and in which error, like success, is so blown up that a miss is as good as a mile. (We often forget that the early Moscow Art Theatre that brought out Chekhov between the years 1898 and 1905 was, by comparison with the big popular theatres of its time, a "little theatre.")

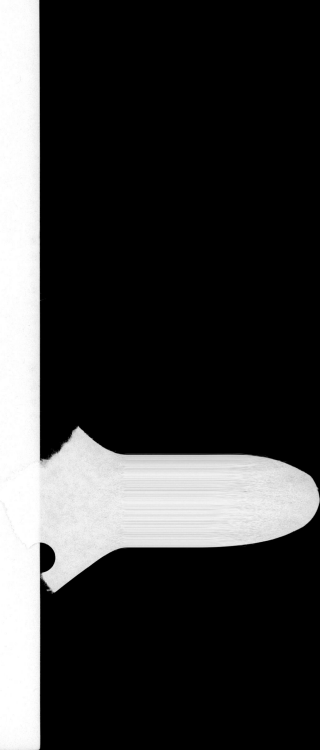

Chekhov in a regular Broadway playhouse is not really Chekhov, whether his plays fail on Broadway or succeed. Actually they have succeeded only with the assistance of stars like Alfred Lunt and Lynn Fontanne, who in addition to having an independent following possess the invaluable gift of being able to invigorate plays with the infectious liveliness of their performances. If the Russian Chekhov is not successful Chekhov in our professional theatres, American Chekhov is even less so. The American equivalents of Chekhov's principal characters and families simply lack the poetic quality, the odd charm, and the complex humanity to be found in *The Sea Gull, Uncle Vanya, The Three Sisters,* or *The Cherry Orchard.* This was apparent when the gifted director Joshua Logan wrote and staged *The Wisteria Trees,* his Southern version of Chekhov's last masterpiece. The production failed to survive on Broadway. Although it was easy enough for Logan to draw parallels between Chekhov's fading gentry and the decaying aristocracy of our post-bellum South the latter lacked the spice of the Russian characters. The family that was Robert Anderson's subject in *All Summer Long* was even less attractive and less endowed with spontaneity or volatility.

While one cannot generalize in speaking of ethnic or national qualities it does seem that the extravagant world of Chekhov, a world he could not have entirely invented, offers a richer supply of attractive, amusing and moving failures than the world of Robert Anderson's *All Summer Long.* The characters of the book were drab and commonplace, unstimulating and unamusing representatives of lower middle-class life.

There is inequality even in failure, and some failures offer themselves as better subjects for humor or sympathy than others. The rare exception is found in the vision of transcendent genius, the genius "who knows," as Alfred Kazin puts it, "that men are not the same everywhere, who believes that each human being is original . . ." or who maintains, as Faulkner does and as Chekhov surely did, an "amused astonishment at how much a human being can take in, how long a road he travels through in his own mind." * Less gifted writers need more overt assistance from their subjects. They do not seem to get much of it in our world, at least not until they appear down in the deep South. For this reason, rather than Walter Kerr's pragmatic observation of Chekhovian failure at the box office, I am inclined to say that he was right in advising our play-

* See the excellent essay "Faulkner in His Fury" in Alfred Kazin's *The Inmost Leaf,* The Noonday Press, 1959; especially pages 271–273.

wrights to stay out of the American cherry orchard. The pickings are likely to be meager, especially when they are put on display in the big Broadway super market.

2

New York reviewers evinced various degrees of affection for *All Summer Long*. The play presents the stalemate of a family engaged in petty interests while its home is being undermined, both literally and symbolically, by erosion. Only the twelve-year-old son, Willie, encouraged and watched over by the elder, temporarily crippled brother Don, makes an effort to save the home. But the stone wall the lad has built all summer long with insufficient strength and resources gives way in the end, and the hapless family is compelled to abandon the house.

A just appraisal of Robert Anderson's second Broadway work must distribute praise and blame. Praise should be given to some excellent details of characterization and feeling; blame to laboriousness in underscoring the lesson and for a general mildness of action and characterization. An excellent argument may be advanced against the requirement of an exciting plot, but only if the author's work on theme and characters provides an inner excitement of its own. *All Summer Long* drifted too long before coming to its conclusion. If no objection could be raised against the expectedness of the conclusion itself—who does not expect Chekhov's Cherry Orchard family to lose its estate—our judgment of the play was nevertheless affected by the degree to which interest was sustained while we were waiting for the blow to fall. How much interest could we take in those who endeavored to avert the blow and failed to do so. How much concern for whether or not the blow would fall? In *All Summer Long* the movement of the play was too uneventful, and some torpor overcame us while we were being languidly carried toward the catastrophe.

The drift of the characters was the very subject of the dramatization, and their lassitude gave an aura to their personality that was distinctly attractive. It was possible to agree with those reviewers who found *All Summer Long* appealing, for Robert Anderson's talent made it possible for us to take some interest in the play's characters, especially in the little boy who patiently erected his pitifully inadequate stone wall against erosion. But it is also true that the characters were not particularly engrossing on their own merits. One of the principals, Don, who encourages his little brother with lectures while indulging his own melancholy, did not wear well. One could only wish that the playwright had managed to make the drifters and their drift more arresting and poignant. More poetry of characterization and symbolism was needed to avoid the mild depressiveness of the family drama. It is a pity that the proper and full employment of a keen sensibility is so difficult and rare on the contemporary American stage with native middle-class characters. Which is perhaps only another way of saying that Chekhovian artistry has a difficult time of it in our theatre.

It is interesting to observe how the sensibilities of a writer like Robert Anderson have fared in this extrovert theatre of ours. Whereas the Chekhovian progression of *All Summer Long* was a descending one, *Tea and Sympathy*, written later but produced earlier on Broadway, had an ascending movement. It also had a sensational conclusion and a dramatic pressure that propelled the action forward in spurts of intrigue, conflict, discoveries, and reversals.

Tea and Sympathy, a work of greater sensitivity than *All Summer Long*, consists of one activated situation after another. An adolescent at a boarding school comes under suspicion of homosexuality because he prefers the refinements of art to the customary manly sports. The insensitivity of his classmates is compounded by the curious relentlessness of his sportsminded schoolmaster and the obtuseness of his father. When the boy is overcome by the realization that he is considered abnormal a classmate prevails upon him to disprove the accusation by going to a prostitute. His failure with her, the cause of which is obviously the coarseness of the woman, nearly destroys his self-confidence. He might resign himself to homosexuality as his natural condition but for the intervention of the wife of the athletic schoolmaster. The schoolmaster's persecution of the boy has become intolerable to her. The play concludes with her taking matters into her own hands. An unloved wife, she puts her athlete-husband in his place by pointing out to him that it is he who is the latent homosexual, a fact that his penchant for going out camping with the boys confirms rather than refutes. In persecuting the suspected adolescent he is really punishing himself as well as trying to suppress his own propensities. Having sent her husband away she then turns her attention to the desperate boy and allays his fears by giving herself to him.

It is hardly necessary to point out that the progression of this play con-

sists of one theatrical reversal after another. We arrive at one high point
when the wife pins the charge of homosexuality on the manly teacher
and at another high, indeed distinctly sensational point, when the woman
offers herself to the adolescent in order to save him from a dangerously
wrong opinion of himself. Under the spell of the action and the attractive
personality of Deborah Kerr the questionable features of this climax were
likely to be overlooked. The boy's libido might easily have failed him
again, for instance, if for no other reason than that she is his schoolmaster's
wife as well as a person who could have overawed him with her dignity.
Even at the considerable risk of forcing the development of events and
of moving toward a hazardous resolution Anderson, abetted by the explosive talent of his director, Elia Kazan, took his drama of adolescence
out of the cherry orchard. Whatever we may think of his means we can
hardly doubt that Robert Anderson's decidedly un-Chekhovian playwriting sustained the interest of his public and secured his sensitivity a
place in the popular American theatre.

It is greatly to Anderson's credit that he was not at all content to have
his say exclusively in the terms of overt and sensational action that first
made him a successful Broadway playwright. *All Summer Long* reached
New York after *Tea and Sympathy*, but the play showed no sign of
having been sensationalized for the Times Square super market. Anderson's last play of the Fifties, *Silent Night, Lonely Night*, was an exercise
in restraint. Not many reviewers appreciated the discipline he imposed
on himself in his story of two lonely adults who find each other on Christ-
mas night only to part the next morning, the hero going to his mentally
disturbed wife, the heroine to her unfaithful husband. There was a finely
rendered sensibility in these characters affectingly played by Henry Fonda
and Barbara Bel Geddes.

Complicating events were sparse in *Silent Night, Lonely Night*. These
could have been supplied easily enough if the author had been willing
to contrive a plot. But he would have regarded such tinkering with the
feelings of his characters or with their limited capacity for action as an
act of sacrilege. He rested his case instead solely on the shy rapprochement of two people and took the calculated risk of exhibiting nothing else
on the stage. It was quite a risk to take on Broadway but it was worth
taking for those of us, apparently a minority, who were held by the
author's finely spun web of feeling and insight. I enroll myself with that

minority, although I believe that ideally *Silent Night, Lonely Night* should have been a long one-act play in two or three scenes. (It is deplorable that playwrights aiming for a Broadway production have to observe a conventional length in their playwriting.)

But the Anglo-Saxon stiffness or restraint in the relationships of the two protagonists, while thoroughly natural in the play, is far removed from the buoyancy and rich variety of tone and mood that enabled Chekhov to turn even stalemate into drama. When the curtain fell on *Silent Night, Lonely Night* one felt that the author had gone as far as it was possible to go with his subject matter and that he had even taken longer than necessary to get there. Chekhov's most representative plays give us the impression that the author's matter is inexhaustible and that he does not need to arrive at a destination because the abundance of life in them is continuous and commanding.

Dramatizing Fiction: *Look Homeward, Angel*

The dramatization of Thomas Wolfe's celebrated novel *Look Homeward, Angel* by the Hollywood scenarist Ketti Frings won both the Drama Critics Circle Award and the Pulitzer Prize. Few playgoers missed the brimming language and egocentric passion of the novel that had to be sacrificed in the stage production. The play was no longer lyrical autobiography; it was basically a vivid family drama whose unifying thread of development was the gradual liberation of young Tom Wolfe from an aggravating family situation and an oppressive environment.

Miss Frings began with a sprawling and effervescent epic; she emerged with a trim but still substantial drama. Sacrificing a great deal of the incidental life of the book was not detrimental to the play, though some experiences were telescoped. The fine stage production was worth the many sacrifices and the occasional forcing of situations. The result was a closely realized personal drama made stirring and meaningful by the obsessiveness of complex human beings locked in conflict.

The mother of *Look Homeward, Angel,* Eliza, was a hard-driving, ruthless woman who tyrannized her family, waged a knockdown battle with her resentful husband, and tried to reduce her seventeen-year-old son, Eugene (the young Tom Wolfe), to the status of a ragged messenger boy. As played by the accomplished actress Jo Van Fleet, she was an unforgettable character. Her husband, Gant, vividly portrayed by the English actor Hugh Griffith, was equally fascinating, though a less forceful character even when on one of his periodic binges, venting his futile resentments against Eliza. Between these two ill-matched parents young Eugene Gant is ground and sharpened. He comes to understand the need of an education, of achieving freedom from the respective morbidities of his parents and the nightmarish environment of his mother's boarding house and its eccentric inmates. He is encouraged by his dying brother, Ben, to go to college, and his urge to leave home for the university at Chapel Hill is intensified by his first disappointment in love. Eugene departs from the tragicomic world of his boyhood and moves toward the destiny that we know awaits him, a destiny he will shape with his memories and hunger for experience. Young Anthony Perkins played Eugene with sensitivity and conviction.

Look Homeward, Angel was greeted with jubilation on Broadway. The general public had reason to be grateful to the dramatist, the cast, the director, George Roy Hill, and the scene designer, Jo Mielziner, whose movable main set provided admirable fluidity for the events in the Gants' boarding house.

There was little complexity or poetry in the Broadway play, but the dramatization would probably have been a fulsome failure if an attempt had been made to use the prodigal character analysis and cumbersome lyricism of Wolfe's large novel on the stage. A spare, occasionally semi-naturalistic treatment was the best choice for the play, and it is interesting that it should have been made by Ketti Frings. Her only previous bout with Broadway had occurred fifteen years earlier when the Theatre Guild presented her *Mr. Sycamore,* a fantasy about a postman who transforms himself into a tree!

The industry of adapting novels continued to thrive throughout the Fifties, not without reason when the writing of plays has generally been so mediocre in comparison with the writing of novels and stories. The standards of contemporary fiction have been higher than those of the drama, and the difference has not been exclusively one of form and style. The *content* of the novel (perhaps because it is relatively easy to pour good matter into it) has given it superiority in modern times, and it is not surprising that playwrights have been adapting modern fiction. It has done the novel no harm and the art of playwriting a great deal of good.

Ketti Frings' dramatization is a prime example of the application of craft to literary material. That the application was more than usually successful suggests adaptive talent on the part of Miss Frings combined with exceptional sympathy for Wolfe. A great deal of European and American fiction of the past is still available for use by our craftsmen. It will be a long time before dramatic writing is so rich in content that it will not seem threadbare by comparison with modern fiction. More playwrights will have to possess Ketti Frings' ability to emerge refreshed from the plunge into the novelist's sea of words; mere transcription of story matter and characterization in books is not enough. Material must be *recreated,* for the difference between something to be read privately and to be displayed publicly is immense. Even when the author of a novel is his own dramatist, as in the case of Faulkner's *Requiem for a Nun,** the problems of transcription are enormous.

Ulysses in Nighttown: Mostel at the Rooftop

Expressionistic stylization so powerfully used in *The Visit* also appeared in the same season in a dramatization of *Ulysses* at the off-Broadway Second Avenue Rooftop Theatre. Although I have always thought *Ulysses* would make an excellent motion picture I would never have believed it was possible to dramatize Joyce's stream-of-consciousness novel for the relatively static stage. Certainly the production at the Rooftop was uneven, but it was impressive and the experiment was patently worth making. The interest with which it was received was a tribute to Joyce, to the producers, to the friendly press, and to New York City itself (which is not the cultural Sahara some people like to think it is). The success of the production was also a tribute to expressionism which supposedly died out as a movement in the theatre a third of a century ago. The technique of dramatic exaggeration and distortion remains effective when properly used.

Ulysses in Nighttown was boldly conceived by Burgess Meredith, who also directed it brilliantly, and adapted by Marjorie Barkentin under the guidance of the distinguished Irish poet Padraic Colum. After an awkward beginning the adaptation was delightful, touching high points

* See elsewhere in Part II.

of comedy, pathos, and fantasy until the one serious decline of interest in the long brothel scene. Pauline Flanagan as Molly Bloom rendered the monologue from the last chapter of the book superbly and such capable actors as Robert Brown playing Stephen Dedalus carried the story to the climactic meeting of Bloom and Stephen in the inferno of Dublin's red-light district. Bloom's lusts, his jealousy of Molly, his imaginary defiance of anti-Semitism, his dreams of greatness, his grief for the remembered loss of a little son; Stephen's pride as an artist, his anguish as the son who refused to pray at his dying mother's bedside; and some unnecessarily unsavory details in Dublin's red-light district all swirled about the stage with expressionist frenzy and fragmentation.

But it was the humanity of the work, not its frenzy, that made the flamboyant theatricality of *Ulysses in Nighttown* rewarding. Much of this interfused life came from that very remarkable actor and mime Zero Mostel. In his performance as Bloom it was simply impossible to distinguish between what was life and what was theatre. Living and performing comprised a single experience, from Mostel's first appearance on the stage to his last, as he stood guard over the drunken Stephen Dedalus. This heavy-set man with a sad-sensual, scowling mask stood beside the collapsed young poet defying the whole hostile world. Immensely dignified after his gross humiliation in the brothel from which they had fled together, each of them fleeing from remembered failures and sense of guilt, the Jewish Ulysses protected the Irish Telemachus in a memorable climax.

How to differentiate between the planned comic pathos of a superb clown and the unplanned pathos of an ordinary, yet also distinctly extraordinary, human being? Mostel provoked a troublesome question for critics of the theatre: how and when do we distinguish between performance and play? For without the compelling performance of Mostel, we might have thought less well of this dramatization and its desultory passages. The great German critic Lessing postulated the principle that, "The great discrimination of a dramatic critic is shown if he knows how to distinguish infallibly, in every case of satisfaction or dissatisfaction, what and how much of this is to be placed to the account of the poet or the actor." How right can we be in practice? Usually we have not had an opportunity to read a new play in advance of the production, and we can get at the work of the writer only through the actor. But how difficult it is to discover where the playwright's work ended and the player's began! Luckily we in the audience are not called upon to render an absolute judgment. We are permitted to experience the play and the performance *together* without having to arrive at a niggling adjudication of credits.

MacLeish's J.B.: Yale and Broadway

I

Undoubtedly the most impressive event of the 1958-59 season was the Alfred de Liagre Broadway production of *J.B.* by Archibald MacLeish. The play was directed by that dynamic master of theatrical effects, Elia Kazan, and the cast included Pat Hingle as an excellent Job and Raymond Massey and Christopher Plummer as memorable representatives of God (Mr. Zuss) and the Devil (Nickles). *J.B.* won great respect and support from press and public, and its success on Broadway was acclaimed as a victory for verse drama.

Usually the nonprofessional stage trails Broadway rather than leads it, and it is interesting that this lofty and austere contemporary version of "The Book of Job" came to Broadway via a university theatre production. In this particular case the leadership came from F. Curtis Canfield, Dean of Yale's School of Drama, whose interest in the work was whetted by excerpts printed in *The Saturday Review of Literature*. He acquired *J.B.* for Yale, gave the play its world première at the University Theatre, and took his production to the Brussels World Fair. Wisely, he refrained from pressing a moral claim to directing the work for Broadway, thus maintaining as clear a distinction as possible between the obligation of a university director (which is to bring out intrinsic values) and the obligation of a Broadway director (which is to deliver a box-office success whenever possible).

Comparisons between the Yale and Broadway productions establish the reality of this distinction. At Yale, *J.B.* was most effective when Mr. Zuss (Zeus, Deus?) and Nickles (Old Nick?) clashed over the main ethical issues; on Broadway, when the afflictions of Job were inflicted on J.B. The morality-play features, the philosophical encounters, and the impersonal elements of the play were dominant on the university stage, whereas the Kazan production favored the dynamics of external action and gave dramatic immediacy to the personal drama. Though the first production could strike the captious critic as too cool or detached, the other could seem rather superheated and hypertheatrical. But there was singular merit in both versions, one notable for its austerity and reflective power, the other for its emotional drama.

In the Broadway production changes in the text resulted in the omission of powerful though decidedly difficult lines of discussion. Cuts made during the pre-Broadway tour were especially apparent in the last scene in which J.B. forgives God (pages 135-140 of the text published by Houghton Mifflin Co.). At Yale the dramatic reversal in the original text provided one of the most provocative twists in the intellectual and quite heterodox action of the university production.

The capacity for forgiveness is a human trait and Man "forgives God." But God's answer to J.B.'s cry for justice in the universe is only an overpowering manifestation of natural force:

> *Planets and Pleiades and cages—*
> *Screaming horses—scales of light—*
> *The wonder and the mystery of the universe—*
> *The unimaginable might of things . . .*

"Who plays the hero, God or him [J.B., Man]? /Is God to be forgiven?" Mr. Zuss asks indignantly after J.B. has, as Nickles admits, given in. "Giving in!" Zuss cried in the original script and production. "You call that arrogant/Smiling, supercilious humility/Giving in to God?" This added conflict between God and Devil was omitted on Broadway. (I believe it was dropped during the pre-Broadway tryout period in Washington.) The Kazan production hurtled toward a conclusion in which J.B. and his wife, who has returned to him, conclude that mankind cannot rely on justice but must trust in its own humanity and love.

The university production showed MacLeish what kind of a play he had written. It also showed Broadway how much theatre there was in it, for many people would have been blind to the theatrical possibilities of this philosophical work in verse. The objective of the Broadway production was to attain the greatest dramatic impact upon the commercial theatre's mixed audience. The production succeeded brilliantly, unavoidably at a sacrifice. The pragmatic principle followed by Broadway productions is that nothing should stand between the audience and the action and emotional drive. For this reason the successive calamities of J.B. were merged with considerable telescoping of the time element, whereas the calamities that befell J.B. in the university production were kept distinct, with God and Devil clashing in debate between the separate episodes.

The direction of each production also showed this different emphasis. In the Kazan scheme God and Devil remained at opposite ends of the stage with J.B. between them as though he were located on earth between Heaven and Hell; whereas the Canfield production provided exciting occasions for God and Devil to approach each other, dramatizing their struggle visibly as well as philosophically. *Their* struggle, rather than J.B.'s, was central in the Yale version. Even the sets emphasized the disparate objectives. The Broadway setting by Boris Aronson offered many planes for movement and actually changed position in the scene when J.B.'s city is wrecked; whereas Donald Oenslager's circus setting at Yale was an austere showcase for argument and philosophical conflict.

Controversy will continue to simmer about *J.B.* for a long time even without invidious comparisons between the original and the Broadway version. It is the kind of controversy that only a work of singular interest arouses, and it is difficult to think of a healthier state of affairs in our theatre which usually generates as little heat as light. The play was on Broadway hardly more than a week when it was apparent that, like *The Cocktail Party* a decade before, it was already browbeating a portion of its public. Some playgoers who could not quite follow the lines appeared to be vaguely impressed; others felt dissatisfied with themselves for not rising to the occasion of a verse drama about God, Man, and Devil. For such people, as Oscar Wilde is reported to have said before the première of *The Importance of Being Earnest,* the question was not whether the play would be a success but whether the audience would be.

The presentation of *J.B.* impressed me as a salutary act which added dignity and luster to the Broadway stage. But as a critic I had serious reservations about both play and production. In his commendable effort to direct his poetic talent into the theatre MacLeish seemed to be functioning as a full-time poet, but because he resolved *J.B.* by means of various undramatized transitions he was only a part-time playwright. Toward the end of the play there was a conspicuous gap between God's voice and J.B.'s change of attitude which veered rapidly from one intellectual position to another. After J.B. submits to God's will in the next-to-last scene, he modifies his submission by maintaining that he can stand alone and can accept life even if there is no justice in the universe. But he also qualifies this position when his wife returns to him, by placing his reliance on human love.

Perhaps I am being unjust, but as the play whirled to its conclusion its argument seemed muddled. In the Broadway version the logic and position of J.B. was the weakest part of the work. For this reason all the trappings—the extensive preparations for the action in a circus tent, for instance, a piece of stage business largely of Kazan's devising—seemed dramatically wasteful. So did the author's dramatic frame of a discussion between a candy butcher and a balloon vendor who assume the roles of God and Devil. Their conversation about Job is characteristic of the discursive character of the work. Kazan's direction reduced this wordiness considerably by vigorous pacing and by means of vivid stage effects, but it was outside his province to supply any action other than stage business.

Staging alone could not overcome structural defects in J.B. There are two levels of interest in the play: the God-Devil conflict and the personal drama of the modern American Job. The conflict between Mr. Zuss and Nickles is largely prologue, epilogue, and interlude for the main action about the tribulations of J.B. But Zuss and Nickles overshadow J.B.; the frame becomes more prominent than the picture. Kazan gave vitality and dramatic dimension to J.B. and his family, but he also embellished the frame with physical details. It was difficult to determine whether frame or picture was more important in the theatrically oriented Broadway production. The main dramatic action was over in the first half of the play; nearly everything that followed dropped from drama to debate and explanation. The Comforters argued in vain, the divine voice (named the Prompter in the program) spoke portentously but ineffectually, and the conclusion when J.B. announced his newly won credo and expressed his rueful acceptance of human life and love was only half-realized.

Because J.B. and the other characters were morality play figures rather than fully realized characters it was impossible for me to subscribe to the generous opinion of those who hailed J.B. as the greatest play of the postwar period. Nevertheless J.B. was an exalted work of the dramatic and poetic imagination in a generally commonplace theatre. Though the poetry was rarely MacLeish's best, its quality was still measurably above the level of dialogue in most American prose drama. The work had what an English reviewer called tragic diction, the absence of which has been considered a major deficiency in the prose realism of our theatre.

J.B. is plainly a morality play, and to require it to provide rounded characters is to ask for something that MacLeish did not intend. It is a contemporary *Everyman* that is half poem and half discussion drama. As poem *J.B.* has mystery at its core, symbolism for its method, and ambiguity as its result. As discussion drama the play inevitably left much unresolved; to expect a solution to the problem of evil that would satisfy men of divergent conviction was to demand more than any contemporary work for the stage could possibly provide. The real test was whether we had experienced any mental stimulation and spiritual invigoration, and the play passed this test for me and for many other playgoers.

The dramatic frame of the circus vendors' decision to dramatize "The Book of Job" and the burden of the senseless misery of man presumably made the play an improvisation on their part. Because such an improvisation relieves the author from absolute commitments, it is convenient for a writer whose mind has only a tenuous connection with religion. In the Bible, the story of Job is an act of *faith*. In *J.B.* the story is the result of the decision of two actors to exercise their unemployed talents in an empty circus tent, in short, it is an act of *theatre*. The ultimate fascinations and limitations of *J.B.* derived from MacLeish's effort to express his alienated modern consciousness of man lost in a universe indifferent to him. Because the endeavor was intense even when not altogether successful, the play was superior to most mid-century American drama in depth and elevation.

2

J.B. cannot be judged outside the theatre for which it was written. It is possible to be troubled by the sudden transitions from the lines of Mr. Zuss and Nickles as circus vendors putting on a show and the lines of the God-mask and Satan-mask that they assume. It is also possible to question the origin of God's voice in his great speech from "The Book of Job"; is it a speech remembered by the actors from their reading of the King James Version, or is it, along with some earlier speeches, God's authentic voice mystically participating in the show that the two vendors have recklessly staged? The answer is that God's voice here and the voices of the God-mask and Satan-mask have the same value as the lines of the vendors, J.B., his wife, and all the other characters of the play within the play. In other words each level of discussion is equally cogent, equally forceful, and equally real as dialogue. The voices of God and Satan, the echoes from "The Book of Job," the discussions of Mr. Zuss and Nickles, and the colloquies of J.B., his family, the Messengers, the would-be Comforters, and the others are all part of an *invention* called *J.B.* written by a man named MacLeish. We waste time worrying about what is real and what isn't in trying to fit *J.B.* to our procrustean concepts of realism. Everything in the play is real because it happens in the theatre.

Readers of the play (which was reviewed in the literary journals chiefly by critics who had not seen it on the stage) might be less inclined to point out inconsistencies of style if they imagined the speakers in the context of dramatic action. The characters either speak poetically rhythmic passages occasioned by their roles or they switch from common speech to such echoes from the Bible and liturgical verse (and T.S. Eliot?) as

> *I only, I alone, to tell thee ...*
> *I who have understood nothing, have known*
> *Nothing, have been answered nothing ...*

In the theatre these inconsistencies, if noticed at all, are harmless; on occasion they even enrich the action and the levels of poetic suggestion. More often they merely fit the tempo or mood of a scene. So do the occasional jingles:

> *If God is God He is not good*
> *If God is good He is not God;*
> *Take the even, take the odd;*

or:

> *Blow on the coal of the heart.*
> *The candles in churches are out.*
> *The lights have gone out in the sky.*

Complaints about the reduction of the majestic story of Job to the commonplaces of modern life and protests against minification (the word for reduction of magnitude used in the *Hudson Review* criticism) have little relevancy in the theatre. I felt no minification while under the spell of either the Yale or Broadway productions. J.B. is unquestionably a commonplace American and is so intended. But he grows under the blows of misfortune and becomes Mankind's representative in the allegorical and theatrical action of the play. He is also a projection both of the vendors' imagination and of an allegory conceived in common modern terms.

In neither case is *J.B.* inadequate for the dramatic intentions of the author (though I regret that he did not give J.B. less platitudinous language in reacting to the early blows against him).

The author's modern interpretation does use minification justifiably in treating the Comforters as modern praters of the respective doctrines of psychological determinism (the psychiatrist), historical necessity (the Communist agitator), and original sin (the cleric). The peddlers of these ideologies are caricatures, but that is what they should be in a play in which scorn for facile solutions of the enigma of Man is an important element (as it also is in "The Book of Job").

One of the outstanding dramatic virtues of *J.B.* is the sudden flaring of indignation and scorn produced by compassion. This tone of protest is sounded early in the play within the play when Nickles, reporting on his traffic with the world, recalls the millions mutilated and slaughtered "for thinking," for . . .

> *Walking round the world in the wrong*
> *Skin, the wrong-shaped noses, eyelids;*
> *Living at the wrong address—London, Berlin, Hiroshima*
> *Wrong night, wrong city.*

There are also theological criticisms of *J.B.* with which it is difficult to quarrel since these are likely to emanate from a religious commitment or position. But again the most suitable testing ground for theatrical criticism is the theatre itself, where the relation of argument to the overall action of the drama is relevant. In this context the author's religious philosophy is neither right nor wrong; it is simply an integral part of the action and emotions of the characters. If the second half of *J.B.* is less satisfactory theatre than the first it is not because the theological opinions expressed in it are confused or ambivalent but because the dramaturgy is imperfect. Action is halted by discussion and the transitions from one attitude to another in the last quarter of the play are hurried over rather than dramatized.

It is tempting to subject *J.B.* to literary analysis. Exploration of this area is pertinent since literary and theatrical considerations are interrelated in the case of poetic drama. But the fact is that literary criticism is apt to find fault with *J.B.* on grounds that lose much of their validity in the theatre. Undoubtedly the reverse is also true. There could be no strong literary objections to the most serious theatrical limitation of *J.B.*

in the theatre, that is, to the long stretches of discourse and infrequency of dramatic episodes.

Between the crossfires of literary, religious, and theatrical judgments it was inevitable that *J.B.* was criticized for succumbing to some of the pitfalls of modern poetic tragedy. For this very reason the production of *J.B.* was one of the two or three truly important events in the mid-century American theatre. How few new American plays had the stature and dimension to be criticized on such grounds!

And These Others

On rereading this New York chronicle I am dismayed; surely our mid-century theatre is in danger of being misrepresented if this report, however long and diversified, is not amplified. In a more comprehensive survey there would also be much to consider from abroad that touched our stage only lightly, for example, the success of Bertolt Brecht's work and of the East German company he helped to develop; the continued productivity of Jean Anouilh in France; the growing European vogue of the four modernists, Beckett, Ionesco, Genet, and Adamov; and the rising reputations of the Swiss writers, Friedrich Duerrenmatt and Max Frisch.

Even if we confine ourselves to the New York scene it is necessary to amplify the record. As I have stated in my preface I have too little to contribute to the appraisal of many of the productions of the last ten years to justify chapters on them, and since even brief comments on the achievement and debris in the theatre during the Fifties would make a very fat book I shall merely skim the record.

I

The American dramatization of *The Diary of Anne Frank* by Albert Hackett and Frances Goodrich was a beautifully executed adaptation, sensitively staged by Garson Kanin and played with touching truthfulness by Susan Strasberg as Anne, Joseph Schildkraut as her father Otto Frank, and a fine supporting cast. The play opened on Broadway on October 5, 1955, instantly captured New York, had many productions abroad, and made a particularly strong impression on the German public. This expertly fashioned play confirms the fact that we are still adept at realistic dramaturgy. In those rare instances when the material to which we apply this tired technique is genuinely stirring our playwrights can create creditable journeymen's work. The adapters of *Anne Frank* had not been considered important playwrights heretofore, but they proved themselves craftsmen and produced a play that a dozen better known dramatists in America would have been pleased to consider their own.

An effective writing team was Jerome Lawrence and Robert E. Lee. In 1955 these collaborators contributed *Inherit the Wind,* a semihistorical drama depicting a celebrated battle with bigotry in the famous monkey trial initiated by Fundamentalist objections to the teaching of evolution in American schools. A pedestrian work except for its touches of folk drama, it was invigorated by its subject matter, by Herman Shumlin's vivacious direction, and by Peter Larkin's stunning multiple-level stage setting. The two authors supplied a livelier but less successful historical study in 1959 with *The Gang's All Here,* a drama of political corruption during the Harding administration. Herman Wouk's *The Caine Mutiny Court-Martial* in 1954, extracted by the author from his Pulitzer Prize novel, *The Caine Mutiny,* was a provocative and exciting trial drama. Though the ending—a complete reversal of point of view—jeopardized the integrity of the play Wouk at least provided tense trial drama on a theme other than those little murders so favored in England, where melodrama has long been a staple of the stage. Another American trial drama, Saul Levitt's *The Andersonville Trial,* revolved around the conflict between military obedience and private conscience. Staged by José Ferrer with Herbert Berghof in the role of the commandant of the horrible Confederate prison camp, this production closed the Fifties with dramatic power and theatrical thunder.

I have offered no separate comment on some plays of our important younger writers. I have had little to say about Tennessee Williams' *Cat on a Hot Tin Roof* except to acknowledge that its vivid characterizing power makes most living playwrights look like anemic pygmies. I must qualify this compliment, however, by saying that if Williams had anything of consequence to say in his family drama he did not manage to get it across. The theme, that it is important to face the truth and that there is a liberating power in taking the blinkers off our emotions, is surely secondary to the sheer drive of life and rebellion against death in the play. There was also very little for me to say about Williams' folksy comedy, *The Rose Tattoo.* The bizarre conduct of Serafina in the latter suggests a sympathetic yet overstrenuous and rather synthetic view of love; it was not altogether clear to me why a writer so gifted made such a fuss about the sexual career of his torrid Sicilian heroine.

I have also neglected *A View from the Bridge*, a drama that proved more impressive in England than in New York. Arthur Miller aspired to tragic and poetic drama in the play, but was only partially successful. He may have been aware of this, for he first felt impelled in the 1955 Broadway version to make his lawyer-narrator point out the parallels to Greek tragedy in his incest drama, and then to moderate the claim in the prologue written for the later two-act London version. Incest tragedy is actually less important in *A View from the Bridge* than the tragedy of an informer who betrays a relative to immigration officers out of jealousy. Miller's concern with the theme of betrayal placed *A View from the Bridge* far outside the area of opportunistic sensationalism. The subjects of honor and integrity have always been a preoccupation of this playwright and they have given elevation to Miller's work. These subjects, which have been largely overlooked or treated condescendingly by many of Miller's contemporaries, form the spine of *A View from the Bridge*; they dignified the work and brought it within the precincts of tragedy.

I should also like to salute William Inge's first Broadway production, *Come Back, Little Sheba*, which the Theatre Guild presented in New York on February 15, 1950. Though it was of more limited range than his later plays of the Fifties this drama of a supposedly resigned man who flares up into alcoholic violence whenever the meanness of his married life overwhelms him was an observant and compassionate work. Most men, Thoreau wrote, "lead lives of quiet desperation." The desperation which drives Doc berserk was painful to watch, but his quiet resignation on returning from the City Hospital was even more terrifying. I recall another sentence by Thoreau: "What is called resignation is confirmed desperation." In the Inge canon *Come Back, Little Sheba* is a little play, but in my opinion it was, on the whole, his most considerable work.

A word is also in order here about the same author's very successful *Bus Stop*, beautifully directed by Harold Clurman. But even my affection for this play must be qualified because I felt that the overly naïve cowboy's wooing of his "chantoosie" inamorata paid reduced dividends as it went along. As usual in an Inge play, it was the darker tonalities that spoke for the playwright who is the modest poet of the American landscape of failure and near-failure. *Bus Stop* drew its life chiefly from its secondary characters. The elder of the two cowboys who has played father to the boy, the sheriff, and the nympholeptic college professor were all hauntingly ambiguous creations. Some day, if left alone by producers, William Inge is going to write a play made up entirely of minor characters and come up with a major masterpiece.

I might also have discussed several plays that dealt with social problems, a genre of writing that fell into considerable disrepute in the Fifties. Tennessee Williams' *Camino Real*, produced in 1953, could rate a separate essay because this imaginative work exemplified the complexities of writing a symbolist drama in the flamboyant, expansive American way. Our extravagant manner, which playwrights once employed in adapting American techniques of vaudeville and burlesque (e.g. Kaufman and Connelly's satire, *Beggar on Horseback,* and John Howard Lawson's vivid farrago of social criticism, *Processional*), still has possibilities. I doubt that a romantic pageant bedecked with literary allusion can accomplish much in the field of contemporary social drama. Certainly Williams and his director, Elia Kazan, were most successful in the burlesque sequences of *Camino Real.*

Usually a more routine realistic procedure prevailed in the area of social drama. We had good honest work of limited ambience during the decade in such plays as Calder Willingham's military-school drama *End as a Man* and Louis Peterson's *Take a Giant Step,* the affecting story of a Negro boy's growing pains. Two other provocative dramatizations were Norman Rosten's *Mister Johnson,* from Joyce Cary's novel about the gap between the white and African Negro worlds and Alfred Hayes's war romance *The Girl on the Via Flaminia.* Also to be remembered is Lorraine Hansberry's vividly authentic picture of Negro life, *A Raisin in the Sun,* of the 1958-59 Broadway season. This play earned critical approbation and popular success with its simple and concentrated realism. Action, environment, and characterization rang true. The young author was completely in rapport with her material, yet intelligently detached in her judgments. Her handling of the crisis within the Negro family was especially admirable; there was control without constraint. Such a touchy issue as the Negro housing problem was treated with skill and incisiveness free from liberal clichés and melodramatic involvements. There was equal restraint in the production, especially in the vital performances of Sidney Poitier, Claudia McNeil, and Ruby Dee.

This socially slanted character drama posed a gently persuasive argument that can be easily misunderstood if summarized. Certainly it sounds insulting and condescending to state the obvious fact that the Negro is also a human being; yet that is the theme of the play. Because the author leaned over backwards in trying to avoid one-sidedness *A Raisin in the Sun* was a play we tended to overrate a little; we had expected tedious propaganda and were entertained by a good slice of life instead.

2

American playwrights are adept at making theatre about the young, and their problems of entering or avoiding the adult world. One of the most appealing plays of the Fifties was *The Member of the Wedding*, which opened on Broadway on January 5, 1950. It was at Tennessee Williams' suggestion that Carson McCullers dramatized her novel. Concerned with "a human condition" and with an "inward play," Mrs. McCullers brought a unique grace to her treatment of the adolescent pains of a little girl who naïvely expects to join her brother and his bride on their honeymoon. The theme of loneliness and the dreamlike effort to overcome it provided all the action on the stage. The inexplicable and irrelevant death of a little boy from encephalitis and (although its source is vaguely social) the equally meaningless death of a Negro youth were strangely affecting. At the end of the play the Negro nurse who has mothered all the young people is alone. Novelistic though these deaths were, Mrs. McCullers avoided sentimentality in spite of all temptations to succumb to it. She gave the decade a fragile little masterpiece that does not call for critical rough-handling or for being classified as part of any trend of the times.

In looking over the field of other plays about human relations there are none I wish to treat in any detail. Arthur Laurents' *The Time of the Cuckoo,* in which Shirley Booth achieved stardom in 1952, was a touching love story realistically ended when the heroine, a vacationing spinster, finds Venetian romance too rich for puritan blood. *In the Summer House,* Jane Bowles' study of a domineering woman and her intimidated daughter, was sensitively written and provided a challenging role for Judith Anderson, one of the very few great actresses of the mid-century theatre.

One play, Paddy Chayefsky's *Middle of the Night,* still gives me some twinges of guilt. In common with members of the New York daily press, I may have underrated it because of irritation with the prosiness of the dialogue and the embarrassment that apparently afflicts many

Americans when confronted with middle-aged romance. Though I still hold no brief for the play as dramatic literature, it still retains a poignant hold on my imagination as a convincing representation of a middle-aged widower's love for his young secretary. The author did not remain content with his success in reportage. He contributed a folksy comedy, *The Tenth Man*, to the 1959-60 season that was greatly appreciated for its touches of fantasy and humor. It was a seductive, if somewhat synthetic, work.

I have omitted detailed comment on almost all of the lighter plays. Only two comedies attained distinction, *The Teahouse of the August Moon*, based by John Patrick on Vern Sneider's novel about the American occupation of Okinawa, and Thornton Wilder's *The Matchmaker*, the latter a masterpiece of literate lunacy. Certainly there are few so literately delightful characters in recent theatrical history as Vandergelder's Irish servant, Malachi, when he explained to the audience why he would not help himself to someone's purse even though his chief occupation had once been to pick up money that didn't belong to him. He had been "engaged in the redistribution of superfluities," he said, but he had acquired another vice since then and could not afford more than one at a time: ". . . nurse one vice in your bosom. Give it the attention it deserves and let your virtues spring modestly around it." In the France of Giraudoux such sallies are apt to be the rule rather than the exception, but their novelty on our stage makes them refreshing.

There were other sorties into the field of literate entertainment: S.N. Behrman's *Jane*, based on a Maugham story; Carolyn Green's *Janus*; Jean Kerr's and Eleanor Brooke's *King of Hearts*, a deflationary comedy about a popular comic-strip artist; Sam and Bella Spewack's free adaptation of Husson's French comedy, *My Three Angels*, in which penal colony convicts protect a friendly family from the venalities of a respectable citizen; Kyle Crichton's comedy of a Philadelphia tycoon, *The Happiest Millionaire*; Leslie Stevens' ingeniously contrived lecture-comedy *The Marriage-Go-Round*; Joseph Fields' and Jerome Chodorov's pleasant adaptation of Eudora Welty's *The Ponder Heart*; N. Richard Nash's folksy play, *The Rainmaker*; *The Pleasure of His Company*, a witty drawing-room comedy by Samuel Taylor and Cornelia Otis Skinner; Gore Vidal's satirical farce, *Visit to a Small Planet*; Kaufman and Teichmann's clever collaboration, *The Solid Gold Cadillac* (starring the unforgettable Josephine Hull, whom, I am proud to say, I was the first producer to star on Broadway); *The Fourposter,* Jan de Hartog's two-character "story of all marriages" (Brooks Atkinson's phrase), in which Jessica Tandy and Hume Cronyn captivated New York; *A Majority of One,* Leonard Spigelgass' comedy of Jewish-Japanese amity, to which Gertrude Berg and Sir Cedric Hardwicke brought great personal charm; Ira Levin's *No Time for Sergeants,* adapted from Mac Hyman's novel; and, finally, George Axelrod's imaginative bit of fluff, *The Seven-Year Itch.* These all deserve mention as polished and well-tailored entertainments of varied quality.

I have also disregarded such melodramas as Maxwell Anderson's *The Bad Seed,* and Joseph Hayes' capably developed crime drama *The Desperate Hours;* and such modern religious plays as Graham Greene's *The Living Room* and the effective dramatization of his novel, *The Power and the Glory.* There were also unclassified oddments: Jack Gelber's mesmeric drama of drug addiction, *The Connection;* Robinson Jeffers' distinguished rendition of the Phaedra legend, *The Cretan Woman;* S.N. Behrman's touching play of New England memories, *The Cold Wind and the Warm;* and *Rashomon,* an esoteric drama imaginatively adapted for the Western stage by Fay and Michael Kanin.

And the musicals! *Silk Stockings, Damn Yankees, Redhead,* the supremely brash *Guys and Dolls, The Pajama Game, Fanny, The King and I, The Music Man, Gypsy, Can-Can, Wonderful Town, Paint Your Wagon, My Fair Lady,* and *Fiorello!* all gave evidence of the efficiency of a form of entertainment that has become peculiarly American. But there was more than old-fashioned musical comedy on Broadway in the Fifties. *Regina,* with Marc Blitzstein's music; *Candide,* with Leonard Bernstein's music and Lillian Hellman's libretto; *West Side Story,* music by Bernstein, and libretto by Arthur Laurents; and *The Consul* and *The Saint of Bleecker Street* by Gian-Carlo Menotti were all examples of musical drama.

I must also mention those plays from England and the Continent that have not been discussed in the preceding chronicle: T.S. Eliot's *The Cocktail Party,* his best modern play, and *The Confidential Clerk,* well written though tiresome; *A Sleep of Prisoners, The Dark Is Light Enough, Venus Observed,* and *The Boy with a Cart* by Christopher Fry; *Tiger at the Gates, Ondine,* and *The Enchanted* by Jean Giraudoux; *Time Re-*

membered, Legend of Lovers, Ardèle, The Fighting Cock, and *Thieves'
Carnival* by Jean Anouilh; and off-Broadway revivals of such older plays
as Chekhov's *Ivanov* and S. Ansky's *The Dybbuk.*

With all these any regular playgoer of the Fifties who could say he
was not sporadically seduced or stimulated by the New York theatre was
simply not being honest with himself! My dissatisfactions with what
Broadway and off-Broadway failed to yield are in themselves a compliment to its perverse vitality as a producer and importer of dramatic art.

The persistent playgoer always hopes for more than he receives, and
the Fifties have merely whetted my appetite for what the future holds.
But I wonder whether I shall be able to manage another decade of
playgoing. One way or another I have been involved with the American
theatre for nearly forty years, virtually all of them for reasons far less
tangible than making a living. It is childishness to persist, and weakness
of flesh and spirit *not* to persist. It has been a terrible, frustrating, and
wonderful life, and there are a great many amusing, wearing, and
remarkable people to thank: producers, stage directors, playwrights, designers, actors, stage managers, musicians, choreographers, dancers,
clowns, stagehands, fellow critics and reviewers, first and second nighters,
company and business managers, theatrical press agents. If a hail and
farewell is premature perhaps it is not too soon to compose an *Envoi.*
How should it read?

Envoi

Our theatre remains what it has been; a Vanity Fair upon which
sometimes the dove descends tentatively with a pentecostal flicker which
we, in our need, consecrate as a flame.

BIBLIOGRAPHICAL NOTE

The plays discussed in this chronicle have all been published in individual volumes, mostly by Random House. The two new O'Neill plays, *Long Day's Journey into Night* and *A Touch of the Poet*, were published by the Yale University Press; Tennessee Williams' plays by New Directions; Arthur Miller's by The Viking Press; John Osborne's plays by Criterion Books in a single volume; Giraudoux' and Anouilh's plays by Hill and Wang; Ionesco's and Beckett's by Grove Press.

A large number of the plays are in anthologies. *New Voices in the American Theatre* is a Modern Library title. In addition Random House has published *The Off-Broadway Theatre*, edited by Richard Cordell and Lowell Matson, which includes the text of *Ulysses in Nighttown*.

The following plays appear in three of my anthologies, issued by Crown Publishers:

Billy Budd, The Member of the Wedding, The Autumn Garden, The Iceman Cometh, Come Back, Little Sheba, Darkness at Noon, and *Summer and Smoke* in *Best American Plays: Third Series,* 1952

I Am a Camera, Cat on a Hot Tin Roof, The Rose Tattoo, A Moon for the Misbegotten, A Hatful of Rain, Picnic, Bus Stop, Tea and Sympathy, A View from the Bridge, The Crucible, Inherit the Wind, and *The Matchmaker* in *Best Plays of the Modern American Theatre: Fourth Series,* 1958

The Lark, A Month in the Country, The Sea Gull, The Madwoman of Chaillot, Ondine, and *Tiger at the Gates* in *Twenty Best European Plays on the American Stage,* 1957.

The Viking Press has published Arthur Miller's *Collected Plays*, 1957, which includes the full-length version of *A View from the Bridge*. Random House has issued Inge's collected plays as *4 Plays by William Inge*, 1958. Crown Publishers has published *The Rope Dancers* by Morton Wishengrad, 1958.

–J.G.

Index

INDEX

317